Library of
Davidson College

Crime and Criminal Justice Under the Third Republic

View of Faces—The Grand Staircase at the Palace of Justice, by Honoré Daumier, first published in *Le Charivari*, February 8, 1848.

Crime and Criminal Justice Under the Third Republic

The Shame of Marianne

Benjamin F. Martin

LOUISIANA STATE UNIVERSITY PRESS
Baton Rouge and London

Copyright © 1990 by Louisiana State University Press
All rights reserved
Manufactured in the United States of America

First Printing
99 98 97 96 95 94 93 92 91 90   5 4 3 2 1

Designer: Sylvia Malik Loftin
Typeface: Trump Mediaeval
Typesetter: G&S Typesetters, Inc.
Printer and binder: Thomson-Shore, Inc.

Library of Congress Cataloging-in-Publication Data
Martin, Benjamin F., 1947–
Crime and criminal justice under the Third Republic: the shame of Marianne/Benjamin F. Martin.
p. cm.
Includes bibliographical references.
ISBN 0-8071-1572-X (alk. paper)
1. Criminal justice, Administration of—France—History—19th century.
2. Criminal justice, Administration of—France—History—20th century.
3. Crime—France—History—19th century. 4. Crime—France—History—20th century. 5. France—History—Third Republic, 1870–1940. I. Title.
HV9960.F7M37 1990
364.944'09'034—dc20   89-27334
                                                                     CIP

The paper in this book meets the guidelines for permanence and durability of the Committee on Production Guidelines for Book Longevity of the Council on Library Resources. ∞

For Janis
Belle Femme

Contents

	Preface and Acknowledgments	xi
	Abbreviations	xv
1	The Crimes	1
2	The Police (I)	39
3	The Police (II)	82
4	The Criminal Procedure	125
5	The Courts	157
6	The Magistrature	191
7	The Bar	234
8	The Punishments	255
	Conclusion	269
	Afterword Gangsters and Anarchists in the Belle Epoque: The Bande à Bonnot	275
	Glossary	319
	Bibliography	325
	Index	353

Tables

1	Felony Defendants, 1871–1940: Totals and Rates	10
2	Rates of Crime by Sex	11
3	Most Commonly Charged Felonies by Sex	12
4	Rates of Crime by Age	14
5	Most Commonly Charged Felonies by Age	16
6	Rates of Crime by Marital Status	18
7	Most Commonly Charged Felonies by Marital Status	20
8	Rates of Crime by Residence	22
9	Most Commonly Charged Felonies by Residence	24
10	Rates of Crime by Degree of Education	26
11	Most Commonly Charged Felonies by Degree of Education	28
12	Rates of Crime by Occupational Category	32
13	Most Commonly Charged Felonies by Occupational Category	34
14	Disposition Practices of the Juges d'Instruction: Rates for Murder, Grand Larceny, and Girl Molestation	36
15	Salaries of Paris Sûreté Personnel, 1870–1910	52
16	Directors of the Paris Sûreté, 1870–1912	54
17	Paris Prefects of Police, 1870–1913	62
18	Directors of the Sûreté Générale, 1871–1940	84
19	Budget of the Sûreté Générale, 1871–1940	86

Tables

20	Personnel of the Sûreté Générale, 1860–1940	87
21	Personnel of the Paris Sûreté, 1890–1940	108
22	Personnel Budget of the Paris Sûreté, 1890–1940	109
23	Directors of the Paris Sûreté / Police Judiciaire, 1912–1941	111
24	Paris Prefects of Police, 1913–1941	120
25	Cours d'Appel, 1800–1940	168
26	The Courts of Paris During the Third Republic	170
27	Personnel of the Bench and Parquet	171
28	Salaries for the Bench and Parquet	172
29	Ministers of Justice, 1870–1940	200
30	Directeurs des Affaires Civiles, Ministère de la Justice, 1870–1940	202
31	Directeurs des Affaires Criminelles, Ministère de la Justice, 1870–1940	203
32	Directeurs du Personnel, Ministère de la Justice, 1870–1940	204
33	Patterns of Senior Judicial Promotion, 1871–1940	218
34	Promotions Within the Magistrature by Political Period, 1871–1940	222
35	Parquet-to-Bench and Out-of-Step Promotions, 1871–1940	231

Preface and Acknowledgments

I began this work on the criminal justice system of Third Republic France because I am fascinated by crime, police methods, and courts (and if this fascination is a perversion, I can at least claim good company in Marc Bloch and many other devotees among historians); because I believe that the manner in which a society investigates, tries, and punishes those charged with crime is a powerful lantern illuminating the dark cellars and closeted secrets of that society; because I am an adherent of history as a narrative (trial descriptions are that par excellence, second only to battles) and as an account of the individual (before an examining magistrate, his life spread out in the documents of instruction, a human is all too human). In 1977, I had completed a biography of Albert de Mun and was considering various future projects when Eugen Weber encouraged me to select "justice" as my compass for surveying the territory of the Third Republic. Since then, David Pinkney, Gordon Wright, Joel Colton, Robert Nye, Steve Hause, Jean-Marie Mayeur, William Logue, and Karen Offen have also lent their support and occasionally apposite suggestions and criticism. Certainly, the first products of this research, *The Hypocrisy of Justice in the Belle Epoque*, several articles, and an essay for the Jewish Museum's distinguished exhibition on the Dreyfus affair, benefited substantially from their attention and inspection.

Preface and Acknowledgments

In this monograph I have chosen to analyze the French criminal justice system—from the crime that forces it to take action, through the police investigation that provides an arrest, through the criminal procedure that formalizes the charges and draws an indictment, through the court trial that ends in a judgment, to the punishment of the guilty by fine, jail, prison, hard labor, deportation, or death. At points during this passage through the judicial perils of Pierre and Pauline, the analysis extends to the principal agents and actors of the system—the police detectives, the magistrates, and the lawyers. If the portrayal on the whole is negative, I can only reply that the French judicial system worked better in theory than in practice, that too many elements were subject to frequent and baleful political pressure, and that in consequence, the honorable and upright were often overwhelmed. The Afterword displays French justice in action through the perspective of a specific and rightly famous case, that of the Bonnot Gang from 1911 to 1913. No one, not criminals, police, magistrates, or even the public, emerges as a hero. And perhaps that is only a proper assessment of a criminal justice system and the criminals who make it necessary.

The research for this book would have been much more difficult or even impossible without the extraordinary assistance of Ségolène de Dainville-Barbiche and Geneviève Le Moël at the Archives Nationales, of Gérard Poisson and Jean-Louis Ginhac at the Archives de la Préfecture de Police, Paris, and of André Cardoso, Sous-Directeur de Personnel for the Police Nationale. Their interest in this subject aroused a willingness to share rich knowledge and to help make available relevant files that would otherwise have remained inaccessible. I am most grateful for these efforts and this kindness.

My thanks go as well to the Andrew W. Mellon Foundation, for supporting the first forays into the archives, and to the Louisiana State University Council on Research, for a summer grant of time and the training to analyze the statistical material I had gathered and to prepare tables drawn from it. Some portions of this book have appeared in print previously as articles. I acknowledge with appreciation permission to adapt and reprint the following: "Sex, Property, and Crime in the Third Republic: A Statistical Introduction," *Historical Reflections/Réflexions Historiques*, XI (Fall, 1984), 323–49; "The Record of Murders: Blood-Stained Dossiers at the Archives de la Préfecture de Police," *Third Republic/Troisième République*, X (Fall, 1980), 1–17; "The Courts, the Magistrature, and Promotions in Third Republic France, 1871–1914," *American Historical Re-*

Preface and Acknowledgments

view, LXXXVII (1982), 977–1009; "The Bande à Bonnot: Les Bandits Tragiques," *Laurels* (American Society of the Legion of Honor Magazine), LIII (Fall, 1982), 73–98; and "The Dreyfus Affair and the Corruption of the French Legal System," in Norman L. Kleeblatt (ed.), *The Dreyfus Affair: Art, Truth, and Justice* (Berkeley: University of California Press, 1987), 37–49. The frontispiece is taken from the illustration for the article in the *American Historical Review*. I first presented the argument of this book in a paper, "Criminal Justice Under the Third Republic," before the Symposium on Fin-de-Siècle France, organized by the Jewish Museum of New York and the New York Council for the Humanities, at the Jewish Museum on November 15, 1987. My research assistants, Connie Sue Evans and Teresa Lynn Nicholson, compiled the index. Leslie E. Phillabaum, Beverly Jarrett, Margaret Dalrymple, and John Easterly of the Louisiana State University Press shepherded the manuscript through publication and by their suggestions significantly improved it.

Abbreviations

AMF	Archives du Ministère des Finances
AN	Archives Nationales
APP	Archives de la Préfecture de Police
JO	*Journal Officiel,* Lois et Décrets
JOC	*Journal Officiel,* Chambre des Députés
JOS	*Journal Officiel,* Sénat

Crime and Criminal Justice Under the Third Republic

1

The Crimes

In 1840, writing the last volume in his history of Cologne, Friedrich Everhard von Mering vented his resentment at France's treatment of his native city during the Napoleonic Wars: "Since time out of mind, the French have always been known as devious, two-faced, sly, insidious, treacherous people, arrogant and cruel in victory and craven in defeat. They were always dangerous confidence-tricksters, practiced swindlers, windbags, babblers, braggarts, hypocrites, liars, and thieves. Just about every child knows that."[1] The words were rank cultural prejudice. Through the nineteenth century the German experience with crime and crime rates was quite similar to that of the French for the principal forms of larceny and fraud. But Mering had a point. The 1830s and 1840s were a time of much crime, and the French did commit at least their share of property offenses. The situation would grow worse during the rest of the century, with the totals and the rates (based on population) increasing significantly. So would the totals and rates for the most common misdemeanor offense of violence against persons—assault and wounding.[2] What

---

1. Friedrich Everhard von Mering, *Zur Geschichte der Stadt Köln am Rhein, von ihrer Gründung bis zur Gegenwart* (Cologne, 1838–40), IV, 224. I am indebted to Susan Vandiver Nicassio and Katherine Anne McGinn, graduate students at Louisiana State University, for pointing out this reference.
2. Howard Zehr, *Crime and the Development of Modern Society: Patterns of Criminality in Nineteenth-Century Germany and France* (Totowa, N.J., 1977), 35–39, 87.

every child in Cologne may have known about these crimes and others is problematical. By the last thirty years of the century, what many a child in France knew was that in addition to theft, fraud, and assault, another crime with a high incidence was the molestation of children, particularly of young girls.

Between 1871 and 1940, a Frenchman charged with a *felony* crime "against property" was, by a large margin, likely to have committed grand larceny. If charged with a felony crime "against persons," he was, again by a large margin, likely to have molested a girl of fifteen years or younger. Whether his age was sixteen or seventy or any point within this range; whether he lived in a rural or an urban district; whether he was a bachelor, a husband, or a widower; whether he had children or was childless; whether he was well-educated or illiterate; whether he was rich or poor, *blouse bleu, commis,* or *patron,* the felonies of the average Frenchman were most often grand larceny and the molestation of young girls. Grand larceny rarely goes unreported, and it represented 50.69 percent of the felonies against property charged during the seventy years of the Third Republic. Statistics for so-called "sex crimes" are believed to be understated because of the embarrassment involved in contacting the police. Even with this caveat, girl molestation accounted for 32.21 percent of the felonies against persons during the same period.

Such statistics emerge from the fundamental source for the study of French crime, the *Compte général de l'administration de la justice criminelle,* issued annually by the Ministry of Justice since 1825. Each volume provides a breakdown—by indictments, convictions, and sentences—for misdemeanors (*délits*) and felonies (*crimes*) tried before the courts during the previous year. The information about misdemeanors is summary, but for felonies, tried before the superior criminal courts (*cours d'assises*), there are tables dividing defendants (*accusés*) into categories by sex, age, marital status, rural or urban residence, degree of education, and occupation.[3] An inevitable distortion results from the use of court records for the study of crime: crimes that remain unsolved or for which there is insufficient evidence to win an indictment are absent, creating what criminologists

3. The statistics for seven years of the period 1871–1940 are not included: The volumes for 1914–18 were not published because of World War I; that for 1939 because of World War II. The Bibliothèque Nationale lacks the volume for 1921, and it is not readily available elsewhere. See my "Sex, Property, and Crime in the Third Republic: A Statistical Introduction," *Historical Reflections/Réflexions Historiques,* XI (1984), 323–49. Some of the findings in that article have been modified to a minor degree through the inclusion of additional statistical material and through revised quantitative techniques.

The Crimes

term the *dark figure.* Yet, without local police statistics, this "dark figure" must remain dark.[4]

There are further admonitions to the study of crime statistics. Any change in legal statutes provokes a change in the statistics and therefore a distortion. The most commonly cited example for the early nineteenth century is the series of laws surrounding the use of state forests. Between 1831 and 1835, infractions reached a zenith, averaging 135,000 a year and accounting for approximately a quarter of all female defendants. After these laws were altered (the last change occurring in 1859), legalizing what had formerly been illegal, an entire category of crime disappeared from the statistics, and the rate for female criminality plummeted—deceptively. Likewise, public drunkenness (*délit d'ivresse*) was first declared illegal in 1873, and the arrests in consequence produced an equally deceptive rise in the rate of (largely) male criminality.[5]

Patterns of enforcement affected the statistics more frequently and less obviously. Howard Zehr suggests that "minor violence and malicious mischief may have been looked upon more lightly in the countryside than in the city," and such traditions as the charivari support this position. Rural inhabitants were (and are) mistrustful of formal legal proceedings and likely to settle differences and grievances privately: "From Justice, Lord, deliver us!" This attitude probably reduced the number of reported crimes against property as well. Robbery is difficult to commit successfully when the robber and his victim are acquainted, and any stranger would be immediately suspect.[6] Enforcement could also vary over time: As Frenchmen during the last years of the nineteenth and the first decade of the twentieth century became ever more concerned about the nation's decreasing

---

4. For an introduction to the problems of utilizing statistics for crime, see Zehr, *Crime and the Development of Modern Society,* 10–30, 157–76, and his summary article, "The Modernization of Crime in Germany and France, 1830–1913," *Journal of Social History,* VIII (1975), 117–41; André Davidovitch, "Criminalité et répression en France depuis un siècle (1851–1952)," *Revue française de sociologie,* II (January, 1961), 30–49; J. J. Tobias, *Crime and Industrial Society in the Nineteenth Century* (New York, 1967), 256–67; V. A. C. Gatrell and T. B. Hadden, "Criminal Statistics and Their Interpretation," in E. A. Wrigley (ed.), *Nineteenth-Century Society: Essays in the Use of Quantitative Methods for the Study of Social Data* (Cambridge, England, 1972), 336–96; Robert A. Nye, "Crime in Modern Societies: Some Research Strategies for Historians," *Journal of Social History,* XI (1978), 491–507; and Michelle Perrot, "Délinquance et système pénitentiaire en France au XIXe siècle," *Annales: Economies, Sociétés, Civilisations,* XXX (January–February, 1975), 67–91.

5. Perrot, "Délinquance et système pénitentiaire," 72–73.

6. Zehr, *Crime and the Development of Modern Society,* 17. On the attitude of rural districts to "state" justice, see Eugen Weber, *Peasants into Frenchmen: The Modernization of Rural France, 1870–1914* (Stanford, 1976), 57–67.

birth rate, the legal authorities reacted by more strictly enforcing laws against abortion and infanticide. The benevolent blindness toward these offenses as practiced by women in earlier decades ceased almost entirely. V. A. C. Gatrell and T. B. Hadden conclude that increased attention to a crime or improved policing has a double impact on the statistics: "It seems likely that their *initial* effect would be to bring more criminals before the courts who might previously have escaped detection; and that, other things being equal, their *subsequent* effect might be reflected in a decline in the rates as the deterrent influence of the new police forces came to be felt."[7]

The statistics for felonies are further distorted by the increasing use during the nineteenth century of *correctionnalisation*, particularly after 1842, when this practice received official sanction. The verdict in a trial before the cour d'assises was rendered by a jury, whereas that before the lower magistracy court (*cour correctionnelle*) was by the three-judge panel. In France, juries were an innovation of the 1789 Revolution and were notoriously indulgent, returning acquittals for more than 28 percent of defendants during the Third Republic. By prosecuting a lesser charge before a cour correctionnelle, where acquittals averaged less than 10 percent, the district prosecutor (*procureur de la République*) was much more likely to secure a guilty verdict. The distortion also appears in the statistics for misdemeanors but is more serious for felonies because in those cases it affects the detailed tables dividing defendants into categories. Consulting only the records for felonies can lead to serious errors. The number of defendants tried before the cours d'assises for grand larceny declined in the nineteenth and twentieth centuries from much higher totals, leading some researchers to conclude that there was a *fall* in the rate of crimes against property. In fact, the combined figures for the cours correctionnelles and the cours d'assises show an increase of approximately 60 percent in the rate of grand larceny during the same period.[8]

For all of their deficiencies, the statistics of the *Compte général* are the best statistics available. Used with circumspection, they pro-

---

7. Perrot, "Délinquance et système pénitentiaire," 73; Davidovitch, "Criminalité et répression," 40–42; Gatrell and Hadden, "Criminal Statistics and Their Interpretation," in Wrigley (ed.), *Nineteenth-Century Society*, 353.

8. For an egregious example of this variety of error, see Charles Tilly *et al.*, *The Rebellious Century, 1830–1930* (Cambridge, Mass., 1975), 79–80. The estimate of a 60 percent increase comes from Zehr, *Crime and the Development of Modern Society*, 36, Table 2.2. On *correctionnalisation* and acquittal rates, see Davidovitch, "Criminalité et répression," 37, 48. I have computed the acquittal rate for the cours d'assises during the Third Republic to be 28.41 percent.

The Crimes

vide at least good approximations for the situation of crime and criminals during the Third Republic. Or to use the argument of Gatrell and Haddon, "Recorded rates are sensitive enough to reflect the otherwise unknowable movements in the 'actual' incidence of criminal activity." Furthermore, these statistics influenced what legal and political leaders—and through them the great majority of educated French men and women—believed about crime and criminals, and from that, about the larger society.[9]

One means of comparing these social judgments during the Third

9. Gatrell and Haddon, "Criminal Statistics and Their Interpretation," in Wrigley (ed.), *Nineteenth-Century Society*, 361. For contemporary perceptions of crime and criminals, see Albert Abbo, *Les Crimes des foules* (Menton, 1910); Louis Albanel, *Le Crime dans la famille* (Paris, 1900); Camille Aymard, *La Profession du crime* (Paris, 1906); A. Bellanger, *Les Théories modernes de la criminalité* (La Chapelle-Montligeon, 1905); Marie-Anatole Bérard des Glajeux, *Souvenirs d'un président d'assises* (Paris, 1892); W. A. Bonger, *Criminalité et conditions économiques* (Amsterdam, 1905); Visoiu Cornateano, *Essai d'une théorie juridique et médico-légale de la préméditation criminelle* (Paris, 1910); Hélie Courtis, *Etude médico-légale des crimes passionels* (Toulouse, 1910); J. Dallemagne, *Les Théories de la criminalité* (Paris, 1896); A. Debierre, *Le Crâne des criminelles* (Lyon, 1895); Dr. Delassus, *Les Théories modernes de la criminalité* (Paris, 1899); Augustin Delvincourt, *La Lutte contre la criminalité dans les temps modernes* (Paris, 1897); Charles Desmaze, *Le Crime et la débauchée à Paris, le divorce* (Paris, 1881); Maurice Duval, *Religion, superstition, et criminalité* (Paris, 1935); Maurice de Fleury, *L'Ame du criminel* (Paris, 1898); Albert Giuliani, *L'Adolescence criminelle* (Villefranche, 1908); Camille Granier, *La Femme criminelle* (Paris, 1906); Roger Grébaut, *De l'alcoolisme dans ses rapports avec la criminalité* (Paris, 1900); J. Grosmolard, *La Lutte contre la criminalité juvénile au XIXe siècle* (Lyon, 1907); Louis Hamon, *Police et criminalité: Impressions d'un vieux policier* (Paris, 1900); Raymond Hesse, *Les Criminels peints par eux-mêmes* (Paris, 1912); Henri Joly, *Le Combat contre le crime* (Paris, 1892), *Le Crime: Étude sociale* (Paris, 1888), *La France criminelle* (Paris, 1889), and *Problèmes de science criminelle* (Paris, 1910); Emile Laurent, *L'Anthropologie criminelle et les nouvelles théories du crime* (2nd ed.; Paris, 1893); Eugène C. F. Ledos, *Les Criminels et la criminalité* (Paris, 1908); Prosper Lemaître, *Criminalité, répression, du sens moral des criminels, prison cellulaire, exposition publique* (Limoges, 1900); Raoul Lévy, *Examen médico-légal d'un jeune criminel de vingt ans poursuivi pour viol et homicide volontaire* (Auxerre, 1907); Cesare Lombroso, *L'Anthropologie criminelle* (3rd ed.; Paris, 1896); J. Maxwell, *Le Concept social du crime, son évolution* (Paris, 1914), and *Le Crime et la société* (Paris, 1909); Lucien Mialane, *La Criminalité juvenile; ses causes, ses remèdes* (Paris, 1926); Edouard Miltgen, *Le Cerveau des criminels* (Clermont-Ferrand, 1938); Monsieur Jean [pseud.], *Les Bas-fonds du crime et de la prostitution* (Paris, 1901); Charles Perrier, *L'Affaire Deluze* (Lyon, 1907), and *Les Criminels, étude concernant 859 condamnés* (Paris, 1900–1905); Raymond de Ryckère, *La Femme en prison et devant la mort* (Lyon, 1898), and *La Servante criminelle* (Paris, 1908); Quintiliano Saldona, *La Criminologie nouvelle* (Paris, 1929); Jean Signorel, *Le Crime et la défense sociale* (Paris, 1912); Henri Thulié, *La Lutte contre la dégénérescence et la criminalité* (Paris, 1912); Georges Pierre Marie Vidal, *Considérations sur l'état actuel de la criminalité en France* (Paris, 1904). See also the contemporary fictional literature, which abounds in stereotypes. An overall introduction is Robert A. Nye, *Crime, Madness, and Politics in Modern France: The Medical Concept of National Decline* (Princeton, 1984).

Republic with the realities of crime (at least as measured by court records) is to analyze the tables in the *Compte général* that classify defendants in felony cases by category (sex, age, marital status, residence, education, and occupation). Unfortunately, there is no similar information for misdemeanors. The following list, along with Table 1, provides preliminary information necessary for such an analysis. The list gives the names of the felonies cited in the detailed tables of the *Compte général*, the article(s) in the *Code pénal* defining the crime, and a brief description of the proscribed behavior.

Part I: Felonies Against Persons

1. Premeditated murder (*assassinat*) (Arts. 296–98). Homicide committed with premeditation or from ambush, usually defined in American law as first-degree murder.
2. Unpremeditated murder (*meutre*) (Art. 295). Homicide committed without premeditation but with a clear desire to kill, often defined in American law as second-degree murder.
3. Parricide (*parricide*) (Art. 299). The homicide, premeditated or not, of a parent or guardian, an act singled out for unusually harsh punishment under the law.
4. Poisoning (*empoisonnement*) (Art. 301). Homicide through poison, an act singled out for unusually harsh punishment after 1682, because it was considered so dangerous, so cowardly, and so difficult to prove.
5. Manslaughter (*blessures et coups suivi de mort*) (Arts. 309[4]–310). Homicide through accident, usually assault and wounding, without a clear desire to kill.
6. Infanticide (*infanticide*) (Art. 300). Homicide committed against a newborn infant.
7. Abortion (*avortement*) (Art. 317). Having an abortion or granting any assistance leading to a successful abortion; reduced to a misdemeanor in 1923.
8. Aggravated assault and wounding (*blessures et coups graves*) (Art. 309[1–3]). Inflicting serious, incapacitating, or permanent injury through assault.
9. Assault and wounding of a parent or guardian (*blessures et coups envers un ascendant*) (Art. 312). Singled out for harsh punishment because of the threat to family order.
10. Rape or sexual assault (*viol ou attentat à la pudeur*) (Arts. 331–33). Rape, attempted rape, or molestation.
11. Girl molestation or statutory rape (*attentat à la pudeur ou viol sur des enfants*) (Arts. 331–33). Illicit fondling of any child

The Crimes

under the age of fifteen, rape of a girl under the age of fifteen, or any sexual relations by consent between a girl under age thirteen and an adult.

12. Illegal restraint (*séquestration de personnes*) (Arts. 341–44). Detaining or imprisoning an individual against his will; in extreme cases defined as kidnapping.
13. Concealment or falsification of birth (*enlèvement, suppression ou supposition d'enfant*) (Art. 345). The crime takes two forms: the concealment of a birth, for whatever reason, and the assumption of a child as one's own when it is not, usually for the purposes of heirship.
14. Seduction or corruption of a minor (*enlèvement et détournement de mineurs*) (Arts. 354–57). Applies primarily to the removal of a girl under the age of sixteen from her parent's protection for the purpose of seduction or corruption.
15. Perjury (*faux témoinage en matière criminelle*) (Arts. 361, 364). Perjury in a felony case.

Part II: Felonies Against Property

16. Fraud in a commercial document (*faux en écriture de commerce*) (Arts. 145–48). Intentional perversion of the truth in a commercial document designed to induce another to part with something of value.
17. Fraud in an official public document (*faux en écriture authentique et publique*) (Arts. 145–48). Intentional perversion of the truth in an official public document designed to induce another to part with something of value.
18. Fraud in a private document (*faux en écriture privée*) (Arts. 150–51). Intentional perversion of the truth in a private document designed to induce another to part with something of value.
19. Abuse of confidence (*abus de confiance*) (Art. 408). Fraudulently misusing to anyone's prejudice valuables handed over for a special object.
20. Extortion (*extorsion de titres ou de signatures*) (Art. 400[1–2]). Obtaining property or consent from someone through the use of actual or threatened violence or fear; blackmail.
21. Fraudulent bankruptcy (*banqueroute frauduleuse*) (Arts. 402–404). Fraudulently entering into a condition of bankruptcy.
22. Embezzlement by a public official (*détournement par un dépositaire de deniers publics*) (Arts. 169–72). Fraudulent appropriation of public funds, usually by a tax collector.
23. Malfeasance by a public official (*soustraction d'actes par un*

dépositaire public) (Arts. 169–72). Fraudulent withholding of official deeds and records by a public official.
24. Corruption of a public official (*concussion ou corruption*) (Arts. 174–75, 177, 179). Offering a bribe to a public official; accepting a bribe if a public official.
25. Theft from the mails (*soustraction, par un employé de la poste, de lettres contenant des valeurs*) (Art. 187). Theft of valuables from the mails by an employee of the post office.
26. Counterfeiting (*fausse monnaie*) (Art. 132). Fraudulent and criminal imitation of money.
27. Aggravated robbery (*vol à l'aide de violences sur les personnes, hors de la voie publique*) (Art. 382). Robbery committed with violence other than on or near a public highway or street.
28. Highway robbery without violence (*vol sur un chemin publique, sans violences*) (Art. 383). Robbery committed without violence on or near a public highway or street.
29. Highway robbery with violence (*vol sur un chemin publique, à l'aide de violences*) (Art. 383). Robbery committed with violence on or near a public highway or street.
30. Theft from a church (*vol dans les églises*) (Arts. 385[2], 386[1]). Larceny committed against church property, an act singled out for harsher punishment because of the notion of sacrilege.
31. Theft by a servant (*vol par un domestique ou homme de service à gages*) (Art. 386[3]). Singled out for harsher punishment because larceny by a servant or an employee carries with it the notion of treachery.
32. Grand larceny (*autres vols qualifiés, passibles de la réclusion, passibles de la peine des travaux forcés*) (Arts. 381, 384–86). Theft aggravated by one or more of the following conditions: committed at night, committed by more than one person, committed while armed, committed through the burglary of an inhabited residence, committed through the assumption of official uniforms or the identity of a public official.
33. Arson of a dwelling (*incendie d'édifices habités*) (Art. 434). Malicious burning of an inhabited residence.
34. Arson of a nondwelling (*incendie d'édifices non-habités*) (Art. 434). Malicious burning of any structure or object not used as a residence.
35. Pillage (*pillage et dégât d'objets mobiliers en bande et à force ouverte*) (Arts. 440–42). Destruction of property by individuals acting as a mob.[10]

10. *Compte général de l'administration de la justice criminelle* (Paris, 1825–);

The Crimes

Table 1 lists, by rank order of frequency, the number of defendants charged with each of these felonies during the Third Republic and the percentage of total felony defendants that each represents. From the table it is immediately clear that only four crimes—grand larceny, girl molestation, unpremeditated murder, and premeditated murder—account for 57.15 percent of the felony charges. By themselves, grand larceny and girl molestation, the most frequently charged felonies, respectively, against property and against persons, combine to contribute 42.35 percent of all the defendants. So many cases of grand larceny would have brought a grim satisfaction to the Cologner von Mering. What astonishes is the prevalence of girl molestation. Detailed analysis of the data will demonstrate that an extremely broad spectrum of Third Republic society was responsible for the elevated levels of these two felonies.

The perception of male and female criminals can be expressed concisely: men were violent, women cunning.[11] The tables from the *Compte général* simply confirm this stereotypical view. Based on statistics for 1871, 1881, 1891, 1901, 1911, 1922, and 1931, men accounted for 83.06 percent of felony defendants, women 16.94 percent. The rate for each felony has been compared with this "normal" average for each sex, and when the rate for any offense is substantially greater than the normal average, it has been labeled a "male crime" or a "female crime." Table 2 displays this information and includes the absolute number of defendants for each crime as cited in the *Compte général* for the specified years.[12]

Emile Garçon (ed.), *Code pénal annoté* (Paris, 1901–11). For additional details consult the *Code*.

11. For additional details, the following are particularly interesting. Grébaut, *De l'alcoolisme*, attributes most male crime to heavy drinking; Desmaze, *Le Crime et la débauchée*, and Monsieur Jean [pseud.], *Les Bas-fonds*, link much female crime, especially murder and theft, to prostitution. Lévy, *Examen médico-légal*, explains "sex crimes" by claiming that the men who committed them were either "animals" or "moral imbeciles." Cornateano, *Essai d'une théorie*, Courtis, *Etude médico-légale*, and Dallemagne, *Les Théories*, assign male and female crimes on a psychological basis. Ryckère's *La Femme* and *La Servante* condemn women as crueler and more prone to criminality than men. Perrier, *Les Criminels*, provides brief analyses of criminals and their crimes.

12. Unfortunately, there is not perfect consistency throughout the *Compte général* in the tables dividing defendants by sex, age, marital status, rural or urban residence, degree of education, and occupation. For example, in the table for sex, the absolute number of cases of girl molestation is 3,014, but in the tables for age, marital status, residence, and education, it is 2,949. These variations are attributable to differences in record keeping, combined with undetected errors in computation and printing. None of the disparities appears significant enough to distort seriously the statistical findings for rates of crime and most commonly charged crimes.

TABLE 1
Felony Defendants, 1871–1940: Totals and Rates (n = 202,018)

Felony	Total	Rate (%)
1. Grand larceny	56,184	27.81
2. Girl molestation	29,369	14.54
3. Murder (unpremeditated)	16,366	8.10
4. Murder (premeditated)	13,542	6.70
5. Theft by a servant	9,664	4.78
6. Infanticide	8,792	4.35
7. Manslaughter	8,260	4.09
8. Arson (dwelling)	6,907	3.42
9. Counterfeiting	5,338	2.65
10. Fraud in commercial document	5,216	2.58
11. Rape	5,109	2.53
12. Aggravated robbery	4,611	2.28
13. Abortion	4,118	2.04
14. Fraud in official public document	3,860	1.91
15. Abuse of confidence	3,780	1.87
16. Arson (nondwelling)	3,338	1.65
17. Fraudulent bankruptcy	3,092	1.53
18. Fraud in private document	3,068	1.52
19. Highway robbery with violence	1,971	.98
20. Aggravated assault and wounding	1,816	.90
21. Theft from a church	1,168	.58
22. Parricide	842	.42
23. Assault and wounding of a parent	763	.38
24. Concealment of birth	749	.37
25. Poisoning	576	.28
26. Extortion	564	.28
27. Corruption (public official)	551	.27
28. Seduction of a minor	507	.25
29. Theft from the mails (PTT employee)	483	.24
30. Embezzlement (public official)	398	.20
31. Highway robbery without violence	363	.18
32. Pillage	279	.14
33. Perjury	184	.09
34. Illegal restraint	176	.09
35. Malfeasance (public official)	14	.01

SOURCE: *Compte général de l'administration de la justice criminelle*, 1871–1913, 1919–20, 1922–38, 1940, statistics for felonies.

The Crimes

TABLE 2
Rates of Crime by Sex (n = 22,507)

Men (normal rate 83.06%)

Felony	No.	Rate (%)
1. Malfeasance (public official)	2	100.00
2. Rape	598	99.50
3. Girl molestation	3,014	99.04
4. Corruption (public official)	43	97.67
5. Highway robbery with violence	256	96.48
6. Aggravated robbery	553	94.58

Women (normal rate 16.94%)

Felony	No.	Rate (%)
1. Infanticide	940	94.89
2. Abortion	748	87.17
3. Concealment of birth	80	82.50
4. Poisoning	53	54.72
5. Extortion	77	38.96
6. Theft by a servant	1,185	27.68

SOURCE: *Compte général de l'administration de la justice criminelle*, 1871, 1881, 1891, 1901, 1911, 1922, 1931, statistics for felonies by sex.

Men, as expected, were charged with the heinous sex crimes and with the forms of larceny aggravated by acts of violence during their commission. The high male rates for malfeasance and corruption by public officials, based on the relatively few of these cases charged, are the result of the overwhelming predominance of men in such positions. Not surprisingly, the highest rates of crime for women were connected with the process of reproduction—infanticides, abortions, and concealments of birth. What strikingly confirmed the prejudice of women's cunning was their high rates of poisonings and extortions, more than three times and two times, respectively, above their normal average. By its denunciation in the Code pénal as treachery, theft by a servant might also be considered cunning. Nevertheless, this contrast between men and women is blurred by a second manner of analyzing the statistics—compiling the most commonly charged crimes for each sex by *total* instead of *rate*. Table 3 displays this information by rank order of frequency for each sex and by number of defendants for each crime.

The findings in Table 3 reveal a similar pattern of criminality for both sexes, with grand larceny, theft by a servant, and various forms

TABLE 3
Most Commonly Charged Felonies by Sex

Men (n = 18,695)

Felony	No.
1. Grand larceny	5,753
2. Girl molestation	2,985
3. Murder (unpremeditated)	1,647
4. Murder (premeditated)	1,268
5. Theft by a servant	857
6. Manslaughter	842

Women (n = 3,812)

Felony	No.
1. Infanticide	892
2. Grand larceny	656
3. Abortion	652
4. Theft by a servant	328
5. Murder (premeditated)	231
6. Arson (dwelling)	167

SOURCE: *Compte général de l'administration de la justice criminelle*, 1871, 1881, 1891, 1901, 1911, 1922, 1931, statistics for felonies by sex.

of homicide (premeditated, unpremeditated, manslaughter, and infanticide) ranking among the most frequently charged crimes for men and women. It appears as well that children were the targets of a singular degree of violence, though in two quite different ways (girl molestation and infanticide). The data from other tables will reinforce this conclusion.

The perceptions and stereotypes associated with age and crime are less clear than those associated with sex. Traditionally, violence (against property as well as persons) and the highest rates of crime are related to youthful criminals, less violent and more clever forms of theft to those of maturity, and girl molestation (for men) and arson (for women) to the old.[13] Table 4 lists the "normal rate" of total felo-

---

13. For additional details, consult the following. Mialane, *La Criminalité juvenile*, and Giuliani, *L'Adolescence criminelle*, treat the problem of criminality among the young, and with Lévy, *Examen médico-légal*, argue that lack of moral instruction was the root cause of juvenile delinquency. Desmaze, *Le Crime et la débauchée*, and Monsieur Jean [pseud.], *Les Bas-fonds*, point to prostitution as the source of most serious crime among men and women under the age of thirty. Aymard, *La Profession du crime*, finds recidivism to be a function of age, and Perrier, *Les Criminels*, supports this thesis through case histories. Debierre, *Le Crâne*, and Dallemagne, *Les Théories*, assert that the age of a criminal was part of the sociological and physical background that would define his crime.

The Crimes

nies by age group, the absolute number of defendants for each crime, and the specific felonies associated with each age group by elevated rate.[14]

The data in Table 4 offer a confirmation of the traditional view. Men and women (the structure of the statistics in the *Compte général* makes it impossible to control for gender) thirty years old or younger were responsible for 49.09 percent of all felonies. No other age group had a high rate of violent crime. Rape is almost exclusively a male crime, and adolescents (sixteen to twenty-one years old) alone accounted for 24.04 percent of the rapes charged; adding young adults from twenty-two to thirty increases the rate to 57.90 percent. This thirty-and-under age group was responsible for 76.63 percent of aggravated robberies, 64.06 percent of highway robberies with violence, 55.63 percent of aggravated cases of assault and wounding, 49.29 percent of manslaughters, 48.80 percent of unpremeditated and 43.49 percent of premeditated murders, and 71.14 percent of infanticides. Defendants thirty-one to sixty years old had a combined felony rate of 46.91 percent. These individuals, much more likely to have held positions of trust, had high rates of "white collar" offenses, including various forms of fraud: fraud in a commercial document (69.50 percent), fraud in an official public document (64.93 percent), fraud in a private document (74.31 percent), abuse of confidence (63.69 percent), and fraudulent bankruptcy (77.91 percent). And defendants in this age range who were public officials had high rates of white collar crime involving abuse of functions: theft from the mails (55.17 percent), corruption (72.72 percent), embezzlement (79.31 percent), and malfeasance (100.00 percent). Persons in this age range also accounted for a large proportion of the perjury cases, 79.99 percent. Significantly for the stereotype, the first elevated rate for girl molestation appears in the fifty-one-to-sixty-year-old segment of the age group, to be continued among the oldest defendants, those sixty-one years and older. This last group also had high rates for arson (both types) and poisoning, crimes often associated with old women.

However much the statistics for elevated rates of crime confirm the traditional stereotypes for age, the figures for the most commonly charged felonies again blur the differences among groups. Table 5 displays this information by rank order of frequency for each age group and by number of defendants for each crime. The most

---

14. The additional numbers in the discussion of Tables 4 and 5 are derived from the same volumes of the *Compte général* as those in the tables.

TABLE 4
Rates of Crime by Age (n = 21,459)

Under 16 (normal rate .78%)

Felony	No.	Rate (%)
1. Arson (dwelling)	647	6.18
2. Arson (nondwelling)	395	4.81
3. Pillage	133	2.26

16–21 (normal rate 16.59%)

Felony	No.	Rate (%)
1. Aggravated robbery	475	35.16
2. Theft from a church	93	27.96
3. Rape	570	24.04
4. Infanticide	856	23.01
5. Theft by a servant	1,172	22.78
6. Highway robbery with violence	256	22.66
7. Grand larceny	6,277	22.66

22–30 (normal rate 31.72%)

Felony	No.	Rate (%)
1. Infanticide	856	48.01
2. Aggravated assault and wounding	151	43.71
3. Counterfeiting	558	41.58
4. Highway robbery without violence	41	41.46
5. Concealment of birth	78	41.03
6. Aggravated robbery	475	40.63
7. Highway robbery with violence	256	40.23

31–40 (normal rate 24.46%)

Felony	No.	Rate (%)
1. Malfeasance (public official)	2	50.00
2. Extortion	77	38.96
3. Illegal restraint	39	38.46
4. Embezzlement (public official)	29	37.93
5. Fraud in commercial document	531	37.48
6. Fraudulent bankruptcy	249	36.55
7. Poisoning	46	34.78
8. Theft from the mails (PTT employee)	29	34.48

41–50 (normal rate 14.82%)

Felony	No.	Rate (%)
1. Malfeasance (public official)	2	50.00
2. Corruption (public official)	33	36.36
3. Fraudulent bankruptcy	249	27.71

The Crimes

TABLE 4
Continued

41–50 (normal rate 14.82%)

Felony	No.	Rate (%)
4. Fraud in private document	327	26.91
5. Perjury	35	25.71
6. Fraud in official public document	305	25.25
7. Abuse of confidence	358	25.14
8. Embezzlement (public official)	29	24.14

51–60 (normal rate 7.63%)

Felony	No.	Rate (%)
1. Perjury	35	28.57
2. Illegal restraint	39	17.95
3. Embezzlement (public official)	29	17.24
4. Girl molestation	2,949	16.01
5. Fraud in private document	327	15.29
6. Corruption (public official)	33	15.15

61 and above (normal rate 4.00%)

Felony	No.	Rate (%)
1. Poisoning	46	15.22
2. Girl molestation	2,949	12.78
3. Arson (dwelling)	647	10.97
4. Illegal restraint	39	10.26
5. Arson (nondwelling)	395	8.10

SOURCE: *Compte général de l'administration de la justice criminelle*, 1871, 1881, 1891, 1901, 1911, 1922, 1931, statistics for felonies by age group.

commonly charged felony against property for all age groups except that of sixty-one years and older was grand larceny; the most commonly charged felony against persons for all age groups except those under sixteen and those between twenty-two and thirty was girl molestation. Premeditated and unpremeditated murder were also very frequent for all age groups, with infanticide linked to the heavy childbearing years, sixteen to thirty. These findings are almost identical to those for most commonly charged felonies by men and by women.

Stereotypes and perceptions of a criminal's marital status paralleled those for his age. Marriage was considered to be a stabilizing influence, and unmarried men and women, usually the youngest element in the society, were presumed to commit more, and more violent, crimes. Married men and women, conversely, would be

TABLE 5
Most Commonly Charged Felonies by Age

Under 16 (n = 166)

Felony	No.
1. Grand larceny	57
2. Arson (dwelling)	40
3. Arson (nondwelling)	19
4. Murder (premeditated)	12
5. Murder (unpremeditated)	9

16–21 (n = 3,560)

Felony	No.
1. Grand larceny	1,397
2. Girl molestation	319
3. Theft by a servant	267
4. Murder (unpremeditated)	249
5. Infanticide	197

22–30 (n = 6,807)

Felony	No.
1. Grand larceny	2,499
2. Murder (unpremeditated)	573
3. Girl molestation	445
4. Murder (premeditated)	436
5. Infanticide	411

31–40 (n = 5,248)

Felony	No.
1. Grand larceny	1,401
2. Girl molestation	679
3. Murder (unpremeditated)	437
4. Murder (premeditated)	380
5. Theft by a servant	275

41–50 (n = 3,181)

Felony	No.
1. Girl molestation	654
2. Grand larceny	610
3. Murder (premeditated)	256
4. Murder (unpremeditated)	233
5. Theft by a servant	153

The Crimes

TABLE 5
Continued

51–60 (n = 1,638)

Felony	No.
1. Girl molestation	472
2. Grand larceny	251
3. Murder (premeditated)	132
4. Murder (unpremeditated)	131
5. Arson (dwelling)	86

61 and above (n = 859)

Felony	No.
1. Girl molestation	377
2. Murder (unpremeditated)	71
Arson (dwelling)	71
4. Grand larceny	62
5. Murder (premeditated)	57

SOURCE: *Compte général de l'administration de la justice criminelle*, 1871, 1881, 1891, 1901, 1911, 1922, 1931, statistics for felonies by age group.

more mature, less violent, and more likely to fall into crimes of fraud as they worked to provide for their families. Widowers and widows would be susceptible to the crimes of the elderly. For the married, widowers, and widows, the presence of children would strengthen the tendency toward stability.[15] Table 6 lists the rate of total felonies by marital status, the absolute number of defendants for each crime, and the specific felonies associated with each status by elevated rate.[16]

To a degree, the data in Table 6 sustain the stereotype. The unmarried did have a high rate for all felonies (56.65 percent) and elevated rates for some violent crimes: aggravated robbery (83.58 percent), in-

15. Albanel, *Le Crime dans la famille*, is an excellent introduction to the stereotype. Mialane, *La Criminalité juvenile*, and Giuliani, *L'Adolescence criminelle*, argue the familiar case that the destruction of the family unit bred crime. Grébaut, *De l'alcoolisme*, insists that unmarried men drank more heavily than married men and therefore committed more crime. Desmaze, *Le Crime et la débauchée*, mounts a similar argument that unmarried women were more apt to enter prostitution and then move to more serious forms of criminality. Delvincourt, *La Lutte*, Debierre, *Le Crâne*, and Dallemagne, *Les Théories*, assert the positive effect of family life upon the reduction of crime.

16. The additional numbers in the discussion of Tables 6 and 7 are derived from the same volumes of the *Compte général* as those in the tables.

TABLE 6
Rates of Crime by Marital Status (n = 21,530)

Unmarried (normal rate 56.65%)

Felony	No.	Rate (%)
1. Aggravated robbery	536	83.58
2. Theft from a church	93	74.19
3. Infanticide	855	73.92
4. Grand larceny	6,275	71.78
5. Concealment of birth	73	67.12
6. Counterfeiting	558	67.03
7. Rape	573	65.45

Married with Children (normal rate 27.73%)

Felony	No.	Rate (%)
1. Embezzlement (public official)	29	65.52
2. Extortion	77	61.04
3. Corruption (public official)	33	60.61
4. Perjury	35	60.00
5. Fraud in a private document	327	57.80
6. Fraudulent bankruptcy	249	53.41
7. Fraud in commercial document	532	49.81
8. Highway robbery without violence	41	48.78

Married Without Children (normal rate 8.46%)

Felony	No.	Rate (%)
1. Extortion	77	20.78
2. Fraudulent bankruptcy	249	18.47
3. Embezzlement (public official)	29	17.24
4. Perjury	35	17.14
5. Fraud in commercial document	532	15.98
6. Illegal restraint	39	15.38
7. Corruption (public official)	33	15.15
8. Fraud in official public document	304	14.14
9. Fraud in private document	327	14.07

Widow(er) with Children (normal rate 5.50%)

Felony	No.	Rate (%)
1. Poisoning	46	34.78
2. Abortion	538	11.90
3. Girl molestation	2,949	10.95
4. Infanticide	855	10.53
5. Illegal restraint	39	10.26
6. Murder (premeditated)	1,460	8.70
7. Arson (dwelling)	647	7.42

The Crimes

TABLE 6
Continued

Widow(er) with Children (normal rate 5.50%)

Felony	No.	Rate (%)
1. Aggravated assault and wounding	152	4.61
2. Poisoning	46	4.35
3. Seduction of a minor	51	3.92
4. Manslaughter	854	3.16
5. Murder (premeditated)	1,460	2.88
6. Fraudulent bankruptcy	249	2.81
7. Abortion	538	2.79

SOURCE: *Compte général de l'administration de la justice criminelle*, 1871, 1881, 1891, 1901, 1911, 1922, 1931, statistics for felonies by marital status.

fanticide (73.92 percent), rape (65.45 percent), highway robbery with violence (62.65 percent), and aggravated assault and wounding (60.53 percent). But they did not have an elevated rate for others: premeditated murder (47.53 percent), unpremeditated murder (54.40 percent), and manslaughter (54.33 percent). It is hardly clear whether these rates are associated more closely to relative youth or to the lack of a spouse. Married men and women, with or without children, were much less violent and accounted for far fewer crimes. Their rates (with and without children, respectively) for all felonies were 27.73 percent and 8.46 percent, but for the forms of fraud and abuse of public office, there were substantial elevations: fraud in a commercial document (49.81 and 15.98 percent), fraud in an official public document (40.13 and 14.14 percent), fraud in a private document (57.80 and 14.07 percent), abuse of confidence (46.93 and 11.73 percent), fraudulent bankruptcy (53.41 and 18.47 percent), corruption (60.61 and 15.15 percent), and embezzlement (65.52 and 17.24 percent). (The sample contained only two cases of malfeasance, both charged against a married man with children.) For widowers and widows, the elevated rates of abortion and infanticide may indicate successful efforts to avoid more children (for themselves or other family members) or the traditional role of older women (and sometimes men) as abortionists and midwives. If widowers and widows were, in fact, the oldest element in society, the high rates of poisoning and girl molestation would not be unusual. The slightly elevated rates of manslaughter and of aggravated assault and wounding are surprising, but may be the result of quarrels.

TABLE 7

Most Commonly Charged Felonies by Marital Status

Unmarried (n = 12,197)

Felony	No.
1. Grand larceny	4,504
2. Girl molestation	1,188
3. Murder (unpremeditated)	927
4. Theft by a servant	700
5. Murder (premeditated)	694
6. Infanticide	632

Married with Children (n = 5,970)

Felony	No.
1. Grand larceny	1,205
2. Girl molestation	1,022
3. Murder (unpremeditated)	480
4. Murder (premeditated)	466
5. Theft by a servant	307

Married Without Children (n = 1,821)

Felony	No.
1. Grand larceny	368
2. Girl molestation	336
3. Murder (unpremeditated)	153
4. Murder (premeditated)	131
5. Theft by a servant	107

Widow(er) with Children (n = 1,184)

Felony	No.
1. Girl molestation	323
2. Grand larceny	154
3. Murder (premeditated)	127
4. Murder (unpremeditated)	102
5. Infanticide	90

Widow(er) Without Children (n = 358)

Felony	No.
1. Girl molestation	80
2. Grand larceny	44
3. Murder (premeditated)	42
Murder (unpremeditated)	42
5. Manslaughter	27

SOURCE: *Compte général de l'administration de la justice criminelle,* 1871, 1881, 1891, 1901, 1911, 1922, 1931, statistics for felonies by marital status.

The Crimes

When the most commonly charged felonies of the marital status groups are calculated, the distinctions fade, as in the instances of the statistics for sex and age. Table 7 displays this information, by rank order of frequency for each status group and by number of defendants for each crime. For all five groups, grand larceny and girl molestation again emerge as the most commonly charged felonies against property and against persons, respectively, with murder following. The presence or absence of children appears to have been almost without influence on the findings.

Statistics categorizing defendants by residence—rural, urban, or vagrant—provide a fourth perspective on the variety and incidence of felonies charged between 1871 and 1940. By the last quarter of the nineteenth century, urban areas were far safer than they had been fifty years earlier, when the *classes dangereuses* described by Louis Chevalier were perceived by the bourgeoisie and aristocracy as waging a form of class warfare, and far safer as well than the urban jungles spawned by late-twentieth-century society. It was the dangers of the city that enveloped rural districts in the romantic notion of a simpler, less fearful existence. Nestled in the happy time when urban life seemed less crime-ridden than it had been or would become, the men and women of the Third Republic had not forgotten some of the frightful past of the city but also had not yet come to hold false assumptions about rural villages. This was the period of France's great urbanization, and if the countryside was deserted by many, it was because the countryside was so eminently desertable. The stereotypical thinking about crime therefore did not distinguish clearly between kinds of rural and urban crimes but between kinds of rural and urban criminals: the brutal but cunning peasant and the ruthless but degenerate urban swindler. Vagrants were denounced, and feared, as dangerous, thieving vagabonds.[17] Table 8 lists the rate

---

17. Debierre, *Le Crâne*, and Dallemagne, *Les Théories*, are examples of the argument that crimes grew out of their sociological background and assert the stereotype. Mialane, *La Criminalité juvenile*, emphasizes the influence of the city on juvenile delinquency. Grébaut, *De l'alcoolisme*, attributes to heavy alcohol consumption the prevalence of crimes against persons in rural areas, a thesis supported by the case histories in Perrier, *Les Criminels*, Abbo, *Les Crimes des foules*, explores the exaggerated fears about mob violence held by urban inhabitants. The statistics for France during this period that Zehr develops in *Crime and the Development of Modern Society*, 41, 59–60, 97–99, suggest that though theft rates rose steadily throughout the nineteenth century, the rate of increase was less after 1880; that there was a fairly strong relationship between theft and levels of urbanism (Pearson $r = 0.66$); and that there was a weaker relationship between assault and battery and wine consumption (Pearson $r = 0.42$).

TABLE 8
Rates of Crime by Residence (n = 21,534)

Rural (normal rate 41.01%)

Felony	No.	Rate (%)
1. Perjury	36	83.33
2. Extortion	77	80.52
3. Poisoning	46	78.26
4. Infanticide	856	73.60
5. Arson (dwelling)	647	72.95
6. Parricide	73	71.23
7. Concealment of birth	73	68.49
8. Arson (nondwelling)	395	68.10

Urban (normal rate 49.32%)

Felony	No.	Rate (%)
1. Corruption (public official)	33	87.88
2. Abuse of confidence	358	77.93
3. Theft from the mails (PTT employee)	29	72.41
4. Abortion	538	70.26
5. Fraud in commercial document	532	69.74
6. Counterfeiting	558	68.46
7. Aggravated robbery	536	67.35
8. Fraudulent bankruptcy	249	63.05

Vagrant (normal rate 9.67%)

Felony	No.	Rate (%)
1. Theft from a church	93	26.88
2. Grand larceny	6,277	20.07
3. Arson (dwelling)	395	18.73
4. Highway robbery with violence	256	15.63
5. Aggravated robbery	536	15.30
6. Counterfeiting	558	13.26
7. Highway robbery without violence	41	12.20
8. Seduction of a minor	51	11.76

SOURCE: *Compte général de l'administration de la justice criminelle*, 1871, 1881, 1891, 1901, 1911, 1922, 1931, statistics for felonies by residence.

of total felonies by residence, the absolute number of defendants for each crime, and the specific felonies associated with each category by elevated rate.[18]

18. The additional numbers in the discussion of Tables 8 and 9 are derived from the same volumes of the *Compte général* as those in the tables.

The Crimes

It is a commonplace of contemporary sociology to associate crimes against property with urban life and to associate crimes against persons with rural life—a criminological variation on the gesellschaft-gemeinschaft contrast. The data for elevated rates in Table 8 offer sure support neither to this hypothesis nor to the stereotype. Although abortion and infanticide were both extreme forms of birth control, abortion dealt with the problem of unwanted pregnancy in a quicker, more sophisticated, more "urban" manner. The "reverse image" rates of the two crimes confirm this impression: 70.26 percent of the defendants in abortion cases came from cities and towns, whereas 73.60 percent of the defendants in infanticide cases came from rural districts. The other felonies associated by elevated rate with urban life were, in fact, crimes against property. For rural areas, the analysis is less straightforward. The crimes with the highest rates were ones of cunning—perjury, extortion, poisoning, and arson—but they were hardly brutal. Rural crime rates did show a greater degree of violence than urban rates, but the differences overall are not extreme: for murder, in premeditated cases, 55.14 and 39.52 percent, in unpremeditated cases, 45.95 and 48.00 percent; for manslaughter, 54.10 and 43.68 percent; for aggravated assault and wounding, 46.71 and 48.03 percent; for rape, 58.81 and 34.03 percent; for girl molestation, 53.00 and 43.13 percent. Instead, the felonies with elevated rates in rural areas were those associated with feuds and grievances in which official justice was ignored or circumvented: parricide is a spectacular example. The crimes of vagrants were the expected ones, largely forms of theft, often aggravated by violence.

The relatively neat dichotomy between urban and rural crimes disappears in the statistics for the most commonly charged felonies. Table 9 displays this information by rank order of frequency for each category of residence and by number of defendants for each crime. As with the statistics for sex, age, and marital status, these findings suggest the pervasiveness in Third Republic society of three major felonies—grand larceny, girl molestation, and forms of murder. They confirm again the degree to which one crime, girl molestation, was the most common offense against persons. Even vagrants, who as strangers might be presumed to have fewer opportunities to approach young girls, committed the crime frequently.

The tables for degree of education are considerably less revealing than the four previous sets. The Ministry of Justice divided defendants crudely into "illiterates," "literates," and the "highly edu-

TABLE 9
Most Commonly Charged Felonies by Residence

Rural (n = 8,832)

Felony	No.
1. Girl molestation	1,563
2. Grand larceny	1,555
3. Murder (premeditated)	805
4. Murder (unpremeditated)	783
5. Infanticide	630

Urban (n = 10,620)

Felony	No.
1. Grand larceny	3,462
2. Girl molestation	1,272
3. Murder (unpremeditated)	818
4. Theft by a servant	727
5. Murder (premeditated)	577

Vagrant (n = 2,082)

Felony	No.
1. Grand larceny	1,260
2. Girl molestation	114
3. Murder (unpremeditated)	103
4. Aggravated robbery	82
5. Murder (premeditated)	78

SOURCE: *Compte général de l'administration de la justice criminelle*, 1871, 1881, 1891, 1901, 1911, 1922, 1931, statistics for felonies by residence.

cated." The first category, illiterates, grew increasingly useless as the free lay public primary education for both sexes voted in the 1880s became a reality in the decade before World War I. It is not difficult to specify the adjectives that would have described the defendants labeled illiterate—female, rural or vagrant, old and poor—but the percentages of the possible combinations remain obscure. Nevertheless, given this composition, it could be presumed that the felonies of the illiterates would be similar to those of women and rural inhabitants (the old and vagrants accounted for relatively few defendants, and no judicial statistics were compiled on the basis of wealth). The second category, literates, was so broad that it was meaningless. By 1914, as the literacy rate surpassed 90 percent, and among the young, who committed a disproportionately high number of crimes, approached 99 percent, the great majority of criminals came within its bounds. The crimes associated with literates would therefore likely be very much a cross section of all felonies. In contrast, the category for the highly educated was extremely narrow, and the felonies associated with it atypical, if only because a higher education was the prerogative of the few. This small segment of the population was not merely better educated but much wealthier and more powerful than any other. The crimes they were likely to commit would be those associated with business, the professions, and public office: abuses of confidence, abuses of function, frauds. Moreover, the percentage of the highly educated who appeared as defendants is surely even lower because their wealth and power protected them from detection or prosecution. These judgments are essentially the same as the stereotypical perceptions held during the Third Republic.[19] Table 10 lists the rate of total felonies by degree of education, the absolute number of defendants for each crime, and the specific felonies associated with each category by elevated rate.

The findings in Table 10 match reasonably well with the presumptions for illiterates. Perjury was the felony with the highest rural rate, and three other "rural crimes"—infanticide, poisoning, and concealment of birth—were strongly associated with women. The other proposed elements in the combination, vagrants and the old, are both suggested by the frequency of arson. The elevated rates for highway robbery and theft from a church may, in fact, indicate that vagrants made up a larger proportion of illiterate defendants than suspected. For literates, despite the comprehensive nature of the category, the findings do not correspond to the rates for all felonies in Table 1. Instead, there is a jumble of crimes best representing four characteristics: an urban (theft from the mails, aggravated robbery, fraudulent bankruptcy, counterfeiting, corruption, and fraud in a commercial document) male (malfeasance, aggravated robbery, and corruption), married (fraudulent bankruptcy, corruption, and fraud in a commercial document) and aged thirty-one to fifty (malfeasance, theft from the mails, fraudulent bankruptcy, illegal restraint, corruption, and fraud in a commercial document). Such a Frenchman did represent an important part of the population. He might even be

---

19. An additional perspective is provided by Abbo, *Les Crimes des foules*, which emphasizes the threat of crime from mobs of illiterate barbarians who had never been exposed to the civilizing influence of the schools. Aymard, *La Profession du crime*, Delvincourt, *La Lutte*, Giuliani, *L'Adolescence criminelle*, Lévy, *Examen médico-légal*, and Mialane, *La Criminalité juvénile*, also insist on the need for additional moral instruction in the system of public primary schools, though there was scant evidence of the efficacy of this proposal.

TABLE 10
Rates of Crime by Degree of Education (n = 21,523)

Illiterates (normal rate 21.48%)

Felony	No.	Rate (%)
1. Perjury	35	54.29
2. Highway robbery without violence	41	36.59
3. Highway robbery with violence	256	35.16
4. Infanticide	856	34.35
5. Theft from a church	93	33.33
6. Poisoning	46	32.61
7. Pillage	133	32.33
8. Arson (dwelling)	647	31.53
9. Concealment of birth	73	31.51
10. Arson (nondwelling)	392	30.87

Literates (normal rate 74.65%)

Felony	No.	Rate (%)
1. Malfeasance (public official)	2	100.00
2. Theft from the mails (PTT employee)	29	86.21
3. Aggravated robbery	536	86.01
4. Fraudulent bankruptcy	249	84.74
5. Illegal restraint	39	84.62
6. Seduction of a minor	51	84.31
7. Counterfeiting	558	83.51
8. Corruption (public official)	33	81.82
9. Murder (unpremeditated)	1,694	81.40
10. Fraud in commercial document	532	80.64

Highly Educated (normal rate 3.87%)

Felony	No.	Rate (%)
1. Embezzlement (public official)	29	44.83
2. Abuse of confidence	358	36.59
3. Fraud in official public document	305	32.13
4. Fraud in commercial document	532	17.86
5. Corruption (public official)	33	15.15
6. Theft from the mails (PTT employee)	29	13.79
7. Fraud in private document	330	12.73
8. Fraudulent bankruptcy	249	8.84
9. Abortion	538	8.55
10. Parricide	73	6.85

SOURCE: *Compte général de l'administration de la justice criminelle*, 1871, 1881, 1891, 1901, 1911, 1922, 1931, statistics for felonies by degree of education.

The Crimes

called the typical citizen of the Third Republic, though never the typical felony criminal. This misleading result probably derives from the concentration of violent felonies, more associated with rural areas and youth, in the statistics for illiterates, with the rates of these crimes consequently reduced for literates. In the case of the highly educated, the only narrowly defined category in this classification, the presumptions and the stereotype are entirely confirmed. The felonies associated with the highly educated are overwhelmingly crimes of men (and the very few women) in commerce, the professions, and positions of public trust.

Despite the awkward categories and the considerable differences among the three groups, when the most commonly charged felonies are calculated for degree of education, the findings are remarkably similar to those for the four previous sets of statistics. Table 11 displays this information by rank order of frequency for each level of education and by number of defendants for each crime. There are no surprises for illiterates and literates: grand larceny, girl molestation, and murder appear in their accustomed positions. The frequency of infanticide among illiterates surely reflects the large number of rural inhabitants in the group. For the highly educated, there is confirmation that they led quite different lives from the rest of the population. For the first time in this form of calculation, grand larceny is surpassed as a felony against property by abuses of confidence and frauds in official public and commercial documents. The relatively low ranking for murder suggests that the educated elite were less violent and had other means of settling disputes. The differentiation ceases with girl molestation. Like all other groups of Frenchmen, the highly educated were very frequently charged with this crime.

A sixth set of statistics in the *Compte général* divides defendants in felony cases into eleven categories by occupation. Here are the categories and their definitions. (A woman without an occupation was placed in the category applicable to her husband.)

1e Classe A: attachés à l'exploitation du sol (bûcherons, charbonniers, mineurs, carriers, terrassiers, cultivateurs, journaliers, manoeuvres). Occupations associated with the utilization of the earth: woodcutters, colliers, miners, quarriers, ditchdiggers, farmers, agricultural day laborers, unskilled laborers.

1e Classe B: attachés à l'exploitation du sol (domestiques de ferme).

TABLE 11

Most Commonly Charged Felonies by Degree of Education

Illiterates (n = 4,624)

Felony	No.
1. Grand larceny	1,428
2. Girl molestation	753
3. Infanticide	294
4. Murder (unpremeditated)	286
Theft by a servant	286
6. Murder (premeditated)	278
7. Arson (dwelling)	204
8. Manslaughter	169
9. Rape	161
10. Arson (nondwelling)	121

Literates (n = 16,067)

Felony	No.
1. Grand larceny	4,771
2. Girl molestation	2,056
3. Murder (unpremeditated)	1,379
4. Murder (premeditated)	1,143
5. Theft by a servant	866
6. Manslaughter	669
7. Infanticide	556
8. Counterfeiting	466
9. Aggravated robbery	461
10. Arson (dwelling)	437

Highly Educated (n = 832)

Felony	No.
1. Girl molestation	140
2. Abuse of confidence	131
3. Fraud in official public document	98
4. Fraud in commercial document	95
5. Grand larceny	78
6. Abortion	46
7. Fraud in private document	42
8. Murder (premeditated)	39
9. Murder (unpremeditated)	29
10. Fraudulent bankruptcy	22

SOURCE: *Compte général de l'administration de la justice criminelle*, 1871, 1881, 1891, 1901, 1911, 1922, 1931, statistics for felonies by degree of education.

The Crimes

	Occupations associated with the utilization of the earth: domestic servants on farms.
2e Classe:	ouvriers chargés de mettre en oeuvre les produits du sol, le fer, etc. (industrie textile, du bois, des métaux, du cuir, des produits chimiques, du bâtiment, de luxe, bijoutiers, etc.). Occupations associated with manufacturing the products of the earth: workers in the textile, wood, metals, leather, chemical, building, and luxury industries.
3e Classe:	alimentation (boulangers, bouchers, meuniers). Occupations associated with the supply of food: bakers, butchers, millers.
4e Classe:	habillement et toilette, ameublement (tailleurs, perruquiers, chapeliers, etc.). Occupations associated with clothing and furnishings: tailors, wigmakers, hat makers, etc.
5e Classe:	commerçants (banquiers, agents d'affaires, fabricants, négociants, marchands colporteurs et forains, employés de commerce). Occupations associated with commerce: bankers, agents and brokers, manufacturers, merchants, shopkeepers, peddlers, stall holders, employees of commercial enterprises.
6e Classe:	transports (employés dans les chemins de fer, mariners, voituriers, commissionnaires). Occupations associated with transportation: railroad workers, sailors, carters, deliverymen.
7e Classe A:	aubergistes, logeurs, hôteliers. Occupations associated with inn keeping, hotel keeping, and the renting of rooms.
7e Classe B:	domestiques attachés à la personne. Personal domestic servants.
8e Classe:	professions libérales (avocats, avoués, clercs; notaires et clercs; huissiers et clercs; médecins, chirurgiens, sages-femmes; pharmaciens, herboristes; clergé, religieuses; professeurs ou instituteurs; artistes; fonctionnaires publics; employés des postes; force publique; propriétaires, rentiers; étudiants; ingénieurs; imprimeurs, typographes). Liberal professions: barristers, solicitors, law clerks; notaries and notary clerks; bailiffs and deputies; physicians, surgeons, and mid-

	wives; pharmacists and herbalists; clergy and religious; professors and teachers; artists; government bureaucrats; postal employees; authorities charged with public order; landowners and men of independent means; students; engineers; printers and typographers.
9e Classe:	gens sans aveu (chiffonniers, saltimbanques, sans profession ou profession inconnue). Vagabonds: ragpickers, (traveling) acrobats, vagrants.[20]

This scheme presents many problems. Established in 1829, when the country was overwhelmingly agrarian, the system of classification was never sufficiently revised to meet the changing economic and social conditions brought by industrialization. Many jobs—more almost every year—did not fit well. The 1e Classe A did not separate farmers who owned their land from the workers they hired; it also included the different types of miners, a reasoning that dated from the time when mining was more agricultural than industrial. Domestic servants on farms, the 1e Classe B, were not combined with personal domestic servants, the 7e Classe B, though a specific form of felony theft applied to them both. The 2e Classe, manufacturing, was burdened by almost every variety of "industrial" worker, without regard for how different work experiences might influence possible criminal behavior. Bakers, butchers, and millers, from the 3e Classe, and tailors, wigmakers, and hatters, from the 4e Classe, all conducted commercial operations yet were rigorously segregated. Neither category could be easily distinguished from the shopkeepers and stall holders listed in the 5e Classe, commerce. The 8e Classe, liberal professions, included groups whose principal characteristic was leisure and the lack of any profession (*propriétaires*, rentiers, and students), as well as bureaucrats of several kinds and the most exalted of the artisans—printers and typographers. Almost inevitably, defendants were forced into categories in an arbitrary manner.

20. *Compte général*, 1871, 1881, 1911, 1922, 1931, statistics for felonies by occupational category. The tables for occupation in the *Compte général* underwent several alterations during the Third Republic, though nothing that approached a true revision. Two of the changes are important for the present analysis. In all of the previous statistical computations involving the detailed tables, I have used seven years (1871, 1881, 1891, 1901, 1911, 1922, and 1931) as the sample. But for the occupational tables, two of these years, 1891 and 1901, are omitted because the statistics published are in an entirely different format that precludes their use. In addition, the published statistics for the years 1911, 1922, and 1931 are in a reorganized form, but one assimilable to that used in 1871 and 1881 and throughout most of the nineteenth century.

The Crimes

Except when viewed in the broadest fashion, such statistical tables should be treated with unusual skepticism.

Notwithstanding these objections and the caveat, it remains interesting to examine the statistics for the most important of the occupational categories, 1e Classe A (agriculture and mining), 2e Classe (manufacturing), 5e Classe (commerce), and 8e Classe (liberal professions). Collectively, they represent 69.66 percent of all felony defendants. The presumptions and stereotypes are relatively clear. Farmers and farm workers, the predominant element in their category, were rural and therefore prone to display rural habits about crime. Through similar deduction, small businessmen, shopkeepers, and stall holders, the bulk of the commercial classification, would tend toward urban crimes. Industrial workers were equally urban, but they were widely presumed to be rougher and more violent, often involved in brawls with their mates and likely to turn to robbery in times of unemployment. The disparate but generally privileged groups listed together as the liberal professions would commit the crimes of the highly educated.[21] Table 12 lists the rate for total felonies by each of these occupational categories, the absolute number of defendants for each crime, and the specific felonies associated with each category by elevated rate.

The findings in Table 12 fully support the presumptions. The rural character of the defendants in the 1e Classe A is substantiated by the high rates of perjury, arson, poisoning, and extortion. Two other "rural crimes" also appear on the list, parricide and the assault and wounding of a parent, which must often have issued from the deep frustration felt by grown sons waiting for their inheritance of land while having to work on it. The businessmen, large and small, of the 5e Classe were charged with the nonviolent swindles and larcenies typical of "urban crimes." The cases of corruption are clearly the result of *paying* a bribe to a public official, because the officials who might have *accepted* it are listed with the 8e Classe. Industrial workers in the 2e Classe did have the anticipated high rates of some violent crimes: manslaughter, unpremeditated murder, girl molestation, and aggravated robbery. Was the elevated rate for counterfeiting a function of particular skills in the working of metals? The list of felonies associated with the defendants from the 8e Classe corre-

21. For additional details about the stereotypes, see Cornateano, *Essai d'une théorie*; Courtis, *Etude médico-légale*; Debierre, *Le Crâne*; and Dallemagne, *Les Théories*. Perrier, *L'Affaire Deluze*, describes what can happen when crime occurs among the highly educated at the upper levels of society.

TABLE 12

Rates of Crime by Occupational Category (n = 14,242)

1e Classe A: Agriculture and Mining (normal rate 28.91%)

Felony	No.	Rate (%)
1. Perjury	11	72.73
2. Assault and wounding of a parent	55	58.18
3. Arson (nondwelling)	121	57.85
4. Parricide	50	52.00
5. Highway robbery with violence	140	50.00
6. Poisoning	31	48.39
7. Extortion	33	45.45

2e Classe: Manufacturing (normal rate 28.33%)

Felony	No.	Rate (%)
1. Counterfeiting	214	50.47
2. Manslaughter	627	39.39
3. Murder (unpremeditated)	1,305	35.63
4. Grand larceny	4,388	33.64
5. Girl molestation	2,150	33.16
6. Aggravated robbery	246	32.11
7. Seduction of a minor	35	28.57

5e Classe: Commerce (normal rate 7.56%)

Felony	No.	Rate (%)
1. Fraudulent bankruptcy	159	53.46
2. Corruption (public official)	5	40.00
3. Fraud in commercial document	450	38.89
4. Abuse of confidence	202	19.31
5. Fraud in private document	167	18.56
6. Highway robbery without violence	31	16.13

8e Classe: Liberal Professions (normal rate 4.86%)

Felony	No.	Rate (%)
1. Malfeasance (public official)	1	100.00
2. Theft from the mails (PTT employee)	16	87.50
3. Embezzlement (public official)	6	83.33
4. Fraud in official public document	118	50.00
5. Corruption (public official)	5	40.00
6. Illegal restraint	33	36.36
7. Abuse of confidence	202	30.20
8. Perjury	11	27.27
9. Abortion	303	12.54
10. Fraud in private document	167	11.98

SOURCE: *Compte général de l'administration de la justice criminelle*, 1871, 1881, 1911, 1922, 1931, statistics for felonies by occupational category.

sponds closely to the list for the highly educated, because an advanced education was necessary for most of the "liberal professions." The two groups even had remarkably similar normal rates for felonies (4.86 and 3.87 percent, respectively).

Few of the differences among the four categories remain when the most commonly charged felonies are calculated. Instead, the prevalence of grand larceny, girl molestation, and murder continues. Table 13 displays this information, by rank order of frequency for each occupational category and by number of defendants for each crime. Despite the anomalous character of the statistics for occupation, it is worth adding that the pattern of grand larceny as the most commonly charged felony against property and girl molestation as the most commonly charged felony against persons is maintained in the calculation for nine of the eleven categories. The exceptions are the 7e Classe B (personal domestic servants)—in which the specific felony "theft by a servant" outranks grand larceny and in which infanticide, often the destiny of a servant girl seduced and then discharged by her employer, is more frequent than girl molestation—and the 9e Classe (vagabonds)—in whose violent world both forms of murder surpass girl molestation.

The statistics from the *Compte général* for the Third Republic present a view of society that cannot be sharply focused. Distortions from the insufficiency of the data, from changing statutes, from varying patterns of enforcement, and from increasing *correctionnalisation* compromise the effort to insist upon the details. Even so, some of the outlines are relatively clear. Certain felonies were indeed associated with sex, age, marital status, residence, degree of education, and occupation. Contemporary prejudices, perceptions, and stereotypes did have a basis in fact. Yet however much the calculation of *rates* for crime might divide Third Republic society into groups, the *totals* for four felonies—grand larceny, girl molestation, premeditated murder, and unpremeditated murder—were so large among all categories that they accounted for almost three out of every five felonies charged. Murders and grand larcenies have been recorded so frequently in every Western society that these crimes are reluctantly acknowledged to be an unfortunate concomitant of civilization. Not so the molestation of young girls, and not so its prevalence during this period.

Is it possible to attribute many of the cases of girl molestation to allegations made in error or out of vengeance? A further set of statis-

TABLE 13

Most Commonly Charged Felonies by Occupational Category

1e Classe A: Agriculture and Mining (n = 4,117)

Felony	No.
1. Grand larceny	1,144
2. Girl molestation	730
3. Murder (unpremeditated)	418
4. Murder (premeditated)	392
5. Arson (dwelling)	231
6. Infanticide	198
7. Manslaughter	197

2e Classe: Manufacturing (n = 4,035)

Felony	No.
1. Grand larceny	1,476
2. Girl molestation	713
3. Murder (unpremeditated)	465
4. Murder (premeditated)	272
5. Manslaughter	247
6. Arson (dwelling)	117
7. Counterfeiting	108

5e Classe: Commerce (n = 1,077)

Felony	No.
1. Grand larceny	226
2. Fraud in commercial document	175
3. Girl molestation	105
4. Theft by a servant	90
5. Murder (unpremeditated)	87
6. Fraudulent bankruptcy	85
7. Murder (premeditated)	50

8e Classe: Liberal Professions (n = 692)

Felony	No.
1. Girl molestation	156
2. Grand larceny	68
3. Abuse of confidence	61
4. Fraud in official public document	59
5. Murder (unpremeditated)	48
6. Murder (premeditated)	43
7. Abortion	38
Theft by a servant	38

SOURCE: *Compte général de l'administration de la justice criminelle,* 1871, 1881, 1911, 1922, 1931, statistics for felonies by occupational category.

tics from the *Compte général* appears to indicate that most of the charges were legitimate. When the office of the procureur de la République received an accusation involving a felony, the case was immediately communicated to an examining magistrate (*juge d'instruction*) for investigation and for the preparation, if appropriate, of an indictment. In approximately three-fifths of all felony investigations (60.65 percent), the juges d'instruction concurred with the initial accusation and recommended prosecution. In another quarter (23.56 percent), they rejected the accusation as ill-founded and ordered the criminal proceedings terminated. For the remaining one-sixth of the cases (15.79 percent), they modified the original complaint to make it either heavier (8.06 percent) or lighter (7.73 percent). If accusations of girl molestation were made mistakenly, frivolously, or vindictively, the rate at which the juges d'instruction dismissed or reduced the charges would have been considerably elevated above the normal rates. The statistics for disposition practice reveal, however, that the charges were maintained or increased in approximately three cases of girl molestation out of four (75.65 percent) and dismissed at a rate (23.73 percent) almost identical to that for all felonies. Table 14 displays this information, listing the rate by disposition practice for total felonies and the rate by disposition practice and the absolute number of cases for the four most common felonies.

Was the high incidence of girl molestation peculiar to France during this period? The recent controversy over Sigmund Freud and the seduction theory suggests not. Freud initially credited his patients' description of sexual violation during childhood but later came to believe that they were relating fantasies universal to all children, from which he constructed his theory of the Oedipus complex, the keystone of the psychoanalytic system. Some of Freud's critics have contended that even after he abandoned his initial conclusions, he worried over the continued evidence of molestation, particularly among the children of the outwardly proper Viennese bourgeoisie.[22] The English equivalent, the upright Victorian, had a barely concealed weakness for pornography, sadism, and child prostitutes. Al-

22. See Jeffrey Moussaieff Masson, *The Assault on Truth: Freud's Suppression of the Seduction Theory* (New York, 1984), especially 14–54, and his "Freud and the Seduction Theory," *Atlantic Monthly*, CCLIII (February, 1984), 33–60. John F. Laffey, "The Problematic Bourgeoisie," *Historical Reflections/Réflexions Historiques*, XI (1984), 153–72, provides an introduction to the issues. See also Larry Wolff, *Postcards from the End of the World: Child Abuse in Freud's Vienna* (New York, 1988).

TABLE 14

Disposition Practices of the Juges d'Instruction: Rates for Murder, Grand Larceny, and Girl Molestation (n = 26,411)

Felony	No.	Unchanged (normal rate 60.65%)	Modified/Heavier (normal rate 8.06%)	Modified/Lighter (normal rate 7.73%)	Rejected (normal rate 23.56%)
Murder (premeditated)	1,903	43.25	27.64	9.14	19.97
Murder (unpremeditated)	1,979	40.83	14.65	15.51	29.01
Grand larceny	5,810	80.17	3.31	9.29	7.23
Girl molestation	4,989	69.23	6.42	.62	23.73

SOURCE: *Compte général de l'administration de la justice criminelle*, 1871, 1876, 1881, 1886, 1891, 1896, 1901, 1906, 1911, 1919, statistics for disposition of felony charges by juges d'instruction. The volume for 1919 was used because the *Compte général* was not published in the years 1914–1918. No statistics for disposition of felony charges by juges d'instruction were published after 1919.

most certainly, then, girl molestation by the upper and middle classes was prevalent in London and Vienna, as well as in Paris. A social-psychological explanation may lie in the context of the so-called "bourgeois marriage," which with its emphasis on arrangements and alliances of property and prestige, to the disparagement of romantic love, frequently left males unsatisfied sexually and sentimentally. Their longing for "passion" could lead them to seek solace in adultery or among prostitutes, but there was also the third alternative of "seducing" (molesting) young girls. The seduction of a *petite fille* could fulfill the ego drive for "virginity" and simultaneously redirect the forbidden impulse of father-daughter incest—though that did occur as well in some instances. The *fruit vert* of servant girls or the daughters of peasants and urban workers was considered fair prey by the class morality of the period.[23]

But every young girl was at risk, not just from socially privileged males but from males of all categories and descriptions, as the statistics of the *Compte général* demonstrate. The obsession of any French family of means, and even those of little means, to cloister their daughters until marriage becomes easy to understand. To determine whether the threat to girls in Austria or England or anywhere else was as overwhelming as in France will require the availability of comparable statistics, with all of the accompanying difficulties of interpretation and of reconciling statutes. It might be contended that the apparent willingness to report this felony, which in France seems to have been much greater than normal for a sex crime, implies a pervasiveness so great that the sense of shame was diminished, that girl molestation had become almost banal. A literary clue lends support: Vladimir Nabokov wrote *Lolita* in France between 1936 and 1939 and then redrafted it into an American setting in the early 1950s. But this indication should also remind that the problem of child abuse and girl molestation in the United States, now recognized to be of immense proportions, was not even admitted until the 1980s.[24]

---

23. Steven Marcus, *The Other Victorians: A Study of Sexuality and Pornography in Mid-Nineteenth-Century England* (London, 1964), especially 59–61, 75, 176–77, 217–22, 252–65; Ronald Pearsall, *The Worm in the Bud: The World of Victorian Sexuality* (London, 1969), 358–66, 430–46; Jesse Richard Pitts, "The Bourgeois Family and French Economic Retardation" (Ph.D. dissertation, Harvard University, 1958), 285–96; Jesse Richard Pitts to Benjamin F. Martin, January 3, 1983 (in author's possession).

24. Vladimir Vladimirovich Nabokov, *Lolita* (Paris, 1955); Alfred Appel, Jr. (ed.), *The Annotated Lolita* (New York, 1970); Andrew Field, *Nabokov: His Life in Art*

Crime and Criminal Justice Under the Third Republic

The question of social sources for crime and an analysis of statistical trends defined the issues examined by the criminologists of the Third Republic. They provided, as well, elements in the preparation of prosecutions by the magistrature. And they represented factors in the ideal police investigation. But for the police, the concern was more with the crime itself than with the motivation. Solving, or better yet, preventing, the crime was work enough.

(Boston, 1967), 323–37. For another literary approach see the haunting short story by Eugène Berjot, "Cécile," which seems to have been first published as a pamphlet in New Orleans in 1859. It has been translated by Bethany S. Oberst as "Cecilia," in *French-American Review*, VI (1982), 103–15. For the American situation see, among the many studies on this topic, Judith Lewis Herman, with Lisa Hirschman, *Father-Daughter Incest* (Cambridge, Mass., 1981); Florence Rush, *The Best Kept Secret: Sexual Abuse of Children* (Englewood Cliffs, N. J., 1980); Clifford L. Linedecker, *Children in Chains* (New York, 1981); D. Kelly Weisberg, *Children of the Night: A Study of Adolescent Prostitution* (Lexington, Mass., 1985).

2

The Police (I)

The argument is familiar: Men and women are determined to live up (or down) to the Hobbesian view of mankind. To preserve order, to deter crime, to arrest criminals, an armed body of citizens charged with enforcing the law is vital. Thus, the police. A typical justification comes from Jacques Lantier, the pseudonymous official of the Fifth Republic's Ministry of the Interior who was earlier a Resistance hero, secret agent, and commissaire in the Police Nationale, France's version of the Federal Bureau of Investigation. Lantier accuses French society of differing little from a primitive, ungovernable horde, prey to collective anguishes, at the mercy of ambitions and appetites, and riddled with minority groups absolutely free from all scruples. He who calls for constraint and repression, writes Lantier, calls for the police; he who calls for tranquillity and order calls for the police.[1] In the confusion of these duties, abuses by the police are born.

Louis Casamayor, the French magistrate who writes most prolifically and philosophically about issues of justice in France today, defines the problem: "To have a strong police, yet not too strong, in that it may be used without fearing it." Why the fear? The police are

---

1. Jacques Lantier [pseud.], *Le Temps des policiers: Trente ans d'abus* (Paris, 1970), 4–17.

part of a corrupt society. If mankind cannot be perfected, neither can the police. Inevitably, legitimate as well as illegitimate activities will be repressed, the innocent will be arrested, the guilty will go free. And the abuses will be tolerated: "We will have to be indulgent and realistic, for man is not perfect. Voilà le grand mot lâché. The result is that small compromises follow upon small concessions, the poison by little doses is easily tolerated, and no one knows quite when society has become infected."[2] The police remain as necessary as their use is a calculated danger. "Cops are not made from choirboys," insisted Louis Lépine, the famous prefect of police during the Belle Epoque.[3]

In France every government from the ancien régime monarchy to the Fifth Republic has combined wariness of police power with recognition of the special security needs within the capital of so centralized a state. The balance point was decided very early. There would be no unitary police system for the entire country, but the organization of the police in Paris would be formidable.

Louis XIV laid the foundation for the security forces in Paris by his edict of March, 1667, appointing a lieutenant general of police. The post, in fact if not in name, was the intendancy of the capital, and among the approximately thirty-five other royal governors, the lieutenant general would rank in prestige below only the intendant of Paris (i.e., of the généralité, which was an entity distinct from the city itself). The powers and responsibilities of the office were very broad. The lieutenant general was supreme in municipal government, held administrative and judicial police powers, supervised the Paris food supply and many other aspects of business and industry, and exercised direction over prisons, sanitation, public institutions, public places, and public health. His was the most absolute authority in France below the rule of the king. Napoleon would find the institution so effective that in 1800 his reorganization of the government bureaucracy would merely rename the office the Paris Prefecture of Police and confirm its traditional duties.

The principal subordinates to the lieutenant general were the inspectors of police. When established in 1708, the office was venal, but in 1740 the original forty inspectorships were suppressed and twenty new ones created at a much higher price, an amount beyond the means of men who would purchase it as a sinecure. There was,

2. Louis Casamayor, *La Police* (Paris, 1973), 75, 136.
3. Cited in Jean Belin, *Trente ans de Sûreté Nationale* (Paris, 1950), 8.

as well, a new requirement that an inspector have attained the rank of officer in the king's army and have five years of experience in addition to the rank. In this clumsy manner the monarchy sought to eliminate incompetent personnel and to rebuild the ranks with more capable men. The effort was successful, and the increasing professionalization of the inspectors permitted specialization of duty. By midcentury, the three or four most accomplished and experienced of the inspectors were assigned to a special criminal investigation unit, the first version of the Sûreté. Other inspectors provided a *service des garnis*, examining daily the rosters of hotels and boardinghouses to collect information about foreigners, travelers, vagrants, or in fact anyone who might come to the attention of the lieutenant general of police. Still more inspectors constituted a *brigade des moeurs*, concentrating on prostitutes, whose presence in Paris was supposedly forbidden by law. Under the lieutenant generalship of Nicholas René Berryer in the early 1750s, the inspectors were instructed to offer prostitutes a limited toleration in return for confining themselves to specific houses, submitting to police surveillance, and, most important, reporting the names of the men who frequented them. The records of the *chambres garnies* and the testimony of the prostitutes enormously simplified the process of locating suspects and filled the primitive files with raw intelligence that could be developed for further investigations. All of the inspectors hired, at their own expense, various informers (*observateurs, mouches,* or *mouchards*) and assistants (*commis* or *préposés*), perhaps three to four hundred in total, who added further information of dubious veracity. Many of the agents were current or former criminals, hired for their expertise within the Paris underworld, but the inspectors also recruited from among the professions and even within the parlements in order to remain informed about all levels of society.[4]

The lieutenant general and the corps of inspectors were assisted in the work of policing Paris by the commissaires of the Châtelet. During the eighteenth century, two or three commissaires were assigned to each of the twenty "quarters" of Paris to serve as both judicial and police officials—judges, fire chiefs, patrolmen, and investigators. It was under the authority of the commissaires, and to the police stations of the quarters (the commissariats), that the lieutenant general

---

4. Alan Williams, *The Police of Paris, 1718–1789* (Baton Rouge, 1979), 94–111, 228–31.

assigned most of the approximately three thousand men of the Paris police. If these three thousand were insufficient to guarantee the security and order of the capital, the lieutenant general could call on the mounted constabulary (*maréchaussée*) of the généralité, the Gardes Françaises and Gardes Suisses, which after 1776 were subject to his direct command. Postrevolutionary France would call the constabulary the gendarmerie, and those troops under the prefect of police the Garde Nationale, Impériale, or Républicaine, depending upon the regime.[5]

The structure of the Paris police elaborated during the eighteenth century was shaken by the ten years of usurpations and reorganizations that followed the 1789 Revolution. Like other elements in the government, the police were subject to experimentation. Courts, trial procedures, the magistrature, and the orders of barristers were cut into new patterns. But the implication that revolutionary justice required a revolutionary police was tempered by the necessity to maintain order and repress criminal activity in Paris. No executive body in the form of the Committee of General Security could run the Paris police for long. Napoleon restored stability by returning to the conception of the lieutenant generalship. The law of 28 Pluviôse VIII (February 17, 1800) instituted a prefect in each department and, in Paris, a prefect of police. Napoleon's system placed the prefect of police in a complicated web of bureaucratic relationships. Some administrative responsibilities for the city of Paris belonged to the prefect of the Seine, the department that included the capital. Important judicial duties were subjected to the public prosecutor of Paris and his parquet. More than a prefect, the Paris prefect of police would be a "ministre sans le titre," even a superminister—in essence, a revival of the lieutenant general of police under a new name but with slightly reduced powers.[6]

Within the Paris Prefecture of Police, the basic division of responsibility is between the patrolmen and the detectives, between the Police municipale, who preserve order and attempt to *prevent* crime, and the Police judiciaire, often called the Sûreté, who *investigate* crimes already committed. The allocation of personnel was weighted heavily toward the maintenance of order. In 1896, for example, of the 8,484 men under the command of the prefect of police, 8,112

---

5. *Ibid.*, 93–94, 137–50.
6. Marcel Levilain, "Histoire de l'organisation des services actifs de la police parisienne" (Thèse droit, l'Université de Paris, 1970), I, 136–37.

(96 percent) were organized in the Police municipale.[7] Discouraging crime through the visibility of street patrols ranked higher than apprehending criminals, and required less physical and mental exertion.

From its beginnings in the mid-1750s among Berryer's inspectors, the Sûreté's ranks were thin. During its first half century, it was rarely assigned more than five inspectors, and those for the task of investigating all the crimes reported to the commissariats. The inadequacy of criminal investigations was apparent, but the solution proposed by high police officials was not to commit more of their men and resources to the Sûreté. Instead, criminals were hired to track down other criminals: It takes a thief . . . ! In 1810 the Sûreté was reorganized under François Eugène Vidocq (1775–1857), who had escaped from a hard-labor prison but whose past was excused because of his extraordinary knowledge about the Parisian underworld. The innovation was emphasized by a physical separation, with the new Sûreté offices on the Rue Sainte-Anne, several blocks from the prefecture and the Palais de Justice. Vidocq's position was anomalous because he was not formally appointed a member of the police. He was also left free to recruit whatever assistants he wanted. At first his staff was four; fifteen years later it was twenty-eight, all of them, like himself, former inmates of French prisons. With these men, Vidocq "controlled" crime in Paris through the highly questionable method of ignoring criminals who would deal with him and cracking down hard on those who would not. Within the prefecture, grave misgivings about these procedures were allayed by their relative effectiveness. Nevertheless, when Vidocq retired in 1829, his personal band of agents was scattered and the Sûreté reintegrated at the prefecture. Twelve regular police inspectors were then placed in charge of criminal investigations. Their inexperience was quickly obvious, and in March, 1832, Vidocq was recalled to head the Sûreté, but this time with the rank of a police official. Slowed by age and forbidden to follow his previous tactics, Vidocq could not guide his neophytes to success. On November 17, 1832, after less than nine months in office, he was dismissed.[8]

Vidocq's departure represented the prefecture's decision that po-

7. Archives de la Préfecture de Police, Paris (hereinafter cited as APP), Budget, Ville de Paris, Préfecture de Police, 1896.
8. Charles Virmaître, *Paris police* (Paris, 1889), 273–323; Léon Améline, *Ce qu'il faut connaître de la police et de ses mystères* (Paris, 1926). See also the romantic and fanciful work of Philip John Stead, *Vidocq: A Biography* (London, 1953), 30–146.

lice work could not be entrusted to crooks, and any criminal conviction would henceforth bar a career in the police. The prefecture also committed new resources to the Sûreté. Within a few months of Vidocq's dismissal, the forces were increased to 31 men: the *chef de la brigade de Sûreté* (director), 1 *inspecteur principal* (principal inspector), 4 *brigadiers* (sergeants), 21 *inspecteurs* (police inspectors), and 4 *commis* (clerks). The number of the detectives increased rapidly, to 150 in 1848 to 300 in 1866. At the same time, Vidocq's legacy was not entirely disavowed. Alliances with the criminal underworld provided important intelligence, as the experience with *mouchards* had proved. The detectives believed that *malfaiteurs* (criminals) were necessary to lead them in their investigations just as firemen used smoke to locate fires. One of France's most famous police officials from the twentieth century would always tell his agents: "Avez-vous des indicateurs [informants]? Non! Alors, faites un autre métier." *Indicateurs*, he insisted in his memoirs, are more important than the clues of Sherlock Holmes, the deduction of Edgar Allan Poe, or the wise theories of Georges Simenon. The unfortunate price paid for this reliance was a blind eye turned toward certain criminal elements and the tolerance of incompetent detectives who could investigate a crime only by turning to *mouchards*. In 1920 the celebrated criminologist Edmond Locard denounced the use of informants as "a blemish on the insignia of the police."[9]

There was no control over the reports provided by the informants, very little means of verifying what Jean Chiappe (prefect of police, 1927–1934) described as "des petits papiers, des délations mesquines, des surveillances sordides." Everything the police learned was squirreled away in the file rooms of the prefecture. The most jealously guarded information constituted the famous "dossiers blancs," which concerned men of status and enumerated details of their private lives. Here was potentially compromising material about politicians, the wealthy, and the celebrated, all of whom could be useful to the police and whose enmity could be deflected by the threat of revelation. When Louis Andrieux became prefect of police in 1879, his own secret dossier, bearing the number 14207, was placed before him. Andrieux spent several hours reading the file and then pronounced it replete with nonsense—even the birth date was

---

9. Virmaître, *Paris police*, 275; Levilain, "Histoire de l'organisation," I, 172–217; Charles Chenevrier, *De la Combe aux Fées à Lurs: Souvenirs et révélations* (Paris, 1962), 23–25; Edmond Locard, *L'Enquête criminelle et les méthodes scientifiques* (Paris, 1920), 8.

in error. But he took the file with him two years later when he retired, had it bound, and placed it in his library out of police reach. When Léon Daudet, considered an enemy of many established politicians friendly to the prefecture, was elected to the Chamber of Deputies in 1920, he learned that his photograph had been circulated to every house of prostitution in Paris with instructions to notify the police if he paid a visit. Louis Lépine, the most famous and popular prefect of police during the Third Republic, defended such tactics, claiming that everything was of interest to his agents.[10]

Like the Sûreté, the Police municipale, the much larger division of the prefecture, underwent reorganizations and grew rapidly in size. The arrondissements of the city of Paris (twelve until an annexation of thirteen surrounding towns in 1859–1860 increased the number to twenty) remained the organizational unit. Every arrondissement was assigned a *commissaire* (police captain), an *officier de paix* (lieutenant), and a *brigadier* (sergeant). Within the arrondissement, there was a further division into four quarters, each with a precinct station, one of which was the central post (*commissariat*) for the arrondissement and the offices of the commissaire, officier de paix, and brigadier. For the precinct, there were three *sous-brigadiers* (corporals), each commanding a brigade of fifteen *sergents de ville* (patrolmen) for an eight-hour shift. In addition to the forces of the arrondissements, five "central brigades" were held in reserve for unusual disturbances. By 1860 the total number of the Police municipale had surpassed 4,600: 116 commissaires de la Seine, 32 officiers de paix, 78 brigadiers, 427 sous-brigadiers, 3,676 sergents de ville, and miscellaneous officials and clerks.

The ranks from sergent de ville through officier de paix were filled mostly with former soldiers, many of them noncommissioned officers who were used to discipline and regimentation. They were dressed in distinctive uniforms: cocked hat and thick serge frock coat, in dark blue, set off by collar numbers in silver embroidery, rows of silver buttons down the coat, and red piping along the trousers. Each wore a sword, the copper hilt gleaming with the Paris coat of arms. The commissaires were appointed by the head of state after a competitive examination and usually came from a slightly higher social level than the men they commanded. As in the eighteenth

10. Jean Chiappe, *Paroles d'ordre* (Paris, 1930), 216; Ernest Raynaud, *La Police des moeurs* (Paris, 1934), 56; Louis Andrieux, *Souvenirs d'un préfet de police* (Paris, 1885), I, 28, 95–101; Léon Daudet, *La Police politique: Ses moyens et ses crimes* (Paris, 1934), 126–27; André Ulmann, *Le Quatrième pouvoir: Police* (Paris, 1935), 89–93.

century, the commissaires were expected to carry out a range of duties. In addition to directing the work of the commissariat, the commissaire was the initial element in the *police judiciaire* through his responsibility to report crimes to the Sûreté. As the highest representative of the government for each arrondissement, he also filled a social and ceremonial role. The commissaire was identified by his tricolor sash and, on formal occasions, by an ornate black uniform with silver braid and stripes.[11]

Outside the twenty arrondissements of Paris, the structure of the police was much less rigorous. In towns with a population under five thousand, the mayor alone decided on the composition of his police force. And because such towns were invariably rural and poor, there was resistance to organizing more than a part-time *garde champêtre*. Once the population surpassed five thousand, the town was required to have, and to pay the salary of, a commissaire, with another commissaire for each additional ten thousand in population. For towns of less than six thousand, the prefect of the department appointed the commissaire; for larger towns the appointment was made by the head of state, acting on the prefect's recommendation. The decree of February 27, 1855, established a uniform classification and pay scale for these commissaires, based on the size and importance of the town to which they were assigned. Even the highest grade was poorly paid (though at Fr 4,800, the salary was more than three times higher than that of the lowest class, Fr 1,440), and the duties were complex and difficult. In maintaining order, the commissaire answered both to the prefect, and through him the Ministry of the Interior, and to the mayor, sometimes receiving conflicting instructions. As an officer of the *police judiciaire*, the commissaire was responsible to the local district attorney and other judicial officials of the Ministry of Justice. To coordinate with the gendarmerie, the commissaire maintained contact with the Ministry of War. As Howard Payne has written, the office was an administrative junction. Applications for the position were always numerous, but the low salary discouraged the kind of candidates who might best fulfill the exacting responsibilities. Most of those appointed were former noncommissioned officers from the military, some former mayors, and a few minor government officials.

The difficulties faced by commissaires in small provincial towns

---

11. Howard C. Payne, *The Police State of Louis Napoleon Bonaparte, 1851–1860* (Seattle, 1966), 128–40.

were mitigated in part by the presence of the gendarmerie and the promise of a system of cantonal commissaires. The gendarmerie, successor to the ancien régime's *maréchaussée*, was an element of the army and was recruited from among noncommissioned officers with at least five years of service. It exercised military police functions for the army and was at the call of the Ministry of the Interior to impose order (taking direction from the prefects and mayors) and of the Ministry of Justice to investigate crimes. By standing instruction, the gendarmerie had to inspect each town twice a month by day, once by night. The cantonal commissaires were established by decree on March 25, 1852, and would have provided a needed coordination for the commissaires of the towns. Unfortunately, because local municipal councils refused to approve the necessary funds, the system developed very slowly and was even abandoned for five years between 1870 and 1875.

In towns with a population of forty thousand or more, the mayor was relieved of all police powers and responsibilities, reducing by one the authorities overseeing the commissaires. The law of July 24, 1867, placed the organization of the police in these large towns under the direction of the Ministry of the Interior, which acted through the prefects. All appointments of personnel, down to the level of patrolman, were made at the prefecture. Mayors and municipal councils were required to appropriate whatever funds the prefects asked. This centralization of police power by the Second Empire would be confirmed by the Third Republic in the law on municipalities of April 5, 1884. The Third Republic would also retain and then greatly elaborate the Second Empire's creation of a *police d'état* for the major cities that would come under strict day-to-day direction by the minister of the interior. Louis Napoleon placed Lyon under the *police d'état* (June, 1851). The Third Republic would extend the system to Marseille (March, 1908), Toulon and La Seyne (November, 1918), Nice (June, 1920), Strasbourg (January, 1922), Mulhouse (February, 1924), Metz (March, 1925), and Algiers (May, 1930).

Within the Ministry of the Interior, responsibility for police matters was assigned to the Direction de la Sûreté générale. The division was created on January 6, 1828, and established in offices along the Rue des Saussaies, adjacent to the ministry on the Place Beauvau. In addition to issuing instructions for the prefects and the *police d'état*, the director of the Sûreté générale oversaw approximately seventy-five commissaires charged with special duties. There were twenty-one *commissaires-inspecteurs de la librairie* (nine at the frontiers, twelve in the large cities) to enforce laws dealing with copyright and book sales and to confiscate publications that infringed political or moral standards. An additional twenty commissaires constituted a "frontier service" to watch for suspicious characters at the principal passenger crossing points for carriages—a role that was made increasingly obsolete by the spread of the rail network. Government officials had early recognized that railroads offered new possibilities for crime and for police intelligence. Railway commissaires were first appointed in 1846, and by 1860, there were thirty-three commissaires on duty, with seventy "police inspectors" serving as assistants. The railway commissaires had their offices in the major rail centers (seven in Paris alone) but spent most of their days riding the great train routes to gather information for the ministry and to investigate crimes committed at stations or on the trains themselves. Although the Direction de la Sûreté générale provided an overall structure for a substantial portion of the police outside of Paris, it could not be considered to constitute a national police force.[12]

Rigor in Paris under the prefecture but only the outline of a state police under the Sûreté générale for the rest of France: This was the structure of police power that had been developed by the time that the Second Empire fell in September, 1870. Although republicans had criticized Louis Napoleon for presiding over a police state, the responsibility of government would temper their idealism. The Third Republic left the sway of the Paris prefect undiminished and slowly extended the scope of the Sûreté générale until it coordinated the investigation of all serious crime beyond the boundaries of the capital and commanded an elite corps of commissaires and inspectors.

Louis Napoleon's last prefect of police, Joachim Piétri, was forced from office on September 4, 1870, by the collapse of the Second Empire. But there followed no purge within the prefecture and no large turnover in the lower echelons. Even the director of the Sûreté, Antoine François Claude, held on to his position. The provisional government of the war-born republic could not dispense with the services of an experienced police, no matter how many of its agents

12. *Ibid.*, 207–32; Etienne Félix Guyon, *L'Organisation de la police en France* (Paris, 1923); Marcel Rougé, *La Sûreté Nationale* (Dijon, 1935), 20–27; Levilain, "Histoire de l'organisation," I, 10–46.

might sympathize with Bonapartism. In turn, police officials exercised a careful neutrality toward the major contenders, republican and monarchist, for domination of the new government. Through this politically troubled decade of the 1870s, represented at the prefecture by the succession of nine different prefects between September, 1870, and July, 1881, the police in Paris maintained their traditional patterns and structures. Any plans for expansion or reorganization were postponed until additional appropriations were available. There was the overwhelming labor of reconstituting, at least in part, some of the dossiers lost when the prefecture files were destroyed on May 28, 1871, in the fires of the Paris Commune's Bloody Week. But the wait for additional funds would be far longer than expected, and though new dossiers were created, most of the information in the old files could never be replaced. Patterns and structures that had been effective in the 1850s and 1860s were increasingly outmoded in the 1870s and 1880s. From unfortunate conditions, unfortunate consequences ensued.

The situation of the Sûreté can be appraised from the memoirs of its director between 1879 and 1884, Gustave Macé. He recalled that his office, at the back of the Palais de Justice on the Quai des Orfèvres (later made famous by Simenon's Inspector Maigret), had only a single antechamber. On his arrival one morning, two prostitutes, two accused murderers, a judge, and the public executioner were waiting for him, all crowded together. During this period, service in the Sûreté, far from a privilege, was reserved for outcasts. The salary was no higher than in the Police municipale, but the chance of having a career broken over an error was much greater in the complications of the Police judiciaire. Nobody *wanted* to belong to the Sûreté. In 1881 the *brigade des moeurs* (vice squad) was joined to Macé's command, providing him with eighty more men, but ones accustomed to nothing except passing time in brothels and bistros. Liaison with other units of the police was nonexistent. Information about an urgent case required two days to arrive from one of the commissariats; for an ordinary case, a week might pass. At a time when telephones were increasingly common in the homes of wealthy Parisians (Alexander Graham Bell took out patents for the telephone in 1876 and 1877), Sûreté agents working away from headquarters but still within Paris had to use the telegraph to contact their superiors. Macé resigned in 1884 because he could not convince the prefecture to carry through essential reforms. He was refused a telephone for his office despite offering to pay for it from his own meager salary of six thousand francs.[13]

Franc-pinching was so severe throughout the Paris police that the prefecture's budget for 1880 included a line item for the feeding of stray cats (Fr 301.76) in the hope of avoiding the much heavier expense of employing an exterminator for the rat-infested Quai des Orfèvres. The commissariats were in even worse condition. Ernest Raynaud, in his memoirs of the "vie intime des commissariats" concerning the years when he began his career in the 1880s, describes the rats, the insects, the smell, the peeling paint, the filth and squalor. By the 1920s, when he published these memoirs, there had been little improvement.[14]

In Macé's time, and after the addition of the brigade des moeurs, the Sûreté was composed of approximately 320 men: the director and his sous-chef (both with the rank of commissaire), 5 inspecteurs principaux, 10 brigadiers, 300 inspecteurs, and 2 clerks. This total would increase slightly, with fluctuations, until the eve of World War I.[15] Within the Sûreté, there were three grand divisions. A small headquarters staff provided command functions and maintained liaison with high officials in the prefecture and with the Police municipale (often very ineffectively). A sizable number of inspecteurs (usually a quarter of the force) served on the délégations judiciaires, working under the *juges d'instruction* (examining magistrates) in the investigation of crimes. The rest of the Sûreté's detectives made up the "brigades," the number and strength of which varied according to the organizational priorities of the director. Invariably, there was a service des garnis, a brigade des moeurs, and a *brigade de la voie publique* (to prowl the streets in ordinary dress, watching for suspicious acts, keeping in contact with informers, and occasionally penetrating gangs of criminals). Homosexuality in Paris was often repressed by the *brigade des pédérastes* (sometimes called the "brigade Baube" for reasons that are now obscure). Every director also constituted a special elite squad for particularly important or difficult cases—Macé called his the "bataillon sacré." Depending upon the need, brigades were established to watch for counterfeit money,

13. Philip John Stead, *The Police of Paris* (London, 1957), 141–45.
14. APP, Budget, Ville de Paris, Préfecture de Police, 1880; Ernest Raynaud, *Souvenirs de police: La Vie intime des commissariats* (Paris, 1926), 72–96.
15. In 1890 the Sûreté numbered 330; in 1895, 372; in 1900, 360; in 1905, 339; and in 1910, 343. The sharp rise in the mid-1890s was a reaction to anarchist crimes. APP, Budget, Ville de Paris, Préfecture de Police, 1890, 1895, 1900, 1905, 1910.

the sale of stolen objects, and various forms of fraud; to pursue particular groups, such as anarchists; or to carry out "special" assignments, such as domestic espionage or blackmail, that could not be officially acknowledged.[16]

The relatively small number of the Sûreté were confronted with an enormous load of work. Every step in the investigation of a crime had to be written up. One retired inspecteur principal claimed that in 1888 alone, the Sûreté received and acted upon 27,903 administrative, and 9,975 judicial, memoranda. In turn it generated 44,399 reports (most of them surely concise) and 7,690 background briefings, made 8,839 arrests, and executed 1,684 surveillances. Even reduced to a daily average, this volume of paper work is impressive, perhaps astounding. Many of the reports survive in the archives of the Prefecture of Police, most of them painstakingly structured and written in the meticulous cursive handwriting of the fin de siècle. It was not merely the investigation of crimes or the intelligence of informers that the inspecteurs recorded. Important politicians insisted that their mistresses be followed. The wives and daughters of the wealthy required the Sûreté to locate missing pets. The inspecteur was occasionally asked to act beyond the law to preserve "honor and peace," as in a case related by Ernest Raynaud: Two adulterers, both prominent, were trysting at the woman's house when the man suffered a fatal heart attack. The inspecteur arranged for the body to be removed and filed a report that the man died elsewhere.[17]

For their work, the men of the Sûreté were paid meanly. Although the records are imprecise, salaries appear to have been essentially constant throughout the 1870s and 1880s (a time of deflation). By 1900, and more so by 1910 (a time of inflation), there was some improvement, but particularly for the inspecteurs, there could have been no luxuries, as Table 15 indicates. Every member of the Sûreté also received a clothing allowance of Fr 450, but he was required to purchase his own revolver and ammunition. The equivalent ranks of the Police municipale were paid the same, but the salaries for the Sûreté were so low in proportion to the dangerous and demanding work that the prefecture provided an additional piecework system of rewards. Depending upon the suspect, a bonus of between one and

16. Virmaître, *Paris police*, 283–96; Georges Aubert, *Organisation et méthodes de la police française* (Tours, 1938), 75–77.
17. Horace Valbel, *La Police de Sûreté en 1889* (Paris, 1889), 34; Pierre Morel, *La Police à Paris* (Paris, 1907), 172; Raynaud, *Souvenirs de police: La Vie intime*, 17–19, 97–125.

TABLE 15
Salaries of Paris Sûreté Personnel, 1870–1910 (in Francs)

Position	1870–1890	1900	1910
Chef de la Sûreté	8,000	9,000	11,000
Sous-chef	6,000	7,000	7,500
Inspecteur principal	2,500	3,200	4,200
Brigadier	2,000	2,100	3,030
Sous-brigadier	—	1,950	2,500
Inspecteur	1,700	1,900	2,420

SOURCES: Charles Virmaître, *Paris police* (Paris, 1889), 300–302; APP, Budget, Ville de Paris, Préfecture de Police, 1900, 1910.

thirty francs was awarded for each arrest, and the detectives divided the amount quarterly. After twenty-five years of service (including time spent in the military), a member of the Paris police was eligible to retire with a pension equal to the average of his salary for the preceding three years. Retirement after between fifteen and twenty-five years was possible, but only with a much-reduced pension figured at the rate of 2 percent of the average salary for the preceding three years multiplied by the years of approved service.[18]

In the late nineteenth century a recruit for the Paris police had to be a native or naturalized citizen of France who had resided in Paris during the preceding two consecutive years. He could be no more than thirty years old (thirty-five if a veteran of the military). He had to be at least 1.67 meters (5'5¾") tall, physically fit, of good character (with no record of arrest), literate, and able to pass a minimal entrance examination. By the time of the Third Republic, the separation of the Police judiciaire from the Police municipale was present almost from the beginning of a recruit's career. Few patrolmen became detectives, and a detective who erred severely was dismissed from the prefecture, not just from the Sûreté. Although all police recruits began work immediately, learning, sometimes awkwardly, through the performance of duty, there was a distinction in the training provided by the two services. New patrolmen spent one morning every third day for four months in a classroom, hearing lectures on writing reports, making arrests, dealing with emergencies,

18. The budget of the prefecture provides no salary schedule by rank before 1890, and on that period see Virmaître, *Paris police*, 300–302. On 1900 and 1910, see APP, Budget, Ville de Paris, Préfecture de Police, for those years. See also Levilain, "Histoire de l'organisation," I, 356–57; Louis Lépine, *Mes Souvenirs* (Paris, 1929), 145–53; and Raymond B. Fosdick, *European Police Systems* (London, 1915), 253.

and presenting the proper image. There were no examinations and no continuing studies. At the Sûreté, new detectives did not receive formal instruction. Their first assignments were to the less critical brigades, in which they were told to learn from the brigadier. They were permitted more challenging work only as they passed a series of examinations in identification methods, the first efforts at scientific police investigation. By the mid-1890s, most of the Paris detective recruits came directly from the army, many of them from business and professional families experiencing an economic hardship that closed off traditional ambitions. The leadership of directors like Macé and Marie François Goron (1887–1894) had by then elevated the reputation of the Sûreté to the point that the Police judiciaire was an attractive career for such a man.[19]

The two highest positions in the Sûreté, director and assistant director, were reserved for police officials with the rank of commissaire. Under the Third Republic, as under previous regimes, appointment was by the head of state after the candidate passed a competitive examination. It was possible, though not usual, for an inspecteur principal or an officier de paix to study for and pass the examination. Instead, the great majority of aspirants, approximately 80 percent, prepared for the *concours* by acting as the *secrétaire* (administrative assistant) to a commissaire. This course guaranteed that the commissaires as a whole would be from a slightly elevated social group, because secrétaires required an outside income and enough political patronage to win appointment. The posts were few in number and received a salary below even that of an inspecteur, but they were the proven pathway to the rank of commissaire.[20]

Between 1870 and 1912, when a reorganization greatly enlarged and thereby altered the character of the Police judiciaire, there were eight directors of the Paris Sûreté (see Table 16). As a group, these men assumed office at an average age of forty-four, left office at fifty-one, and had an average tenure of eighty-one months, the last figure slightly skewed by Claude's long term. However much it sought neutrality, the prefecture was subject to the changing political complexion of the Third Republic, as the appointments demonstrate. The first three directors, Claude, Jacob, and Macé, were monarchists; the last three before 1912, Goron, Cochefert, and Hamard, were Radicals. (The political leanings of Kuhn and Taylor cannot be deter-

19. Fosdick, *European Police Systems*, 217–19, 296–304.
20. Aubert, *Organisation et méthodes*, 66–74.

TABLE 16
Directors of the Paris Sûreté, 1870–1912

Chef du service	Dates of Service
Antoine François Claude	January 15, 1858–July 10, 1875
Etienne Eugène Léopold Jacob	July 11, 1875–February 16, 1879
Gustave Placide Macé	February 16, 1879–March 15, 1884
Théophile Jean Kuhn	April 1, 1884–November 28, 1885
Hippolyte Ernest Auguste Taylor	November 28, 1885–November 13, 1887
Marie François Goron	November 14, 1887–July 6, 1894
Armand Constant Théophile Cochefert	July 6, 1894–November 16, 1902
Octave Henri Adéodat Hamard	November 17, 1902–January 1, 1912

SOURCES: APP, E A/88, Claude; E A/89, Jacob; 26169, Jacob; B A/1165, Macé; E A/89, Macé; 31900, Macé; E A/90, Taylor; E A/89, Goron; 42472, Goron; E A/88, Cochefert; 47940, Cochefert; E A/89, Hamard; 56248, Hamard. No dossier exists for Kuhn, but scattered references to him can be found in E A/90, Taylor.

mined.) Information about the social origins, education, and wealth of these men is incomplete, but to the extent it is available, they appear largely characteristic of the prefecture's commissaires. Jacob is the major exception. Of the eight, he alone came from a well-established bourgeois family with a tradition of working in the government bureaucracy, and he earned the credentials sufficient to teach for a time at the Lycée of Sens in Reims. The other seven were from the petite bourgeoisie, or in Macé's case, a middle-class family down on its luck. Macé, Cochefert, and Hamard had their baccalaureates; Kuhn, Taylor, and Goron completed only a primary school certificate. All but Jacob had to scramble economically to survive the period as a secrétaire (Macé would begin his career as an inspecteur), but they were accustomed to enough money to realize that the privations were an investment. Macé and Hamard made advantageous marriages that eased their situations.[21]

The Third Republic's first director of the Sûreté was a holdover from the Second Empire. Antoine François Claude, as a young man in Paris during the 1820s, became friends with Adolphe Thiers, who

21. APP, E A/88, Claude; E A/89, Jacob; 26169, Jacob; B A/1165, Macé; E A/89, Macé; 31900, Macé; E A/90, Taylor, E A/89, Goron; 42472, Goron; E A/88, Cochefert; 47940, Cochefert; E A/89, Hamard; 56248, Hamard. There is no dossier at the Archives de la Préfecture de Police, Paris, for Kuhn, but scattered references to him can be found in E A/90, Taylor.

helped him obtain a position in the clerk's office of the Tribunal de la Seine. Aided by Thiers's prominence under the July Monarchy, Claude was promoted to chief clerk in 1837, but working with the magistracy was becoming too tame for him. In 1845 he won appointment as a commissaire de police in Meaux, and he was assigned to the prefecture as the commissaire for Passy in January, 1848, just before the 1848 revolution. The Second Republic revoked him for royalism, and Claude took his revenge by becoming a secret agent for Louis Napoleon. After the Bonapartist victory in the presidential election of December, 1848, Claude was rewarded with a post on the délégations judiciaires of the Paris Sûreté. In 1857 he filed a report warning of the danger to the emperor from anarchist attacks, and the Orsini bomb of January 14, 1858, made Claude appear clairvoyant. On the following day, the director of the Sûreté was dismissed and Claude installed as his successor.

Claude was to remain as director of the Sûreté for seventeen and a half years. A short, stocky man with a square, clean-shaven face when most government bureaucrats were cultivating an "imperial," Claude revealed his long training with the magistrature in his absolute unwillingness to tolerate dishonest detectives. He was convinced that diligence and intelligence would produce superior police investigations. He also recognized the value of informants. The system worked well under his administration, and the emperor placed considerable trust in him. The disaster of the Franco-Prussian War brought down the Second Empire, but the prefect of police in the new provisional government, Count Emile de Kératry, retained Claude for his efficiency and probity. During the next months, Claude's patron Thiers emerged as the most important political figure in defeated France. Thiers confirmed Claude's continuance at the Sûreté and insisted that he remain at his post during the Paris Commune in the futile hope of preventing the Sûreté files from falling to the Communards. Claude was arrested by the Commune and saved from execution only by the triumph of Thiers's forces. The files of the Sûreté were burned in the flames of the fighting. Claude remained director of the Sûreté until mid-1875 and then retired to suburban Vincennes, on the east side of Paris. His successors, Jacob and Macé, came there to consult him about difficult cases. He died on April 1, 1880. The death date should be taken as a warning: Claude did not write the memoirs attributed to him.[22]

22. APP, E A/88, Claude.

Like Claude, Etienne Eugène Léopold Jacob (1831–1893) was a monarchist and began his career in the police as a commissaire outside Paris, but these were the only similarities the two men shared. Jacob was a dry, wiry man with a long nose, thin lips, and a blond beard. His family was wealthy, and he was educated at the Lycée Louis-le-Grand. After passing his baccalaureate, Jacob taught briefly in Reims. His appointment as commissaire for the Ministry of the Interior came in 1859, and he managed to transfer to the prefecture in 1867, where he held a series of administrative posts until his elevation to director of the Sûreté in July, 1875. Little in Jacob's career appeared to have prepared him for the position. In addition, his dossier contained two letters of censure for venal favoritism, and his constant requests for leave betrayed an incapacity for sustained work. Almost certainly, the path was cleared by his father, who held a political appointment in the prefecture. But this patronage was not proof against ineptitude in such public view. Any successor to Claude would have seemed an epigone, but Jacob was simply too much inferior to his tasks. Moreover, as a symbol of monarchist favoritism at a time when the republicans were increasingly dominating the government, he was a particularly easy target for criticism. On February 3, 1879, Jacob requested retirement, at the age of forty-seven, claiming to be tired and ill. The request was granted the following day.[23]

Jacob was followed by one of the Sûreté's most famous directors, Gustave Placide Macé (1835–1904), a thin, balding, ascetic man who always wore small, round spectacles. The son and grandson of police officers, Macé was one of the few commissaires to begin a career in the police as a simple inspecteur. He was only eighteen years old when his father died unexpectedly. The family was in economic crisis, and he was compelled to forgo his plan to seek a post as a secrétaire. Macé's superiors in the police encouraged him to pursue his ambitions, but he was not able to pass the *concours* for commissaire until 1868. The fifteen years as an inspecteur and brigadier were hardly wasted, though, for Macé honed his detective skills in hundreds of criminal investigations. He moved up rapidly after 1868 and was an obvious candidate to succeed Jacob in 1879.

Macé's experience was instrumental in restoring to the Sûreté some of the efficiency lost under Jacob, but there were limits to what

---

23. APP, E A/89, Jacob; 26169, Jacob. See in particular the letters of censure from 1866 and 1867, and the recommendation from his father, all in 26169, Jacob.

could be done. The files lost in 1871 cost the police valuable background intelligence and made the tracking of repeat offenders much more difficult. The knowledge that the Paris police were operating under the handicap of having lost their archives attracted criminals from all over Europe to the city. In his memoirs Macé claims that the number of crimes in Paris by foreigners was very much above average during the 1870s and 1880s. In December, 1882, to help identify recidivists, Macé permitted a prefecture clerk, Alphonse Bertillon, to experiment with *anthropométrie*—measuring certain physical features of everyone who was arrested and entering the data, along with frontal and profile photographs, on a file card. The procedure permitted the police to single out professional criminals who committed many crimes and were arrested frequently. Bertillon would be recognized as a pioneer criminologist and given direction of a new division within the prefecture, the Identité judiciaire (identity department). For Macé, however, the Bertillon system could yield only meager returns until arrests built up the number of cards. For the short term, he knew from his long years as a detective that the Sûreté required modern equipment and better-trained men. His insistence on telephone links for the Sûreté came to symbolize his budget demands, and after the prefecture repeatedly rejected his proposals, he resigned angrily in mid-March, 1884.

Did politics also play a role in Macé's departure? The Republic was by now solidly in the hands of the republicans, and Macé's devotion to monarchism certainly undercut his influence at the prefecture. Although his performance at the Sûreté was highly praised, some of the Radical politicians gratuitously fashioned and spread malicious rumors about him. Macé rightly considered himself ill used, and with less justification believed that his good name had been tainted. On April 13, 1884, a month after his resignation, he printed up and circulated widely an open letter addressed to Henri Brisson, president of the Chamber of Deputies, protesting against the treatment he had received from certain Radicals. Macé also planned revenge through his memoirs. He hurriedly wrote a polemical first volume, *La Police parisienne*, by the early fall of 1884. Advance copies went to thirty-four newspapers, sixty-eight senators and deputies, and twelve bureaucrats in the Ministry of the Interior, all of whom he counted on to support his accusations. Monarchist newspapers published Macé's frequent and sarcastic criticism of his successors at the Sûreté, Kuhn and Taylor. His vindictive anger eventually led him to take an active role in the Boulangist conspiracy. In November, 1884, the Radical newspaper *La Lanterne* claimed that Macé was prepared to become the prefect of police if the Orléanist pretender, the Count of Paris, could restore the monarchy. By the late 1880s, the allegation was probably true.[24]

The successors whom Macé pilloried, Théophile Jean Kuhn and Hippolyte Ernest Auguste Taylor, served only briefly and unsuccessfully as directors of the Sûreté. Little information exists about Kuhn because no dossier for him can be located in the archives at the Prefecture of Police. He was a florid, violent man who raged at both superiors and subordinates until a heart attack as he sat behind his desk killed him after eighteen months in office. Ernest Taylor (1838–1908) took over in late 1885 under difficult circumstances. Perhaps the undated photograph in his dossier was taken early in his two-year tenure: A narrow-faced man with a high, broad forehead and thick moustache looks out through melancholy, worried eyes. Arrests were down, and morale among the detectives was low. Kuhn had made high officials in the prefecture unfriendly toward the Sûreté. Taylor was apparently chosen director because of a reputation as a placater. He did calm tensions, but he was an extremely poor choice. His sickly constitution was weakened by the stress of his new position, and he had to delegate too much authority. He was also too cautious to be an effective leader, insisting on written orders whenever the Sûreté was given a delicate assignment. By August, 1886, newspapers from the extreme Left to the extreme Right carried strident criticism of the Sûreté's inability to solve important crimes and claimed that the detectives openly mocked Taylor's failures. Despite his circumspection, Taylor was caught up by scandal in November, 1887, when the prefecture, at the request of Jules Grévy, president of the republic, destroyed the evidence of bribery and corruption against Grévy's son-in-law Daniel Wilson, a member of the Chamber of Deputies.[25]

On November 14, 1887, the day after Taylor's departure, the short, wiry sous-chef of the Sûreté, Marie François Goron (1847–1933),

---

24. Gustave Placide Macé, *La Police parisienne, aventuriers de génie* (Paris, 1884), 25–36; APP, B A/1165, Macé; E A/89, Macé; 31900, Macé. Macé was angry at an attack by Radical deputy Eugène Dellatre (Seine) before the Chamber of Deputies, on January 21, 1884. The reports of royalist activity come from B A/1165, July 4, 1885–January 20, 1889. The clipping from *La Lanterne*, November 26, 1884, is in E A/89, Macé.

25. APP, E A/90, Taylor. The file contains numerous newspaper clippings.

was promoted to become the new director. It was another step in a long and picaresque life. Born in Rennes, Goron completed his primary schooling and joined the army in 1865. By the time he left military service in 1871, he had been stationed in Martinique and Algeria, fought in the Franco-Prussian War, and won a battlefield commission. He returned to Rennes to work eight years as a wholesale merchant. He made enough money to pass the following two years traveling in Paraguay and Argentina. Back in France, he used contacts with Radical politicians to obtain an appointment as a secrétaire in March, 1881, and was made a commissaire in 1885. His energy and ability were so obvious that he was rapidly advanced to sous-chef of the Sûreté in 1886, and less than a year later he succeeded Taylor in the wake of the Grévy-Wilson scandal.

At the age of forty, Goron was the youngest man ever to head the Sûreté, and as director he exhibited the vigor that characterized his entire life. He would be less an administrator and more the top detective of Paris. During his six and a half years in office, the Sûreté was unusually successful in solving important crimes. Quite often Goron himself led the investigation, sometimes traveling outside Paris, a few times outside France, to evaluate clues and evidence. The Paris press particularly praised his work in tracing the murderers of the bailiff Gouffé in 1890. Goron's broad face, with its combative expression, thick, curly moustache, and black hair combed smartly back, became well-known through front-page photographs. From his detectives, Goron insisted on the hard work and thoroughness he asked of himself. In return, he argued for more liberal expense allowances from the prefecture. Because of his own experience with investigations that took him outside of Paris, he tried, to no avail, to centralize information from provincial police forces. And like Macé, he unsuccessfully demanded telephones.

In June, 1894, accusations appeared in the press that Goron had not pursued vigorously enough certain links to politicians in the Panama Canal scandal. It was alleged that he was too close to Radical politicians compromised in the case. Goron reacted by requesting a transfer to the commissariat of the Gaillon-Vivienne district, an extremely desirable post two blocks from the Bourse. He served there until September, 1895, and then retired with a pension. Taking his son as a partner, he opened a private detective agency. He also published his memoirs—the best of any Sûreté director—and several crime novels loosely based on his own experiences. During World

War I, though in his late sixties, Goron held an administrative position with military intelligence.[26]

There was no effort to find another director for the Sûreté exactly in Goron's mold. Instead, the choice fell on the corpulent, desk-bound Armand Constant Théophile Cochefert (1850–1911). Although he was egregiously overweight—it was said that he frequently ate a dozen hard-boiled eggs while interrogating a witness—Cochefert was an able police official. He became a secrétaire in 1879, passed the examination for commissaire in 1884 with a distinguished score (28 of a possible 30), and was assigned to the délégations judiciaires in 1891. Two years later he was promoted to be a *commissaire divisionnaire* (administrative supervisor) for Parisian commissaires.

At the head of the Sûreté, Cochefert was as easygoing and tolerant as Goron had been compulsive and driving. He rarely ventured from his office to take personal charge of his brigades, but he was shrewd in his analysis of a case and quickly won the respect of his men. At first, there appeared to be no loss in efficiency. The army had the assistance of the Sûreté in the investigation of espionage during the fall of 1894, and Cochefert himself was present when Alfred Dreyfus was arrested. Detectives from the Sûreté completed the controversial inquiry into the Panama Canal scandal (though some politicians and newspapers insisted that the detectives destroyed the most incriminating evidence). Anarchist circles were penetrated, and "propaganda by the deed" reduced. Cochefert did direct the capture of some important criminals, but perhaps because he kept to his office, the prefecture finally installed telephone lines for the Sûreté, more than fifteen years after Macé had first requested them. Unfortunately, Cochefert's methods permitted a slackness that became embarrassingly public in November, 1902, during the Humbert affair. The prefecture moved Cochefert to the post of *contrôleur général* (police superintendant), a promotion, and quietly retired him the following July.[27]

Cochefert's replacement was Octave Henri Adéodat Hamard (1861–19?), a dapper and handsome man who had served as sous-chef of the Sûreté for the preceding six months and who quickly

---

26. APP, E A/89, Goron; 42472, Goron; Marie François Goron, *Les Mémoires de M. Goron* (Paris, 1897), II, 338–59, III, 132–331; IV, 1–102, 366–420.

27. APP, E A/88, Cochefert; 47940, Cochefert. See my *The Hypocrisy of Justice in the Belle Epoque* (Baton Rouge, 1984), 107.

reinvigorated it. Like Goron, he was young (forty-one years old on assuming office) and took an active part in all important investigations. His bravery was unquestioned. Even a serious knife wound during an arrest in 1907 did not reduce his readiness to take personal charge of his elite brigade. Hamard was born at Châtillon-Coligny in the Loiret, passed his baccalaureate after attending the Lycée d'Orléans, and served in the army artillery. When he applied for appointment as a secrétaire, a letter of recommendation from the powerful Radical deputy Alphonse Cochery was decisive at the prefecture. In April, 1888, just before taking up his duties, he married Marie Célébar, whose small inheritance made the low salary of a secrétaire more bearable.

From the beginning, Hamard's performance was highly praised by his superiors, particularly his firmness in cases involving anarchists. He became a commissaire in 1893 and provided coordination between the prefecture and the Sûreté until 1902, when he was called to be sous-chef. In Hamard's nine years as director the Sûreté performed adequately, improving on Cochefert's tenure but not equaling Goron's. The most frequent criticism was that Hamard's ties to the Radical party were too tight—that in certain delicate cases, good police work was sacrificed to political expediency. Certainly, the manner in which the Sûreté handled the final inquiry into the Humbert affair in 1902–1903 and investigated the death of Gabriel Syveton in 1905 (officially termed a suicide) and the murders of the Steinheil affair in 1908 was unusual. But Hamard easily survived any complaints. Although he flaunted his allegiance to the Radicals by declaring an interest in running for office, he decided to remain with the prefecture, and on January 1, 1912, in a large reorganization, he was promoted to directeur des recherches, a doubling of his authority.[28]

When the prefecture acted to appoint, promote, dismiss, or retire personnel, when it fulfilled or rejected budgetary requests, when it reorganized or not departments, divisions, or entire services, when it issued standing regulations and carried out police activities, it was acting in the name of the Paris prefect of police. Between 1870 and 1913, fifteen different men, one of them twice, held this position of "ministre sans le titre" (see Table 17). Each of the prefects had his own agenda for the prefecture, but all agreed that order was the ini-

28. APP, E A/89, Hamard; 56248, Hamard. See Martin, *The Hypocrisy of Justice*, 24–35, 76.

TABLE 17
Paris Prefects of Police, 1870–1913

Prefect of Police	Dates of Service	Previous Position
Emile de Kératry	September 4, 1870–October 11, 1870	Conseiller d'Etat
Edmond Adam	October 11, 1870–November 2, 1870	
Guillaume Cresson	November 2, 1870–February 11, 1871	Avocat, Cour d'appel de Paris
Albert Choppin	February 16, 1871–March 3, 1871	Avocat, Cour d'appel de Paris
Louis Valentin	March 3, 1871–November 17, 1871	Army general
Léon Renault	November 17, 1871–February 9, 1876	Secrétaire-général to the prefect of police
Félix Voisin	February 9, 1876–December 17, 1877	Deputy for Seine-et-Marne
Albert Gigot	December 17, 1877–March 4, 1879	Prefect for Meurthe-et-Moselle
Louis Andrieux	March 4, 1879–July 16, 1881	Deputy for Bouches-du-Rhône, founder of *Le Petit Parisien*
Jean Camescasse	July 16, 1881–April 23, 1885	Former prefect
Arthur Gragnon	April 23, 1885–November 17, 1887	Secrétaire-général to the prefect of police
Léon Bourgeois	November 17, 1887–March 10, 1888	Directeur, Affaires départementales, Ministry of the Interior
Henry Lozé	March 10, 1888–July 11, 1893	Prefect for Somme
Louis Lépine	July 11, 1893–October 14, 1897	Prefect for Seine-et-Oise
Charles Blanc	October 14, 1897–June 23, 1899	Directeur, Sûreté Générale
Louis Lépine	June 23, 1899–March 29, 1913	Governor-general of Algeria

SOURCE: *Journal Officiel*, Lois et Décrets, 1870–1913

tial entry. This meant priority in attention and funds to the Police municipale. Few of the prefects interested themselves in the Sûreté, leaving the Police judiciaire to subordinates and, in the best of cases, to the director of the Sûreté himself. The prefects who did intervene in criminal investigations did so disastrously.

Louis Andrieux, prefect of police from March, 1879, to July, 1881, was appointed largely because of his friendship with Léon Gambetta and the daring to fight a duel with the redoubtable Bonapartist Paul de Cassagnac. His experience with crime had come from writing about it in his newspaper, *Le Petit Parisien*, but he believed himself competent to dispatch detectives all over Europe on his own authority while denying a proper operating budget to Macé. The detectives cheered when Interior Minister Ernest Constans dismissed Andrieux but remarked with displeasure that two of his assistants, Contrôleur général Boissenot and Commissaire divisionnaire Clément, held on to their positions. Boissenot and Clément had established a network of informants throughout the prefecture and the commissariats through which they exercised an administrative blackmail. Because Macé opposed them, they sabotaged many of his requests, placing the Sûreté at the mercy of a personal vendetta. Of the next four prefects of police who followed Andrieux—Jean Camescasse, Arthur Gragnon, Léon Bourgeois, and Henry Lozé—only Gragnon proposed to cashier Boissenot and Clément, at the urgent recommendation of his secrétaire général, Louis Lépine. But Gragnon also interfered with the Sûreté, in the Jules Grévy–Daniel Wilson scandal, and that cost him the prefecture before he followed Lépine's advice. Almost five and a half years later, in July, 1893, Lépine became prefect of of police himself, and one of his first acts was to dismiss the two. Unfortunately, one of his own closest assistants, Louis Puibaraud, was only slightly less outrageous in seeking influence. Ernest Raynaud recalled that many commissaires were relieved when Puibaraud died suddenly in 1903.

The square on the Ile de la Cité bounded by the Tribunal de Commerce, the Hôpital de l'Hôtel Dieu, the Seine River, and the prefecture bears the name Place Louis Lépine. No other street or square honors a prefect of police. In two terms, from July, 1893, to October, 1897, and from June, 1899, to March, 1913, Louis Jean Baptiste Lépine (1846–1933) ruled the prefecture for eighteen years, one quarter of the Third Republic's life and more than twice as long as the next longest terms (of almost seven years, by Jean Chiappe, April, 1927, to February, 1934, and Roger Langéron, March, 1934, to

February, 1941). A small, angular man with a short white beard who dressed most frequently in a bowler hat and morning coat, Lépine would have given the impression of a dandy but for his volatile temperament, emphatic gestures, and enormous energy. As an attorney in Lyon during the early 1870s, he was noted for his ardent republicanism, particularly at the crisis of Seize Mai. He was rewarded by the offer of an administrative career in the Ministry of the Interior. An apprenticeship as prefect or subprefect in the provinces, and the brief period as secrétaire général under Gragnon prepared him for the Paris prefecture. The twenty-month gap in his tenure came when he was sent to calm unrest in Algeria as governor-general.

As prefect of police, Lépine identified strongly with his men. He left his office door open to maintain contact with the ranks. He set aside special hours to hear complaints from anyone on the force. He established a charity for the widows and orphans of policemen. The Sûreté was allowed to do its work without much interference, but Lépine placed his own mark on the Police municipale. He organized it into marching formations, imposed military discipline, issued the now familiar white truncheons, and demanded courtesy to the public. Whenever there was a crisis of order, Lépine left the prefecture to take personal command. The patrolmen called him the Prefect of the Streets and acclaimed him. He created the first river patrol for the Seine and developed a brigade of police on bicycles. Under his authority, the prefecture published a two-volume directory of police procedure. Relationships with the public prosecutor and his parquet and with the municipal council of Paris and the prefect of the Seine were improved. The police gained widespread public esteem. Lépine was simply an extraordinary administrator.[29]

Because there were criminals in Paris, there was the Sûreté, with the assignment to investigate crimes. The structure and leadership of the prefecture and the Sûreté itself were means (better or worse) to that end. To read through a file at the police archives is to follow an inspecteur as he interviews witnesses, gathers evidence, consults informers, arrests suspects, and puzzles over disjointed facts. It is to learn what crimes preoccupied the Sûreté, how an inquiry was

---

29. Levilain, "Histoire de l'organisation," I, 302–22; Ernest Raynaud, *Souvenirs de police, au temps de Félix Faure* (Paris, 1925), 88–123, 315–17; Raynaud, *Souvenirs de police: La Vie intime*, 37–71; Stead, *The Police of Paris*, 148–52; Louis Lépine (ed.), *Répertoire de police administrative et judiciaire* (Paris, 1896–99).

The Police (I)

mounted and conducted, why some cases were solved and others shelved. And it is to discover a social history of crime written from the perspective of the police, often a history of men and women, criminals and victims, who lived on the margin of life and whose world comes alive through one of the few records many of them left behind, the dispassionate analysis of these reports.

Octave Simoni was an Italian immigrant, seventy-nine years old, living alone on the Rue Basfroi. He made a decent living by carving religious objects from wood, which his daughter sold in her shop several blocks away. He seemed to be happy, and no one in this predominantly Italian quarter had a word to speak against him. In November, 1877, he was murdered. Three years earlier, a thief had robbed him of two hundred francs, but he had refused to report the crime. Instead, he secretly borrowed the same amount from a neighbor in order to claim that nothing had happened. Simoni assuaged his pride, but he began to take a new precaution. At night he would leave his curtains open to make any crime more visible. His daughter checked on him often each week, and during a visit on November 8 he promised to bring some of his completed votives to her shop two days later. When he did not come, she grew worried and went to his apartment. Through the open curtains of the bedroom window, she could see nothing amiss, but his kitchen was dark and had no exterior openings. With the aid of the concierge, the daughter managed to enter the apartment. Her father was seated at the table in the kitchen, his head slumped to one side, his clothes soaked with blood. The Sûreté was called, and within three days the killers were arrested—Henri Cantaluppi, Charles Bambanas, and their girlfriend, Méanal Mazarri. They were in their early twenties, and both men were unemployed. Like Simoni thirty years before, they had left their native Italy and come to Paris to find their fortune. When fate brought them poverty, they decided to steal. Simoni's resistance led them to murder. The Italian community of Paris had been Simoni's link to his homeland; now it was the breeding ground for his murder.[30]

Other dossiers in the archives contain records of far grislier crimes, often from the poorest sections of Paris and its suburbs. In late 1875 a woman in her midfifties known simply as La Bonnereu vanished. The man with whom she lived, Toussaint Léon Gervais, told every-

---

30. APP, B A/1612, Crimes, dos. Simoni. See also my "The Record of Murders: Blood-Stained Dossiers at the Archives de la Préfecture de Police," *Third Republic / Troisième République,* X (Fall, 1980), 1–17.

one that his mistress had grown tired of him and had taken up housekeeping with another man across the city. But when Gervais quickly married a much younger woman and began to spend more money than usual, rumors circulated that La Bonnereu must have had some small savings and that Gervais had murdered her for them. In February, 1876, the Sûreté finally took an interest in the gossip, and inspecteurs dug up Gervais' cellar. They found the body of La Bonnereu; she had been half-strangled and then buried alive. Gervais was executed for his crime. There is no record of his young wife's fate.[31]

The case of Sébastien Joseph Billoir from 1876 is notorious. Billoir made his living selling sawdust and shared a two-room apartment in Saint Ouen with a slattern named Marie La Manach. Near midnight on November 6, 1876, La Manach returned drunk to their rooms, where Billoir was waiting for her. She staggered across the floor, knocked over a table, and broke his one prized possession, a decorated wooden cup. As she bent down to pick up the pieces, the enraged Billoir kicked her squarely in the chest. To his horror, she fell dead. Panicking, and fearing that the police would not believe that he had never meant to kill her, he conceived an awful plan. He spread sawdust thickly on the floor and hacked La Manach's body into four pieces, head and breast, abdomen, and two legs. He wrapped each up in paper and threw them into the Seine. On the following day, he sold the sawdust, which had absorbed the blood. Unfortunately for Billoir, a witness saw him casting strange objects into the river. When the pieces of La Manach were recovered further down the Seine by bargemen, the witness stepped forward. Billoir was tried on March 14–15, 1877, for premeditated murder. Any hope he might have had to avoid either conviction or the death penalty was ended when the jury were shown photographs of the dismembered La Manach. Just before his execution six weeks later, on April 27, there was a recognition that the sentence had been based on emotion. Some clamor arose for a reprieve. It was not loud enough. The photographs remain in the file, as gruesome today as they were a century ago.[32]

Children make their appearance in the police dossiers most often as pathetic victims. Little Marie-Jeanne, four years old, was the daughter of Victor and Stéphanie Moyaux. The marriage fell apart in early 1876, when Victor, a failure in business and facing fraud charges, learned that his wife had taken a lover. Nothing seemed left

---

31. APP, B A/1612, Crimes, dos. La Bonnereu.
32. APP, B A/81, Crimes, dos. La Manach.

for him but Marie-Jeanne, but Stéphanie asked for sole custody of her. He went into hiding with his daughter, certain that the courts would find against him. Ironically, as his despair and bitterness grew, he vented his frustrations on the child. On February 3, 1877, he beat her so badly that she died. Crazed with guilt and anger, he bought a pistol, searched out his wife, and killed her with two bullets through the chest.[33]

Children could also suffer as instruments of revenge. Jean Vodable lived with a prostitute, Pauline Malfilâtre, and her child, Alexandrine, who was twelve years old. In November, 1879, Vodable and Malfilâtre quarreled, and she forced him to leave. Three weeks later he asked to move back into the apartment, but Malfilâtre haughtily refused. Vodable swore a terrible vengeance and took it against Alexandrine. He entered the apartment with a skeleton key when the child was alone; then he raped and murdered her. The absolutely chilling touch was to place the body beneath her mother's bed. The Sûreté suspected Vodable immediately and had no difficulty locating him. As soon as he was hungry, he surrendered himself at the prefecture in return for the promise of a good meal. He was executed in July, 1880.[34]

Usually, the children who were murdered were so young that they were helpless before their assailants. In February, 1881, Félix Lemaître, a young man afflicted with the dangerous combination of poverty and delusions of grandeur, decided to become notorious by killing a child. He lured six-year-old Jean Schaonen, the son of poor day laborers, to his room, stabbed him twice fatally, and then reported the act, with great sangfroid, to the Sûreté. Other cases were horrifically similar. In June, 1877, Pierre Jean Welker, who was twenty-one, brought Marie Joséphine Ekerlé, the eight-year-old daughter of a friend, to his room, where he raped and strangled her. Likewise, in April, 1880, Louis Menesclou, who at the age of nineteen already had a considerable reputation as a troublemaker, enticed Louise Deu, four years old, into a wooded area with the promise of flowers. He committed rape and murder before cutting her small body into thirty-five pieces, all of which he carried back to his lodging.[35]

Such delinquents as Lemaître, Welker, and Menesclou often joined criminal gangs. The most famous of these was led by Emile Abadie

33. APP, B A/81, Crimes, dos. Moyaux.
34. APP, B A/84, Crimes, dos. Malfilâtre; Goron, *Les Mémoires*, II, 428–56.
35. APP, B A/1612, Crimes, dos. Schaonen; B A/497, Faits divers, dos. Ekerlé; B A/1612, Crimes, dos. Deu.

and included Michel Knobloch, Paul Kirial, and Pierre Giles. They were responsible for a number of brutal robberies and murders in early 1879 before their arrest, conviction, and execution. Their great notoriety came not from the crimes but from their background of middle-class homes and education at excellent Catholic schools. They were such unlikely criminals that the Sûreté initially doubted its own investigation. Ten years later, in 1889, a gang led by Joseph Allorto carried out similar crimes but received much less public attention because all of the members were from the working class. The Sûreté had a much easier time with the Allorto gang because the various members informed on each other in a vain effort to gain lenient treatment.[36]

The gang leader who received the most individual publicity was François Meerholtz, known as the Pasha of the Glacière (the *glacière* was the old Paris fortifications where his favorite hiding places were located). Meerholtz led a gang of young toughs in their late teens and early twenties who wore identical tattoos reading MORT AUX VACHES! (Kill the pigs!). The Sûreté ascribed a number of crimes to them but gained the evidence for their eventual arrest and conviction only in April, 1884, after the group rape of a young prostitute, Antoinette Prévost, turned into murder. After they kicked her unconscious, they pushed her off the *glacière,* and her head struck a rock as she fell.[37]

One feature of Parisian crime between 1870 and 1900 was that whether robbery was committed by an individual or by a group, it was frequently accompanied by murder. The need to incapacitate a victim long enough to take his valuables cannot explain why so many who were robbed were also stabbed, shot, or strangled. Was there a class warfare by a criminal element from the lower orders against the bourgeoisie and aristocracy, as Louis Chevalier has discovered for the 1830s? The cases in the police archives for the first thirty years of the Third Republic do not lend themselves readily to this hypothesis. More often, it was a working-class criminal robbing and murdering a working-class victim, or a bourgeois criminal and a bourgeois victim. Sheer viciousness sometimes appears to provide a sufficient interpretation. On April 20, 1878, Louis Martin, a fashionable antique dealer burdened with overdue debts on his merchandise and shop, suddenly decided to end his problems through theft. He

36. APP, B A/1612, Crimes, dos. Basengaud, dos. Lecercle; B A/84, Crimes, dos. Bourdon; Goron, *Les Mémoires,* II, 360–427.
37. APP, B A/1612, Crimes, dos. Prévost.

attacked a bank clerk, Louis Sébalte, who passed the shop doorway each afternoon carrying certain receipts to the Société Générale office. Martin could have knocked out Sébalte with a blow to the head but instead cut his throat. In February, 1885, two young men, Henri Mayer and Paul Gaspard, took Fr 105.90 from a poor woodworker, Joseph Delauney. It was simple for them to overpower Delauney, who was seventy-five years old, but they killed him as well, beating him to death with brass knuckles.[38]

During this period a number of middle-aged women were murdered as they slept in their beds: In March, 1877, Mme Marguerite Lachaud was strangled; in April, 1885, Mme Laure Cornet stabbed; in November, 1886, Mme Louise Loyon stabbed; in March, 1888, the widow Vinchon strangled; in January, 1889, the widow Roux stabbed; in December, 1891, the Baroness Emilie Dellard shot; in June, 1896, the Baroness Hermine de Valley strangled. In all seven cases, robbery appeared to be the original motive. The Sûreté was able to solve five of them, and in the three investigations under Goron, the murderous thief was a soldier on leave needing money to return to his unit. Confession by the guilt-ridden Gustave Schumacher closed the case of the widow Vinchon and provided a clue to solve future murders, because Goron had been initially unwilling to believe a soldier capable of such dishonor. In the murder of the widow Roux, Corporal Fulgence Benjamin Géomay was always the prime suspect. A search of his hotel room in Paris turned up only a friend from his unit and a naked prostitute. Goron tracked Géomay back to his post and obtained an order to return him to Paris. Confronted with the corpse, Géomay broke down and confessed. The case of the Baroness Dellard was much more difficult. Goron finally traced a knife and overcoat found near the murder to shops in Lyon, where Lieutenant Louis Anastay was stationed. The victim's son, Paul Dellard, an official at the Ministry of War, knew Anastay as a family friend and recalled that he had offered no condolences. This small piece of information convinced Goron to concentrate on Anastay, and the investigation eventually provided the evidence for his arrest.[39]

38. Louis Chevalier, *Classes laborieuses et classes dangereuses à Paris pendant la première moitié du XIXe siècle* (Paris, 1958); APP, B A/1612, Crimes, dos. Sébalte; dos. Delauney.

39. APP, B A/81, Crimes, dos. Lachaud; B A/1612, Crimes, dos. Cornet; B A/82, Crimes, dos. Loyson; B A/84, Crimes, dos. Vinchon; dos. Roux; B A/85, Crimes, dos. Dellard; B A/1612, Crimes, dos. de Valley; Goron, *Les Mémoires*, II, 252–337; Ernest Raynaud, *Souvenirs de police, au temps de Ravachol* (Paris, 1923), 270–86.

There were crimes that take on more clearly the aspect of poor against rich. Barthélemy Quiblier had worked as the concierge at the *hôtel* of Poulin de La Dreux for several years when a bout of drunkenness brought his dismissal. Quiblier had little cause for resentment because he was given three months' notice in which to find another position, but instead of looking for work, he plotted revenge. On his last night at the *hôtel*, January 15, 1881, he fired on the La Dreux family with a pistol as they sat at dinner. He missed everyone but had greater success shooting himself with the next bullet and died three weeks later in a prison hospital. Another case comes from March, 1888. At the age of twenty-nine, Charles Auguste Mathelin was drunk, debauched, and out of work. Etienne Oudin and his wife were members of a charity group and thought to rehabilitate Mathelin by offering him work on their estate. While Mme Oudin was away, Mathelin knocked down his much older employer and strangled him. With cunning, he hung the body from a tree, making Oudin appear a suicide. At first, the Sûreté did not suspect Mathelin, but he unwittingly proclaimed his guilt by immediately paying off all of his debts on the day after the murder and then squandering four hundred francs in a spree with prostitutes.[40]

A far more interesting and less unsavory crime began on July 26, 1889, when the bailiff Gouffé disappeared. Forty-eight years old, a widower with three daughters, known as a womanizer, and suspected of illegal enterprises, Gouffé was last seen escorting an attractive brunette, much later identified as Gabrielle Bompard. She lured him back to her rooms, where she and her lover, Michel Eyraud, sprang a trap. As Gouffé began to fondle her, Bompard playfully looped a curtain about his neck, and Eyraud pulled a rope attached to the curtain through a pulley. The bailiff was abruptly jerked three feet above the floor, his feet dangling and his neck broken. Eyraud and Bompard had planned their crime carefully. Long before renting the rooms on the Rue Tronson-du-Coudray and equipping one of them with a pulley, they had purchased a large leather trunk in London. As soon as they were certain that Gouffé was dead, they stripped off his clothing, sewed his body into a sack, and placed the sack into the trunk. Using Gouffé's keys, they entered his office on the Rue Montmartre and stole the large sum of money he kept there. On the next day, acting as ordinary travelers, they took the trunk with them on the train to Lyon. At the station, they hired a carriage and drove sev-

40. APP, B A/1612, Crimes, dos. Quiblier; B A/84, Crimes, dos. Oudin.

The Police (I)

eral miles toward the village of Millery, where they found a deserted field to drop the trunk, with the body inside. After returning the carriage, they set off on quite wide-ranging travels.

In Paris, Gouffé's daughters reported him missing, though there was no immediate alarm because he was known to go on brief excursions with a new conquest. His description was not sent out beyond the Paris suburbs, and when farmers at Millery discovered the trunk and body on August 12, police officials in Lyon had no reason to send an account to the prefecture in Paris. Because there were no clothes to assist in identification and Gouffé was unknown in Lyon, the body was buried in the city cemetery after only a cursory investigation. The sole remaining clue in the case was the trunk. Goron accidentally learned about these developments when he saw a Lyon newspaper, and instinct led him to offer the Sûreté's assistance. In January, 1890, the trunk was traced to a London shop. The body was then exhumed and sent to the Paris Institut Médico-légal, where police surgeons identified it as Gouffé. The London shop records made Bompard and Eyraud the prime suspects, and the hunt for them began. Bompard voluntarily surrendered to the Paris Police in April, 1890. Three months later, Eyraud was arrested in Havana and extradited. At their trial in December, both were found guilty, with Eyraud drawing a sentence of death, Bompard of twenty years in prison. Although the jury unanimously recommended that extenuating circumstances spare Eyraud from execution, the justices rejected the plea. So would François Sadi-Carnot, the president of the Republic, who had the final right to commute a sentence of death. There were rumors that the minister of the interior, Ernest Constans, a man of dangerous and dubious reputation, had been compromised by papers in Gouffé's office, papers that Eyraud presumably saw. Constans, it was said, insisted on Eyraud's death. Perhaps Bompard also saw the papers, with the payment for her silence being her release after only thirteen years in prison. On February 3, 1891, as he was led to the guillotine, Eyraud shouted: "Constans est un assassin! Il est plus assassin que moi!"[41]

If the Gouffé affair proved that the Sûreté could occasionally unravel the secrets of even the most well-planned and baffling crimes, the series of violent deaths among prostitutes between 1878 and 1893 indicated that many criminals could still escape its detection.

---

41. APP, B A/85, Crimes, dos. Gouffé. A dramatization of this case, "La Malle à Gouffé," was broadcast by French television on September 16, 1968.

There is no evidence that a French Jack the Ripper stalked Paris, for the crimes were quite different, and a few, but only a few, were solved. Neither is there any indication that the Sûreté spent less time and effort investigating the murders of *filles publiques* than they did inquiring into the murders of baronesses in their beds. The dossiers are crammed with reports, and the Paris press was a constant goad. In many of the cases, the Sûreté could assume that the assailant was a client of the prostitute. But in most instances, these women had so many clients—with reasons to remain anonymous—that it was impossible to find them all, if any could be located. From the records of the investigations, much can be learned about the life and the women of prostitution. For some, there was the glitter of high connections and an address in a respectable neighborhood. For others, there was the fear of working the streets near the railroad stations, a constant threat of violence, and the need to find and service several men a night because no one of them would be able to afford a high fee.

Most often, the murder of a common prostitute was extremely difficult to solve. These women did not have a fixed clientele, and they had few bonds to others in the neighborhood. There was usually too little evidence and too many suspects. On May 27, 1878, the concierge at 134 Rue du Faubourg Saint Martin discovered the body of twenty-five-year-old Caroline Meuris, who was known to bring clients from the nearby Gare de l'Est back to her room. Someone had strangled her. Another young prostitute, Marie Ursule Fellerath, twenty-three years old, who lived on the Passage Saulnier near the Grands Boulevards, was stabbed to death on February 22, 1879. In both cases, the Sûreté's investigation focused on a sometime lover, but there was never enough evidence to make an arrest. On March 20, 1892, Lucie Dubois was found in her room on the Rue Taitbout, not far from the Gare Saint Lazare, her throat cut and her left eye crushed. She was thirty-eight years old and had been a registered prostitute for nine years. The semiprecious jewels she wore and the small amount of money she hid in her room were not taken. Ten months later, on January 27, 1893, there was a similar murder only two blocks away on the Rue Saint Lazare. A second prostitute in her late thirties, Louise Lamier, was the victim. Her throat had been slashed, and there was no evidence of robbery. Inspecteurs from the Sûreté assumed that a man who traveled to Paris occasionally by train committed both murders, but a long investigation produced not a single suspect. The isolation and ostracism of most prostitutes was a significant handicap in these inquiries. Witnesses did not step forward. The crime did not engage local solidarity. When the victim had some links to her quarter, the Sûreté had a greater probability of success. Marguerite Dubois was a thin and pathetic woman in her early forties who attracted clients only because she charged so little to prostitute herself as she worked the streets near the Gare de l'Est. She lived alone without a steady lover and kept her room on the Rue Payenne of the Marais district meticulously clean and neat. The artisan families who rented the other rooms in the house knew that she was a prostitute, but some of them respected her effort to maintain small proprieties. On March 18, 1889, she was killed by a knife thrust between her shoulder blades. Her neighbors alerted Sûreté inspecteurs to Eugène Sauer, a bronze worker whose wife had sought shelter with Marguerite Dubois after quarreling with him. The investigation led to Sauer's arrest and conviction.[42]

The Sûreté could not deploy its forces more effectively when the murdered prostitute attracted her clients from the higher classes. Such women had business with fewer men, but they were men who had reputation at stake in the disclosure of their names and would cooperate with the police only circumspectly. A demimondaine kept apart from the other inhabitants of her building and was usually regarded as a mysterious figure. On July 21, 1885, when Hélène Stein was discovered strangled in her apartment on the Rue Bergère, her neighbors in this excellent quarter not far from the Bourse were shocked by her murder but even more so by the details of her life. Certain clues pointed toward one client, but not enough for an arrest, and the investigation was dropped after six weeks. Marie Aguétant was a beautiful young prostitute who was maintained in an apartment on the Champs-Elysées by several wealthy aristocrats. She was murdered on January 14, 1886, by Frederick Prado y Ribo, but the Sûreté solved the case only in the summer of 1888 and then because Prado's mistress betrayed him.

The most sensational murder of a demimondaine occurred during the night of March 18–19, 1887. When inspecteurs from the Sûreté were called to an opulent apartment on the Rue Montaigne, a block from the Seine River and the Place de l'Alma, they discovered the bodies of three women dead from gunshot wounds—Marie Re-

---

42. APP, B A/81, Crimes, dos. Meuris; B A/1612, Crimes, dos. Fellerath, dos. Dubois, dos. Lamier; B A/84, Crimes, dos. Dubois. See also Andrieux, *Souvenirs*, I, 114–24.

gnault, who was forty years old and called herself Mme Régine de Montille; her maid, Antoinette Guemeret; and the maid's eleven-year-old daughter. Goron, then sous-chef of the Sûreté, took charge of the case. A file at the prefecture identified a circle of proper bourgeois businessmen as Regnault's clients. Goron's investigation revealed that she had experimented as well with lesbian relationships and also sought out rough, lower-class lovers. A self-righteous inspecteur found several sexual aids in the apartment and indignantly burned them. Another discovery, the calling cards of some recent clients, provided a critical clue. The Sûreté made inquiries and singled one man out for having left Paris, Henri Pranzini. He was caught in Marseille on March 23 attempting to sell Marie Regnault's jewels. Ironically, the Marseille police made the arrest based on information they had read in newspaper accounts of the case, because the Sûreté had neglected to send a description of the jewels beyond the Paris suburbs. Goron's work was not completed. Pranzini had cleverly fabricated evidence to confuse the police, implicating a certain Gaston Geissler. The service des garnis discovered a registration under that name, but a search of the hotel room produced only the man's valise. Goron traced Geissler to Vienna, where the valise had been manufactured, and then to Breslau, where he learned that Geissler was the alias of Georg Guttentag. Better record keeping by the prefecture would have spared Goron his long travels. Since the early evening of March 18, several hours before the murders, Guttentag had been in the Mazas prison, in Paris itself, entirely innocent of anything but vagrancy.[43]

In his memoirs Marie François Goron described a typical day in his tenure as director of Sûreté. Awakened before dawn with the news of a stabbing death, he dressed quickly and left his apartment in the Palais de Justice to meet the procureur de la République (district attorney) and a juge d'instruction at the Paris morgue, on the southwest corner of the Ile de la Cité. At 7:30 A.M. the victim's widow arrived to make an identification, and Goron directed two inspecteurs to begin the investigation with the man's drinking mates. By 8 A.M. he reached his office on the Quai des Orfèvres, where he rapidly looked through the approximately three hundred letters heaped on his desk. A few were ludicrous, such as the one suggesting that if

---

43. APP, B A/1612, Crimes, dos. Stein; B A/82, Crimes, dos. Aguétant; B A/83, Crimes, dos. Regnault. See also Goron, *Les Mémoires*, II, 1–251.

The Police (I)

the police performed songs and dances, criminals would gather to watch and reveal crimes in their expressions. Other letters were anonymous denunciations, often by vengeful women, or offered to provide information in return for money. Most of the mail was official correspondence from other services of the prefecture, the Paris parquet, and other parquets and police forces throughout France. Outside Goron's office, his inspecteurs principaux and brigadiers gathered to make their morning reports. After a strategy session with them, he had to hasten through the corridors to the daily 10 A.M. meeting with the prefect of police, which lasted until noon. Reporters wanting news about the latest crimes waited for him as he returned to his office. To escape them, he ate his lunch back in his apartment.

Consultations with several juges d'instruction began the afternoon. Once back in his own office, Goron kept a series of appointments. Men and women asked his advice, often because they were victims of extortion. Each month during his seven years as director, a woman claiming to be the daughter of the Empress Eugénie demanded to see him. Another time, a woman insisted that she was the granddaughter of the Duchesse de Berry and that the proof was a fleur-de-lis on her hip; Goron had trouble convincing her not to lift her skirt. One afternoon, he had to examine candidates for the post of public executioner: a Protestant preacher warring with his church, a postman wanting the position because he would not have to work every day, and a butcher arguing that his trade had provided him with the requisite skills. By the end of the afternoon, the clerks had completed reports based on the morning's official mail. Goron had to sign each, and as he quickly scanned them, he complained that three-quarters were poorly drawn. In the midst of that work, a message arrived about a gaffe. One of the brigades had arrested the wrong man, and Goron had to make amends personally.[44]

Even allowing for hyperbole by Goron, the director of the Sûreté was encumbered with meetings and paper work, and similar burdens rested on all of the ranks, particularly before the 1912 reorganization. Coordination with the juges d'instruction was a particular trial for the detectives. The Sûreté began an investigation and the compilation of a dossier as soon as a crime was reported. On the following day, that dossier was handed to a senior official of the Paris parquet, and he arranged for the appointment of a juge d'instruction

---

44. Goron, *Les Mémoires*, IV, 1–80.

who would have sole authority to order searches, seizures, and warrants for the case. A juge d'instruction could confine himself to this role, merely presiding over the investigation until a suspect was arrested and an indictment could be drawn. But if he insisted on directing the inquiry, inspecteurs working on the case confronted a delicate problem of authority. Legally, any member of the Police judiciare, including the director of the Sûreté, was subordinate to a juge d'instruction, but few juges d'instruction understood police methods. As Louis Andrieux wrote caustically in his memoirs, "In Paris, no juge d'instruction has ever found the traces of a criminal." A tacit compromise existed: Inspecteurs resigned themselves to constant interference from the juge d'instruction but turned to Sûreté superiors for guidance in the conduct of an investigation.[45]

Juges d'instruction shared a misconception common outside the prefecture—that the Sûreté practiced scientific detection, that it solved crimes through the careful amassing of many clues and the rational drawing of conclusions from them, à la Sherlock Holmes. Evidence was collected from the scene of a crime, and statements were taken from witnesses. Such reports filled the dossiers. Goron once dreamed the solution to a crime and another time traced a criminal through a lost button. But the Sûreté's inspecteurs preferred to rely more on a traditional tool, the informant. In a parody of Jesus Christ, Andrieux warned all criminals, "Remember that whenever two or more of you are gathered together, I shall be among you." The Sûreté kept professional informers on the prefecture's payroll. Letters arrived daily with denunciations. Mistresses delivered lovers. Gang members turned traitor. The reliance on informers was so great that in 1920, Edmond Locard could write, with only slight exaggeration, that the practice was "almost universally the entire art of the detective."[46]

The prostitutes of Paris were another major source of information for the Sûreté. No law specifically empowered the prefecture to oversee prostitution in the capital, but prefects of police referred to a ruling by the Tribunal de la Seine on December 3, 1847, for their authority, exercised since the Restoration, to issue regulations and sanctions. The primary measure of control was registration. A prostitute who met this requirement was officially recognized as a *fille*

---

45. Andrieux, *Souvenirs*, I, 111; Lépine, *Mes souvenirs*, 162–63.
46. Andrieux, *Souvenirs*, I, 29–34; Goron, *Les Mémoires*, II, 338–59, III, 276–77, IV, 102–55; Lépine, *Mes souvenirs*, 170; Stead, *The Police of Paris*, 137–39; Marcel Le Clère, *Histoire de la police* (Paris, 1964), 90–99; Locard, *L'Enquête criminelle*, 8.

publique soumise and pledged to adhere to certain rules, the most important of which was an examination every fifteen days by a medical officer from the prefecture. Prostitutes who were free from venereal disease received a white card to display to clients; those with an active infection were given a red card. The *police des moeurs* (vice squad) strictly enforced the medical inspection but relaxed all of the other rules for registered prostitutes in return for information about their clients. Until 1900, for example, *filles publiques soumises* were required to reside and work in brothels (*maisons closes* or *maisons de tolérance*), which were not to be owned or directed by men. In fact, at least half of the registered prostitutes in Paris operated outside of brothels, and the brothels almost always had male owners. Louis Lépine was simply regularizing this situation in 1900 when he authorized *maisons de rendez-vous*, rented rooms or apartments in which prostitutes did not reside but merely came to work. There remained many other rules to ignore in exchange for information.[47]

The opportunity for the police to apply pressure was even greater in dealing with unregistered prostitutes (*filles insoumises*). In 1870, there were 3,359 registered prostitutes on the prefecture's rolls; in 1914 the total had more than doubled to 6,827. But these numbers represented only a small proportion (10 to 20 percent) of the estimated 35,000 to 40,000 prostitutes actually in Paris throughout the period. Some of the unregistered prostitutes were young girls who had come from the provinces with a male friend and were abandoned. More were laundry and shop girls (and women) unable to survive on a weekly wage of eight francs. Along the streets of the Faubourgs Saint Denis and Saint Martin, in the Bois de Boulogne, the Bois de Vincennes, and the Jardin des Plantes, near the Place Maubert and the Boulevards de Grenelle and Charonne, prostitutes as young as twelve years and as old as fifty sold themselves for forty sous. Most of their clients were drunken workers. Physicians attached to the prefecture estimated that 40 percent of the unregistered prostitutes (in comparison with 2 percent of the registered ones) had active venereal diseases. For that reason alone, the police des moeurs tracked down and arrested large numbers of them. The women were sent to the Saint Lazare prison for a medical examination, and treatment if found infected. Those arrested for the first

47. Henri Dupoy, *La Police des moeurs et la liberté individuelle* (Paris, 1913), 25–80; Stead, *The Police of Paris*, 139–41; Theodore Zeldin, *France, 1848–1945* (Oxford, 1973–77), I, 307–309.

time were then released. A second offense meant mandatory registration as a *fille publique* and the stigmatization that implied. The system had many possibilities for abuse. The existence and actions of the police des moeurs were defended by frequent statements from the prefecture linking illegal prostitution to much more serious crimes, particularly grand larceny and even murder. But with so many *filles insoumises*, the practical issue was control, not repression. In the margin for connivance, illegal prostitution could be exploited for the uses of criminal investigations. Unregistered prostitutes could exchange secrets about their clients and rumors they heard of crimes for relative freedom from police harassment. And there were even a few instances in which the police des moeurs arrested women who had no connection with prostitution and threatened to brand them as *filles publiques* to force them or their relatives to reveal information needed by the Sûreté.[48]

One form of corruption engendered another. Once informants or evidence provided a suspect and an arrest was made, the Sûreté turned to a second method of "solving" crimes—extracting a confession. In the parlance of the Quai des Orfèvres, to interrogate a suspect was "to cook" (*cuisiner*) him, and behind the "kitchen" doors of the police, the suspect had no right to an attorney. That had to await questioning by the juge d'instruction. Some cases presented little difficulty. The man or woman might confess readily, sometimes delaying only until promised a good meal. More often the detectives encountered a stubborn refusal to respond or an absolute denial of guilt. If the suspect had no connections, he might be beaten until he admitted every charge, guilty or not. Certain special or difficult interrogations took place in the appropriately dubbed "room of spontaneous confessions." Early in the nineteenth century, each time a policeman recognized a suspected criminal, he was rewarded with a package of tobacco. By a curious evolution the expression *passage à tabac* came to be applied to these police brutalities.[49]

48. Jill Harsin, *Policing Prostitution in Nineteenth-Century Paris* (Princeton, 1985), especially 241–42, 267–68, 361–63; Alain Corbin, *Les Filles de noce: Misère sexuelle et prostitution (19e et 20e siècles)* (Paris, 1978). See also O. Commenge, *La Prostitution clandestine à Paris* (Paris, 1890), 314–36; Léon Bizzard, *Souvenirs d'un médecin de la Préfecture de Police et des prisons de Paris, 1914–1918* (Paris, 1925), 165–267; Desmaze, *Le Crime et la débauchée*, 76–77; Monsieur Jean [pseud.], *Les Bas-fonds*, 4–86; Grébaut, *De l'alcoolisme*, 36–43; Andrieux, *Souvenirs*, I, 66–70, II, 16–33; Lépine, *Mes souvenirs*, 142–44; Dupoy, *La Police des moeurs*, 93–94.

49. Marc A. Bishoff, *La Police scientifique* (Paris, 1938), 9; Goron, *Les Mémoires*, IV, 81–102; Locard, *L'Enquête criminelle*, 14; Aubert, *Organisation et méthodes*, 116–23.

The Police (I)

Three services within the prefecture provided specialized support to the Sûreté in criminal investigations. Physicians and technicians evaluated the evidence of forensic medicine through the Laboratoire de toxicologie, which tested for poisons and drugs, and the Institut Médico-légal, where autopsies were performed. The prefecture began the practice of retaining scientists and physicians for this assistance early in the nineteenth century, with mixed results. During the 1870s alone, two investigations involving suspected poisoning were seriously mishandled. It was only with the case of the bailiff Gouffé in 1890 that these services proved the value of forensic pathology and received appropriate recognition, from both the police and the public. During the Belle Epoque, Dr. Victor Balthazard, of the toxicology laboratory, and Dr. Charles Paul, the medical examiner, would become famous through their testimony at sensational trials. The third service of the prefecture for scientific detection was the Identité judiciare, and it is associated indisputably with the name Alphonse Bertillon.[50]

The precursor of the Identité judiciaire was a set of rooms in the prefecture storing dossiers of individual criminals sought or arrested by the Sûreté. The singular feature was a phonetic classification that permitted identification of the name despite variations in orthography or pronunciation. In 1870, Gustave Macé, then commissaire for the Notre Dame district, suggested the addition of photographs to the dossiers, but this process had hardly been initiated when the 1871 fire destroyed almost all of the files. The massive work of creating a new collection of dossiers began, and on March 15, 1879, Alphonse Bertillon was hired as a clerk in the division. At five feet ten inches, he was tall for a Frenchman of the period. His slender build, short beard, and rapidly receding hair at the temples presented the appearance of an academic. He had been born in Paris in 1853. At school he was an indifferent pupil who was finally expelled from his lycée in Versailles. To the great surprise of his father, Louis Adolphe Bertillon, a respected anthropologist, he nevertheless managed to pass the examination for the baccalaureate in 1873. He spent the following three years serving his compulsory tour in the army, bored by his fellow soldiers, and then three more years as a French master at an English boarding school, humiliated by his students. There were lonely hours to fill, and imitating his father, Bertillon began a serious study of human skeletons.

50. Aubert, *Organisation et méthodes*, 78–80, 124–29; APP, B A/1612, Crimes, dos. Moreau, dos. Danval.

As a clerk in the prefecture, Bertillon learned that the identification of professional criminals had posed great difficulty for the police since the branding of convicts had been ended in 1809. The value of the dossiers was limited by the ease with which aliases could be adopted or physical appearance altered through disguise. The photographs added since 1870 were of poor quality and not taken from a standard pose. The problem aroused Bertillon's curiosity, and he thought to solve it by devising a classification of certain unchanging physical characteristics, such as the ear. In October, 1879, he presented his theory to Macé, who thought it improbable, and Andrieux, who dismissed it entirely. But his father encouraged him to broaden his thinking by incorporating his studies of the human skeleton. Within three years, Bertillon was able to elaborate a much more complete program, a set of bodily measurements that, taken together, would distinguish one individual from any other: 1) length and breadth of head, 2) length and breadth of right ear, 3) length from elbow to end of middle finger, 4) length of middle and ring fingers, 5) length of left foot, 6) height, 7) length of trunk, and 8) length of outstretched arms, middle fingertip to middle fingertip. These measurements, which Bertillon called *anthropométrie*, would be supplemented by photographs taken in two standard poses, frontal and profile, and a description of warts, scars, hair, and eyes. Andrieux's successor as prefect, Jean Camescasse, believed that the system deserved a trial, and beginning in December, 1882, Bertillon was given three months in which to identify a suspect entirely through measurement. On February 19, 1883, he succeeded, proving that a man calling himself Dupont had been arrested and measured under the name Martin on December 15, 1882, only two days after the experiment had begun. The prefecture maintained *anthropométrie* in a provisional status for five more years, during which it proved invaluable to the Sûreté. Bertillon was rewarded properly on February 1, 1888, when he was given charge of a new permanent department, the Identité judiciaire. His achievement was so undeniable that France's greatest scientist, Louis Pasteur, attended the formal inauguration.

During the next quarter century until his death in 1914, Bertillon established himself as a pioneer in criminology and transformed the Identité judiciaire into the first modern crime laboratory. Objects at the scene of a crime could be photographed to scale through his invention of metric photography. Under his direction, a machine was engineered to measure the strength used in forcing a door or win-

The Police (I)

dow. He perfected the taking of plaster casts from footprints and tire marks. There was a disastrous experimentation with graphological analysis in the Dreyfus affair—Bertillon incorrectly identified Dreyfus as the author of the *bordereau*—which briefly damaged his reputation and from which he gained a permanent aversion to such pseudosciences. Ironically, he was also a principal contributor to the development of the identification system that would supersede his own *anthropométrie*. In 1880, Henry Faulds, a Scottish physician working in Japan, invented fingerprinting. By the late 1890s, Francis Galton and William Herschel in Great Britain and Bertillon in France perfected methods for taking fingerprint evidence and for matching that evidence to the fingerprints of a suspect. In 1902, after a decision by the Tribunal de la Seine, the Identité judiciaire celebrated the distinction of Henri Léon Scheffer, the first man convicted solely from having left his fingerprints at the scene of a crime. Bertillon originally believed that fingerprints would be merely an auxiliary to *anthropométrie*, but by the end of his life, he realized that his system, cumbersome, hard to teach, and difficult to index, would probably die with him. An indication had come when the *Mona Lisa* was stolen from the Louvre in 1911. The Sûreté took fingerprint evidence from the empty frame, and the fingerprints of the thief, Vincenzo Peruggia, were actually in a dossier at the Identité judiciaire, but they were not located until after his capture because the dossier was filed by his measurements.[51]

In 1911 the Prefecture of Police and the Sûreté were not remarkably different from what they had been in 1870. The number of patrolmen and detectives was slightly larger, and salaries were higher, partly because of inflation, but there was little technological innovation. The Police municipale formed its bicycle brigade at a time when automobiles were becoming common in Paris. The Sûreté was more comfortable with informants and brutal interrogations than with scientific detection. Even Bertillon's signal contribution, *anthropométrie*, appeared dated. Strong leadership from men like Lépine and Goron could summon exceptional performances. But a new form of motorized anarchist banditry breaking out in December, 1911, would reveal the compelling necessity for renovation and modernization.

51. Morel, *La Police à Paris*, 217–20. The basic biography is by Henry F. T. Rhodes, *Alphonse Bertillon: Father of Scientific Detection* (London, 1956). See also Le Clère, *Histoire de la police*, 100–102; Fosdick, *European Police Systems*, 319–26; Locard, *L'Enquête criminelle*, 127.

3

The Police (II)

The reorganization and modernization that came to the Paris Prefecture of Police in 1912 and 1913 were preceded by changes in the Sûreté Générale. By early 1907, government officials had grown alarmed at statistics from the Ministry of Justice for crimes and arrests outside the jurisdiction of the Paris prefecture: Between 1896 and 1906, reported crimes had surged 19 percent (from 87,073 to 103,419), but arrests had declined 56 percent (from 43,448 to 24,393). Clearly, the local police forces throughout France, usually undermanned and lacking national coordination, were often no longer sufficient. There could be only limited assistance from the Sûreté Générale's network of special commissaires, whose responsibilities were narrowly focused. As discussion proceeded about possible remedies and reforms, public opinion was inflamed by the outrages of the Pollet gang in the Nord—8 murders, 10 armed robberies, and 104 burglaries within seven months. Georges Clemenceau, the premier and minister of the interior, then took personal initiative. On December 30, 1907, he ordered the creation of twelve mobile brigades within the Sûreté Générale to provide special assistance to local police in difficult investigations.[1]

Until the creation of the mobile brigades, the Third Republic had

---

1. Henry Buisson, *La Police, son histoire* (Vichy, 1949), 268–76; Marcel Montarron, *L'Histoire vraie des brigades mobiles* (Paris, 1976), 15–16.

left the Sûreté Générale relatively undeveloped and neglected. There had been a slow increase in the budget and the number of personnel for the service, but the organizational structure of commissaires and inspecteurs established during the Second Empire was not altered until 1889 and not greatly then. For two years, from February, 1874, to February, 1876, the Sûreté Générale was detached from the direct control of the Ministry of the Interior and placed under the supervision of the Paris prefect of police, Léon Renault. Thereafter, until 1907, there were eighteen changes of command, with the average tenure of office only twenty months, an insufficient time to imprint a distinctive mark (see Table 18). Although Emile Honoré Cazelles provided a limited stability by serving as director for sixty-one months, the total was compiled during three terms over a period of twelve years from 1880 to 1892. René Cavard headed the Sûreté Générale for seventy-five months, from December, 1899, to March, 1906, but until March 31, 1903, he bore only the title sous-directeur and found his power over the service and his influence within the Ministry of the Interior relatively limited. Eight of the eighteen directors, almost half, were former prefects who regarded the post as merely another step in an administrative career with the Ministry of the Interior, and certainly one inferior to the Paris prefecture. When Arthur Gragnon was dismissed in November, 1887, as prefect of the Paris police for his part in the Grévy-Wilson scandal, he needed another year of service to qualify for his government pension. The Ministry of the Interior permitted him to earn it by serving as director of the Sûreté Générale from April, 1888, to April, 1889.

During the thirty-six years from 1871 to 1907, the budget at the disposal of the Sûreté Générale's director increased 69 percent, from Fr 3,092,875 to Fr 5,239,690 (see Table 19). In 1871, 18 percent of the total, Fr 546,820, went to pay the salaries of the 179 special-duty commissaires and inspecteurs, who made an average salary of Fr 3,054. Another 18 percent, Fr 546,055, was allocated for administrative offices in Paris and for the cost of mounting investigations, principally the reimbursement to agents for legitimate expenses. The rest of the budget, Fr 2,000,000 (64 percent), was designated "dépenses secrètes de sûreté publique" and was used to pay informers and agents provocateurs. Outside of the Sûreté Générale's hierarchy, only the president of the Republic was told how the secret funds were spent, and the names of these undercover operatives were not revealed even to him. By 1907 the secret funds had been reduced to Fr 1,000,000 and represented only 19 percent of the budget. Salaries for 411 special-duty commissaires and inspecteurs, by then called collectively the

TABLE 18
Directors of the Sûreté Générale, 1871–1940

Director	Dates of Service	Previous Position
de Nervaux	November 18, 1871–February 17, 1874	Chef de bureau, Ministry of the Interior
Léon Renault	February 17, 1874–February 9, 1876	Conseiller d'Etat
de Boislisle	February 9, 1876–May 19, 1877	Chef de bureau, Ministry of the Interior
Paul Le Roux de Bretagne	May 19, 1877–December 18, 1877	Chef de bureau, Ministry of the Interior
Alfred Boucher-Cadart	December 18, 1877–March 9, 1880	Magistrate
Emile Honoré Cazelles	March 9, 1880–May 1, 1882	Directeur de l'administration pénitentiaire, Ministry of the Interior
Emile Schnerb	May 1, 1882–April 1, 1884	Prefect for Maine-et-Loire
(Position vacant)	April 1, 1884–September 30, 1884	
Paul Louis Wallet	September 30, 1884–April 16, 1885	Chef-adjoint du cabinet, Ministry of the Interior
Levaillant	April 16, 1885–April 10, 1888	Prefect for Doubs
Arthur Gragnon	April 10, 1888–April 3, 1889	Former prefect of police
Emile Honoré Cazelles	April 3, 1889–March 8, 1890	Conseiller d'Etat
Christian	March 8, 1890–March 25, 1890	Prefect for Somme
Emile Honoré Cazelles	March 25, 1890–March 4, 1892	Conseiller d'Etat
Henri Soinoury	March 4, 1892–March 7, 1893	Secrétaire-général to the prefect of police
Alfred Lucien Fournier	March 7, 1893–October 6, 1894	Prefect for Oran
Henri Poirson	October 6, 1894–June 25, 1896	Prefect for Morbihan
Charles Blanc	June 25, 1896–October 14, 1897	Prefect for Deux-Sèvres
Léopold Viguié	October 14, 1897–December 21, 1899	Prefect for Charente
René Cavard	December 21, 1899–March 15, 1906	Contrôleur-général, Sûreté Générale (Sous-directeur until March 31, 1903; Directeur thereafter)
Henry Huart	March 15, 1906–January 30, 1907	Prefect for Marne
Célestin Hennion	January 30, 1907–March 29, 1913	Commissaire principal, Sûreté Générale

Name	Dates	Position
Pujalet	March 29, 1913–May 15, 1914	Former contrôleur-général, Sûreté Générale
Henri Richard	May 16, 1914–October 19, 1916	Conseiller d'Etat
Louis Hudelo	October 19, 1916–June 3, 1917	Prefect for Gard
Leymarie	June 3, 1917–August 24, 1917	Directeur du personnel, Ministry of the Interior
Bouju	August 24, 1917–November 23, 1917	Prefect for Côtes-du-Nord
Georges Maringer	November 23, 1917–August 10, 1918	Conseiller d'Etat
André Labussière	August 10, 1918–July 29, 1921	Chef de bureau, Ministry of the Interior
Durand	July 29, 1921–March 1, 1923	Directeur du personnel, Ministry of Welfare
Marlier	March 1, 1923–July 8, 1924	Directeur du cabinet to the prefect of police
Jean Chiappe	July 8, 1924–April 14, 1927	Directeur du contrôle, Ministry of the Interior
Renard	April 14, 1927–February 19, 1929	Prefect for Constantine
Paul Roquère	February 19, 1929–December 23, 1930	Conseiller d'Etat
Georges Thomé	December 23, 1930–April 3, 1931	Prefect for Gironde
Léon Noël	April 3, 1931–January 30, 1932	Prefect for Haut-Rhin
Pierre Julien	January 30, 1932–June 18, 1932	Directeur du personnel et de l'administration, Ministry of the Interior
Georges Thomé	June 18, 1932–February 3, 1934	Directeur du contrôle, Ministry of the Interior
Antoine François Geay	February 3, 1934–March 13, 1934	Directeur du personnel et de l'administration, Ministry of the Interior
Jean Berthoin	March 13, 1934–October 15, 1934	Prefect for Haute Garonne
Magny	October 15, 1934–September 26, 1936	Prefect for Bouches-du-Rhône
Pierre Moitessier	September 26, 1936–May 31, 1938	Prefect for Gard
Amédée Bussière	May 31, 1938–May 19, 1940	Prefect for Oise
Winter	May 19, 1940–June 18, 1940	Inspecteur-général des services administratifs, Ministry of the Interior
Didkowski	June 18, 1940–August 8, 1940	Prefect for Pyrénées-Orientales

SOURCE: *Journal Officiel*, Lois et Décrets, 1871–1940

TABLE 19
Budget of the Sûreté Générale, 1871–1940 (in Francs)

Year	Amount	Year	Amount
1871	3,092,875	1918	9,683,441
1875	3,867,100	1919	12,017,526
1880	3,992,026	1920	27,742,000
1885	4,425,855	1921	32,910,977
1890	3,480,013	1922	30,738,965
1895	4,600,000	1923	29,835,200
1900	4,800,900	1924	no data
1901	4,955,900	1925	38,935,100
1902	5,212,900	1926	37,262,000
1903	5,212,900	1927	53,225,880
1904	5,212,900	1928	61,881,404
1905	5,112,900	1929	71,598,124
1906	4,844,700	1930	78,222,634
1907	5,239,690	1931	80,479,754
1908	6,506,369	1932	101,131,810
1909	6,407,290	1933	100,283,362
1910	6,634,290	1934	100,857,328
1911	7,014,705	1935	51,028,250
1912	7,379,044	1936	54,992,559
1913	8,356,425	1937	76,309,263
1914	9,124,506	1938	83,302,341
1915	9,003,690	1939	94,886,649
1916	9,254,373	1940	128,849,106
1917	10,783,507		

SOURCE: Archives du Ministère des Finances, annual reports, 1871–1940.

Police spéciale, accounted for 25 percent, Fr 1,318,000 (with the average salary Fr 3,200). Although the cost of investigations and administration had risen to Fr 652,000, that figure took only 12 percent of the budget. The remainder, 43 percent, Fr 2,269,690, was devoured by the expense of providing the police force for all the Department of the Seine outside the city limits of Paris and the immediate suburbs, which were under the jurisdiction of the Paris prefecture. When the Sûreté Générale first assumed this responsibility in 1878, the cost was Fr 458,000, at that time a mere 11 percent of its budget.[2]

2. Lucien Zimmer, *Un septennat policier* (Paris, 1967), 220–30; Archives du Ministère des Finances (hereinafter cited as AMF), Budget, Ministère de l'Intérieur, Sûreté Générale, 1871–1934; Budget, Ministère de l'Intérieur, Sûreté Nationale, 1935–40.

The Police (II)

When measured against the needs of the service, the funds available in the budget were simply inadequate. The 144 special commissaires and inspecteurs of 1860, when the Sûreté Générale was last reorganized under the Second Empire, had become 411 in 1907, an increase of 185 percent (and one of 129 percent over the total of 179 in 1871; see Table 20). These agents repressed crime and gathered police intelligence through their surveillance of the railroads. But during the period, there was an enormous extension of the French rail network and an even more enormous expansion in ridership. The increase in the number of commissaires and inspecteurs was entirely insufficient to keep pace. The popularity of bicycles, and soon after 1900 of automobiles, offered new mobility and therefore new opportunities for crime, for which the Sûreté Générale was unprepared

TABLE 20
Personnel of the Sûreté Générale, 1860–1940

Year	Personnel	Year	Personnel
1860	144	1917	649
1871	179	1918	576
1875	169	1919	714
1880	189	1920	1,057
1885	242	1921	1,057
1890	236	1922	1,161
1895	387	1923	1,161
1900	431	1924	no data
1901	421	1925	1,161
1902	436	1926	1,098
1903	436	1927	1,203
1904	436	1928	1,204
1905	417	1929	1,304
1906	411	1930	1,303
1907	411	1931	1,337
1908	534	1932	1,402
1909	531	1933	1,389
1910	531	1934	1,389
1911	596	1935	1,298
1912	650	1936	1,401
1913	661	1937	1,647
1914	738	1938	1,729
1915	614	1939	1,985
1916	614	1940	2,347

SOURCE: AMF, annual reports, 1860–1940.

and poorly organized. Too many of the special agents were men of inferior quality. Salaries remained almost constant from 1871 to 1907, with the average (Fr 3,000 to 3,200) an amount comparable with the salary of an inspecteur principal of the Paris Police. Outstanding men were difficult to recruit for a career of frequent travel, long hours, sometimes dangerous work, and mediocre income. The Sûreté Générale eagerly, occasionally too eagerly, sought better agents. By 1887 the entire written examination for the position of commissaire was waived for candidates with a baccalaureate. In 1886, Pierre Marie Kuehn was appointed an inspecteur to oversee a frontier crossing at Belfort after a cursory investigation into his seemingly impressive background. Six months later, he was discovered to be a German spy. Such a lapse is comprehensible because the hierarchy labored under severe deficiencies. In Paris the director of the Sûreté Générale had a staff of approximately forty men, including his closest assistants, department heads, and all the clerks, with which to administer the service and to deal with a correspondence of at least six hundred letters each day. The offices, located on the Rue des Saussaies and later expanding around the corner to the Rue Cambacérès, were ill-arranged along labyrinthine corridors. There were never enough employees or sufficient funds to maintain such fundamental activities as archives, clippings from the press, central files for convicted or suspected criminals and for foreign nationals living in France, a full-time crime laboratory, or accountants to assist in investigations of white-collar or financial crimes.[3]

The Third Republic's only reorganization of the Sûreté Générale before 1907 began eighteen years earlier in 1889, when the division of special-duty agents by function (surveillance of the railroads, the frontier crossings, and book sales) was replaced by a division on the basis of geography. Commissaires and inspecteurs were assigned either to the "Police spéciale de la frontière," in the border departments, or to the "Police spéciale de l'intérieur," in the central parts of France. The change indicated that they were responsible for a wider variety of functions, not merely a few or a single one. In 1895 the geographical distinction was removed, and all special-duty agents of the Sûreté Générale were designated the "Police spéciale."

Clemenceau's order on December 30, 1907, altered this structure

3. F. Euvrard, *Historique de l'institution des commissaires de police, son origine, leurs prérogatives* (Montpellier, 1911), 110–14; Rougé, *La Sûreté Nationale*, 27–49; APP, E A/66, Kuehn.

fundamentally. From the 411 special-duty commissaires and inspecteurs, 183 were chosen to constitute twelve mobile brigades, varying in strength from 13 to 18 men each and stationed strategically throughout the country: Paris, Lille, Caen, Nantes, Tours, Limoges, Bordeaux, Toulouse, Marseille, Lyon, Dijon, and Châlons-sur-Marne. While remaining under the command of the Sûreté Générale's director, and above him the minister of the interior, the mobile brigades were charged with supporting local authorities in the investigation of major crimes if their intervention was requested by the *procureur général* (attorney general) of the judicial district (*ressort*). The director of the Sûreté Générale since January 30, 1907, Célestin Hennion, had served in the hierarchy at the Rue des Saussaies and knew well what inadequacies existed. He had strongly recommended the reorganization to Clemenceau and now assigned his closest associate, Joseph Sébille, to oversee the new forces with the title contrôleur-général des services des recherches. Hennion and Sébille conceived the mobile brigades as an elite and successfully demanded for them extraordinary treatment: an average salary of Fr 3,600, free postage, free access to all trains, telephones, and bicycles, and in Paris at least, the rudiments of a crime laboratory. The first automobiles, four luxurious Dions Boutons, were given to the Paris brigade in 1911. The other brigades had to wait until 1912 and 1913 to receive less glamorous Panhards and Levassoes. By then, there were three additional brigades, and the "Police mobile" numbered 321 men, an increase of 75 percent. During World War I, the force was slowly reduced from 347 in 1914 to 246 in 1918. As the mobile brigades marked the end of their first decade, their success could be measured by an astounding record of arrests: 7,955 for felonies, 48,078 for misdemeanors.[4]

The rapid expansion of the mobile brigades provided immediate opportunities for such talented young recruits as Jean Belin, who would eventually become a *contrôleur-général* (principal superintendent) in the criminal investigation division of the Sûreté Générale. Born at Dijon in 1896, Belin passed his baccalaureate and completed his military service by 1907. He won a position as a secrétaire in 1908 with the Paris prefecture, and he hoped for an assignment to

---

4. Euvrard, *Historique de l'institution*, 183–86; Buisson, *La Police*, 268–76; Rougé, *La Sûreté Nationale*, 183–89; Montarron, *L'Histoire vraie*, 43–49; Aubert, *Organisation et méthodes*, 45–50; Jacques Gandon, *Le Rôle de la police dans la recherche des preuves des infractions* (Bergerac, 1944), 108–18.

the Sûreté while he prepared for the commissaire examination. Unfortunately, his height, five feet seven inches, ran afoul of Louis Lépine's dictum that detectives, in order to be less noticeable in a crowd, should never be taller than five feet six inches. The extra inch was sufficient to disqualify Belin from the Quai des Orfèvres, and he was sent to the commissariat at Montrouge, a suburb on the southern rim of Paris, to serve as an administrative assistant. Belin came to know the district intimately, but the work was routine, too many cases involving a concierge irate at her building's tenants. The announcement in April, 1912, that the Paris brigade of the Sûreté Générale was looking for applicants attracted him, and he requested an interview with the brigade commander, Commissaire Jacques Faivre. Already almost a legend within the Sûreté Générale for his austerity and uncompromising standards, Faivre was fifty-six years old and closely resembled the current premier, Raymond Poincaré, in both appearance and nervous tension. He decided immediately to offer Belin an appointment as a commissaire but warned him: "A mobile brigade is not a commissariat. Here, we work! What is needed here is work! But no fiascoes, especially no fiascoes!"

Belin joined the brigade at the beginning of May, 1912, just as the Paris police and the mobile brigade were tracking down the last members of the notorious Bonnot gang of anarchist bank robbers and murderers. During the chase, Faivre had permitted no holidays and had slept every night on a cot in his office next to the telephone. When one of the inspecteurs requested four days of leave to get married, Faivre responded acidly, "That's two too many for such foolishness" as he reluctantly approved an absence for forty-eight hours. It was a dangerous time to be a novice detective, and Belin was uneasy because he was almost the double of one suspect, Eugène Dieudonné. But his instincts were sure and his courage manifest. On May 12 he was able to ambush the last two members of the Bonnot gang, Octave Garnier and René Valet. During a lonely reconnaissance in the dark along a road south of Paris, Belin spotted their automobile and gave chase in his until they shot out his tires. Garnier and Valet would finally be cornered and killed two days later in a hideout only four miles away.[5]

This first decade was the period of glory for the mobile brigades. Besides compiling the extraordinary record of arrests, the new units made critical contributions in several of the most important crimi-

5. Belin, *Trente ans*, 1–52; Montarron, *L'Histoire vraie*, 16–30.

nal investigations, particularly tracking down in December, 1914, Vincenzo and Michele Lancelotti and Françoise Seguenot for complicity with Vincenzo Peruggia in the theft of the *Mona Lisa* and in August, 1917, unraveling the treasonous activities of Paul Bolo-Pasha. On April 11, 1919, Belin made the sensational arrest of Henri-Désiré Landru, thief, confidence man, and modern bluebeard, who had killed eleven "fiancées" in the preceding five years and disposed of their bodies in his furnace. Almost incredibly, Belin solved the case only six days after his assignment to it. In his memoirs he would recall how each of his investigations had required him to "change his skin, to enter into the personality of the victim and the personality of the criminal." He would also write: "I have loved my profession passionately. To it I sacrificed my health and my life. For me, it was a priesthood." Belin was unusually talented and dedicated, but he was not alone. The mobile brigades had fulfilled the high expectations of their commander, Joseph Sébille, and had become an elite corps of detectives. Through them, the Sûreté Générale developed a reputation as the nerve center and brain of a national police.[6] But with the retrospective knowledge that during the 1920s and 1930s the Sûreté Générale would be crippled by budgetary restrictions and disgraced by corruption and politicization, this conclusion appears to have been premature and the achievements precarious.

At the end of World War I, André Labussière, who had been named director of the Sûreté Générale three months earlier on August 10, 1918, identified five priorities for the service. The needs of the military had forced the mobilization of many commissaires and inspecteurs, leaving the Sûreté Générale with only 576 men in 1918, the smallest number since 1910. As they were released from the armed services, the former police personnel would have to be attracted back to their positions. There would have to be additional recruits as well. Two new mobile brigades, bringing the total to seventeen, would be formed, one to serve the restored provinces of Alsace and Lorraine, the other to supplement the thinly stretched units in the northern half of the country. The emphasis on the Police mobile since 1907 had led to a relative neglect and partial depletion of the Police spéciale, which would have to be remedied. The Ministry of the Interior also planned to extend to certain "strategic" cities the *police d'état* that had been imposed on Marseille in 1908. Both

---

6. Montarron, *L'Histoire vraie*, 31–43, 50–81; Belin, *Trente ans*, 21–36, 78–157, the quotations from 78, 127.

projects would require a large expansion in the ranks of commissaires and inspecteurs. New recruits and veterans alike would have to be trained in criminological techniques, many developed before 1914 by Alphonse Bertillon but not yet widely known outside Paris. Bertillon's protégé, Gaston Edmond Bayle, and the new French genius in the scientific detection of crime, Edmond Locard of Lyon, were highly critical of the Sûreté Générale's slowness to master important modern methods. Finally, there was an urgent need to repair, refurbish, and replace the service's equipment, for which there had been little money during the war years since 1914.[7]

Unfortunately, France's victory on the battlefield came to seem very much like a defeat as inflation was rampant and the national budget almost permanently out of balance during the next two decades. The appropriation to the Sûreté Générale increased 85 percent from 1907 to 1918, from Fr 5,239,690 to Fr 9,683,411; from 1918 to 1934, when there would be a major reorganization of the service, the increase would be 942 percent, to Fr 100,857,328 (see Table 19). Until the stabilization of the franc in 1926 by the Poincaré ministry at one-fifth of its prewar value, inflation increased much more swiftly than the appropriation; after 1926, it increased merely somewhat more swiftly. The cost of administration and investigations remained a relatively constant fraction of the service's budget, 12 percent in 1907, 14 percent in 1918 (Fr 1,384,400) and 1934 (Fr 13,863,290). Providing the police forces for the Department of the Seine—outside the jurisdiction of the Paris prefecture—already took 43 percent of the budget in 1907, would rise to 54 percent in 1918 (Fr 5,237,041), and would fall slightly to 48 percent by 1934 (Fr 48,194,038). In 1918 the Sûreté Générale was receiving Fr 1,000,000 for undercover operatives, the same amount as in 1907. By 1934 the allocation was Fr 3,800,000, and what had represented 19 percent of the budget in 1907 and 10 percent in 1918 became only 4 percent.[8]

By far the largest budgetary increase after the war, 1,597 percent, went for salaries, from Fr 2,062,000 in 1918 to Fr 35,000,000 in 1934. The average salary of commissaires and inspecteurs (Fr 3,580 in 1918, Fr 25,198 in 1934) rose at a much slower rate, 604 percent, because the service expanded from 576 men to 1,389, nearly two and a half times the personnel of 1918. The ranks of the Police mobile and

7. Montarron, *L'Histoire vraie*, 82–107; Gandon, *Le Rôle de la police*, 58–62, 108–21.
8. AMF, Budget, Sûreté Générale, 1918–34; Alfred Sauvy, *Histoire économique de la France entre les deux guerres* (Paris, 1965–67), I, 331–43, II, 392–411.

The Police (II)

Police spéciale were enlarged in part because of the requirements detailed by Labussière, but also because the governments of postwar France needed to find employment for demobilized soldiers. Five-sixths of the new positions were set aside for veterans, with their army service constituting the primary test of their suitability for police work. The Sûreté Générale was able to rerecruit most of the commissaires and inspecteurs it had lost to mobilization and to complete a major expansion. By 1920, the Police mobile was enlarged from 246 men to 407, and by 1934 to 489, an overall increase of 99 percent. Two additional mobile brigades were formed, and the manpower of all the brigades was almost doubled. The growth of the Police spéciale was an even greater 172 percent, from 330 men in 1918 to 650 in 1920 and to 900 in 1934. State police control was extended to seven cities: to the strategic Mediterranean ports, Toulon and La Seyne (November 14, 1918) and Nice (June 26, 1920); to cities of the new northeastern frontier, Strasbourg (January 10, 1922), Mulhouse (February 12, 1924), and Metz (March 17, 1925); and to Algiers (May 14, 1930). But with salaries lagging behind the pace of inflation and the restricted pool of candidates, the new personnel were more in the mold of the pre-1908 Sûreté Générale than of the mobile brigades in their glorious first decade. There were few men of Jean Belin's capacity among them.

The entry requirements for the Sûreté Générale had never been strict. Until 1887, there was a formal written and oral examination of applicants, much like the one administered by the Prefecture of Police, but almost everyone was passed. After 1887 the pretense of an examination was dropped. Any candidate with a baccalaureate or higher degree was routinely given provisional appointment as a commissaire and, barring scandal or disaster, confirmed in that rank after twelve months. A primary school certificate was sufficient for a probationer at the level of inspecteur. Beginning in 1919, even these minor requirements were attenuated. A noncommissioned officer released from the army at the rank of sergeant could henceforth qualify for appointment as a commissaire regardless of his education merely by passing an aptitude test. An enlisted man could become an inspecteur if he had served four years in the army and passed a similar test. According to the published regulations of the Sûreté Générale, all new recruits were to spend eleven months studying police techniques at training schools established in 1895 at Lyon and Bordeaux. The courses were not rigorous, and any recruit having previous experience with the Paris prefecture, the gendarmerie, or a local police force was normally excused. Belin, for example, was never required to undergo additional training. During the 1920s and early 1930s the regulation was often disregarded altogether, especially for veterans, who adapted poorly to confinement in formal classes. The result was a corps of detectives whose military discipline and physical development might have prepared them well to be members of the Police municipale in Paris but who, as members of the Sûreté Générale, were largely ignorant of their craft and almost entirely so of modern scientific criminology.[9]

As the budget of the service lost ground to inflation, this lack of training was complemented by the almost complete inability of the Sûreté Générale to replace or refurbish facilities and equipment. At the headquarters on the Rue des Saussaies, prewar conditions actually grew worse. There was still no elevator, and the number of telephones was extremely limited. The staff remained so small that plans for a central file system and photograph bank had to be postponed indefinitely. The mass of correspondence overwhelmed the secretaries and bureaucratic procedures so thoroughly that accurate notations were not kept of the arrival and dispatch of letters. Papers overflowed desks and cabinets. Offices were cleaned irregularly; filth was everywhere. When Jean Belin once brought a suspect to the Rue des Saussaies in the mid-1920s for questioning, he had great difficulty convincing the man that they were in the headquarters of the Sûreté Générale: "He told me afterward that he honestly believed that he had fallen into the hands of blackmailers. He would never have believed that the French police could work in such surroundings." As late as 1934 the Sûreté Générale did not have a single airplane of its own and had to borrow what it needed from the French air force. At any moment, half of its automobiles were out of working order. Some inspecteurs were still issued bicycles. For all of France the service had only eight radio-receiving units. Delays in the delivery of telegrams were so flagrant that some messages from Marseille to Paris required four days to arrive. And in the provinces, conditions appear to have been even worse. In 1923, when Louis Marin, a conservative member of the Chamber of Deputies, surveyed one hundred commissaires chosen at random, he discovered that twenty-four had no telephone, thirty-one shared an extension with the local

---

9. Ulmann, *Le Quatrième pouvoir*, 184–90; Euvrard, *Historique de l'institution*, 110–24; Gandon, *Le Rôle de la police*, 18–22; Aubert, *Organisation et méthodes*, 80–88.

mayor's office, and forty-five were connected to a party line with other subscribers.[10]

Marcel Sicot was one of the new recruits taken from the military after World War I, though he was far from typical of their generally mediocre quality. By 1959 he was secretary-general of Interpol, the culmination of a career in the police that had begun thirty-nine years earlier in December, 1920, when he was appointed a provisional commissaire of the Police spéciale. Born the son of a gendarme in Brittany in 1899, Sicot joined the army at age eighteen immediately after passing the baccalaureate examinations and was wounded in fighting along the western front. After recovering at a military hospital, he applied to the Sûreté Générale. Because of his youth, he was given some seasoning in the Paris area before he was sent in February, 1921, to serve in the French occupation zone of the Rhineland. Any idealism he might have retained upon entering the service was tarnished in these fifteen months. At the Rue des Saussaies and the suburb commissariats, he was impressed by the lack of telephones and the amount of dust. Life in the capital seemed to have been altered distinctly by the experience of the war. The city was dirtier, men and women more shameless, the gaiety and lighthearted hypocrisy of the Belle Epoque replaced by a more frantic yet more calculated corruption. Older and more experienced colleagues taught him by example that the police found more criminals through informers and links to the demimonde and underworld than through scientific detection. They warned him about the dangers of interrogating suspects—men would accuse him of inflicting a *passage à tabac*, women of sexual abuse—while proving that these accusations were not always false. And yet the Sûreté Générale worried about maintaining a proper public image to the extent of forbidding him to live with his mistress.

In 1924, Sicot was transferred to Beauvais, where he had direction of the commissariat. In addition to the traditional responsibilities of a railway commissaire, he was assigned to supply reports on any social, political, or economic movements in the entire Department of the Oise. Before assuming these duties, Sicot had never even passed through Beauvais and was so unfamiliar with the region that he had

---

10. Belin, *Trente ans*, 288–89; Paul Allard, *L'Anarchie de la police* (Paris, 1934), 23–94; Rougé, *La Sûreté Nationale*, 27–49, 57–64; Ulmann, *Le Quatrième pouvoir*, 190–97. See also the debate in the Chamber of Deputies in *Journal Officiel*, Chambre des Députés (hereinafter cited as *JOC*), Débats parlementaires, May 6, 1934.

to read a tourist guide for the Ile-de-France as background. The entire support provided to the commissariat by the Sûreté Générale was a *carte de circulation* permitting free train travel throughout the Oise and funds to purchase a bicycle. During the next ten years, Sicot served at three other commissariats: Vitré (Ille-et-Vilaine) and Granville (Manche), where in both cases he had a telephone, and Versailles (Seine-et-Oise), where he finally had a typewriter for his reports. Reflecting upon his career with the Sûreté Générale, he wrote in 1959 with irony, "I have had to contend with the realities of life, conventions, prejudices, traditions, laws, codes, regulations, canons of discipline, and the wrath of superiors."[11]

By the mid-1920s it was clear that the goals established for the Sûreté Générale by Labussière in 1918 would be realized only in part. Most of the demobilized commissaires and inspecteurs were reintegrated. And so many new recruits were added that the initial plans for expansion had to be revised to accommodate them all. Unfortunately, far too many of these recruits were of such mediocre quality that the benfits of expansion were undermined. The service remained resistant to modern detective science. Few of the older agents and fewer still of the new were sent to the classes at Bordeaux or at Lyon, where Edmond Locard vainly continued to call for a change in attitude. The renewal of equipment was all but completely neglected. The fate of these objectives reflected the priorities of France's postwar cabinets and legislatures, which were parsimonious (by necessity, given the economic conditions) except in providing employment for veterans—who had to accept limited salaries. The interests of the Sûreté Générale suffered also because of frequent changes of command. In late July, 1921, Labussière was promoted to preside over departmental and district administration within the Ministry of the Interior. After his departure, there were ten directors in the next thirteen years, a period that ended with the reforms initiated in March and April, 1934. Their average tenure was fifteen months. No Célestin Hennion was present to provide continuity of leadership or to argue over a long period for the changes necessary in the Sûreté Générale.

A further problem was a crippling corruption at the center of the service, at the headquarters in Paris. Like the Prefecture of Police, the Sûreté Générale had long maintained dossiers (called "les roses" at the Rue des Saussaies from the distinctive color of the paper) in

11. Marcel Sicot, *Servitude et grandeur policières: Quarante ans à la Sûreté* (Paris, 1959), 8–160, the quotation from 8.

which sensitive details about the private lives of prominent men and women were enumerated. This information had frequently been used to advantage in the investigation of crimes and in deflecting criticism. In the 1920s it came to be increasingly the source of extortion, through which a few agents supplemented their salaries or won extraordinary political favors. The testimony on this subject by Léon Daudet, the malignant editorialist of *L'Action française*, would be suspect if it were not corroborated over and over. He called the Sûreté Générale an "association of *malfaiteurs*" and claimed that "blackmail is their most important function." Such activity and other forms of corruption gained enormous impetus while Jean Chiappe served as director from July 8, 1924, to April 14, 1927, the longest tenure (thirty-three months) between 1921 and 1934. Jean Belin learned firsthand about the new standards of behavior when an investigation of fraud brought one of Chiappe's political friends under suspicion. Chiappe demanded that Belin falsify a deposition and, when he refused, threatened him with dismissal. Only Belin's reputation as the agent who had arrested Landru saved him, and he understood that he could not oppose Chiappe directly: "In a struggle between us, it would have been a pot of iron smashing against a pot of clay." For Chiappe had too many important allies and was rapidly making himself all-powerful in the hierarchy of the Ministry of the Interior. When he left the Rue de Saussaies, it was to become prefect of police.[12]

The web of corruption was spun out of secrets and illicit needs, out of informers, blackmail, and influence. Some of the Sûreté Générale's agents skittered through the strands, fattening like swollen spiders on the entangled victims. Lucien Mariani, an inspecteur at Lille, trafficked in drugs and practiced extortion so openly that his cowed superiors recommended him for a promotion in August, 1934, even though five months earlier the local procureur de la République had named him as a principal suspect in a criminal investigation. When the web was torn, when victims threatened embarrassing revelations while struggling to wriggle free, it had to be rewoven, the weak points covered and reinforced. Pierre Bonny, an inspecteur attached to the headquarters in Paris, was entrusted with many of these sensitive assignments, ones that Belin described as "missions no other detective, I avow, would have undertaken." Within the

12. Allard, *L'Anarchie de la police*, 60–67; Daudet, *La Police politique*, 69–70, 129–30, 153–54; Zimmer, *Un septennat policier*, 11–28; André Benoist, *Au nom de la loi, ouvrez!* (Paris, 1961), 122–75; Belin, *Trente ans*, 167–69.

service, it was widely believed that Bonny's activities included murder. For them, he was paid an additional six thousand to ten thousand francs each month for "expenses."[13]

This network of blatant corruption and vicious debasement came to public view in late 1933 and early 1934. One force of detectives from the Sûreté Générale was searching for a swindler known to them as Serge Alexandre while other agents from the service and from the Paris prefecture were protecting him and concealing his true identity—Alexandre ("Sacha") Stavisky, under which he had been arrested for fraud in 1926. Stavisky was a prominent figure in the demimonde of Paris. With money from various illegal enterprises, he had bought the Empire Theater, a string of racehorses, and the control of newspapers at all points of the political compass. Bearing a currency that included information and blackmail as well as francs, he also knew how to buy those consciences that were for sale among politicians and magistrates and police. His circle was rumored to include Jean Chiappe and members of the Paris parquet and the Sûreté Générale. Through them, Stavisky was granted provisional liberty while the case against him was under preparation, and through them, the trial was postponed nineteen separate times. During this freedom, his activities generated forty-five police reports, but no action was taken against him.

In December, 1933, when Stavisky mishandled a major embezzlement at Bayonne involving municipal bonds, his name and past became headlines in Paris. As public indignation mounted, any connection to him became a liability. From the Paris prefecture, he received a false passport and advice to flee abroad. But at the Rue des Saussaies, officials who had previously protected Stavisky now demanded that he be located. The reason was quickly apparent. On January 8, 1934, three inspecteurs, led by Charles Chenevrier, tracked him to a villa above Chamonix and heard him fire shots as they forced the door. Stavisky had attempted suicide but only wounded himself. He was left without medical aid for more than an hour while he died slowly. It is fair to suggest that Chenevrier and his men would have shot Stavisky themselves, if he had not saved them the trouble, to prevent his making embarrassing revelations.[14]

13. Belin, *Trente ans,* 169; Ulmann, *Le Quatrième pouvoir,* 51–66, 184–95; Rougé, *La Sûreté Nationale,* 65–105.
14. APP, E A/85, Affaire Stavisky; *JOC,* Documents parlementaires, 1935, No. 4886; Martin, *The Hypocrisy of Justice,* 225–28; Marcel Montarron, *Tout ce joli monde: Souvenirs* (Paris, 1965), 148–51.

The Police (II)

Charles Chenevrier had joined the Sûreté Générale in 1925 at the age of twenty-three and was singled out early for special attention by Paul Gabrielli, who commanded the mobile brigade for the Paris region and was known as the Tiger because of his resemblance to Georges Clemenceau. Chenevrier justified a rapid advancement by successfully investigating several particularly difficult cases. Confidently employing Locard's scientific methods, he had an unusual talent for carefully preparing his arrests, frequently taking his suspects entirely by surprise in bed with a mistress or as they were standing in line to purchase tickets for a movie. His renown as a detective rivaled that of his sometime friend Jean Belin, and as late as 1954, when he solved the mystery of the multiple murders at Lurs, he was recognized as one of France's *premiers flics*. In the early 1930s he edged toward those elements of the Sûreté Générale involved in corruption. By his conduct in the villa at Chamonix, Chenevrier forever stained his record but forestalled the absolute blackening of many reputations, perhaps including his own.[15]

The revelations of the Stavisky affair touched cabinet ministers and judicial authorities as well as police officials. Even the premier, Camille Chautemps, was implicated through his brother Pierre Chautemps, who was an attorney for one of Stavisky's companies, and his brother-in-law Antoine Pressard, who as procureur de la République for the capital presided over the Paris parquet, which had postponed Stavisky's trial nineteen times. Demonstrations in the steets against the Chautemps ministry quickly became riots that the Police municipale had grave difficulty controlling. Almost in fear, Chautemps resigned on January 27, 1934. He was replaced as premier by Edouard Daladier, whose curious conception of reform meant promoting the administrators of the seriously compromised police as the least troublesome means of removing them from their locus of power. Chiappe was offered the plum of government service, the governor-generalship of Morocco. Georges Thomé, the less influential director of the Sûreté Générale, was appointed, ludicrously, to head the Comédie-Française. The riots continued and reached a peak on the night of February 6, fueled partly by the outrage of Chiappe's political friends at his removal from the prefecture and made more dangerous by the inexperience and slight audacity of his successor, Adrien Bonnefoy-Sibour. Daladier resigned on the following day.

15. Chenevrier, *De la Combe aux Fées à Lurs*, 12–18; Montarron, *L'Histoire vraie*, 108–23, 190–231.

With the government humiliated and the nation seemingly in crisis, Gaston Doumergue, the president of the Republic from 1924 to 1931, agreed to form a broad-based cabinet of national unity.

Daladier's choice to take command of the Sûreté Générale was Antoine François Geay, who moved from the relative tranquillity at the Ministry of the Interior, where he had been director of personnel and general administration. He was unprepared for the discord and the degree of rot he discovered at the Rue des Saussaies. When faced with a critical situation of his own after only eighteen days in office, he turned as indecisive as Bonnefoy-Sibour at the prefecture. On February 21, the body of Albert Prince, a *substitut* (assistant prosecutor) in Pressard's office, was discovered dismembered on the railroad tracks at the village of Combe aux Fées, not far from Dijon to which he had traveled on a mysterious errand the previous evening. Prince had been rumored to hold evidence proving Pressard's complicity, and perhaps that of even higher officials, with Stavisky. A contrary rumor ran that Prince had acted alone in postponing Stavisky's trial dates but had used Pressard's name to cover these improprieties.

Geay ordered Jean Belin to carry out an investigation for the Sûreté Générale. Although Belin arrived in Dijon less than twelve hours after the discovery of the body, he learned, with shock, that the procureur de la République, Alphonse Barra, and the juge d'instruction assigned to the case, Jean Rabut, had already decided to rule the death a suicide—despite evidence that Prince had been tied to the tracks and that his body contained traces of incapacitating drugs. Barra and Rabut were furious at Belin's intervention, and with reason. They had proceeded with a carelessness better labeled incompetence. The locomotive that had presumably run over Prince was by then in the rail yard of the Gare de Lyon in Paris, but no request had been sent to place it under judicial seal. The position of the body on the tracks had not been photographed. Fingerprints had been taken haphazardly. All of Prince's personal effects—which notably did not include incriminating papers—had been returned to his widow before Belin's arrival. Was this performance simply an egregious example of the sloppy work that Locard had denounced without effect? Or was it a conscious attempt to conceal the murder of a man who, had he remained alive, might have been extremely "awkward"? There were too many contrary signs for Belin to draw a firm conclusion, and that was the report he made to Geay.

The director of the Sûreté Générale appeared initially to support the finding of the local investigation. Doing so obviated the need to track down a murderer and avoided the charge that the murderer was acting for highly placed officials and might even be operating behind the cover of the police. The reaction of the Paris press made this position untenable. Even the most serious-minded newspapers questioned the verdict of suicide and carried public opinion with them. The more sensational press hired private detectives to conduct inquiries, with *Paris-Soir* retaining the former chief of Scotland Yard, Sir Basil Thompson. Although the evidence is circumstantial, it seems that at this point Geay panicked and demanded a new official version of the case. Belin was clearly an inappropriate choice for the assignment; Chenevrier could not be used in a delicate situation so soon after his equivocal conduct at Chamonix. The obvious candidate was Pierre Bonny, but he had been suspended from his duties on January 27 because his association with Stavisky had been altogether too blatant. Belin's rectitude could not be easily undermined. Chenevrier could not be quickly rehabilitated. But Bonny could be reinstated and was, on March 2. He mounted a whirlwind investigation that ended two days later with charges against three minor criminals, whom Bonny claimed murdered Prince during a robbery and then camouflaged the crime to make the death appear a suicide. None of the three ever went to trial, because they all had perfect, unbreakable alibis. Their release attracted much less attention than their arrest, for which Bonny received a promotion. Was Prince murdered, whether as part of another crime or to prevent his possible revelations? Did he commit suicide because he was Stavisky's contact within the Paris parquet or because he believed that he would be made the scapegoat for his superior? And if the latter, did he arrange the complicated and horrible details to render his death mysterious and thereby hope to clear his name? The truth about the Prince affair can never be known, partly because the evidence was so badly mishandled, but also because Bonny, who offered his special talents promiscuously, served the Germans during World War II and was shot as a collaborator in 1944.[16]

The Stavisky and Prince affairs seriously besmirched the reputation of Third Republic government because the blame and responsibility were smeared across the full face of the national administration. And afterward, the major protagonists escaped with few sanctions. By resigning their ministerial positions (but not their leg-

16. Belin, *Trente ans*, 186–203; Montarron, *Tout ce joli monde*, 152–60; Martin, *The Hypocrisy of Justice*, 228.

islative seats), the Chautemps cabinet avoided any serious inquiry into their roles. Chiappe and Thomé were offered promotion to ease regret at losing their control of the prefecture and the Sûreté Générale. On February 27, less than a week after Prince's body was discovered, Antoine Pressard was appointed to the Cour de Cassation as a *conseiller* (associate justice). He would have less power than as procureur de la République for Paris, but the prestige of his new post was almost as great in the judicial world, and the transfer could hardly be considered a serious demotion. This semblance of action was typical of the Doumergue ministry, which could not muster the vigor to deal seriously even with the most critical question raised by the Stavisky and Prince affairs—the role of the police. The scandals appeared to demonstrate a festering corruption and perhaps that some segments of the security forces were out of control. Albert Sarraut, Doumergue's minister of the interior, made a proper start by sending Geay back to the peace of his former position and replacing him with Jean Berthoin, who had distinguished himself as prefect of the Haute Garonne. But the broad restructuring of the Sûreté Générale that Sarraut announced on April 28 was cosmetic and left the service little changed in its essentials.

The report that the minister of the interior submitted to the legislature along with his recommendations for change was carefully drafted to allay public disquiet. Sarraut conceded that there had been "certain shortcomings and individual acts of negligence," but he attributed the Sûreté Générale's failures primarily to insufficient funding and to organizational defects exacerbated by inadequate accommodations on the Rue des Saussaies. Deflecting attention from the charges of corruption, his recital of dismal working conditions was familiar to every agent and to all who had dealings with the Sûreté Générale: Parisian and provincial offices that were "absolutely unhealthy," desks surrounded by piles of dossiers that "reach to the ceiling and spill into the hallways," buildings "haphazardly purchased or rented although ill-suited to administrative needs," offices linked by "a labyrinth of dark and malodorous corridors," a "skeletal" hierarchy so overwhelmed by paperwork that it was unable effectively to oversee the service.

Sarraut argued that these deficiencies, while grave, could be remedied through two major actions. The construction of a new building on the Rue des Saussaies would, for the first time, provide the Sûreté Générale with an appropriate headquarters. In clean, commodious, well-ordered offices, the work of the service would proceed more smoothly and efficiently. This issue of furnishings and accommodations was, he insisted, the critical initial step, which, once taken, would ensure the success of the second one, a restructuring of the Sûreté Générale hierarchy. There was no need for new administrators; a redeployment of the existing staff was sufficient. One high official would be designated the inspecteur général and assigned to establish and maintain the close cooperation with the Paris prefecture that had always been lacking. Eight other officials would hold the title contrôleur général (some already did so) and would oversee specific activities of the service, which itself would be slightly reorganized to fit the shape of the new hierarchy. In the arrangement of responsibilities, particular emphasis would fall on the creation of a central dossier file, bureaus for translation and press clippings, a unit to investigate financial crimes (all of which had been needed for decades), and a division to monitor espionage attempts (a measure of the anxiety the Doumergue ministry felt toward the National Socialist government in Germany). The director of the Sûreté Générale would be insulated from day-to-day operations and concerned more with overall policy. Left unsaid was the idea that the agents of the service would be less subject to direct political pressure.

For the implementation of his proposals, Sarraut promised an extraordinary appropriation of Fr 4,132,000. That would cover the physical costs of restoring and improving the Sûreté Générale. To heal the psychological wounds and to indicate a break with past methods, he declared that the service would henceforth be called the Sûreté Nationale. With a new name, a new structure, a new building, and a new morale, the *braves gens* of the Sûreté Nationale would be prepared to assume all of their responsibilities "without weakness." Sarraut concluded his report with stirring praise for the work of the commissaires and inspecteurs who had compiled a "roll of honor"—forty-five thousand arrests, twenty per day, since 1927—in spite of the organizational inadequacies that impeded them. These men could not, he declaimed, be held responsible for the failures of a few and deserved the means to continue their brilliant record of service.[17]

Established institutions resist rapid changes: The Sûreté Nationale remained largely what it had been, both good and bad, before the modification of name. And so in August, 1934, the notorious in-

17. Report of April 28, 1934, published in the *Journal Officiel*, Lois et Décrets, (hereinafter cited as *JO*), May 6, 1934. See also Rougé, *La Sûreté Nationale*, 27–55.

specteur Lucien Mariani was given a promotion despite (or because of) his illicit activities. But there were signs other than the rapid rise of the five-story office building that Sarraut's proposals might generate momentum for needed reforms. As part of the effort to coordinate more effectively with the Paris prefecture, the new inspecteur général, Ernest Helly, negotiated the transfer of the Paris suburb commissariats to the control of the Police municipale. The contrôleur général for personnel, Raoul Cadiot, stiffened the recruiting requirements by returning to the pre-1919 standards. Candidates for the rank of commissaire had to have the baccalaureate; for the rank of inspecteur, a primary school certificate. There was also a conscious effort to limit the number of former noncommissioned officers from the military. All recruits were to attend revitalized police technique academies in Bordeaux and Lyon, and even after that, they were to serve in a closely monitored provisional status for nine months. Georges Gayet, one of the contrôleurs généraux for criminal investigations, established a financial crimes unit and, when the new building was ready for occupancy in late February, 1935, ensured that all of the various card and dossier files were at least placed in the same room. The move to modern quarters provided the occasion for the current minister of the interior, Marcel Régnier, in Pierre-Etienne Flandin's cabinet, to alter the structure of the Sûreté Nationale hierarchy beneath the level of director from that established by Sarraut. In place of a single inspecteur général and eight contrôleurs généraux, Régnier decreed two *directeurs adjoints*, to which six *chefs du service* would report. By removing the director from daily operations, Sarraut's system had diffused authority too severely. Régnier's restored a centralized power to the director and his closest subordinates (and with it the old danger of political pressure). It was with this organization that the Sûreté Nationale finished the last years of the Third Republic.[18]

During the first five of those years, 1935 through 1939, the appropriation to the service increased 80 percent over that of 1934 (if the funding for the suburb commissariats of the Seine in the 1934 budget is subtracted), from Fr 52,663,291 to Fr 94,886,649. For 1940,

---

18. The name of the service was changed officially on July 1, 1934. On Mariani see Ulmann, *Le Quatrième pouvoir*, 63–66. The transfer of the suburban commissariats to the Paris prefecture became effective on June 25, 1934. On recruitment see Gandon, *Le Rôle de la police*, 18–22, and Aubert, *Organisation et méthodes*, 33–37. On other changes see Rougé, *La Sûreté Nationale*, 49–64, 131–50, and the report of March 1, 1935, by Marcel Régnier, published in *JO*, March 2, 1935.

with the Sûreté Nationale on a war footing, the appropriation jumped to Fr 128,849,106, a 145 percent increase over 1934 and up 36 percent in a single year alone. Most of the increase from 1934 to 1939, Fr 13,863,290 to Fr 47,503,691—243 percent—was in the category of administration and investigations, with a significant amount going toward the long-postponed purchase of new equipment. The budget for salaries, by contrast, increased only 25 percent, from Fr 35,000,000 to Fr 43,782,958, at the same time that the number of personnel rose 43 percent, from 1,389 to 1,985. The average salary in 1939 was only 88 percent of what it had been in 1934—Fr 22,056 compared with Fr 25,198—a clear example of the effort by French legislators to fight the inflation of these years through the deflation of paychecks to government workers. Undercover operations were stigmatized by the Stavisky and Prince scandals, and funds for them were actually cut 5 percent between 1934 and 1939, from Fr 3,800,000 to Fr 3,600,000. With the advent of war, any delicacy about secret operations was ignored, and the amount rose to Fr 15,000,000, a 317 percent increase over 1939. As the service geared up for the crisis, there were clear priorities: Administration and investigations received Fr 67,013,460, up 41 percent over 1939 and 383 percent over 1934, while salaries were allocated Fr 46,835,646, up 7 percent over 1939 and 34 percent over 1934. For 1940 the Sûreté Nationale added 362 inspecteurs and commissaires, pushing salaries down even further, to an average of Fr 19,955, 79 percent of what they had been in 1934.[19]

In the transition from Sûreté Générale to Sûreté Nationale, the Police spéciale were merged with the Police mobile. The purchase of new equipment, particularly more automobiles, gave to all of the inspecteurs and commissaires the kind of mobility that only the Police mobile had possessed previously and made the distinction meaningless. More than any other action, this vastly increased appropriation for administration and investigations, including the modern office building and the opportunity to establish new divisions and facilities, permitted the men (and the few women, added first in 1930 as typists) to perform their work more efficiently. The change in recruitment, though welcome, would show an effect only slowly. Coordination with the Paris prefecture was always compromised by mutual competition and mistrust. The restructuring of the hierarchy at the Rue des Saussaies could not eliminate politicization (if that was its aim), which had been a tradition of the service since its

19. AMF, Budget, Sûreté Générale, 1934; Budget, Sûreté Nationale, 1935–40.

establishment during the Second Empire. One propagandist for reform, Marcel Rougé, could write in 1935 that political pressure was "the true evil at the Sûreté Nationale, the gangrene that must be extirpated immediately for fear that it will spread to the healthy parts of the organism." But the essence of the service was the corps of outstanding individual agents, men such as Jean Belin and Marcel Sicot, who persevered during the worst years and would do so during the better. They suppressed the outbreak of political terrorism by the Cagoule in 1937, tracked down the brutal murderer Bruno Weidmann, and solved thousands of less sensational crimes. All they asked was the means to pursue their duties.[20]

Such "means"—more personnel, better equipment, improved organization—brought necessary renovation and modernization to the Paris Sûreté in 1912 and 1913. During the last half of 1911, the prefect of police, Louis Lépine, and the director of the Sûreté, Octave Hamard, won approval from the Ministry of the Interior to increase substantially the number of detectives in the service, from 360 to 458, and to provide for their salaries by raising the budget for personnel from Fr 916,501 to Fr 1,148,526. This need was evident to the police hierarchy, and the outrages of the Bonnot gang in December, 1911, provided a convincing public justification. The addition of nearly a hundred new detectives to the Sûreté (an increase of 27 percent) altered the balance of the director's responsibilities. Although he had always had to juggle the roles of administrator and chief of detectives, the administrative functions became increasingly dominant.

Hamard would have made the transition easily, but on January 1, 1912, he was elevated to Lépine's inner circle of advisers as directeur des recherches. His replacement at the Sûreté, Xavier Guichard, had made a reputation as a brave leader of the elite criminal brigade that investigated the most serious crimes. Unfortunately, Guichard's education (primary schooling only) and capacity for administration were limited, and he was also arrogant and headstrong. His most serious qualification for this advancement was a devotion to the Radical party, a political opinion often rewarded while Joseph Caillaux was premier. During the first three months of 1912, Guichard botched

---

20. There were eight *dames dactylos* in 1930, twelve in 1940. See Rougé, *La Sûreté Nationale,* 219; Montarron, *L'Histoire vraie,* 154–213; Belin, *Trente ans,* 253–87; Sicot, *Servitude et grandeur,* 161–90.

the hunt for the members of the Bonnot gang so thoroughly that the legislature hastily voted an extraordinary appropriation of Fr 259,093 to purchase additional equipment for the Paris Sûreté (plus an additional Fr 540,030 for the Sûreté Générale). A month later, in April, he forgot himself so completely that he slapped and threatened a suspect while in the full view of a large crowd. In an official evaluation filed on March 27, 1912, Hamard noted his successor's appropriate political views (which matched his own) and next described him as having fulfilled his duties "with zeal and intelligence"—but then struck out these last four words. Lépine refused to act under pressure and took no action against Guichard before retiring at the end of March, 1913. The new prefect, Célestin Hennion, permitted Guichard to remain at his post another six months, until August 31, but it was still the briefest tenure of a Sûreté director during the Third Republic.[21]

Hennion, who had sponsored the mobile brigades while director of the Sûreté Générale, retained Guichard while planning a reorganization of the detectives. He regarded the supplementary men and equipment in 1912 as only a beginning, and armed with the prestige acquired through brilliant success at the Rue des Saussaies, he could confidently expect that his requests would be granted. The Sûreté gained 215 more men in 1913 and another 161 in 1914, raising the total to 834 at the outbreak of World War I (see Table 21). The budget for personnel rose to Fr 2,354,318 (an increase of 157 percent over 1911), and average salaries were up as well, to Fr 2,822 (an increase of 11 percent over 1911; see Table 22). The equipment budget for any division is difficult to extrapolate from the overall budget of the prefecture, but for the Sûreté it appears to have increased approximately 18 percent between 1911 and 1914.

Hennion proposed to use the added men and equipment to implement a significant decentralization of the Sûreté. For more than a century and a half, the detectives had operated entirely from headquarters, where they received their orders and filed their reports. This centralization permitted the prefecture to impose a control over every criminal investigation, confining the independence of the Sûreté agents and describing the limits of the case. It also produced

---

21. APP, Budget, Ville de Paris, Préfecture de Police, 1911–12; 56248, Hamard; E A/89, Guichard; 75067, Guichard, with the evaluation by Hamard (March 27, 1912) and a defense by Lépine (February 17, 1913); *JOC*, Débats parlementaires, March 26, 1912.

TABLE 21
Personnel of the Paris Sûreté, 1890–1940

Year	Personnel	Year	Personnel
1890	330	1917	891
1894	370	1918	891
1895	370	1919	891
1896	370	1920	908
1897	370	1921	903
1898	360	1922	830
1899	373	1923	830
1900	360	1924	766
1901	366	1925	766
1902	365	1926	766
1903	339	1927	766
1904	339	1928	766
1905	339	1929	765
1906	339	1930	760
1907	339	1931	765
1908	341	1932	765
1909	341	1933	765
1910	343	1934	765
1911	360	1935	765
1912	458	1936	765
1913	673	1937	765
1914	834	1938	819
1915	901	1939	819
1916	891	1940	842

SOURCE: APP, Budget, Ville de Paris, Préfecture de Police, 1890–1940.

stultification and delay. When rapid communications were impossible or unreliable, this restraint was valuable, even essential. By 1913 it was appropriate only for the more serious or delicate crimes. Hennion's reorganization paired the twenty arrondissements of Paris into ten districts, each to receive a force of fifty detectives under the command of a commissaire and to have the responsibility for all initial investigations within the district. Police inquiries into misdemeanors and some felonies, most of them relatively uncomplicated larcenies, would take place at this level. Grave crimes of violence, large-scale frauds, and any case with unusual, and particularly political, overtones were to be referred by the district commissaire of detectives to the Quai des Orfèvres. There the Sûreté would maintain its traditional special brigades, the elite criminal squad and

TABLE 22
Personnel Budget of the Paris Sûreté, 1890–1940 (in Francs)

Year	Amount	Year	Amount
1890	568,800	1917	2,475,617
1894	694,654	1918	2,418,664
1895	701,203	1919	4,939,074
1896	704,360	1920	5,086,944
1897	710,148	1921	7,624,970
1898	710,313	1922	6,727,000
1899	707,280	1923	6,755,000
1900	716,216	1924	7,655,000
1901	845,430	1925	8,319,375
1902	802,834	1926	12,935,200
1903	774,738	1927	11,395,200
1904	777,709	1928	13,725,600
1905	704,135	1929	14,537,700
1906	780,854	1930	15,500,000
1907	786,622	1931	19,247,000
1908	799,412	1932	19,145,000
1909	809,967	1933	18,941,100
1910	878,394	1934	19,956,500
1911	916,501	1935	19,685,000
1912	1,148,526	1936	17,500,000
1913	1,727,736	1937	19,080,000
1914	2,354,318	1938	21,501,000
1915	2,435,193	1939	22,645,000
1916	2,471,341	1940	21,194,000

SOURCE: APP, Budget, Ville de Paris, Préfecture de Police, 1890–1940.

units trained in the unraveling of confidence schemes and swindles. The brigade des moeurs, the brigade de la voie publique, and the service des garnis would also be based at the Quai des Orfèvres and continue to gather information from prostitutes, police spies, and hotel clerks. Although these central brigades would remain under the personal control of the Sûreté's director, Hennion granted their leaders an expanded freedom of maneuver by ordering a reduction in the number and frequency of required reports and by declaring privately that he would tolerate petty infringements of police regulations governing investigations.

Through this decentralization, Hennion wanted to free the Quai des Orfèvres to concentrate on major crimes and on the accumulation of intelligence. Although the plan would initially deplete the agents assigned to the headquarters of the Sûreté, he intended that the addition of new personnel would restore the central brigades to their previous strength. The reorganization had such support at the Ministry of the Interior that from 1913 through 1919 the Paris Sûreté would have more detectives than the Sûreté Générale's Police spéciale and Police mobile combined. The first stage of the plan went into effect on September 1, 1913, when Hennion replaced Guichard with Paul Mouton, a magistrate from the Ministry of Justice who had displayed unusual administrative skill as secretary-general of the Paris parquet. The service also received a new official name, the Police judiciaire, though common parlance inside and outside the prefecture continued to refer to the Sûreté. The 673 detectives assigned to the Police judiciaire in 1913 were not sufficient for Mouton to carry through the decentralization immediately: If 500 were assigned to the districts, there would have been only 173 for the central brigades. Full implementation was delayed until 1914, when a new complement of 161 detectives permitted assigning 334 men to the Quai des Orfèvres. Hennion completed executing his list of changes for the Police judiciaire in February, 1914, soon after the death of Alphonse Bertillon, when he made small adjustments in the routine of the Identité judiciaire that he had hesitated to propose while the legendary criminologist was still alive.[22]

The ten districts of the decentralized Police judiciaire also served as the new organizational base for the Police municipale. In a rearrangement that was primarily administrative, ten commissaires divisionnaires took the place of the twenty commissaires who had directed the twenty arrondissement commissariats. The basic structure of the Police municipale remained unaltered. A company of patrolmen, under the command of an officier de paix seconded by brigadiers and sous-brigadiers, continued to be stationed in each arrondissement, its forces divided among four precincts. The approxi-

---

22. APP, Budget, Ville de Paris, Préfecture de Police, 1911–19; Levilain, "Histoire de l'organisation," I, 136–37, 237–81; Fosdick, *European Police Systems*, 286–88; Le Clère, *Histoire de la police*, 109–10; Pierre Vohl, *La Police française* (5th ed.; Paris, 1936), 59. Under Hennion's plan, the Sûreté (Police judiciaire) partitioned Paris into the following districts: District 1 (1st and 8th arrondissements), District 2 (2nd and 3rd arrondissements), District 3 (4th and 12th arrondissements), District 4 (5th and 13th arrondissements), District 5 (6th and 14th arrondissements), District 6 (7th and 15th arrondissements), District 7 (9th and 18th arrondissements), District 8 (10th and 19th arrondissements), District 9 (11th and 20th arrondissements), District 10 (16th and 17th arrondissements). On Mouton, whose personnel dossier was retained by the Ministry of Justice, see Archives Nationales (hereinafter cited as AN), BB 6 II, 1092, dos. Paul Henri Mouton.

The Police (II)

TABLE 23
Directors of the Paris Sûreté/Police Judiciaire, 1912–1941

Chef du service	Dates of Service
Paul Eugène Xavier Guichard	January 1, 1912–August 31, 1913
Paul Henri Mouton	September 1, 1913–October 15, 1919
Charles Louis Alfred Ducrocq	October 16, 1919–July 31, 1923
Louis Ernest Lacambre	August 1, 1923–May 31, 1928
André Benoist	June 1, 1928–April 4, 1930
Paul Eugène Xavier Guichard	April 5, 1930–March 31, 1934
Charles Hubert Meyer	April 1, 1934–February 28, 1941

SOURCES: APP, E A/89, Guichard; 75067, Guichard; 65450, Ducrocq; 69513, Lacambre; 74408, Benoist; E A/89, Meyer; E A/181, Meyer; 82932, Meyer; AN, BB 6 II, 1092, dos. Mouton.

mate strength of the companies, twenty for the arrondissements and five in reserve at the prefecture, had grown steadily from 180 men in 1860 to 320 by the 1890s. It remained stable at this level until the end of World War I, when there was a rapid augmentation to 500 by 1926 and 560 by 1938. The total personnel of the Police municipale increased from about 4,600 in 1860 to 8,378 in 1915 and 14,424 in 1938. In contrast, the number of detectives at the Police judiciaire reached a peak of 908 in 1920 and, with variations, declined through most of the 1920s and 1930s, though never dipping below 760 men. Hennion's health failed after more than seven years of enormous responsibilities, and he took the opportunity to retire when the prefecture was placed under military authority on September 2, 1914, as part of the wartime government in Paris. Emile Laurent, the secretary-general of the prefecture since 1892, was selected to succeed him and completed his projects faithfully with a minimum of interference from army officials. It was Hennion's organizational structure for the two divisions of the Paris police that would last until the end of the Third Republic.[23]

Six men directed the Police judiciaire from the beginning of its expansion in 1912 through 1941 (Guichard served twice; see Table 23). They had a different task from their eight predecessors because the detectives were now more to be managed than led. Guichard's disasters in 1912 and his dismissal in 1913 were an admonition. The premium would be less on leadership and more on administrative abil-

23. APP, Budget, Ville de Paris, Préfecture de Police, 1870–1940; Levilain, "Histoire de l'organisation," I, 358–59; Fosdick, *European Police Systems*, 126–33; Stead, *The Police of Paris*, 153–54.

ity, a talent that comes most frequently through longer experience and greater age. The new demands of the position help to account for the changes in the statistical characteristics of the directors. Between 1870 and 1912, they had assumed office at an average age of forty-four and left it at fifty-one; between 1912 and 1941, they would assume office at an average age of fifty-two and leave it at fifty-six (for the entire Third Republic, the averages are forty-eight and fifty-three, respectively). The average tenure was shorter by thirty-one months (two years, seven months), and the principal cause was the removal of directors for incompetence or corruption (Guichard twice and André Benoist). Before 1912 the average tenure had been eighty-one months (six years, nine months); afterward, it was fifty months (four years, two months), though eliminating Claude's long term from the computation leaves the difference between the two periods a mere twelve months. The constants were greater than the slight dissimilarities. The conspicuous example of Guichard, whose allegiance to the Radical party covered some of his professional failings, and the less clear case of Charles Ducrocq, whose conservatism and Catholicism appealed to the Bloc National, indicate that political connections continued to count and could not be neglected. The director was still likely to be a rough-and-tumble policeman with lower-middle-class origins and only a primary education. That is why greater experience and age were necessary after 1912—because background and education did not provide a proper preparation. Mouton and Ducrocq had law degrees and some independent income, but they were exceptions, as Jacob had been earlier. And most independent incomes from securities were made meaningless by the inflation of the 1920s and 1930s.[24]

The unfortunate Xavier Guichard was not one of the exceptions. He was born in 1870, the son of a physician who had few patients and who died in 1881, leaving behind a wife and two children. The household had little money, and Guichard left school to work at age fifteen. After completing his military service in 1891, he managed to secure an appointment as a secrétaire and joined the prefecture. Somehow he scraped together enough money to survive the long years until 1903, when he finally reached the rank of commissaire. His superiors noted his slow progress but also his willingness to work hard. He became known for his courage and for an arrogance

24. APP, E A/89, Guichard; 75067, Guichard; 65450, Ducrocq; 69513, Lacambre; 74408, Benoist; E A/89, Meyer; E A/181, Meyer; 82932, Meyer; AN, BB 6 II, 1092, dos. Mouton.

that increased as he gained more authority. Along with police methods, he learned the value of appropriate political opinions. The success of the Radical party brought him promotions until he was made director of the Sûreté in January, 1912, at the young age of forty-one. There he could do nothing right. Throughout the first months of 1912 he bungled the Bonnot gang investigation, and in late April, when he was finally close to capturing all of the bandits, he excited intense criticism in the press by publicly roughing up a minor figure in the case. After Hennion replaced him on September 1, 1913, Guichard found himself almost banished, sent away from the Quai des Orfèvres itself to command the Seventh Division of detectives in the Ninth and Eighteenth arrondissements.[25]

Hennion's choice for a successor was Paul Henri Mouton, a member of the judicial bureaucracy who had left a promising career as an attorney in Toulouse to join the magistrature in 1895. After serving as a substitut at Bernay and a juge d'instruction at Soissons and Pontoise, he was appointed the procureur de la République for Meaux. From there he was called in 1910 to be the secretary-general of the Paris parquet, a role in which his administrative talent attracted Hennion's attention. Mouton had the background and education that Guichard had lacked. Born into an upper-middle-class family in Carcassonne, he had passed his baccalaureate and taken a *licence ès lois* at Toulouse. He welcomed this unorthodox assignment away from his ministry because he had a particular interest in criminal investigations, almost a fascination, that had led him into the magistrature and to write a book, *De la recherche de vérité dans les enquêtes de police* (1903). Mouton was not anxious to lead these investigations personally, only to arrange for their success. Despite wartime disruptions, he patiently and skillfully carried through the decentralization and changes Hennion devised. When he left the Police judiciaire in October, 1919, to accept an appointment as a conseiller on the Cour d'appel de Paris, the system worked with indisputable smoothness and efficiency.[26]

At Mouton's departure, the Police judiciaire passed back to the control of a veteran detective, Charles Ducrocq, who had served as assistant director at the Quai des Orfèvres since 1914. Although as stocky and bluff as Mouton had been elegant and refined, Ducrocq had the same education, a baccalaureate and a *licence ès lois*, and

25. APP, E A/89, Guichard; 75067, Guichard, with newspaper clippings about several embarrassing incidents.
26. AN, BB 6 II, 1092, dos. Mouton.

was almost as fine an administrator. His dossier contained letters of recommendation from René Waldeck-Rousseau and unusually strong praise from superiors—"zèle constant et une intelligence remarquable." Yet promotions came to Ducrocq slower than to some others; Guichard, for example, was three years younger. The cause was Ducrocq's identification as a conservative and a practicing Catholic during a time of government-sponsored anticlericalism. A revival of nationalism and religious sentiment after 1911 eliminated his politics and his religion as a handicap, and after the war the political mood that would carry the Bloc National to dominance in the elections of November, 1919, made them an asset. As director, Ducrocq needed all of his talents. During the years of the war the total of detectives assigned to the Police judiciare was maintained at a high level, even while that of the Sûreté Générale was permitted to drop significantly. Sharp repression of crime contributed to calm and confidence in the capital, and the detectives also kept a close surveillance over political groups having different ideas about the conduct of the fighting. After 1920 the need to reinforce the Sûreté Générale coincided with an end to the specific wartime exigencies. The result for the Police judiciare was a slight reduction in its personnel (by 7 percent between 1919 and 1923) and the failure of its budget to keep pace with inflation. Under these circumstances Ducrocq had to struggle to uphold the standards established under Mouton's tenure. He was successful in the main, but the frustrations exhausted him, and he retired in July, 1923, after only four years as director.[27]

Ducrocq's decision to leave the Quai des Orfèvres was hastened by the knowledge that the personnel total of the Police judiciaire was to be reduced still further in 1924, to 766 detectives, a decrease of 8 percent in a single year and 16 percent from the record level of 908 in 1920. Mouton and Ducrocq had securely entrenched Hennion's system. What the service, with its thinned ranks, needed next was vigorous execution, and thus Louis Lacambre was chosen as director. Lacambre was fifty-five years old and had served with the prefecture for thirty of them. Since 1919 he had been a commissaire divisionnaire of notable ability and activity. There was no mistaking the contrast with his two predecessors. He had completed only a primary education, and his superiors noted as late as 1917 his lack of "culture générale et valeur intellectuelle." But he was a robust, thor-

---

27. APP, 65450, Ducrocq. See especially the evaluation dated 1910, remarking on his identification as a "Catholique."

ough administrator who knew how to organize criminal investigations. He was also sufficiently bold to have complained formally in 1911 of having been advanced less rapidly than the favored Xavier Guichard, who had joined the prefecture two years later than Lacambre. Impressed by this audacity, Louis Lépine, then prefect, gave Lacambre a raise in salary. As director, Lacambre stabilized the detective force at the number of 766 men and prevented any serious deterioration in the work of the Police judiciaire.[28]

Rumors of police corruption are frequently spread by those who seek a scapegoat for their misfortunes, whether they are criminals or the prey of criminals. However much individual patrolmen or detectives may have blackmailed informants, petty hoodlums, and prostitutes, there had been little basis for charges of major corruption against the Paris police in the two decades since the bizarre investigation of the Steinheil affair murders in 1908. This record changed after Lacambre's retirement in 1928.

The new director of the Police judiciaire was André Benoist, a small, slender man who had the mien of an intellectual, but whose dark and penetrating gaze held a frightening power. Throughout an extraordinary career he would mix remarkable accomplishments with striking indiscretions. Benoist joined the prefecture as an inspecteur in 1901 at the age of twenty-four. In the next six years he was cited for bravery twelve times. The degree of his education is uncertain, but he was to demonstrate unusual mental acuity. In 1907 he abruptly resigned, and the next seven years are a complete blank in his record. When war broke out in 1914, he asked to rejoin the prefecture and was assigned to work as an undercover agent investigating possible subversive activities. A year later the army recruited him for its own intelligence apparatus. From 1916 to 1919 he served as director of espionage for the French, and then the Allied, army in the Balkans. He personally undertook dangerous missions in Macedonia and Albania, once destroying an entire network of Bulgarian spies who menaced Allied communications. In 1919, however, he was sent back to France in disgrace, accused of taking bribes from Russian Jewish refugees fleeing the Bolsheviks. For three years Benoist disappeared again, this time probably to carry out more secret operations for military intelligence. He carefully made important friendships, and when he surfaced in 1922, he was made a com-

---

28. APP, 69513, Lacambre. Of special note is the formal complaint to Lépine about Guichard, June 16, 1911, and Lépine's reply, November 24, 1911.

missaire in the Police spéciale at Lille upon the personal insistence of Paul-Julien de Cassagnac, a leading conservative politician. Two years afterward, he was assigned to Paris as a high-ranking liaison officer between the Rue des Saussaies and the prefecture. He won the favor of Jean Chiappe, who was then the director of the Sûreté Générale. When Chiappe became prefect of police in April, 1927, he kept Benoist on his staff and at the end of May, 1928, appointed him director of the Police judiciaire.

To a series of important positions within the Ministry of the Interior, Chiappe brought skillful, effective administration and a taint of corruption that spread among subordinates. Under Benoist's leadership the Police judiciaire quickly acquired an unsavory reputation for venality, with the director himself viewed as purchasable. During a tenure of twenty-two months, Benoist was implicated in two major financial scandals. Marthe Hanau, an accomplished swindler, apparently paid him Fr 75,000 to keep police detectives from inquiring into the doubtful enterprises she publicized through a seemingly respectable weekly, the *Gazette du Franc et des Nations*. The bribe came too late, because an inquiry had already been opened under Lacambre that would unravel Hanau's schemes by the end of 1928. Benoist also involved himself in the intrigues of Albert Oustric, a banker who specialized in floating stocks of questionable quality, driving up the price through paid endorsements, and selling before the inevitable collapse. Benoist's complicity prevented an investigation into these manipulations until early 1930, when Oustric's bank failed. Soon afterward, on April 4, Benoist prudently announced his retirement. Even when he was brought to trial on May 26, 1933, for his part in the Oustric affair, he arrogantly explained away all of the charges against him. His acquittal three days later was regarded by many as having been politically motivated.[29]

Chiappe chose Xavier Guichard to succeed Benoist. During the seventeen years since his inadequate performance in 1912 and 1913, Guichard had learned administration, first as a commissaire divisionnaire and then as a member of the upper bureaucracy of the prefecture, having become contrôleur général adjoint in 1919 and inspecteur général des services in 1930. He had not neglected his political connections to the Radical party, and though Chiappe spread

29. APP, 74408, Benoist. See Benoist's memoirs, *Les Mystères de la police: Révélations par son ancien directeur* (Paris, 1935), and *Au nom de la loi*, especially 122–75. For a hostile version see Ulmann, *Le Quatrième pouvoir*, 69–81. Benoist refurbished his reputation through heroic service in the Resistance during World War II.

The Police (II)

his network of friendships widely indeed, his roots were among the Radicals. Guichard failed to learn the lesson of Benoist's premature retirement, and he continued to overlook, if not actually permit, the corruption that had become blatant under his predecessor. It was this attitude, combined with loyalty to Chiappe and to Radical politicians, that would sully Guichard's second term as director of the Police judiciaire. When the Stavisky affair broke open in the first week of January, 1934, he delayed arresting some of the principal figures, particularly the minister of colonies, Albert Dalimier, who was clearly implicated. Guichard quickly realized that he had committed a serious tactical error and on January 22 declared his intention to retire on April 1, claiming that he had planned to do so since the previous December. When this decision was announced officially on March 12, the Paris press correctly interpreted it as a disgrace. Guichard appealed for superiors to defend his record, but with Chiappe no longer prefect, they refused.[30]

A year later, on March 2, 1935, Guichard was called before the Tribunal de la Seine as a witness in the trial of a police detective, a certain Loublié, who was charged with undisguised, gangsterlike extortion. Guichard defended the willingness of detectives to accept "une gratification" and testified that all of Loublié's alleged crimes had taken place during "special assignments" for Chiappe, whose "authority completely sheltered this subordinate." Loublié was, in effect, the prefecture's Pierre Bonny. To convict Loublié was to attack Chiappe, who retained formidable influence. The panel of judges preferred to dismiss the case. Here was proof public of how thoroughly the decay had penetrated. The new administration of the prefecture under Roger Langéron, who assumed office in mid-March, 1934, had concluded that every member of the Police judiciaire would have to be considered potentially contaminated. For Guichard's successor, Langéron looked among the senior administrators of the Police municipale and chose its assistant director, Charles Meyer. He would serve through the fall of the Third Republic and bring a new discipline that at least forced the extortion and bribery out of sight. There were no more major scandals, but Meyer could not hope to eliminate a corruption that had become habitual.[31]

Such behavior was entirely consonant with the tone set by Chiappe

30. APP, 75067, Guichard, especially the correspondence about his retirement, dated January 22–March 13, 1934.
31. Ulmann, *Le Quatrième pouvoir*, 51–62; APP, E A/89, Meyer; E A/181, Meyer; 82932, Meyer.

as prefect, a period of seven years that marked the summit of his remarkable ascent within the Ministry of the Interior. Born in Ajaccio, Corsica, Chiappe joined the bureaucracy of the Place Beauvau in 1899, at the age of twenty-one, as a *rédacteur* (head clerk). The Radical party had come that year to dominate French politics through its fortuitous position in the Dreyfus affair, and Chiappe made obvious his allegiance to Radical programs and Radical politicians. Even with the proper sentiments, advancement was slow, but in 1916 he was promoted to *chef de bureau* (bureau chief) because of his friendship with Louis Malvy, an important younger Radical leader and minister of the interior since June, 1914. When Malvy was accused of treason by Georges Clemenceau during the crisis of 1917, Chiappe defended his patron and continued to do so even after Malvy's trial before the Senate in August, 1918, and banishment for having "betrayed the duties of his office." For this misplaced fidelity, Chiappe was relegated to a minor post in the accounting section of the ministry. He languished there until the victory of the Cartel des Gauches in 1924 returned the Place Beauvau to Radical control. The new minister of the interior, Camille Chautemps, provided a suitable reparation, promoting him to director of the Sûreté Générale, a spectacular elevation.

During thirty-three months at the Rue des Saussaies (July, 1924–April, 1927), Chiappe encouraged the spread of extortion and other forms of criminality among the agents by condoning these acts and by constructing a personal network of informers, confidence men, and detectives willing to carry out any assignment. Stavisky and Bonny were only two recruits. Investigations were misdirected, charges fabricated, documents falsified, privileged information divulged, serious crimes of violence committed—all for a fee. And it was this attitude toward the law and this manner of directing a police detective force that Chiappe brought to the prefecture.

Sleekly and smoothly, Chiappe built a fortress of popularity and political connections about his new fiefdom. He ensured broad support within police ranks by founding a charity for the families of disabled or deceased patrolmen, the Maison de Santé du Gardien de la Paix, with his wife, Marcelle, as executrix. By loudly proclaiming his determination to suppress any breach of public order, he appealed to propertied Parisians panicked at the fear of bolshevism. After its enormous demonstrations in August, 1927, protesting the execution of Nicola Sacco and Bartolomeo Vanzetti in the United States, Chiappe made an example of the Communist party by banning all of its future mass meetings. The middle class also applauded a well-publicized enforcement of traffic regulations in the capital and an effort to drive prostitutes from the streets. Chiappe's position was solidified by his close relationship to Chautemps, who was minister of the interior eight times between 1924 and 1934 and premier twice. Chiappe also took care to make friends among the politicians of groups to the right of the Radicals.

This facade of order, propriety, and decency concealed the foulest rot. Chiappe maintained and expanded the network and techniques of corruption that he had perfected at the Sûreté Générale. The Maison de Santé provided a cover for extortion: A bank check to the prefect's favorite charity could make incriminating evidence disappear. More than ever before, prostitution represented a source of bribery, not a crime, with regular payments from the prostitutes through the vice squad to the police hierarchy. The directors of the Police judiciaire under Chiappe, Benoist and Guichard, committed the detective force to these schemes while making their own venal bargains. Lucien Zimmer, Chiappe's closest administrative aide, acted as an overall coordinator of corrupt practices. No patrolman or detective could dare to protest. Chautemps's influence prevented any rebellion against Chiappe at the Ministry of the Interior or within the Radical party. The prefect of police had become the head of a crime syndicate.

There can be no wondering why Chiappe failed to arrest Stavisky when the scandal became public, no wondering why he blocked an investigation that might prove the complicity of Chautemps, no wondering why Daladier hesitated to dismiss Chiappe and sought to placate him by offering the governor-generalship of Morocco. With Corsican pride Chiappe rejected the consolation prize. Entering the first available elections, he exploited his continuing popularity in Paris to win office as a *conseiller municipal* (alderman) on May 5, 1935, and his fellow conseillers municipaux immediately voted him the chairman of the city council. In August, 1936, he was elected to the Chamber of Deputies from the wealthy Sixteenth Arrondissement of the capital. At the Palais Bourbon, Chiappe was as haughty as at the prefecture. After the military disasters of June, 1940, he declared his allegiance to Philippe Pétain and the government at Vichy. Five months later, in November, he accepted an appointment as high commissioner for Syria and Libya. He departed for Damascus by air on November 27. Although the plane was clearly marked, Italian gunners shot it down over the Mediterranean Sea. Chiappe's

TABLE 24
Paris Prefects of Police, 1913–1941

Prefect of Police	Dates of Service	Previous Position
Célestin Hennion	March 29, 1913–September 2, 1914	Directeur, Sûreté Générale
Emile Laurent	September 2, 1914–June 3, 1917	Secrétaire-général to the prefect of police
Louis Hudelo	June 3, 1917–November 23, 1917	Directeur, Sûreté Générale
Fernand Raux	November 23, 1917–May 13, 1921	Prefect for Oise
Robert Leullier	May 13, 1921–July 9, 1922	Prefect for Pas-de-Calais
Armand Naudin	July 9, 1922–August 2, 1924	Prefect for Nord
Alfred Morain	August 2, 1924–April 14, 1927	Prefect for Nord
Jean Chiappe	April 14, 1927–February 4, 1934	Directeur, Sûreté Générale; secrétaire-général, Ministry of the Interior
Adrien Bonnefoy-Sibour	February 4, 1934–March 17, 1934	Prefect for Seine-et-Oise
Roger Langéron	March 17, 1934–February 27, 1941	Prefect for Nord

SOURCE: *Journal Officiel*, Lois et Décrets, 1913–1941.

body was never recovered. Whether the Italians fired by mistake or on command has never been determined, but like Bonny, Chiappe would not survive to tell his secrets.[32]

Chiappe was France's most controversial prefect of police. The other nine men who held that position between Louis Lépine's resignation in March, 1913, and the destruction of the Third Republic in July, 1940, were hardly controversial at all (see Table 24). Like their predecessors, their primary concern was for order and the maintenance of the Police municipale. Three of the ten moved directly from the Rue des Saussaies to the prefecture and took an unusual interest in the Police judiciaire, with effects as beneficial under Célestin Hennion and Louis Hudelo as they were disastrous under Chiappe. All were men of broad administrative experience. Emile Laurent was appointed after serving as secretary-general of the Paris prefecture for twenty-two years. Fernand Raux, Robert Leullier, Armand Naudin, Alfred Morain, Adrien Bonnefoy-Sibour, and Roger Langéron had the preparation of long careers with the Ministry of the Interior as departmental prefects. Three—Naudin, Morain, and Bonnefoy-Sibour—had law degrees. But this appropriate background and training were twice insufficient: Chiappe used his to perfect deceits; Bonnefoy-Sibour's lack of sangfroid during the riots of February 6, 1934, was so manifest that he had to be replaced six weeks later.[33]

In the aftermath of the Stavisky affair, there was much criticism of the Paris police and, once it decreased, some proposals for reform. It was clear that not everything was rotten, that much of the edifice was sound. Even during the worst excesses committed by Benoist and Guichard at the Police judiciaire, some of the detectives managed to retain their integrity. Chief among them was the head of the criminal brigade, Georges Victor Massu, whose methods may have been part of the inspiration for Georges Simenon's fictional commissaire, Jules Maigret. The legislature was willing to appropriate more money. By 1939, the last year of peace, the budget of the Police

32. Ulmann, *Le Quatrième pouvoir*, 101–81, provides an excellent, though inimical, summary of Chiappe's career and the accusations made against him. Benoist's view from the Police judiciaire is in *Au nom de la loi*, 122–50, 177–255. Zimmer defends himself and Chiappe in *Un septennat policier*, 8–48, 184–97. For the Stavisky affair, see APP, E A/85, Affaire Stavisky, and the Rapport général in *JOC*, Documents parlementaires, 1935, No. 4886.

33. See the standard biographical sources, such as G. Ruffy (ed.), *Qui êtes-vous? Annuaire des contemporains, notices biographiques* (Paris, 1924).

judiciaire for personnel had been raised to Fr 22,645,000, a 13 percent increase over 1934. The number of detectives was up 7 percent, from 765 to 819, and average salaries 6 percent, from Fr 26,086 to Fr 27,650. For 1940, with the expectation of wartime conditions, the detective force was enlarged to 842, though in the name of national sacrifice the budget for personnel was dropped to Fr 2,194,000, and with it, average salaries to Fr 25,171. The Ministry of the Interior proposed nothing for the prefecture approaching the Sarraut-Régnier reorganization of the Sûreté Générale/Sûreté Nationale. Langéron, the prefect of police from mid-March, 1934 until February, 1941, was merely authorized to make whatever changes he believed necessary. Besides replacing the major administrators compromised by the Stavisky affair, he acted only to restrict the recruitment of former noncommissioned officers and to limit the immunity extended to men such as Stavisky who became "permanent informers." Langéron was unwilling to go beyond these modest internal reforms because he believed that the police should retreat, bind their wounds, and recover with as little public exposure as possible.[34]

From the world outside the prefecture, there was pressure for additional reform and even for a major purging of the police apparatus. Public opinion was roused by the appearance of two searching and comprehensive indictments, Paul Allard's *L'Anarchie de la police* (1934) and André Ulmann's *Le Quatrième pouvoir: Police* (1935), both of which denounced the pervasive acceptance of bribes, the use of brutality in the questioning of suspects, the unexplained "police crimes," and the flagitious connection between certain politicians and certain police officials. Allard and Ulmann cited the corrupt payments between prostitutes and the vice squad and called bribery so common that even to obtain a *carte de séjour* might require a *pourboire* of Fr 2,500 to Fr 5,000. They documented cases of the *passage à tabac* so severe that the suspect died from his beatings. While acknowledging that agents like Bonny and Loublié were exceptions, they recalled how frequently men who knew too many secrets had died mysteriously or "committed suicide" or simply disappeared for-

---

34. On Massu see Montarron, *L'Histoire vraie*, 124–53, and his memoirs, *Souvenirs du commissaire Massu: Aveux, Quai des Orfèvres* (Paris, 1949). On the origins of Jules Maigret see Fenton Bresler, *The Mystery of Georges Simenon: A Biography* (London, 1983), 66–68, 81–87. For the appropriations see AMF, Budget, Sûreté Générale, 1934; Budget, Sûreté Nationale, 1935–40. On Langéron and the minor reforms see Gandon, *Le Rôle de la police*, 36–38; Ulmann, *Le Quatrième pouvoir*, 82–100; and Marcel Ludovic Guillaume, *Trente-sept ans avec le pègre* (Paris, 1938), 188.

ever. Stavisky and Prince were only the most recent. They claimed that patrolmen and detectives who seemed unwilling to tolerate this conduct were warned privately to resign because otherwise some accident might befall them.[35]

Ulmann insisted accurately that many of these abuses stemmed from links between men, and occasionally women, with political power or affluence, and the individual police agents they recruited to watch over their dubious investments in the demimonde, whether sexual or financial. Occasionally the client could be sheltered behind the law. In his memoirs Charles Pherdac, a commissaire during the last two decades of the nineteenth century, recalled having once been requested to verify an act of adultery between a famous general and a cabaret dancer. Pherdac evaded this responsibility because the general had been awarded the Grande-Croix of the Légion d'honneur, and by regulations dating from April 20, 1810, only a procureur général could search the person or the dwelling of such a dignitary. In other circumstances, more positive action was required. When Violette Nozière was brought to trial in October, 1934, for the murder of her father and the attempted murder of her mother a year earlier, none of the wealthy businessmen who had enjoyed her as a teenaged mistress were called to testify, and the police held their names a close secret. As a result of such efforts to protect the powerful, the police were tempted by extortion and thereby gained enormous illicit influence.[36]

Some of the circumstances of the Stavisky affair, particularly the failure of the Sûreté Générale and the Police judiciaire to exchange information about current investigations, strengthened the long-standing argument that the police apparatus in France should be unified, as it had been from February, 1874, to February, 1876, when the Sûreté Générale was placed under the direct supervision of the Paris prefect. The great caution against unification was that the concentration of police power would be too much in too few hands, but certainly there needed to be more cooperation. In the years immediately before the Stavisky affair, the relationship had been characterized as the "guerre des deux polices." When asked to explain why the Police judiciaire did not share a dossier on Stavisky with the

---

35. See, in particular, Allard, *L'Anarchie de la police*, 4–22; Ulmann, *Le Quatrième pouvoir*, 82–100, 198–235; and Aubert, *Organisation et méthodes*, 157–60.
36. Ulmann, *Le Quatrième pouvoir*, 36–50; Charles Pherdac, *Les Jeux de l'amour et de la police: Souvenirs d'un commissaire* (Paris, 1908), 15–22.

Sûreté Générale, Jean Chiappe had replied: "Nontransmission [to the Rue des Saussaies] is explained by standard procedure in such matters." The Sarraut reforms in 1934 envisioned a closer coordination between the two services, but the improvement was minimal.[37]

Just as reform came with difficulty, if at all, to the Rue des Saussaies, so it came with difficulty, if at all, to the Paris prefecture. Marcel Guillaume, a commissaire in the Police judiciaire with thirty-seven years of experience, was not far from Langéron's attitude when he wrote in 1938, "The police want only to work in peace according to their consciences." For him and for some of his fellow detectives and patrolmen, that avowal might have been a sufficient standard. But the history of the police under the Third Republic had demonstrated that trusting the consciences of individual policemen and police officials was dangerous. The police would not reform themselves, and they would stubbornly resist any reform from outside.[38]

Ulmann raised a final pertinent question to which there was no clear answer. The magistrature was the one governmental bureaucracy in constant contact with the police. Why had the prosecutors and judges not demanded reforms? All of the correlative questions were disturbing. Could the magistrates have remained unaware of—or indifferent to—police corruption? Were they aware but afraid of police power? Or had the magistrature itself become so corrupt that it was incapable of leading any reform?[39]

---

37. Allard, *L'Anarchie de la police*, 4–22, the quotations from 6, 17; Ulmann, *Le Quatrième pouvoir*, 270–78; Aubert, *Organisation et méthodes*, 145–49; Zimmer, *Un septennat policier*, 220–30.
38. Guillaume, *Trente-sept ans*, 190.
39. Ulmann, *Le Quatrième pouvoir*, 256–57.

4

The Criminal Procedure

An American legal scholar offers this cautious summation of the central problem confronting criminal procedure:

> More perhaps than any other societal institution, a criminal justice system involves the use of blatant governmental power and authority to coerce and control individual conduct. On the one hand, it seeks to put into practice a society's highest aspirations for doing justice within a procedurally fair system; on the other, it reflects the society's deepest fears and phobias.
>
> To maintain order, protect the society and its individual citizens, their persons, privacy, and property, the governmental power must to some extent itself invade or interfere with the interests and freedom of the citizenry at large. How much governmental interference is justified under particular socio-economic, cultural circumstances is a question of policy, a question of choice for the body politic to make.

More than eighty years earlier, a French attorney put the issue more bluntly, saying justice must "reassure the innocent as much as it makes the guilty tremble." And the belletrist René Benjamin rejected the notion that the dilemma could be bridged at all. "Justice," he wrote, "is not just and will never be so."[1]

---

1. George W. Pugh, "An Introductory Analysis of Characteristic Aspects of American Criminal Justice with Comparative Comments as to the French System," *Revue de la recherche juridique droit prospectif,* V (1985), 625–26; G. Andrier, *Intervention du défenseur dans l'instruction préparatoire* (Paris, 1903), 2; René Benjamin, *Le Palais et ses gens de justice* (Paris, 1919), 4.

The oldest form of criminal procedure in France had its origin in feudal custom. The victim of a crime went before a judge to make a formal accusation and demand a specific punishment. This judge might be a representative of the king or, more likely during the Middle Ages, a nobleman with the right to administer high justice. Seeking redress required courage, for the accused had the right of a "judicial duel" to the death with the accuser or with any witnesses against him. Even if the accuser survived the combat, the judge might decide that he had lost the duel and was condemned, according to a rule borrowed from Roman law, to suffer the penalty he had demanded for the accused. This form of criminal procedure could have little effect in punishing crime and little appeal to weak victims and witnesses. By the 1300s its use had become infrequent, and with the decline of feudalism, it would disappear entirely.

A new procedure had evolved, one providing greater safety for the accuser, who was required merely to "denounce" a crime and to offer to produce or name witnesses. The judge who received the denunciation was not compelled to convene a trial, as he was for a formal accusation. Instead, he opened an *information* (a judicial investigation), heard witnesses, and if the evidence appeared substantial enough to warrant a trial, only then summoned or arrested the accused. In essence the "denunciation" was only an accusation with a greater role for the judge and protection for the accuser and the witnesses. But these very differences made the new procedure popular and effective. Control of criminal acts moved increasingly into the hands of judicial officials, and as royal powers were extended and took over the entire process of justice, this responsibility became an indispensable part of the king's authority. An additional inducement for the victim was his right under this procedure to bring a civil suit, as *partie civile* (civil party), for damages as the state prosecuted the accused in a criminal action. The denunciation was supplemented by two variants. No specific accuser was necessary when the reputation of an alleged criminal was known through *clameur publique* (common report). An information could be opened, and if the rumors were confirmed by evidence, an arrest made. If the criminal was apprehended *en flagrant délit*, in the act or immediately afterward, the judge could immediately hold a trial and order sentence without a prior information. In all three instances the judge was becoming a species of public prosecutor, assuming the task of drawing up a case against the accused.

When judges merely adjudicated, criminal procedure advanced according to the *ordinary* method: The trial was a public inquest (unless a judicial duel was demanded), with the accused permitted to conduct an unhindered defense, particularly through the calling of favorable witnesses. As the judges adopted the practice of preparing pretrial summaries of the evidence, a belief grew in the necessity for new means to lay bare the truth. Thus originated the *extraordinary* method: To eliminate the possibility that the accused might escape his proper condemnation, he was denied effective defense and became subject to torture. The information was withheld from him entirely, and all of the proceedings, from the testimony of the witnesses through the trial and sentence itself, were conducted in secret. The witnesses were heard three times: first by an examiner, who reduced the declarations to writing; then by the judge, who verified the depositions in a proceeding known as the *récolement;* and finally in confrontation with the accused, who could object to their testimony but could not call any witnesses of his own. The accused was required to submit to an interrogation under oath, and if found guilty in spite of his denials, he suffered an additional penalty for perjury. When the accused claimed an alibi, the judge was morally bound to investigate it, but only the judge, and not the defendant, decided what evidence to gather for this defense. The accused could be tortured; the rationale was that a confession was necessary for complete proof of guilt. Any confession made under torture had to be repeated after the accused recovered. If it was then recanted, he was retortured; if he confirmed it, his condemnation was certain. Even after a confession, he was subject to further torture to discover whether he had committed other crimes or had accomplices.

The Royal Ordinance of 1498 under Louis XII gave this evolution in judicial procedure its first statutory form. Each criminal case was to begin with an investigation by a judge—an information, interrogations, and if appropriate, citation or arrest of the accused. The judge was then to submit his work to a *procureur du roi* (royal procurator), who was responsible for filing charges in the name of the king. These provisions were amplified in April, 1539, by the Ordinance of Villers-Cotterêts, issued by François I and written by his chancellor, Guillaume Poyet. In definitively setting the pattern for criminal procedure in France during the remainder of the ancien régime, the ordinance required that two magistrates participate in the preparation of every criminal case, the judge (called the *lieutenant criminel*) to conduct the examination of evidence and the procureur du roi to make the claims and petitions. This role for the procureur du roi represented the first clear delineation of a public prosecutorial function.

The 1539 ordinance specified the treatment of the accused after his arrest. He was to be interrogated under oath (the *serment*) by the lieutenant criminel, without the aid of counsel and without any knowledge of the information compiled against him, while a clerk recorded his replies. If he admitted his guilt, the confession and any mitigating circumstances were communicated to the procureur du roi and to any partie civile, who prepared in response written petitions demanding punishment and damages. After considering the report of the lieutenant criminel and the pleadings, a panel of (usually three) *conseillers* (judges) imposed sentence. If during the interrogation the accused insisted on his innocence, and in some instances even when he confessed, the lieutenant criminel ordered either the ordinary, which after 1539 was permitted only for very minor matters, or the extraordinary procedure.

By the terms of the 1539 ordinance, when the extraordinary procedure was followed (as it was in all serious cases), each witness was interrogated a second time before the lieutenant criminel (the *récolement*) and then confronted with the accused. Each interrogation took place "in secret"—in the chamber of the lieutenant criminel with only a clerk, and the accused during confrontations, present. The accused was not permitted to have legal counsel or to call witnesses of his own. He could offer an objection, such as bias, to a witness against him, but only *before* hearing the testimony. The records of the lieutenant criminel's investigation were then passed to the procureur du roi, along with any petition from the accused alleging an alibi. The procureur du roi examined the evidence for this defense and prepared a report. The defense was thus in the hands of the prosecution. If the testimony of the witnesses appeared to prove the case against the accused, the procureur du roi could seek a confession by asking the court (the panel of conseillers) to order torture. No confession was admissable unless repeated in the absence of torture. Whether or not the accused confessed, the final step in the extraordinary procedure was for the conseillers to consider the charges. The report submitted by the lieutenant criminel was often of such bulk that one of the conseillers had to act as *rapporteur*, to summarize it for the rest of the panel. The court also had written petitions from the procureur du roi and any partie civile. The accused appeared before the conseillers and knelt on a hard wooden bench (the *sellette*) while they interrogated him. After deliberating, the court rendered its judgment, almost invariably without explanation. The 1539 ordinance emphasized secrecy to such a degree that even the decision was disclosed to the accused alone.

Throughout the extraordinary procedure, the accused remained jailed without provision for bail. Mounting an effective defense, even if he were innocent, was extremely difficult. Often he learned the charges against him only when confronting the witnesses. He could not examine the evidence. The procureur du roi assessed his alibi. Legal counsel was absolutely prohibited. He faced torture. Yet this harsh form of criminal procedure appears to have been generally accepted in early modern France. Every level of society had suffered through the anarchy and the rife brigandage and banditry that characterized the late Middle Ages and the Hundred Years' War. Contemporary accounts emphasize a longing for peace and for greater security. They also stress a savage desire to repress crime and disorder. Guillaume Poyet's predecessor as chancellor, Antoine du Bourg, introduced the wheel and other cruel punishments to France from Germany earlier in the sixteenth century. Some legal scholars raised objections, but the elements they criticized—the secrecy, the emphasis on written documents instead of oral testimony, and the immense power of the judges—were the very ones that made the procedure so ferocious as a deterrent to crime.[2]

The instrument was sufficiently effective to impress Jean Baptiste Colbert a century and a quarter later. In 1664 and 1665 he recommended to Louis XIV modifications in criminal procedure but limited them to additions and clarifications, not changes in structure. Following five years of discussion, the king implemented these revisions through the ordinance of 1670. The two magistrates involved in the preparation of a criminal case, the lieutenant criminel and the procureur du roi, were given stricter definitions for their respective areas of competence. To eliminate some potential for abuses of procedure, new requirements of form were imposed. The court panels,

---

2. Adhémar Esmein, *Histoire de la procédure criminelle en France, et spécialement de la procédure inquisitoire depuis le XIIIe siècle jusqu'à nos jours* (Paris, 1882), translated by John Simpson as *A History of Continental Criminal Procedure with Special Reference to France* (Boston, 1913), 121–79. See also John A. Carey, *Judicial Reform in France Before the Revolution of 1789* (Cambridge, Mass., 1981), 12–23. The best summary and bibliography of current work is Philippe Robert and René Lévy, "Histoire et question pénale," *Revue d'histoire moderne et contemporaine*, XXXII (1985), 481–526.

largely unregulated before, acquired specific rules for composition, verdicts, and appeals.

The 1670 ordinance unambiguously asserted the state's public prosecutorial function. A victim could seek vengeance only through monetary damages, and in doing so, he made himself liable for all the expenses of the judicial proceedings, though he could demand reimbursement in his action against the accused. If there were no partie civile, the state paid the costs of justice. Because the available funds could support only a few prosecutions, the lieutenant criminel had the discretion not to pursue an accusation if the victim refused to act as partie civile. When the lieutenant criminel did undertake an information, he now had to maintain more careful records. His presence with a *greffier* (an official clerk of court) was obligatory at all interrogations. The 1670 ordinance prescribed the oath administered to the witness, the form of the questions, the manner of reading the depositions drawn by the greffier, and even a prohibition of interlineations and the ratification of erasures. If the information justified an arrest or summons, the lieutenant criminel was to inform the procureur du roi, who had the responsibility for ordering it. The two magistrates therefore had to work together early in the case. Once summoned or arrested, the accused had to be interrogated by the lieutenant criminel within twenty-four hours. Otherwise, the conduct of the information, interrogations, and confrontations was not altered from the ordinance of 1539. When these procedures were completed, the case was said to have been *instruit* (examined), and from that appellation, the lieutenant criminel came to be called the *juge d'instruction* (examining magistrate).

The procureur du roi received the instruction of the case and prepared his written petitions for charges and sentences. The instruction next passed to the panel of conseillers, one of whom was designated the *juge rapporteur* (reporting magistrate) to summarize it for the others. The 1670 ordinance made this written summation mandatory and granted the juge rapporteur the power to order the *question préparatoire* (preparatory torture) to elicit a confession if the evidence appeared heavily weighted toward guilt. The court panel, which the ordinance specified as three conseillers for a trial at the original jurisdiction, seven for an appeal, then considered the written documents of the case and interrogated the accused. If the conseillers decided for conviction, they could not impose the maximum penalty unless the verdict was passed by a majority of two votes (and thus had been unanimous at the initial trial). If the panel voted

The Criminal Procedure

against conviction, it chose among three possible judgments. An outright acquittal declared the accusation baseless and permitted the accused to bring suit against any partie civile. A finding of *mise hors de cour* (putting out of court) was an acquittal through lack of proof and left the accused under suspicion and with no right to seek damages. The decision *plus ample information* meant a strong suspicion of guilt and compelled the accused to remain in custody for a period while further investigation took place. The 1670 ordinance provided a basis for appealing all decisions of criminal procedure, and appeal was automatic in any serious condemnation (imposition of death or corporal punishment). For the accused, an appeal offered the possibility of a defense, because the procedure did not necessarily require secrecy or forbid counsel. But the procureur du roi could also appeal if he thought the sentence too lenient, and the partie civile could appeal an award it considered too small.

When evaluating the evidence of a case, the court panel invoked the theory of proof—standards for conviction that had evolved since the Middle Ages. In the feudal courts, proof was uncomplicated. If the accused confessed, he was guilty; if he claimed innocence, he could be convicted only through defeat in a judicial duel or through the testimony of two eyewitnesses. During the thirteenth century, jurists began to burden this simplicity with complications. Proof, it was argued, had to be demonstrated in two stages. The first step was the establishment of the *corpus delicti*, the fact that a crime had actually occurred. This proof was supplied through physical evidence (such as a body with wounds in a murder case) or through technical knowledge (such as from a physician in a poisoning case). The second step was to ascertain the guilt of the accused, and for that, a confession was no longer regarded as enough, because it might be extorted through force or contrived by skillfully manipulating responses from an interrogation. Instead, evidence for guilt was divided into three classes—complete proof, proximate presumptions, and remote presumptions. *Complete proof* could come only from two eyewitnesses whose competence and objectivity were unchallenged or from documentary evidence expressly mentioning the crime and authenticated or signed by the accused. Complete proof obliged the panel to condemn. The testimony of a single eyewitness, a document not acknowledged by the accused but attributed to him by an expert, an extrajudicial confession denied by the accused but confirmed by two competent witnesses—such were *proximate presumptions*, also called "half-proofs." By themselves, proximate presumptions, however numerous, were not sufficient for a conviction in a serious case, though they might be so in a less serious one. But the addition of a confession to proximate presumptions was the equivalent of complete proof, and the acceptability of the *question préparatoire* derived from that equation. The 1670 ordinance permitted the *question préparatoire* only when the proximate presumptions were strong, but the testimony of a single witness could meet that qualification. The conseillors could also consider *remote presumptions*, which might be based on evidence as circumstantial as the relations of the accused with his neighbors or the tremor of his voice. Unsupported, remote presumptions were inadequate for a conviction but could be the basis for a judgment of *plus ample information.*

Through its additions and clarifications the 1670 ordinance brought a greater uniformity to the practice of criminal justice: The *process* of the procedure was standardized, at least in theory. The lieutenants criminels were specifically forbidden to delegate the duties of interrogation. The designation of forms and the presence of a greffier ensured some measure of fairness for the accused during the instruction of the case. Tighter rules were applied to the deliberations and pronouncements of the court panels, and the evolution in the theory of proof that guided them became statutory. The ordinance was unfortunately silent about how the *question préparatoire* was to be applied and provided no classification of penalties, leaving each jurisdiction to establish for itself the measure of pain and suffering to be inflicted upon the accused and the condemned.

Had he seen it in practice, the system would have caused Colbert some dismay. The most sincere effort to make the documents of justice standard and accurate had to founder on the lack of training for greffiers, some of whom could barely take notes during the interrogations and had to prepare a haphazard transcript later. Bribery subverted the secrecy of the extraordinary procedure: A jailer or greffier could inform an accused of the charges against him; some jailers even arranged for an accused to meet with legal counsel. Although the ordinance threatened the nullity of a prosecution in which the prescribed forms were violated, lieutenants criminels delegated duties or assumed the responsibility of a procureur du roi in ordering an arrest. Court panels compromised the objectivity of their deliberations by permitting the lieutenant criminel to act as the juge rapporteur. Worst of all, criminal justice was fatally handicapped by the chronic shortage of money necessary for it to function effectively. The lieutenants criminels could open informations for only a small number of the cases that came to their attention. If there was no partie civile to assume the costs, there could often be no case. Because justice could not be certain, it had to be severely exemplary; thus the threat of torture and the promise of cruel afflictive punishments for the condemned. In spirit as well as structure, the ordinance of 1670 was not far removed from that of 1539.[3]

The practice of the system in rural France can be glimpsed from a recent study of two *sénéchaussées* in the Périgord, Libourne and Bazas. Funds were so short that magistrates could prosecute at state expense fewer than a quarter of the cases that came to their attention. The choice fell on those crimes that most threatened the early modern sense of public order (homicide, vagabondage, highway robbery, and larceny involving livestock or articles from a church) and public morality (infanticide, bestiality, and the rape of a minor). Prosecutions for crimes regarded less gravely (other sexual or moral offenses, physical assault, verbal outrage, and most thefts) depended upon the participation of a partie civile to assume the costs, and the threat of suit for reparation if the verdict were outright acquittal. Under the circumstances, there was not much incentive to report any but the most serious or repeated crimes. Many rural hamlets were far from a court seat, and peasants were reluctant to deal with royal officials, whether financial, military, or judicial. They preferred personal revenge and turned to the law only if that failed. For some minor crimes, they arranged mediation through a notary or a priest for an out-of-court settlement, with the threat of filing charges held as an inducement.

Most criminals were arrested *en flagrant délit* or because of a *clameur publique*. If victims did not report other offenses, official justice seldom learned of them. When a serious crime was discovered but no witnesses stepped forward, the magistrates had little means of inquiry. The undermanned *maréchaussée* could not provide even an effective rural constabulary, much less conduct criminal investigations. The lieutenant criminel might order a *monitoire*, under which, on three consecutive Sundays, priests warned from the pulpit that anyone withholding knowledge about a crime would be excommunicated. But the result was often a wave of unrelated denunciations, and in some parts of France peasants believed that the reading of a *monitoire* would cause hail to destroy their crops.

3. Esmein, *Continental Criminal Procedure*, 183–285.

Once an arrest was made, justice proceeded slowly. In Libourne and Bazas, the average length of time between the filing of a complaint and a final judgment of guilt or innocence was 310 days, though there was enormous variation. One trial for murder lasted almost eleven years, whereas another took only four days, certainly the result of an apprehension *en flagrant délit*. The overall conviction rate of 12 percent in criminal cases is difficult to evaluate. The figure is artificially low because the accused often settled out of court with a partie civile instead of waiting for a definitive verdict. For cases in which the state commonly prosecuted, the rate was much higher—47.2 percent for homicide, for instance. At least in these two jurisdictions, the magistrates were extremely cautious about ordering the *question préparatoire*. At Libourne, in 717 criminal cases involving 1,529 defendants between 1696 and 1780, there was only a single application. Instead of requiring torture, the court elected to impose the lesser penalties permitted when complete proof was unavailable but proximate presumptions were strong.[4]

The depiction of criminal justice in the eighteenth century is not altered greatly when the view is shifted to the most urban of settings, the court of the Châtelet in Paris. Because the magistrates were conveniently close and the capital had the rudiments of an effective police force, the option of personal revenge appears to have had less appeal to victims, and the number of crimes reported out of the total committed was probably greater. But the salient features of the criminal procedure were the same as in rural France: prosecutions limited by the availability of funds or the presence of a partie civile, long delays, and, particularly after midcentury, the relative absence of preparatory torture.[5]

The 1670 ordinance assumed torture to be an integral element in the discovery and prosecution of crime, an assumption that matched the public temper of its time. Even the refined sensibilities of the Marquise de Sévigné were not offended, and in her famous letters she wrote of torture unconcernedly. The Enlightenment altered this

4. Julius R. Ruff, *Crime, Justice, and Public Order in Old Regime France: The Sénéchaussées of Libourne and Bazas, 1696–1789* (London, 1984), 44–58.
5. Porphyre Petrovitch [pseud.], "Recherches sur la criminalité à Paris dans la seconde moitié du XVIIIe siècle," in André Abbiateci *et al.*, *Crimes et criminalité en France sous l'Ancien Régime, 17e et 18e siècles*, Cahiers des Annales, XXXIII (Paris, 1971), 187–261. Porphyre Petrovitch is the pseudonym of a group of students who carried out a research project on the records of the court of the Châtelet in Paris under the direction of François Billacois.

supposition within cultivated circles. Led by Baron de Montesquieu, himself chief justice of the parlement at Bordeaux, the philosophes condemned as unreasonable (the key criticism) a criminal procedure in which the prosecution counted for everything and the defense for nothing. They found in the Roman republic and England, respectively, their favorite classical and modern societies, a procedure with public trials, a free defense, and judgment by jurors. Beccaria's *Dei delitti e delle pene* (1764), which appeared in French late in 1765, had a significant influence through its cogent criticism of early modern judicial practices, especially secrecy and torture. Voltaire, engaged by his intervention in the Calas and La Barre cases, supplied the telling anecdotes that accomplish as much as careful reasoning. Although some jurists mounted a justification of traditional methods, Louis XVI acknowledged the need for reform, and on August 24, 1780, he prohibited ordering the *question préparatoire*. During the next six years, public opinion was incited by a series of grisly judicial decisions that betrayed an arrogant cruelty. Sensing a popular issue to use in its struggle against the pretensions of the parlements, the monarchy prepared further modifications in criminal procedure that the king announced during the *lit de justice* of May 8, 1788. The use of the *sellette* and the infliction of torture after conviction to wring additional confessions and the names of accomplices were forbidden. At the level of appeal (that is, before the parlements), capital punishment could no longer be imposed without a majority of three judges, and capital sentences would by right come under royal review. All verdicts were to be made public—if for conviction, specifying the crimes; if for acquittal, printed and posted at the expense of the procureur du roi or the partie civile.

Issued twenty years earlier, these royal reforms might have been sufficient, but by 1788, the very system established through the ordinances of 1539 and 1670 had come under question. The cahiers de doléances, drawn up early the following year during the elections for the Estates General, called for changes in criminal procedure that represented not reform but revolution. The request that all torture, the *sellette*, and the *serment* of the accused be abolished was expected and had been largely answered. But the cahiers also asked for open proceedings, for bail in all but serious crimes, for the right of legal counsel for the accused, and for that counsel to have an equal status with the lieutenant criminel in the preparation of the instruction. And as the most fundamental innovation, lay jurors were proposed to evaluate guilt or innocence, leaving to the panel of judges only the imposition of sentence.[6] In the crucible of the next ten years, when the French Revolution recast every aspect of administration, these petitions from the cahiers would be swirled and mixed in different combinations, among themselves and with elements of the traditional system.

The Revolution's first experiment with criminal procedure came in the decree of October 8–9, 1789, which substantially modified the rules for instruction under the 1670 ordinance by permitting counsel for the accused and ending the secrecy of proceedings. During the information process, when the lieutenant criminel verified the complaint and decided whether an arrest was justified, two *adjoints*, citizens appointed by their municipalities and sworn to confidence, would serve as representatives of the public to prevent judicial abuse. After the information was completed, their role ended, but if the lieutenant criminel asked for an arrest, all further instruction of the case was open to anyone. Once arrested or summoned, the accused was informed of the complaint against him. He was permitted the legal counsel of his choice, and if he were indigent, the court appointed one for him. His interrogation before the lieutenant criminel was not under oath, and the questioning of any witnesses had to be in his presence. The lieutenant criminel was required to provide without charge a summation of all testimony and evidence to the accused and his counsel. Throughout the instruction, the accused could challenge the competency of witnesses, compel the hearing of his own witnesses, and plead justificative facts.

This open instruction, with its provision for the accused to have counsel and to mount a defense from the outset, realized one of the fundamental reforms asked by the philosophes and the cahiers. It was accompanied by less extensive changes in the second phase of the procedure. The lieutenant criminel continued to submit his instruction of the case first to the procureur du roi, who formulated the state's charges, and to any partie civile, who petitioned for damages, and then to the panel of conseillers, who appointed a rapporteur. But when the court convened to consider the summation and the pleadings and to interrogate the accused, the counsel could speak in his behalf. There was an absolute prohibition against the

6. Esmein, *Continental Criminal Procedure*, 351–402; Antoinette Wills, *Crime and Punishment in Revolutionary Paris* (Westport, Conn., 1981), 3–28.

The Criminal Procedure

use of torture or the *sellette*. Although the conseillers could retire to deliberate, they had to announce their verdict publicly. A sentence of death or afflictive punishment required unanimity at the original jurisdiction, and four-fifths and two-thirds, respectively, of the panel on appeal. The theory of proof was left unmentioned. Except for the introduction of counsel to the court's deliberations, these changes essentially recapitulated the royal reforms of the *lit de justice* of May, 1788. Taken as a whole, this first experiment effectively retained the 1670 system as a framework within which specific traditional abuses could be ameliorated. Two years later, by the laws of September 16 and 29, 1791, the Revolution abandoned such a moderate approach and definitively overturned the 1670 system by altering the entire criminal procedure and introducing trial by jury.

This radical departure from French tradition was carefully structured to fit the new territorial administrative units created in 1790. Initial responsibility in the case of a crime fell to the *juge de paix* (justice of the peace), who was installed in each of the approximately 4,700 cantons. His task was to begin a preliminary investigation (essentially an information) whenever a crime was discovered, a victim filed a complaint, or a "virtuous" citizen reported suspicious activity (a *dénonciation civique*). If the juge de paix concluded that probable cause existed against the accused, he ordered an arrest and, as the second stage in the procedure, sent him before the *jury d'accusation* (grand jury) that sat at the *arrondissement* (district) level. A recommendation by the juge de paix to drop charges could be opposed by the victim or the *dénonciateur civique*, who had the right to insist upon a further hearing.

The jury d'accusation, eight male citizens chosen by lot from a list of property owners ("active citizens" as defined in the 1791 constitution), heard cases brought forward from the cantons. These laymen were led by one of the conseillers from the *tribunal civil* (district civil court, of which there were approximately 350), who served as *directeur* of the grand jury for six months in rotation. The directeur received the records of the information and carried out a more extensive investigation, almost an instruction, of his own. If sufficient grounds for prosecution were lacking, he ordered the release of the accused. If they were present, he drew up an *acte d'accusation* (an indictment), a document similar to the summation previously prepared by the juge rapporteur, and placed it before the grand jury, which examined the evidence, heard the witnesses, and decided by a majority vote whether to bind the accused for prosecution.

A *délit* (misdemeanor) was tried before the *tribunal de police correctionnelle* (district police court), composed of (usually) three juges de paix and two lay judges chosen by the local administrative council for their background in legal matters. All *crimes* were sent before the *tribunal criminel* (departmental criminal court). There the role of the public prosecutor was divided between two officials, the *accusateur public* (public accuser), who argued the case against the accused before the court, and the *commissaire du roi* (king's commissioner), who demanded the application of punishment if the accused were found guilty. The bench was made up of four judges, the *président* and three *assesseurs* (presiding judge and associate judges), but they only imposed sentence, because at the tribunal criminel the verdict was rendered by twelve jurors chosen from a list of "active citizens" in a complicated fashion that permitted the accused a large number of peremptory challenges. The trial itself was public and oral, with both the accusateur public and the counsel for the accused presenting evidence and interrogating witnesses. At the conclusion the jurymen were asked to respond yes or no to a series of questions, with their decision based on personal conviction—the theory of legal proofs was repudiated entirely. In a private room, each juror appeared individually before the président, the commissaire du roi, and the jury foreman to swear his vote and to place a white or black ball in a box. After the jurors reassembled, the box was opened and the votes officially counted. Ten votes out of twelve were required for condemnation. The foreman declared the verdict in open court, and there was no basis for appealing this jury decision other than on the misapplication of law or for improper procedure. If the jury found the accused guilty, the panel of judges retired to deliberate and then returned to announce a sentence.

The provisions of the procedure set forth in the laws of September, 1791, were an extraordinary departure from French tradition and went far beyond the most radical petition of the cahiers, trial by jurors. The institution of the jury d'accusation removed from the magistrature the determination of whether a criminal complaint represented a prima facie case and left that to the untutored wisdom of eight laymen. The public prosecutorial function was weakened by the division of its duties between two officials and by the right of private individuals (the victim or the *dénonciateur civique*) to require a further instruction despite the findings of the juge de paix—a direct infringement of the state's sole authority to pursue criminal charges. The conseillers lost their role of deciding facts (which went

The Criminal Procedure

to the trial jury) as well as interpreting law. In the National Assembly the debate over the proposed changes recognized how fundamentally the new procedure differed from the old, but the partially applicable example of England was cited as justification and carried the vote.

This system of criminal justice, like the rest of the Constitution of 1791, was best suited to a period of calm. What followed was war against a coalition of European powers, the fall of the monarchy, the execution of the king, the rapid growth of counterrevolution, and outbreaks of insurrection against the Jacobin government in Paris. On September 17, 1793, the Convention adopted the Law of Suspects, which permitted the arbitrary arrest of anyone whose actions or opinions could be construed as counterrevolutionary. Before the new Revolutionary Tribunals, stern summary justice was imposed for political dissent, and all the more so after the law of 22 Prairial II (June 10, 1794), which made the hearing of witnesses optional and limited the possible verdicts to acquittal and death. Although the intent was to define and punish "political crime," the transgression of procedures affected criminal justice as well. Where rebellion raged, grand juries were "temporarily" replaced by juges d'instruction, and everywhere, rights of the accused were abridged. The Thermidorean Reaction brought an end to the greatest excesses of the Terror—the law of 22 Prairial was repealed on 10 Thermidor II (July 28, 1794)—but the insurrectionary regions continued to be treated exceptionally.

Fifteen months later, as the Convention prepared to adjourn and transfer power to the government of the Directory, it enacted the judicial law of 3 Brumaire IV (October 25, 1795). The legislation was typically Thermidorean—early revolutionary idealism tempered by the experience of the Year II: It maintained most of the 1791 procedure while making adjustments to avoid possible laxity or abuse. The directeur of the jury d'accusation, whose term was reduced from six months to three, was now to hear witnesses in secret during his instruction, though the open testimony before the juges de paix and the grand jury itself remained unchanged. When a case was brought forward from the cantons, the directeur no longer had the authority to order a release on insufficient grounds. If he concluded that the complaint was a *délit*, it could be tried in the district police court, but otherwise he had to place it before the grand jury. The law eliminated the peculiar stipulation permitting a victim or a *dénonciateur civique* to demand hearings and reemphasized the partie civile. Finally, the tribunal criminel gained an additional assesseur (for a total of four), and the président was given the responsibility to interrogate the accused in secret within twenty-four hours of his entering the court's jurisdiction after having been bound over by the jury d'accusation.[7]

During four more years, making a total of a decade, the liberal experimentation with a criminal procedure of open instruction and trial by jury continued, having coincided with (and of course derived from) the crisis of order in France associated with turbulent revolutionary change. Moments of great political passion, internal revolt, and war along the borders generated the chaos in which a concomitant brigandage flourished. The most infamous of the bandits were the so-called *chauffeurs*, who applied fire to the feet of their victims to encourage revelations about hidden treasures, but they had many imitators or worse. The new and inexperienced juges de paix, the time-consuming rules of form, the multiple layers of the instruction, the distracting presence of counsel for the accused, and the often timid citizens serving as grand jurors and trial jurors made an effective response all but impossible. Secrecy and torture, the methods formerly invoked to clothe justice in oppressive and arbitrary robes, had been specifically debarred. Witnesses were afraid to testify, juries afraid to convict. There seemed to be a return to the conditions of late medieval France that had made the 1539 ordinance so welcome.

The call for a restoration of stability and order was answered by the dominion Napoleon Bonaparte established over the Revolution beginning in November, 1799. For when Bonaparte turned to the problems of criminal justice, he reversed many of the changes since 1791 and brought back aspects of the 1670 ordinance. By the law of 27 Ventôse VIII (March 18, 1800), the tribunaux civils were transformed into *tribunaux de première instance* (lower tribunals), each with one or more *cours correctionnelles* (correctional courts) to replace the tribunaux de police correctionnelle. *Délits* were now to be tried before a three-judge panel that determined the verdict and imposed the sentence. At the level of the tribunal criminel, the public prosecutor's office was unified by eliminating the accusateur public and adding his responsibilities to those of the *commissaire du pouvoir exécutif* (the name had been altered after the deposition of Louis XVI). Further legislation on 7 Pluviôse IX (January 27, 1801)

7. Esmein, *Continental Criminal Procedure*, 402–36.

The Criminal Procedure

endowed the new prosecutor with the authority of the ancien régime's procureur du roi: He was to act in the name of the state upon all criminal complaints, captures *en flagrant délit,* and *clameurs publiques.* Any role for the juges de paix except as minor assistants was excluded. The prosecutor had a new power as well, the *mandat de dépôt,* the right to arrest any accused and to imprison him pending a full investigation of the case.

For that investigation, the law of 7 Pluviôse abolished the office of directeur for the jury d'accusation and revived that of the juge d'instruction. He would hear the accused and the witnesses separately and in secret. During the instruction, the accused no longer had the right to counsel and at the outset was not informed of the charge against him. The only concession was the juge d'instruction's duty to provide the accused with affidavits from the witnesses. When the juge d'instruction completed his work, he could order liberty for the accused if the charge appeared unfounded, trial before a cour correctionnelle if the evidence was for a *délit,* or a presentation of the case before the jury d'accusation if the instruction confirmed a *crime.* The commissaire du pouvoir exécutif, but not the accused, could appeal this order. The jury d'accusation heard no oral testimony or argument. The case was introduced entirely through documents. The grand jurors read and then voted—almost always for prosecution because the instruction could not be countered by a defense. This decision bound the accused to be tried before the tribunal criminel, the bench and jury of which were unchanged from 1795. There, the accused finally had the right of counsel and the possibility of proving his innocence.

The weakness of the trial jury was addressed eleven days later by the law of 18 Pluviôse IX (February 7, 1801), which established a special summary court for thirty-two of the departments (the ones where crime was most rampant), with jurisdiction over the cases particularly likely to make a juror's heart timorous: highway robbery, aggravated robbery, grand larceny, arson, seditious assembly, attempts to corrupt soldiers or conscripts, assaults on the recipients of *biens nationaux,* murder by armed groups, and any crime committed by vagabonds or escaped prisoners. The proceedings remained public, with an oral trial and the right to counsel, but the verdict, which was not subject to appeal, would be rendered by an eight-member panel composed of the président and two assesseurs from the tribunal criminel, three military officers holding at least the rank of captain, and two citizens with legal training. As First Consul, Bonaparte alone had the authority to appoint the officers and the citizens. Creation of these special courts was favored even by many supporters of the trial jury because they feared that the institution might become fatally discredited by continued proof of its ineffectiveness.

The retreat from the fundamental reforms in effect since 1791 was demonstrably attributable to the crisis of order. But the debates of the redactors whom Bonaparte assembled in 1805 to draft a revised criminal code revealed considerable sentiment for a return to the spirit of the 1670 ordinance. The version of the code adopted in December, 1808, and made effective on April 28, 1810, established an awkward compromise between the procedures of the ancien régime and the Revolution: a secret, written preliminary instruction, followed by an open, oral trial before a jury.

The law of 7 Pluviôse IX had restored the preparation of a criminal case to the control of two powerful magistrates, their responsibilities clearly separate. The 1808 criminal code confirmed this reversion to the 1670 procedure: The *procureur impérial* (the new title of the commissaire du pouvoir exécutif) formulated the charges, the juge d'instruction investigated them. The instruction was mandatory for all cases in which a *crime* might have been committed, optional for a *délit*. All steps of the investigation belonged to the juge d'instruction alone, and he had to be entrusted with the case as soon as a criminal complaint was lodged—an exception being made for an arrest *en flagrant délit*, when the procureur impérial could initiate the instruction to confirm ephemeral evidence.

The rules of the instruction recalled the 1670 ordinance so completely that a lieutenant criminel of the ancien régime would have been comfortable working within them. The Revolution had granted an accused the right to counsel during the instruction, to know the charges against him, to see the depositions of the witnesses, and even to be present when the witnesses were interrogated. None of these reforms survived in the 1808 code. Assisted only by his greffier, the juge d'instruction separately questioned the accused and the witnesses against him. Although the accused could suggest the hearing of justificative witnesses, the juge d'instruction was not required to call them. The accused could not contest the juge d'instruction's choice of an expert to report on specific evidence and had no right either to confront the expert or to have a counterexpert act officially. The presence of the accused was obligatory at all searches and seizures of his property, and he was entitled to furnish explanations,

The Criminal Procedure

to identify any objects, and to initial the official seals. If he were charged only with a *délit*, had a fixed address and no previous conviction, he *might* be permitted provisional release during the instruction; otherwise, and particularly if the charge were a *crime*, the 1808 code absolutely prohibited it.

In April, 1810, concurrently with the introduction of the revised procedure, Bonaparte abolished the tribunal criminel and in its place created the *cour d'assises* (assizes court), a panel of three justices and a jury of twelve men, convened quarterly in (usually) the departmental capitals. The minister of justice in Paris selected the président (presiding justice) for the cour d'assises from the *cour d'appel* (court of appeals, a creation of the 27 Ventôse VIII law) for the *ressort* (jurisdiction). The chief justice of the cour d'appel chose two *assesseurs* (associate justices) from his conseillers if the cour d'assises were convened in the town that was the seat of the appeals court, and from the *juges* (judges) of the nearest tribunal de première instance if it convened elsewhere.

The grand jury was another casualty of the 1808 code. When the instruction was complete, it was to be reviewed by the *chambre du conseil* (council chamber), a three-member panel made up of two juges from the closest lower tribunal and the juge d'instruction for the case, whose conclusions could hardly be disregarded and were rarely opposed. A finding by the chambre du conseil that the instruction disclosed serious evidence against the accused sent the case before the redactors' substitute for the grand jury, the *chambre des mises en accusation* (indictment court)—five conseillers from the cour d'appel for the *ressort*. After considering the written instruction and a recommendation from the procureur impérial for charges, the indictment court voted either to release the accused, to order him before a lower tribunal to be tried for a *délit*, or to issue a decree of *renvoi*, binding the accused for trial before the cour d'assises. The chambre des mises en accusation also functioned as an appeal board for complaints by the accused against the juge d'instruction and decided whether to permit provisional liberty for an accused meeting the qualifications.

After the chambre des mises en accusation issued a decree of *renvoi*, the procureur général (the attorney general of the cour d'appel) drew up the state's final acte d'accusation (bill of indictment). The rights of defense for the accused began formally only at that point in the procedure. Within the next twenty-four hours, the président of the cour d'assises was required to interview the accused in secret. Although the interview often became an interrogation, the président had to fulfill solemn magisterial responsibilities: to present the accused with a copy of the acte d'accusation, to inform him officially that he could retain a legal counsel or have the court appoint one, and to advise him that the decree of *renvoi* could be contested before the *Cour de Cassation* (the court of final appeal, created in 1790). During the time left before the trial, the accused had free communication with his counsel, and the defense received, without charge, a duplicate of each document, deposition, and affidavit used during the instruction. These provisions for the defense were guaranteed only when the charge was a *crime*, but they were often observed for the more serious *délits*.

Once the trial began, the rights of the defense were, at least theoretically, the same as the rights of the prosecution. Subject to the rules of procedure and the decisions of the presiding justice, both called witnesses, introduced evidence, and addressed the court. The defense had the last word and presumably the last impression on the jury. The prefect in each department drew up a highly restricted list of the reputedly upright and stern from which the jurors were chosen. The lower classes were systematically excluded. Challenge to a potential juror by the defense was sharply limited. During the trial, jurors were permitted to see the documents and other evidence involved in the case but not the transcribed interrogations from the instruction of either the accused or the witnesses, for they were required to testify orally or not at all. An exception was made if the declarations in court varied from a previous written deposition, and this discrepancy could be brought to the jury's attention. When the prosecution and the defense rested their cases, the jurors were told that they should decide the verdict on the basis of "moral proof," as ordained by Article 342 of the 1808 code.

> The law does not ask the jury to account for the means by which they are convinced. It does not prescribe to them rules on which they must particularly base the fulness and sufficiency of proof. It enjoins them to interrogate themselves in silence and meditation, and to seek in the sincerity of their conscience for the impression made upon their reason by the proofs brought against the accused and his pleas in defense. The law does not say to them: "You will hold as true such a fact attested by such and such a number of witnesses"; . . . it only asks them this one question, comprising the whole measure of their duties: "Are you thoroughly convinced [Avez-vous la conviction intime]?"

This verdict was definitive: It was not subject to appeal except on issues of law, and if for acquittal, it could not be tainted by a finding of *mise hors de cour* or *plus ample information*.[8]

Scholars of comparative law emphasize that the Anglo-Saxon system of criminal justice is primarily "accusatory," whereas the French system is "inquisitorial." Under Anglo-Saxon procedures the truth of a charge must be established in open court where the defendant stands innocent until proven guilty. The basic principle of the French system is that a pretrial inquiry, the instruction, is to place before the court all the facts concerning both the offense and the person alleged to have committed it. The accused cannot be compelled to testify before the juge d'instruction, but an innocent accused has an obvious interest in permitting the facts in his favor to be fully investigated. A refusal to cooperate is viewed with suspicion because the primary object of the instruction is to avoid the trial of an innocent man. Whatever the conclusions of the juge d'instruction, a jury must be convinced that the charges are true. But the juge d'instruction's recommendation of an indictment after a detailed investigation tends to make the court and the jury regard the accused as guilty until proven innocent.

The pretrial investigation was the result of an intricate collaboration among the Police judiciaire, the juge d'instruction, and the public prosecutor, who after the Napoleonic reorganizations might best be designated the district attorney. Officially titled the procureur impérial during the First and Second Empires, the procureur royal under the Restoration and the July Monarchy, and, after September 4, 1870, the procureur de la République, the district attorney directed the *parquet*—the prosecutorial functions—within the jurisdiction of a tribunal de première instance. The term arose from the placement of the prosecutor as well as the judges on the parquet floor laid down for the court during the Middle Ages, with everyone else relegated to the stone blocks beyond. As such, his responsibilities were large. He received all complaints of alleged offenses from the public and from the police and, through his authority to direct the Police judiciaire or to assume police powers himself, took the steps necessary to investigate these complaints as well as anything unusual,

---

8. *Ibid.*, 437–527, the translation of Article 342 from p. 516; Andrier, *Intervention du défenseur*, 59–66.

such as sudden deaths, fires, and explosions. Once having investigated, he had wide discretion to overlook an offense or to declare it a *délit*, but if he concluded that a *crime* had been committed, he was required to turn over the inquiry to a juge d'instruction. When *délits* came to trial before the cour correctionnelle and *contraventions* (misdemeanors of a very minor sort) before the *tribunal de police* (police court), the procureur or one of his *substituts* (assistant prosecutors) presented the case for the state, petitioned for a specific sentence, assured that the sentence was applied in case of a conviction, and could appeal a verdict of acquittal. There were also duties outside criminal law, particularly to conduct certain affairs of minors and the incapacitated, to participate in the oversight of avocats (barristers) belonging to the local bar, and to act on protests from the public about overzealous police. To assure the carrying out of these functions, the procureur was on call *en permanence.*

The procureur was appointed by the minister of justice and was under the immediate supervision of the *procureur général* (attorney general) for the *ressort*. He was expected to consult with his superiors about important investigations, and all the more so if political complications might be involved. For cases of a certain type or for an individual trial, the ministry could require that the procureur adopt a specific argument or tone in his written briefs and petitions to the court. He was free to present his own opinion in the oral argument, but to depart from the line established for him was to risk dismissal or at least the disapproval that would retard or eliminate further promotion. Within this web of responsibility and subordination, the procureur had to maneuver carefully.

His position was most straightforward in the *enquête flagrante,* an investigation undertaken by the procureur when the offense was reported to him immediately upon *discovery* (no matter when it was committed). In this situation the procureur was vested with wide powers usually reserved to a juge d'instruction. After visiting the scene of the offense, he could order police inquiries, searches, seizures, and the expert examination of evidence. If a suspect had been captured *en flagrant délit,* the procureur signed a mandat de dépôt, ordering confinement to jail. If there were merely presumptions against the suspect, the procureur was permitted to order arrest and detainment (*garde à vue*) for twenty-four hours, renewable once, to facilitate questioning by the police. When the garde à vue expired, the procureur could either free the suspect and drop the investigation; cite him to appear in police court charged with a *contraven-*

tion; classify the offense as a *délit* and send the suspect before the cour correctionnelle; or issue a *réquisitoire introductif,* which declared that evidence of a *crime* was present and that the case was to be examined by a juge d'instruction. If no suspect was immediately apparent, the procureur might pursue his investigation for as long as two or three weeks if the Police judiciaire was making progress. But after that period he had to decide whether to conclude the inquiries or to turn them over to a juge d'instruction for continuation.

The procureur's authority was more ambiguous in other situations. When the report of an offense was so delayed that an enquête flagrante could not be justified, the procureur was forced to pursue his investigation as either an *enquête préliminaire* or an *enquête officieuse.* If as an *enquête préliminaire,* the procureur's powers were distinctly limited. He could require expert examinations but had to have written permission from any suspect for searches and seizures and could not order a garde à vue. Without the cooperation of the suspect, the only way to make further inquiries was to transfer the investigation to a juge d'instruction. The right for any victim of an offense (or his heirs or dependents) to file suit as the partie civile against the suspect raised further limitations. Even if the procureur did not believe that a complete investigation would reveal the commission of a crime, the partie civile could insist on the appointment of a juge d'instruction by furnishing a deposit, returned if the juge d'instruction recommended an indictment, to cover judicial expenses. An *enquête officieuse*—extralegal inquiries carried out on the condition that they have no official character—was even further hedged about with restrictions. The procureur proceeded in this manner when a preliminary view was necessary, particularly in "difficult" cases in which discretion might be fatally limited by a formal investigation. The information was supplied by individual agents of the Police judiciaire, who ensured that their accounts did not enter the records by submitting them as *rapports* (summaries) rather than as *procès-verbaux* (official reports).[9]

The formal attributes of the procureur's office endowed him with significant coercive powers. The prosecution of *délits* and *contra-*

---

9. A. V. Sheehan, *Criminal Procedure in Scotland and France: A Comparative Study* (Edinburgh, 1975), 9–43; Franck Duvoisin Mazorie, *La Liberté individuelle dans le procès pénal* (Montpellier, 1913), 70–112; Louis Caullet, *Des fonctions du procureur de la République et de ses auxiliaires au point de vue de la police judiciaire* (Paris, 1909); Henri Nadau, *Des enquêtes officieuses dans l'instruction criminelle* (Trévoux, 1913), 9–63, 309–14.

ventions belonged to him alone, and he initiated the investigation of *crimes*. Through the garde à vue, he could direct a potentially fierce repression under which suspects were entirely at the mercy of the police. The use of the enquête officieuse permitted him some latitude to establish the setting of a subsequent official investigation. Even so, his authority was limited in comparison with that of the juge d'instruction. One of the cherished anecdotes of nineteenth-century French baccalaureate examinations involves the question "Who is the most powerful man in France?" Candidates invariably replied, "The president of the Republic." The correct answer was the juge d'instruction. Before the relatively minor limitations imposed by the law of December 8, 1897, the juge d'instruction could order searches, seizures, and arrests without fear of being countermanded. He operated as a one-man grand jury for crimes, and during the unlimited time that he conducted his instruction of the case, he could keep all of the details secret from the defense and hold the accused in custody, without access to an attorney, for as long as he chose. After 1897 the juge d'instruction had to bring charges against those he arrested within twenty-four hours (a French version of habeas corpus), had to advise those arrested of their right to legal counsel and provide summaries of his investigations to the defense, and could hold an accused incommunicado (except for visits by his attorney) for only ten days (renewable once).

When the investigation by the Police judiciaire and the procureur indicated that a *crime* had been committed, the procureur prepared a réquisitoire introductif, naming, if possible, a suspect. The *président* (chief judge) of the tribunal de première instance, upon the unofficial recommendation of the procureur, then appointed one of the juges d'instruction for the jurisdiction to the case. Once appointed, he could not be removed except upon the extremely rare demand of the procureur supported by the président. A juge d'instruction was frequently asked to assume the inquiries into a serious *délit* because of its potential complications and because of his authority to issue a warrant maintaining the suspect in custody. During his instruction of the case, the juge had to maintain coordination with the Police judiciaire, who carried out the searches, seizures, and arrests that he ordered and who were theoretically to take no independent action without his approval, and with the procureur, who had to issue a *réquisitoire aux fins d'inculpation* whenever a formal designation of an accused (*inculpé*) was made. If the investigation revealed offenses not connected to the original *crime* or *délit* for which the juge d'in-

The Criminal Procedure

struction was appointed, he had to receive a separate commission to pursue them. And if there were a partie civile, the juge d'instruction had to investigate the civil law aspects of the case, because any award for damages would be determined at the conclusion of a trial on criminal charges.

As soon as the investigation produced an inculpé, the juge d'instruction compelled his appearance for interrogation if he were not already in jail because of a mandat de dépôt from the procureur during an enquête flagrante. When the severest penalty was a fine and when the danger of flight was limited, the juge d'instruction could issue a *mandat de comparution* (summons to appear). But if the offense was punishable by imprisonment, the inculpé had to be taken into custody through a *mandat d'amener* (arrest warrant), though the law adhered to the old French tradition that an arrest could not be made at a private residence after 8 P.M. or before 6 A.M. A *mandat d'arrêt* (fugitive arrest warrant) became applicable if the inculpé could not be located and was at least presumably seeking to avoid apprehension. Once in custody, he was questioned briefly (but not under oath, the *serment* having disappeared forever during the Revolution) by the juge d'instruction, who decided whether to issue a mandat de dépôt committing the inculpé to jail for the duration of the instruction. The 1808 code prohibited provisional liberty unless the charge was a *délit* and the inculpé's present and past met stringent conditions. This rigor was eased considerably by the law of July 14, 1865, which granted an inculpé charged with a *délit* the absolute right to provisional liberty with no imposition of bail unless he had been previously convicted of a crime or condemned to prison for more than a year, and authorized the juge d'instruction to permit provisional liberty at his discretion—usually exercised with great reluctance and only after consulting with the procureur and any partie civile—if the charge was a *crime*. The juge d'instruction could also pronounce the *mise au secret* for the inculpé (hold him incommunicado), which, under the same law of July 14, 1865, required a renewal of the order every ten days and a report to the procureur if it was to be continued.

As the juge d'instruction carried out his investigation, he directed experts to examine critical evidence and ordered the Police judiciaire to conduct searches and seizures under the formal title *commissions rogatoires*. In his office he interrogated witnesses under oath, and when the testimony was in conflict, he might confront two or more of them. During these interrogations, a *procès-verbal* was maintained by a greffier, to whom the juge d'instruction dictated both the question and what of the witness's reply he wanted to have retained. The procureur (and the attorney for the partie civile if applicable) could suggest areas of inquiry and even specific questions for the witnesses, but the juge d'instruction alone determined the conduct of the investigation. When he questioned the inculpé, he confronted him with reports, evidence, and witnesses, encouraging him to offer rebuttal and to present his own version. The inculpé could not be compelled to make any statement at all, but the juge d'instruction counseled him that a refusal to tell what he knew would inevitably be viewed with suspicion, both during the instruction and at a later trial. Without the contribution of the inculpé, the dossier would be weighted heavily, perhaps too heavily, by the "facts" of the evidence. The juge d'instruction sought to add balance through an exploration of the inculpé's background and character that might reveal motivation; he was seeking not merely to solve the case but to comprehend it, and to assess the guilt of the inculpé not only for the *crimes* or *délits* charged but for his entire life and within the context of that life.[10]

This description was an idealized portrait of the juge d'instruction at work: Despite the similarity of functions, he was no longer the repressive lieutenant criminel of the ancien régime, but an ingenious, sedulous investigator, of unquestioned probity, sifting through manifold explanations to deduce the truth in all of its complexity. A modern critic, Louis Casamayor, responds that the juge d'instruction found (and finds) "only the truth he *wants* to discover." For the juge d'instruction was a relatively junior member of the judicial bureaucracy, the rank itself not a high one and the magistrate fairly young. A vast difference existed between the ideal of an impartial instruction and the reality of a magistrate who believed, most often correctly, that his future promotion depended on demonstrating rigor toward crime by recommending a high percentage of indictments.[11]

Confounding the supposition of justice with the actuality of prose-

---

10. Sheehan, *Criminal Procedure*, 43–58; Esmein, *Continental Criminal Procedure*, 543–45; Mazorie, *La Liberté individuelle*, 43–57, 69; Maurice Deis, *De la délégation des actes de l'instruction criminelle et des commissions rogatoires en droit pénal* (Lyon, 1895).

11. Louis Casamayor, *Les Juges* (Paris, 1956), 77; Herbert W. Halton, *Etude sur la procédure criminelle en Angleterre et en France* (Paris, 1898), 64–86; Benjamin F. Martin, "The Courts, the Magistrature, and Promotions in Third Republic France, 1871–1914," *American Historical Review*, LXXXVII (1982), 977–1009.

cution, Odilon Barrot wrote in 1871, "compromised the liberty, the honor, and even the life" of a French citizen. Barrot, a liberal under the July Monarchy and a leader of the "banquet campaign" that produced the 1848 revolution, urged the new Third Republic to end abuses within the judicial system tolerated by previous regimes of the nineteenth century. In fact, the Second Empire had already made a start on criminal procedure with the law of July 14, 1865, which slightly limited the extraordinary powers of the juge d'instruction in matters of preventive detention and the mise au secret. The Third Republic did not turn to this question until October, 1878, when Jules Dufaure, premier and minister of justice, created a commission of jurisconsults to frame legislation revising the process of instruction in a less restrictive, more public manner. Their report of November, 1879, recommended 213 changes in the regulations governing the juges d'instruction, which collectively would effect three principal reforms: the inculpé could have legal counsel beside him during any interrogation by the juge d'instruction and would be permitted access to all documents pertaining to the instruction (a significant step toward what United States courts define as "discovery"); the inculpé and his counsel could require the juge d'instruction to pursue inquiries and to question witnesses tending to disprove the charges under investigation; and the inculpé could challenge the methods and conduct of the juge d'instruction by appealing to the chambre des mises en accusation. Dufaure presented these proposals to the legislature, but obstinate disagreement prevented adoption despite intermittent consideration for five years between 1879 and 1884. The Senate insisted on deleting the right of an inculpé to counsel during interrogation, but the Chamber of Deputies adamantly refused to compromise the original formula in any fashion. Perhaps during this period of economic malaise and acrimonious debate over Jules Ferry's imperial adventures, judicial reform did not generate sufficient public support.[12]

An opportune moment to revive the issue did not arrive until nearly thirteen years later, in the spring of 1897, when publicity about abusive instructions incited opinion much as the egregious cruelty of the parlements had done in the 1780s. Before the Chamber

12. Odilon Barrot, *De l'organisation judiciaire en France* (Paris, 1871), 186. For similar sentiments about the judicial system from another prominent reformer, see Lucien-Anatole Prévost-Paradol, *La France nouvelle* (Paris, 1868), 180–84. On the Dufaure proposals see Esmein, *Continental Criminal Procedure*, 547–55, and Andrier, *Intervention du défenseur*, 78–88.

of Deputies on April 5, René Viviani, a Republican Socialist, eloquently denounced the 1808 criminal code as a barely modernized version of the 1670 ordinance and aroused righteous indignation by describing a recent case tried before the cour d'assises of the Seine. In August, 1896, an old woman had been found murdered at her house, and on the basis of slight evidence the police arrested a certain Pélissier, who had lodged with her, and his mistress, a Mme Choquard. The juge d'instruction for the case, a magistrate named Danion, ordered the mise au secret for both and renewed it every ten days for a period of fourteen weeks. He then released Choquard but kept Pélissier in custody for fifteen weeks more while he completed an instruction charging him with *assassinat* (premeditated murder). The chambre des mises en accusation endorsed Danion's findings and ordered a trial before the cour d'assises. When the proceedings began in late March, 1897, Choquard testified that during the weeks she had been held mise au secret, agents of the Police judiciaire, perhaps with the knowledge of the juge d'instruction, sought her testimony against Pélissier, alternately threatening her with violence or promising a bribe. This accusation, made under oath in open court, so shocked the *avocat général* (solicitor general) directing the prosecution that he refused to proceed further and asked the jury to return a verdict of acquittal.

Calling Pélissier hardly the only victim of judicial abuse, Viviani also cited the example of Félix Martin, who was starved by his warders until he confessed to charges subsequently rejected by a jury, and of a juge d'instruction at Bayeux known to beat inculpés and witnesses as he interrogated them. Henri Mougeot, a Radical Republican (Gauche démocratique), then contributed the pathetic story of a Parisian *négociant* (wholesale merchant) arrested in error and ordered mise au secret. The juge d'instruction for the case neglected to interrogate him not merely within the required twenty-four hours but for five days, leaving the man without knowledge of the charges against him and in such despair that he committed suicide. Mougeot asked for an opening of instructions to public view and insisted that the minister of justice, Jean-Baptiste Darlan, act decisively to end abuses of procedure.

Darlan replied that the cabinet of Jules Méline, in which he served, favored reforms similar to those recommended by Dufaure in 1879. This stimulus led Ernest Constans, the chairman of the Senate's committee on judicial matters, to draft a law incorporating the main elements of the Dufaure proposal and adding others that appeared particularly relevant after the Viviani and Mougeot revelations. The senators approved this bill on June 10 by the overwhelming vote of 226 to 4, as the *rapporteur* (floor leader), Jean Dupuy, emphasized the cabinet's backing. Action in the Chamber of Deputies was delayed by an adjournment from July to October, but the deputies adopted it on November 12 by a voice vote—an indication that opposition was all but nonexistent. Félix Faure, as president of the Republic, signed the legislation on December 8, 1897, and it came to bear that date as its appellation.[13]

The new law made six important changes in the rules for a criminal instruction. First, as soon as an individual was formally designated an inculpé, he had to be warned of his right to remain silent during any interrogation before the juge d'instruction and of his right to legal counsel, the one of his choice if he could afford the fee or a counsel appointed for him if he were indigent. No questioning about the specific details of the case could begin until counsel for the inculpé had been arranged. Second, because the inculpé could have his counsel with him during every interrogation, the juge d'instruction had to give the counsel twenty-four hours' notice beforehand. Physical abuse of the inculpé became much less likely, and he could no longer be subjected to interrogation without warning. Third, though a prohibition against speaking without the consent of the juge d'instruction or indicating in any fashion how the inculpé should respond to a question closely circumscribed the conduct of the counsel during the interrogation, the defense gained important new advantages. The formal transcript of the interrogation had to carry notation of a refusal to permit comments by the counsel, and inquiries suggested by the counsel to the juge d'instruction were made part of the official documents of the case, thus all but ensuring that he would act upon them, because his refusal could be appealed to the chambre des mises en accusation. The greffier was required to provide the counsel with a copy of the transcript no later than the evening of the day on which the inculpé was interrogated and to notify the counsel of any order to the Police judiciaire issued as part of the investigation. All of the evidence and documents, formerly held in secret, were now open to the counsel's inspection in the office of the juge d'instruction. Fourth, the juge d'instruction could impose the

13. The text of the law appears in JO, December 10, 1897. For the discussions and votes see *JOC*, Débats parlementaires, April 5, November 12, 1897, and *Journal Officiel*, Sénat (hereinafter cited as *JOS*), Débats parlementaires, June 10, 1897.

mise au secret upon an inculpé, but the order was limited to a tenday period, renewable only once, and could not apply to the counsel, who was free to visit the inculpé as frequently as necessary. Fifth, anyone arrested through a *mandat* from a juge d'instruction had to be interrogated by him, or by a substitute when the arrest was made in another jurisdiction, within twenty-four hours; if this was not done, he was to be released and the responsible magistrate punished. Sixth, a juge d'instruction could not sit as a member of a cour correctionnelle (as frequently occurred in provincial areas where the judicial bureaucracy was thin) in judgment of a case he had instructed and declared a *délit*.[14]

The law of December 8, 1897, did not eliminate all the abuses present in too many criminal investigations. The right to counsel, and with it the implied guarantee against physical intimidation, did not apply to questioning by the police, who continued to treat suspects who fell into their hands with customary brutality. There was no limitation on the juge d'instruction's competence to order searches and seizures, and a proposal in 1909 to restrict them to the possessions of an inculpé never attracted broad support. The position on provisional liberty from 1865 remained unaltered, leaving the juge d'instruction, an obviously interested party, to rule on every case involving a *crime*. The 1897 reforms did enable the counsel to present a preliminary defense during the process of instruction, but under confining conditions. However much he might advise the inculpé in advance, once the interrogation began, the counsel was little more than an observer. He could not commission experts to dispute the reports from the experts of the juge d'instruction. Barred altogether from the juge d'instruction's interrogation of witnesses, he was prevented from asking them the questions most important to the defense and had to rely on depositions for their testimony. An unscrupulous juge d'instruction could hear some witnesses "informally" and avoid the requirement for a *procès-verbal* and its inclusion among the documents of the case. The only solution to this problem of discovery in a system where the pretrial investigation remained so completely in the hands of the juge d'instruction was to permit the counsel to be present at all interrogations. Alexandre Ribot spoke for this remedy before the Chamber of Deputies in Feb-

14. Esmein, *Continental Criminal Procedure*, 555–56; Mazorie, *La Liberté individuelle*, 113–22; Andrier, *Intervention du défenseur*, 89–120; G. Abadie, *L'Avocat devant le juge d'instruction* (Gaillac, 1898).

ruary, 1909, but to no effect. Legislators believed that the 1897 reform of criminal procedure was sufficient, and that opinion prevailed for the duration of the Third Republic.[15]

The juge d'instruction worked without a time limit—an investigation lasting three months was rapid, one lasting six months or more, slow. He then passed the dossier of the case to the procureur for comment. In the interests of justice (as well as to maintain his chances for promotion), a juge d'instruction could not ignore the opinion of a magistrate ranking above him in the judicial bureaucracy, but the procureur's recommendation was not binding. The juge d'instruction alone took responsibility for the ruling to classify the charge as a *délit*, to authorize an *ordonnance de non-lieu* dismissing the charges and freeing the inculpé if he were in custody, or to approve an *ordonnance de renvoi* seeking an indictment for trial before the cour d'assises. The counsel for the inculpé was notified by registered mail.

When the decision was to dismiss the charges, an inculpé who had been held in custody could ask damages from the state or bring suit against a partie civile for malicious accusation. When it was to seek an indictment, the case went before the chambre des mises en accusation. The 1808 code had provided for an intermediate level, the chambre du conseil, between the juge d'instruction and the chambre des mises en accusation, but the law of July 17, 1856, eliminated that body as superfluous because it merely endorsed the juge d'instruction's action. After the juge d'instruction signed an ordonnance de renvoi, the dossier of the investigation was sent to the procureur général. Within the following forty-eight hours, the procureur général and the counsels for the inculpé and any partie civile had to submit written pleadings to the chambre des mises en accusation, which heard no oral arguments. One of its five justices prepared a summary of the pleadings, and by majority vote, this indictment court decided to issue an ordonnance de non-lieu, (rarely) to send the case before a cour correctionnelle to be tried as a *délit*, or to sanction an *arrêt de*

15. Esmein, *Continental Criminal Procedure*, 556–59; Andrier, *Intervention du défenseur*, 121–65; Mazorie, *La Liberté individuelle*, 123–244; Henry Millié, *Le Guide du Palais de Justice* (Paris, 1906), 47–66; Paul Saillard, *Le Rôle de l'avocat en matière criminelle* (Paris, 1904), 71–127. For the proposal on searches and seizures see *JOC*, Débats parlementaires, February 18, 1909, and *JOS*, Débats parlementaires, March 2, 1909. On Ribot's intervention see *JOC*, Débats parlementaires, February 9, 1909. The memoires of Jacques Batigne, *Un juge récidive* (Paris, 1974), 25–97, 185–201, portray a juge d'instruction at his tasks.

renvoi, mise en accusation, which bound the *inculpé*, now officially termed the *prévenu* (the indicted), over for prosecution before the cour d'assises. When the *prévenu* appeared at his trial, he would be called the *accusé* (defendant). The decision of the chambre des mises en accusation was not subject to appeal.[16]

Having experienced the justice of the police and the justice of criminal procedure, the *prévenu* was finally to face the justice of the assizes court. Whatever the conclusions of the Police judiciaire, the procureur, the juge d'instruction, and the chambre des mises en accusation, a jury remained to be convinced of his guilt. The very shift in terminology from *inculpé* to *accusé* implied to the jury that this guilt could already be presumed, but guilt was one thing, conviction another.

16. Sheehan, *Criminal Procedure*, 58–68; Esmein, *Continental Criminal Procedure*, 542; Halton, *Etude sur la procédure criminelle*, 95–115; Mazorie, *La Liberté individuelle*, 227–44; Saillard, *Le Rôle de l'avocat*, 128–37.

5

The Courts

On November 3, 1909, while interrogating Marguerite Steinheil during her trial for murder, Bernard Théodore de Valles, the presiding justice, fell under the spell of her emotional responses and admitted, "In perhaps no other case have we felt so clearly the fear of judicial error." In July, 1914, midway through Henriette Caillaux's trial on the charge of murdering *Le Figaro*'s editor to prevent the publication of documents injurious to her husband, the prominent politician Joseph Caillaux, Louis Albanel, who was presiding, called an unscheduled recess when it appeared that the defense might collapse. Louis Dagoury, an associate justice, angrily turned on Albanel and cried: "You dishonor us! You are a wretch!"[1] Courtrooms were frequently the source of high drama during the Third Republic because there the private conclusions of the juge d'instruction came under public scrutiny, and particularly so before the cour d'assises, where the verdict was rendered by a jury and the penalties after conviction were severe.

Prior to the Revolution of 1789, the system of courts in France was a jumble of confusing, sometimes conflicting, jurisdictions. Confronted by a bewildering number of seigniorial, municipal, and ec-

---

1. Martin, *The Hypocrisy of Justice,* 47, 93; Martin, "The Courts, the Magistrature, and Promotions," 991–92, 995.

clesiastical courts, feudal monarchs from the thirteenth century onward made diminishing the sphere of nonroyal justice a crucial element in their program of consolidation and centralization. The task of extending royal control fell to the king's deputy in each district—called a *bailli* in the north, a *sénéchal* in the south—though presiding over the itinerant assizes courts called *bailliages* and *sénéchaussées* was only one of his extensive responsibilities. By the sixteenth century the bailliages and sénéchaussées evolved into tribunals of the first instance (hearing both civil and criminal cases) in the most important towns. There were thirty-six of these royal courts in 1328, eighty-six in 1500, and more than four hundred by 1789. Professional magistrates, the *lieutenants généraux*, were increasingly appointed to be judges, and the Ordinance of Blois in 1570 investing them with the judicial authority previously exercised by the baillis and sénéchaux formally defined what had already become fact.

As French monarchs imposed the bailliages and sénéchaussées, their jurists advanced the theory of *cas royaux*—that these royal courts should exercise sole jurisdiction over crimes breaching the peace or touching the rights of the king. The category ultimately comprised most of the traditional felonies (murder, rape, abortion, highway robbery), crimes threatening the financial order (counterfeiting, false bankruptcy, usury), and affronts to royal or religious authority (high treason, sacrilege, heresy, popular disturbances) and drastically limited the competence of seigniorial or municipal courts to administer "high justice"—the penalties of mutilation or death. Through a further claim, *prévention*—the monarch's responsibility to assure prompt justice—a royal judge could hear a case in which the nonroyal court with original jurisdiction had not initiated proceedings. The principle of *justice retenue* completed these pretensions: As the source of judicial authority, the monarch could intervene in any process or trial at any point through annulling court decrees (*cassation*), reducing penalties (*lettres de réduction* and *lettres d'abolition*), or granting pardons (*lettres de grâce*).

Through the *cas royaux* and *prévention,* the bailliages and sénéchaussées became the original jurisdiction for ever more crimes and suits. They also heard appeals from a network of lower courts, the *prévôtés*, which tried civil and criminal cases of a minor sort. Thirteen parlements were the courts of appeal for the bailliages and sénéchaussées. Through this hierarchy of courts, the monarchs gained control of the administration of law in France. As justice became identified so clearly with the power of the king, society invested magisterial positions with great dignity and made them coveted. That quality converted even the minor ones into a lucrative source of income for the crown when Louis XI in 1467 declared them venal and the purchasers *inamovible* (irremovable). The press of office seekers was so great that Louis XII and François I succumbed to the temptation to put even the highest judicial positions up for sale.

This decision brought enormous and unsuspected problems. The price of magisterial office was substantial: The post of lieutenant général for a bailliage or sénéchaussée was valued at 25,000 livres, and even the lowest positions cost at least 1,000 livres (at a time when the annual income of most artisans was approximately 250 livres). Purchasers received from the crown only a small monetary return on their investment, *gages*, amounting to 3 percent or less a year. To secure the income appropriate to the dignity of the office, venal judges collected *épices* (fees of justice or court costs) at each stage in the proceedings. There was a natural inclination to draw out civil cases in which the *épices* were greatest and easiest to impose through complications in the law and to disregard criminal cases because of the smaller fees assigned to them.

Under this system, civil suits often lasted a generation and meant financial ruin for all but the judges and lawyers. Neglect of criminal justice contributed to mounting disorder and an increase in banditry. For the crown, the former was tolerable, the latter absolutely not. In response, François I's chancellor, Guillaume Poyet, drew up the Ordinance of Villers-Cotterêts (1539), which stiffened and made more uniform the procedure in criminal cases, and the king decreed in 1536 the creation of summary courts, the *prévôtés des maréchaux*, to try without appeal accusations of highway and armed robbery, burglary, and riot. These crimes became a special category, *cas prévôtaux*, falling exclusively under the jurisdiction of the *maréchaussée*, the undermanned mounted rural police force. Louis XV extended the purview of the prévôtés des maréchaux in 1731 to the trial of certain categories of society, principally vagabonds, whatever the accusation. To hasten final judgment for civil cases involving relatively moderate monetary claims (up to five hundred livres of capital or twenty livres of rent), Henri II in 1551 and 1552 inserted 60 new courts, a number ultimately growing to 120, called *présidiaux* between the level of the bailliages and sénéchaussées and that of the parlements. A présidial heard the appeal of these civil cases and rendered a judgment that could not be taken before the parlements. It also exercised an important function in criminal justice, providing a definitive decision on whether a crime was a cas prévôtal or was to be tried before a bailliage or sénéchaussée.

The instruction of a cas prévôtal was prepared by the *maréchaussée*'s regional brigade lieutenant, who rarely had any formal training in law, with assistance from an assesseur, who was required to have a legal education. These two men then deliberated with five judges taken from local courts to impose a final judgment. Acquittals were rare and proceedings rapid, exactly the justice envisioned when François I created the summary courts. Safeguards for the accused were considerably greater in a criminal case coming before a bailliage or sénéchaussée, particularly the slow pace and the right to appeal the verdict to a parlement. The 1539 ordinance required that a special magistrate, the *lieutenant criminel*, carry out the instruction. Despite the harsh procedure and threat of torture, the accused had some additional protection through the theory of proof and the independence of the judicial panel that would render judgment.

As the competence of the bailliages and sénéchaussées expanded, so did the royal magistrature, until its number at this level grew to approximately 2,700. The original successor to the bailli or sénéchal, the lieutenant général, came to preside over a body of new judicial officers. For civil cases, he acquired a deputy, the *lieutenant particulier*, and to fill out the trial panels, a varying number of *conseillers* (associate judges). After the Ordinance of Villers-Cotterêts in 1539, criminal justice fell under the jurisdiction of the lieutenant criminel (sometimes called the *lieutenant général criminel*) and his own deputy, the *lieutenant particulier assesseur criminel*, who were responsible for preparing the instructions. The presentation of criminal cases before a panel of conseillers belonged to the *procureur du roi* (royal procurator) and his assistants, the *avocats du roi* (royal solicitors). There was also a fringe of lesser officials, *sergents* (sergeants at arms) and *huissiers* (bailiffs) and *greffiers* (clerks of court). Before the end of the sixteenth century, the bailliages and sénéchaussées established separate chambers to hear civil and criminal cases, with conseillers specializing in one or the other. At the level of the présidiaux, where judges sat seven to a panel and there could be as many as five or six panels, the increase in magistrates was particularly striking, to nearly 4,500 for the 120 courts. A *premier président* (chief justice) oversaw the présidial, and a *président* (presiding justice) directed each panel of conseillers. With approximately 1,000 magistrates, the parlements had even larger numbers: In 1767 the

The Courts

parlement of Bordeaux alone counted 117 court officials, from premier président to huissiers. The vastly larger magistrature represented not only the complete victory of royal justice but enormous income for the king at the time each judicial office was sold.

The apparent success was grievously flawed. The system of royal justice worked none too well, and the magistrates, whose purchase of office swelled the king's treasury at the time of the transaction, demonstrated their independence repeatedly. By the middle of the eighteenth century the problems of the judicial system were so obvious that some of the magistrates themselves, as well as Louis XV's ministers Henri François d'Aguesseau and René Nicolas de Maupeou, called for substantial reforms. To pile up *épices*, courts permitted three or four appeals of original civil, and certain criminal, verdicts. Because an appeal was permitted on the basis of fact as well as law, the same evidence was heard over and over, consuming time, patience, and, most important, money. The présidiaux, designed to provide a rapid final judgment for many civil suits, passed into desuetude as an inflation of 345 percent between 1550 and 1770 removed all but the most minor cases from their jurisdiction. The parlements had always detested the slight encroachment made upon their *épices* by the présidiaux and were able to block any increase of the capital limit of five hundred livres for présidial competence until Louis XVI raised it in stages betwen 1774 and 1777 to two thousand livres. The inactivity of the présidiaux, and thus the lack of *épices* for the magistrates, had made seats on the courts so worthless even for social prestige that no purchaser could be found for a vacancy at any price. Judicial reformers called for the replacement of *épices* with state salaries but that implied greater state control, an intrusion that magistrates had escaped through the assertion of property rights in office.

The magistrates of the parlements, the parlementaires, were the wealthiest and most powerful of the judicial officials, with the most to lose from any change, and they led the opposition to reform. During the eighteenth century they had become the spokesmen for an aristocratic resurgence that claimed the right to limit the power of the king by refusing to register as an enforceable law any royal edict they opposed. This attempted usurpation led Maupeou in 1771 to exile the parlements and to create a new hierarchy of courts with magistrates appointed by the king, serving at his pleasure, and paid by the state. A widespread misapprehension among the literate public that the parlements were the guardians of liberty against a tyrannical, spent, and discredited monarch quickened a dangerous opposition to Louis XV during his final three years. In 1774 the newly crowned Louis XVI naïvely sought to repair the throne's popularity by dismissing Maupeou, restoring the parlements, and disbanding the new courts. He would rue his decision within two years, but he would never find the resolve, the skill, or the minister to repeat the energetic action taken by his grandfather and Maupeou.[2]

The Revolution's National Assembly had the audacity to go much further, to re-create the judicial system in accordance with "enlightened" ideals—that justice be equal, free, and open to all, that magistrates be elected representatives of the sovereign people, and that degradation be ended as a punishment. The initial step, as essential as momentous, came during the evening session of August 4, 1789, when the Assembly abolished privilege and so dismantled the framework of the ancien régime. Property in office, and thus the venality of judicial positions, was ended, though with the promise of compensation. Having cleared the way for fundamental change, the Assembly voted a year later, on August 16, 1790, to approve a structure of civil courts designed to fit the new territorial administrative units.

At the base of the system, each canton was to have a *juge de paix* (justice of the peace), whose primary responsibility was to preside over local arbitration panels seeking the resolution of disputes short of formal litigation. For civil suits that were filed, the juge de paix's jurisdiction extended only to cases involving less than fifty livres. His decision could be appealed to the Revolution's replacement for the bailliages and sénéchaussées—the *tribunal civil* (district civil court), a panel of five judges (a président and four conseillers) at the level of the *arrondissement* (district). The tribunal civil heard all civil cases beyond the competence of the juge de paix, and in those involving less than one hundred livres, its judgment was final; if the

---

2. Ruff, *Crime, Justice, and Public Order in Old Regime France*, 24–37; Carey, *Judicial Reform in France Before the Revolution of 1789*, 8–12, 21–23, 69–96; Roland Mousnier, *Les Institutions de la France sous la monarchie absolue* (Paris, 1974–80), II, 249–72. For background see F. Autrand, *Naissance d'un grand corps de l'Etat: Les Gens du Parlement de Paris, 1345–1454* (Paris, 1981); Frédéric Bluche, *Les Magistrats du Parlement de Paris au XVIIIe siècle, 1715–1771* (Besançon, 1960); Iain A. Cameron, *Crime and Repression in the Auvergne and the Guyenne, 1720–1790* (New York, 1981); Nicole Castan, *Justice et répression en Languedoc à l'époque des Lumières* (Paris, 1980); Jonathan Dewald, *The Formation of a Provincial Nobility: The Magistrates of the Parlement of Rouen, 1499–1610* (Princeton, 1980); Maurice Gresset, *Gens de justice à Besançon, 1674–1789* (Paris, 1978).

case involved a hundred livres or more, the ruling could be appealed once to the tribunal civil of a neighboring arrondissement. The National Assembly's refusal to constitute a superior jurisdiction, special courts of appeal, was the result of bitter hostility toward the parlements, which had made themselves odious to reformers during the early 1780s through infamous sentences in criminal justice and during 1788 through the defense of noble privilege, particularly the ruling on September 25 that the Estates General should meet as it had in 1614. The juges de paix and the judges of the tribunaux civils were to have salaries from the state and to be chosen by the vote of "active citizens"—the juges de paix for terms of two years, the judges for terms of six years—with the right of reelection. The crucial difference between the two levels was that no qualification other than the trust of the electorate was asked of the juges de paix; the président and conseillers of the tribunaux civils were required to have served at least five years either as a judge or as a lawyer and, thus, to have had a formal legal education. This issue of technical training and experience established a professional boundary that defined the magistrature through the exclusion of the juges de paix.

In a series of laws enacted on January 20, July 19, September 16 (the most important), and September 29, 1791, the National Assembly partially enlisted the structure of civil courts for the system of criminal justice. *Contraventions*, the most minor violations, were heard by a panel of local administrative officials in each *commune* (town). *Délits* (misdemeanors) were judged by the *tribunal de police correctionnelle* (district police court), consisting of several juges de paix (usually three) and two lay judges chosen by local officials for having some legal background. *Crimes* (felonies) came before the *tribunal criminel* (departmental criminal court) after a formal indictment by the *jury d'accusation* (grand jury). The bench of the tribunal criminel was a panel of four judges—the président, elected by the "active citizens" of the department, and three assesseurs, chosen from among the conseillers of the tribunaux civils. The *accusateur public* (public accuser), elected in the same manner as the président, presented the case for the prosecution. The *commissaire du roi* (king's commissioner), appointed by the state as its representative, proposed the sentence if there were a conviction. That verdict was the responsibility of a twelve-man *jury de jugement* (trial jury). At all three levels the proceedings were public and oral, with the accused having the right to counsel and to present a formal defense. The procedure for hearing *contraventions* and *délits* was concise without being summary. Before the tribunal criminel, the presence of the jury and the need for greater precautions because of the severity of possible sentences required a substantially more complex trial.

The National Assembly also created two special national courts. The Tribunal de Cassation (court of final appeal) was established by the law of November 27, 1790, with a bench of forty-two justices, elected regionally, to hear appeals of civil and criminal cases brought on questions of improper procedure or the misapplication of law. Its role was limited to "breaking" (*casser;* thus the name) a previous verdict and requiring a retrial at the original jurisdiction. The Haute Cour de la Nation (High Court of the Nation) was fashioned by the law of May 10, 1791, to try offenses committed by ministers of state and other officials as prescribed in the Constitution of 1791. The court had its seat in Orléans and was composed of a four-judge bench and a jury of 24 drawn randomly from 166 veniremen, all chosen through complicated indirect elections.

The National Assembly's legislation swept away the royal judicial system of the ancien régime. The prévôtés, the prévôtés des maréchaux, the bailliages and sénéchaussées, the présidiaux, the parlements—all were abolished, and with them the special *tribunaux d'exception,* which had existed to try the special cases of the specially privileged. Venality and property in office were displaced by an elected magistrature of approximately 2,850 judges and prosecutors. Most of the former magistrates never served again. The need for *épices* vanished with the institution of state salaries, and justice became available to all through the elimination of court costs. Degrading penalties, such as the pillory and branding, were ended. In September, 1791, new rules of procedure made criminal justice less terrifying and condemnations less inevitable.

The Revolution's civil courts functioned well during the first half decade of their existence, and the election of juges de paix and conseillers gained general approval in many sections of the country. Unfortunately, the liberalized criminal justice system was little match for the turbulence of these years. By 1793, summary tribunals frequently arrogated the responsibilities of the departmental criminal courts, or a juge d'instruction replaced the jury d'accusation. As the Thermidoreans tried to restore stability, they retreated from the National Assembly's most advanced positions. Criminal procedure was tightened by the law of 3 Brumaire IV (October 25, 1795). Two months earlier, in the Constitution of 5 Fructidor III (August 22,

The Courts

1795), the structure of courts was altered to permit only a single tribunal civil for each department instead of one for each arrondissement. The inevitable result of this centralization was an increase in the expense of civil justice through the costs of travel and delay, which even many middle-class litigants could not easily afford. The change eliminated more than a thousand judges, and for the remainder, the constitution reduced the term of office from six years to five and neglected to specify any technical qualifications. Most important, without legislative sanction, the new government of the Directory began to fill vacant judgeships by appointment, continuing a subordination of the judiciary to the power of the state well established by the Committee of Public Safety and the Revolutionary Tribunals.

The Thermidoreans made changes in the judiciary hesitantly; Bonaparte would do so enthusiastically. The law of 27 Ventôse VIII (March 18, 1800) restored a civil court to each arrondissement and added to its jurisdiction the responsibility for judging *délits*, which was removed from the tribunal de police correctionnelle. A juge de paix would preside over minor judicial proceedings in each canton, with competence only over *contraventions*. The court at the arrondissement level was now to be called the *tribunal de première instance* (lower tribunal), not only because it heard misdemeanor cases, which went before its *cours correctionnelles* (correctional courts), and civil suits "in the first instance," but also because Bonaparte created a superior jurisdiction for the first time since 1790— twenty-nine *cours d'appel* (courts of appeal), approximately one for every three departments. The resemblance to the parlements was unmistakable, even to the point of the heightened importance of the Cour d'appel de Paris, which heard appeals from seven departments. Except for its name, the Cour (formerly Tribunal) de Cassation remained unaltered. The sole change for the departmental tribunaux criminels was the assignment of permanent assesseurs. As First Consul, Bonaparte reserved for himself the appointment of all the magistrates for all the courts beneath the Cour de Cassation, the members of which would be named by the Senate. The juges de paix, whose status had been reduced, would continue to be chosen through local elections. Two and a half years later, in the Constitution of 16 Thermidor X (August 4, 1802), Bonaparte abolished these two exceptions. All judicial officials, high and low, were subject to his power of appointment and advancement. A provision in the law of 27 Ventôse VIII promising irremovability for judges (though not for prosecutors or juges d'instruction) offered only a meager reassurance that independence of thought and action would be respected. On April 28, 1810, the new penal and criminal codes became effective, and at the same time, cours d'assises replaced the tribunaux criminels. With this Napoleonic reorganization, the French judicial system assumed the form it would retain for the next 116 years.[3]

In the National Assembly's legislation, a juge de paix for each canton was an essential component in the judicial structure: He was conciliator and arbitrator, judge of minor civil suits, the initial step in criminal procedure, and a member of the bench for the trial of *délits*. Napoleon reduced this competence, and no succeeding regime restored it. The juge de paix retained his role in conciliation and gained administrative responsibilities, such as verifying signatures and approving adoptions, but his judicial power was limited to deciding civil cases involving up to three hundred francs and, as the sole judge of the tribunal de police correctionnelle, trying offenses classified as *contraventions*, punishable by up to a fine of fifteen francs or five days in the local jail.

The verdict of a juge de paix could be appealed to the tribunal de première instance of the arrondissement. The number of the tribunaux ranged up and down throughout the nineteenth and twentieth centuries according to France's success in war. The Third Republic counted 359 in 1871 and 365 in 1919. The most important of them was the Tribunal de la Seine, which included in its *ressort* (jurisdiction) all the arrondissements of Paris and the surrounding *banlieue*. Some judges of the tribunaux heard civil cases, either originally or on appeal from the juges de paix, and the number of civil chambers and the size of the bench varied with the court and its location. Other chambers consisted of three-judge panels composing cours correctionnelles to try *délits* and to hear appeals from the tribunaux de police correctionnelle. The tribunal de première instance had no jury, and its decision could be taken to the cour d'appel of the jurisdiction on the basis of fact or law. The *président* (chief judge) of the tribunal presided over one of the chambers; the presiding judges for the other chambers held the title *vice-président*. The other members of the chambers were simply called *juges* (judges). The *procureur de la République* (district attorney) and his *substituts* (as-

3. Esmein, *Continental Criminal Procedure*, 402–527.

sistant prosecutors) formed the *parquet* (the prosecutorial office). The court was completed by one or more *juges d'instruction* (examining magistrates). The combined number of these magistrates was dependent upon the population of the arrondissement but could not be fewer than five (président, two juges, juge d'instruction, and procureur de la République) or more than fifteen, with an exception for the Tribunal de la Seine, the total for which was never less than forty-nine and surpassed one hundred by 1850 and two hundred by 1914. The rationale for multijudge panels came partly from tradition, because the tribunaux de première instance and the earlier tribunaux civils were successors to the bailliages and sénéchaussées, and partly from a belief during the 1789 Revolution that a plurality of judges ensured more democratic courts, the juges de paix aside. Napoleon might have been tempted to remake the courts with a single judge, but the appearance of a long bench appealed to his sense of grandeur.

The cours d'appel were France's only true superior jurisdiction. Napoleon created twenty-nine of them in 1800. By 1811, when his empire was at its height, there were thirty-six; after his defeat in 1814, twenty-seven. To honor his birthplace, he established a cour d'appel at Ajaccio; the Restoration moved it to Bastia. The Second Empire added a cour d'appel at Chambéry in 1862 after victory in Italy and lost the cours d'appel at Metz and Colmar in 1870 after defeat by Prussia. The Third Republic inherited twenty-six in 1871 and regained Colmar in 1919 (see Table 25).

The cours d'appel recalled the judicial characteristics of the parlements (but not their political pretensions) in the right to hear appeals, in the long benches and generally large number of attached magistrates, and even in their location: Of the thirteen parlementaire seats in 1789, only Dôle did not receive an appellate court. As with the parlements, the most important cour d'appel was that of Paris, not only because it sat in the capital but because it had jurisdiction over seven departments, two more than any other appellate court. Each cour d'appel was divided into permanent standing chambers to impose judgment in various types of cases. One or more *chambres civiles* heard appeals from the tribunaux de première instance and the *tribunaux de commerce* (commercial courts, solely for business law). A *chambre criminelle* reviewed cases from the cours correctionnelles. The *chambre des mises en accusation* acted as the grand jury for crimes within the *ressort*, examining the conclusions of the juges d'instruction and, if appropriate, issuing indict-

Table 25
Cours d'Appel, 1800–1940

Cour d'Appel	Dates	Cour d'Appel	Dates
Agen	1800–1940	Hamburg	1811–1814
Aix (P)	1800–1940	Liège	1800–1814
Ajaccio	1800–1819	Limoges	1800–1940
Amiens	1800–1940	Lyon	1800–1940
Angers	1800–1940	Metz (P)	1800–1870
Bastia	1820–1940	Montpellier	1800–1940
Besançon	1800–1940	Nancy (P)	1800–1940
Bordeaux (P)	1800–1940	Nîmes	1800–1940
Bourges	1800–1940	Orléans	1800–1940
Brussels	1800–1814	Paris (P)	1800–1940
Caen (P)	1800–1940	Pau (P)	1800–1940
Chambéry	1862–1940	Poitiers	1800–1940
Colmar	1800–1870, 1919–1940	Rennes (P)	1800–1940
Dijon (P)	1800–1940	Riom	1800–1940
Douai (P)	1800–1940	Rome	1800–1814
Florence	1809–1814	Rouen	1800–1940
Genoa	1806–1814	Toulouse (P)	1800–1940
Grenoble (P)	1800–1940	Trier	1802–1814
Hague, The	1811–1814	Turin	1802–1814

SOURCES: *Almanach National*, 1800–1919; *Journal Officiel*, Lois et Décrets, 1920–1940.
(P) indicates the seat of a parlement

ments. A *chambre des vacances* sat during the annual court recess from August 15 to October 15. Each chamber had its own panel of justices made up of a *président de chambre* (presiding justice) and a varying number of *conseillers* (associate justices); beginning in 1919 and only on the Cour d'appel de Paris, one of the conseillers was designated the *vice-président*. The *premier président* (chief justice) could sit with, and preside over, any chamber of the cour d'appel.

For criminal justice, the three-judge panel of the cour d'assises was drawn from the bench of the cour d'appel when the assizes convened at the seat of the appellate court. When the cour d'assises met in another arrondissement of the *ressort*, the *président* (presiding justice) of the panel came from the bench of the cour d'appel, the two *assesseurs* (associate justices) from the arrondissement's tribunal de première instance. The minister of justice chose the président of the cour d'assises; the premier président of the cour d'appel named the assesseurs. In a trial before la cour d'assises, the prési-

The Courts

dent had enormous power over the proceedings and the imposition of sentences, but a twelve-man jury rendered the verdict, which could not be appealed on the basis of fact. The head of the cour d'appel's parquet, the *procureur général* (attorney general), supervised all felony prosecutions. He was seconded by *substituts généraux* (assistant attorneys general), who prepared the individual cases, and *avocats généraux* (solicitors general), who presented the state's charges before the cour d'assises.

The Cour de Cassation heard appeals brought on the basis of law and procedure and ordered retrials if appropriate, but it could not be considered a French "supreme court" because it lacked the power to reverse a verdict. The court was organized in three chambers, one each for civil cases, for criminal cases, and for the decision of which cases to accept for review. A chamber consisted of a *président de chambre* (presiding justice) and fifteen *conseillers* (associate justices). The *premier président* (chief justice) sat with and presided over any chamber of his choice. There were so many judges because the National Assembly originally planned to have one from each department and reluctantly reduced that total by approximately half. The parquet was composed of the *procureur général* (attorney general) and six *avocats généraux* (solicitors general) to make presentations before the bench. Cases could be referred to the court by the defense, by the prosecution, or by the minister of justice, who could act "in the interest of law" to request a clarification or interpretation even if the case at hand was moot. Finally, the Cour de Cassation acted as the disciplinary board for any magistrate accused of malfeasance or dereliction of duty.[4] (On the organization of the courts of Paris, see Table 26.)

The number of judges and prosecutors assigned to these civil and criminal courts increased slowly during the nineteenth century until it reached approximately 3,400; about 1,000 more served in various bureaucratic functions at the Ministry of Justice or on special administrative courts. In 1883 there was a reduction of 614 judges as part of the Third Republic's purge of magistrates with monarchical

---

4. For an introduction to the French judicial system as a whole, see, in particular, Raoul de La Grasserie, *De la justice en France et à l'étranger au XXe siècle* (Paris, 1914), and René David and Henry P. de Vries, *The French Legal System: An Introduction to Civil Law Systems* (New York, 1958). For specific details, see R. C. K. Ensor, *Courts and Judges in France, Germany, and England* (Oxford, 1933), 25–51, 110–12; Gaston Leroy, *Le Juge unique et la réforme de notre organisation judiciaire* (Paris, 1907), 87–106, 137–42; and the *Almanach National*, 1800–1919, a valuable source for judicial structure and organization.

TABLE 26
The Courts of Paris During the Third Republic

Court	Bench	Parquet	Total Number in 1880	1910	1930
Cour de Cassation	Premier président		1	1	1
	Présidents de chambre		3	3	3
	Conseillers		45	45	45
		Procureur général	1	1	1
		Avocats généraux	6	6	6
Cour d'Appel de Paris	Premier président		1	1	1
	Présidents de chambre		7	10	12
	Vice-présidents de chambre (next in line to preside)		—	—	12
	Conseillers		64	73	77
		Procureur général	1	1	1
		Avocats généraux	7	8	10
		Substituts généraux	11	12	16
Tribunal de la Seine	Président		1	1	1
	Vice-présidents		11	12	17
	Présidents de la section (next in line to preside)		—	14	17
	Juges		62	69	105
	Juges d'instruction		25	31	40
		Procureur de la République	1	1	1
		Substituts	26	32	47

SOURCES: *Almanach National*, 1880, 1910; *Journal Officiel*, Lois et Décrets, 1930.

The Courts

TABLE 27
Personnel of the Bench and Parquet

Court and Position	1883	1919	1926
Cour de Cassation			
Premier président	1	1	1
Président de chambre	3	3	3
Conseiller	45	45	45
Procureur général	1	1	1
Avocat général	6	6	6
Cours d'appel			
Premier président	26	26	27
Président de chambre	59	62	65
Vice-président de chambre	—	10	10
Conseiller	427	322	336
Procureur général	26	26	27
Avocat général	57	43	45
Substitut général	55	50	52
Tribunaux de Première Instance			
Président	359	359	138
Vice-président	60	68	149
Président de la section	—	14	17
Juge d'instruction	391	154	261
Juge	627	590	558
Procureur de la République	359	359	138
Substitut	276	207	330
TOTALS	2,778	2,346	2,209

SOURCE: *Journal Officiel*, Lois et Décrets, 1883, 1919, 1926.

or clerical sympathies. The level remained relatively constant at 2,800 until the exigencies of World War I caused so many vacancies, and prevented their being filled, that it dropped below 2,400. The return of Alsace and Lorraine in 1919, adding 113 positions (23 on the cour d'appel at Colmar and 90 on the six tribunaux de première instance) and the recovery of the early 1920s permitted new judicial appointments that raised the number above 2,600 until a reorganization of the tribunaux in 1926 eliminated 393 magistrates and left the total for the courts at approximately 2,200 during the remainder of the Third Republic (see Table 27). Except for the positions on the three Parisian courts and the highest levels of the provincial ones, the magistrates were meanly paid (see Table 28).

TABLE 28
Salaries for Bench and Parquet (in Francs)

Court and Position	1883	1919	1927
Cour de Cassation			
Premier président	30,000	30,000	80,000
Président de chambre	25,000	25,000	75,000
Conseiller	18,000	18,000	60,000
Procureur général	30,000	30,000	80,000
Avocat général	18,000	18,000	60,000
Cour d'Appel de Paris			
Premier président	25,000	25,000	75,000
Président de chambre	13,750	15,000	50,000
Vice-président de chambre	—	14,500	46,000
Conseiller	11,000	13,500	40,000
Procureur général	25,000	25,000	75,000
Avocat général	13,200	14,500	48,000
Substitut général	11,000	13,500	40,000
Cours d'Appel de Province			
Premier président	18,000	18,000	54,000
Président de chambre	10,000	13,000	38,000
Conseiller	7,000	10,000	32,000
Procureur général	18,000	18,000	54,000
Avocat général	8,000	11,000	34,000
Substitut général	6,000	9,000	32,000

Tribunal de la Seine

Président	20,000	65,000
Vice-président	10,000	38,000
Président de la section	—	36,000
Juge d'instruction	10,000	38,000
Juge	8,000	34,000
Procureur de la République	20,000	65,000
Substitut	8,000	34,000
Juge suppléant	1,500	14,000

Tribunaux de Province

Président	5,000–10,000	8,000–13,000	24,000–38,000
Vice-président	4,000–7,000	7,000–10,000	19,000–32,000
Juge d'instruction	3,500–6,500	7,500–9,500	18,000–28,000
Juge	3,000–6,000	5,000–9,000	16,000–24,000
Procureur de la République	5,000–10,000	8,000–13,000	24,000–38,000
Substitut	2,800–5,000	5,000–8,000	16,000–24,000
Juge suppléant	500	4,000	14,000

SOURCE: *Journal Officiel*, Lois et Décrets, 1883, 1919, 1927.

Criticism directed at the number and the salaries of the magistrates was frequent. In the 1870s and early 1880s, there were suggestions that some posts of juge and substitut on the tribunaux and of conseiller on the cours d'appel be abolished because the case load was insufficient to justify them and because compensation might then be raised for the rest. In 1883 the legislature eliminated nearly one-sixth of the positions (all on the bench) and did increase the salaries paid to the lowest-ranking magistrates by from 8 to 40 percent. Other critics assailed the French tradition of multiple judges and compared them unfavorably with their English and American counterparts. A *juge unique* (single judge), so the argument went, would less easily conceal a lack of capacity and would be more clearly and personally responsible for his decisions. No minister of justice during the Third Republic seriously considered such a radical revision of the established structure, but in September, 1926, there was a reorganization of the tribunaux de première instance, which were moved from the level of the arrondissement to the *chef-lieu* (chief town) of each department. The Thermidoreans had made the same change in August, 1795. The problem of transportation, critical then, had been solved, claimed Louis Barthou, the minister of justice, by trains and automobiles, and there would not be any delay in the rendering of justice, because the new tribunaux départementaux would be large courts with many chambers. The great advantage of the reorganization would come not from a saving of money—there would be little of that, for the displaced magistrates were promised absorption into the judicial bureaucracy—but from a centralization that would permit the ministry to oversee the process of justice more tightly. The change was never popular, and three years later the old system was restored by placing a chamber of the tribunal départemental in each arrondissement.[5]

The cour correctionnelle of the tribunal de première instance tried all charges of *délit*, the cases reaching the court through four separate routes. First, by the law of July 14, 1865, the procureur could

---

5. For examples, among many, of the reform proposals, see Georges Picot, *La Réforme judiciaire en France* (Paris, 1881), 267–97; Paul Philouze, *Etude sur l'organisation de nos institutions judiciaires* (Paris, 1882), 8–11; and Leroy, *Le Juge unique*, 123–30. See also the *JO* for the laws of August 30, 1883 (the republican purge), April 28, 1919 (postwar conditions in the courts), July 25, 1923 (the judicial organization of Alsace and Lorraine), September 3, 1926 (the creation of the tribunaux départementaux), and August 22, 1929 (placing a chamber of the tribunal départemental in each arrondissement).

send anyone apprehended *en flagrant délit* before the cour correctionnelle for an immediate trial. Upon request, the accused was granted a delay of up to three days in which to prepare a defense, but capture in the act ensured conviction. Second, the accused could have been arrested and charged with a *délit* only after a police investigation, and in this circumstance his case came before the court in the normal progression of the trial docket. Third, a juge d'instruction or the chambre des mises en accusation could conclude that an offense initially classified as a possible felony was actually a *délit*. Fourth, a juge d'instruction could "correctionalize" a case, ordering that it be tried before the cour correctionnelle instead of the cour d'assises despite his determination that a felony had been committed.

Correctionnalisation mitigated the possible penalties—the cour correctionnelle could not impose a sentence of death, forced labor, or imprisonment for longer than five years—but avoided both the cost and the uncertainty of a jury trial. During the Third Republic, juries acquitted approximately 28 percent of the defendants before them, the three-judge panels of the cours correctionnelles only 10 percent. The procureur and any victim of the crime had to concur in the juge d'instruction's decision to correctionalize; the accused was not consulted. *Correctionnalisation* was first adopted by the parquets in the 1820s as a means of guaranteeing more convictions, and a memorandum from the Ministry of Justice on August 16, 1842, officially endorsed it. The legislature of the Second Empire rebelled against this ministerial intrusion onto the specific provisions of criminal law and on May 13, 1864, prohibited the practice. Within two years the parquets quietly resumed it, partly to gain more convictions, partly to spare some defendants the draconian penalties of the cour d'assises. On January 12, 1871, Adolphe Crémieux, the Jacobin minister of justice in the provisional government of national defense, renewed the injunction against correctionalizing and claimed that the guilty were escaping punishment of sufficient severity. The cours d'assises were immediately overwhelmed by a sudden increase in cases. Less than three months later, on April 5, 1871, Jules Dufaure, premier and minister of justice for the first cabinet of the Third Republic, revoked Crémieux's order and gave the formal, and lasting, sanction of the government to *correctionnalisation*.

Besides the panel of judges, the principal participants in a trial before the cour correctionnelle were the prosecution, usually represented by a substitut; often a partie civile; and the defense. For an accused who was indigent, the law of January 30, 1851, directed that the state appoint an "official defender" and assume as well the obligation of the defense to pay the expenses of its witnesses. The trial began with the *interrogatoire* (interrogation) of the accused by the presiding judge, who used as his guide the dossier compiled by the parquet. The prosecutor, the attorney for any partie civile, and the defense attorney could then examine the accused, always through the presiding judge by means of the formula, "Monsieur le président, veut-il m'autoriser à poser une question?" The accused was not under oath and could refuse to answer, but this refusal was liable to comment by the prosecution and the partie civile. The court then heard witnesses for the defense, with all questions again through the presiding judge. Children aged less than sixteen years and anyone with a criminal record, related to the accused, or having a direct personal interest in the case could not give sworn testimony, and their evidence was to that extent discounted by the judges. The prosecution normally did not present its witnesses, because their written depositions were available to the judges in the dossier. If testimony for the defense contradicted an affidavit for the prosecution, the presiding judge could confront the two witnesses before the court in an attempt to determine the truth. Witnesses were required to give evidence "spontaneously" (without notes), and until they were called, they were prevented from conversing or from hearing the proceedings. Apart from these rules, the judges had broad power throughout the trial to obtain as many of the facts in the case as possible. After the witnesses had testified, the prosecution, the partie civile, and finally the defense made closing statements. The judges retired only briefly before returning to declare a verdict that was announced as if unanimous, because no public dissenting vote was permitted. If for conviction, the panel imposed a sentence and made any award to the partie civile immediately; if for acquittal, the accused was informed that he could bring suit against the partie civile for false accusation. To simplify an appeal by the prosecution or the defense, the law of June 13, 1856, required a stenographic record of the trial, which most often lasted less than two hours.[6]

6. Henri Koral, *Essai de théorie générale de correctionnalisation des crimes* (2nd ed.; Paris, 1919), 1–7; Davidovitch, "Criminalité et répression," 37, 48; Esmein, *Continental Criminal Procedure*, 535–39, 544–45; Sheehan, *Criminal Procedure*, 5–8, 70–81; P. Viguié, *Essai sur la nature juridique des crimes punis de peines correctionnelles et des délits punis de peines de simple police en vertu d'excuses légales ou de circonstances atténuantes* (Toulouse, 1914); Jean Terral, *De la complicité des crimes et délits non-intentionnels* (Toulouse, 1905).

The Courts

The trial procedures before the cour d'assises were much more complex because the evidence had to be presented to an untrained jury and because the penalties after conviction—imprisonment for five years or more, forced labor, or death—were severe. The court staged a species of morality play. The purpose of the trial was to judge the accused after an inexorable revelation of his life and of the misdeeds that placed him in this pass. The quest was for the whole truth, with virtually no evidence except hearsay ruled out as irrelevant or inadmissable. No confession of guilt at any point was sufficient to halt the process. The heavy presumption of culpability borne by the accused from the decision of the juge d'instruction to seek an indictment did not guarantee conviction. Ultimately, the charge to the jury, "Avez-vous la conviction intime?" implied that emotion counted more than reason in their verdict, that the quality of evidence was more important than the quantity, that a single witness might carry more weight than all the rest of the case, and that justice was cut to fit the individual more than the crime.

The cour d'assises was convened quarterly in the chef-lieu of each department and remained in session as long as necessary to try all felony charges for which there were indictments. The minister of justice had the right to name the président of the cour d'assises, but he could delegate that responsibility to the premier président of the cour d'appel for the *ressort*. In a memorandum of December 14, 1906, the ministry declared that it would exercise its prerogative only "exceptionally," by which it meant in cases with political implications, such as that of Henriette Caillaux before the cour d'assises of the Seine in July, 1914. The premier président of the cour d'appel always named the assesseurs—justices from his court if the cour d'assises met at its seat, judges from the district's tribunal de première instance otherwise. The président of the cour d'assises was almost always a conseiller (the premier président or a président de chambre of the cour d'appel was appointed rarely), and he was acutely aware that the avocat général presenting the case for the prosecution had a salary superior to his and ranked slightly higher in the judicial hierarchy. Promotion for the conseiller might depend upon his conduct of the trial and, particularly, upon his attitude toward the prosecution. To lessen a perception of potentially improper influence on the bench, some judicial reformers recommended appointing a président de chambre to preside over the assizes or, better yet, creating for the cours d'assises a pool of judges specially trained in criminal law whose assignments and promotions could not be affected by the parquet.

Once appointed, the président of the cour d'assises was responsible for the pretrial procedures. He reviewed any evidence that the Police judiciaire had discovered since the decree of *renvoi* (binding over for trial) by the chambre des mises en accusation and could order a further investigation if appropriate. As soon as the procureur général drew up the prosecution's final *acte d'accusation* (bill of indictment), the président interviewed the accused in private, usually at the jail, to specify his rights and to ensure his access to legal counsel. Forty-eight hours before the court was to hear the case, he transmitted the names of the potential jurors to the defense, and twenty-four hours before, a complete list of all subpoenaed witnesses to the prosecution, the defense, and any partie civile.

When the court convened, the first act was to impanel a jury. The prosecution was permitted four peremptory challenges, the defense five. For a trial that would last more than two or three days, additional jurors were often chosen to supplement the initial twelve. After the jury took an oath to render justice, a huissier convoked the witnesses en masse before the court and then segregated them in waiting rooms outside, as at the cour correctionnelle. The trial itself commenced with the greffier's reading of the acte d'accusation—usually so rapidly that the jury could barely understand him. Even so, the first impression made upon the jury was this recital of the prosecution's case, to which the defense could not make immediate rebuttal. The jury could also not fail to notice that the avocat général wore a judicial gown identical to those of the président and the assesseurs, that he entered and exited with them through the same side door, and that their tables rested on a platform raised slightly above the rest of the court—implying that the justices were allied with the prosecution against the defense.[7]

The second stage of the trial was the hearing of testimony and the presentation of evidence, in a manner comprehensible to the jury

---

7. For comprehensive information about the cour d'assises see Jacques Brissaud, *Guide-formulaire de la cour d'assises* (Paris, 1935); Alec Mellor, *La Pratique du procès pénal, plaintes et constitutions de partie civile* (Paris, 1959); and Jean Chaprat, *La Composition écrite: Aide-Mémoire sous forme de plans détaillés, droit pénal et procédure pénale* (2nd ed.; Paris, 1941). On the selection of the président, the pretrial procedures, and the initial stage of the trial, see Millié, *Le Guide du Palais*, 47–64; Jean Cruppi, *La Cour d'assises* (Paris, 1898), 109–70; Fernand Baudat, *De la réforme de la procédure pénale à l'audience* (Paris, 1910), 8–14; and Henry Charropin, *De la participation du jury à l'application de la peine* (Poitiers, 1909), 11–25.

and not merely to judges already familiar with the case through study of the dossier. It began with the interrogatoire, and when the accused stepped to the witness bar, there was a moment of drama second only to the jury's announcement of the verdict. In this moment the accused had his first and most important chance to vindicate himself before the jury, and the jury had its first and most enduring impression of the accused. The questioning was carried out as before the cour correctionnelle—by the président and then by the prosecution, any partie civile, and the defense through the président—but at much greater length in order to inform the jury as fully as possible. The président drew upon the dossier compiled by the juge d'instruction for the case, and many of his questions concerned the early life of the accused and any prior accusations and convictions, whether or not they had a bearing on the current charge. The conduct of the président during the interrogatoire was so often clearly prosecutorial that the Ministry of Justice repeatedly recommended prudence and moderation. The severe handling of Marguerite Steinheil in 1909 and of the Bande à Bonnot in 1913, both before the cour d'assises of the Seine, attracted wide notice because the cases themselves were sensational. But there were many other instances of abuse. In 1910, for example, one président demanded of an accused, "Mais avouez donc que vous êtes un assassin!" and another reacted to a response with "C'est inadmissible!" The defense attorney was not permitted to protest the président's questions or those of the prosecution and partie civile, and it was difficult for him to counter the effect of a harsh interrogatoire through his own. As before the cour correctionnelle, the accused was not under oath and could refuse to answer, but doing so always had a negative impact on the jury. The best strategy for him was to brave the questions while using his replies to establish a version of the evidence favorable for the defense.[8]

After the interrogatoire, the prosecution, the partie civile, and the defense could each introduce physical evidence and present experts to argue conclusions from it. Each could subpoena, and the court compel to testify under oath (with the same exceptions as before the cour correctionnelle), anyone with even the most tangential relationship to the case unless he had the right of professional secrecy,

---

8. Sheehan, *Criminal Procedure*, 24–26, 81–85; Saillard, *Le Rôle de l'avocat*, 141–92. On the cases in 1910, see Baudat, *De la réforme*, 29, and on Marguerite Steinheil, Martin, *The Hypocrisy of Justice*, 45–53. On the Bande à Bonnot, see Esmein, *Continental Criminal Procedure*, 562, and the Afterword of the present work.

as lawyers had about their clients, physicians about their patients, priests about the confessional, and juges d'instruction about their investigations. In principle a witness was to testify by relating all that he could recall without the prompting of questions, which would be asked only to elicit further detail. But in practice the président conducted a close interrogation, and after he was finished, the prosecution, partie civile, and defense posed questions through him, each asking the witness whatever it wished, without reference to the questions of the others. For that reason the Anglo-Saxon practice of direct examination followed by cross-examination never developed in France. In its place, once a witness was excused, the defense could comment about his testimony and his integrity almost to the point of slander and could request the président to resolve discrepancies by confronting two witnesses before the court or a witness and the accused. The président usually permitted these confrontations because a denial was frequently the basis of an appeal to the Cour de Cassation. With much less chance for success, the defense could also petition for a *transport sur lieux*—for the entire court to visit a location associated with the case, such as the scene of the crime, to provide the jury with information and perspective that photographs and words could not convey.[9]

When all of the evidence had been presented, when all of the witnesses and experts had testified, and when all of the confrontations had been completed, the court heard final arguments. The avocat général spoke first, and in his *réquisitoire* (the concluding indictment) he summarized the case against the accused, criticized the contentions of the defense, and asked the jury to weigh the impact of the crime upon society and the degree to which the particular accused, based on his character and his record, should be punished for rending the social fabric. His peroration was invariably an admonition to deter criminal depredations by returning a verdict of guilty. If there were a partie civile, his attorney presented an appeal for damages, most often by dilating upon the réquisitoire. In the *plaidoirie* (the pleading), the defense attorney insisted—usually at great length and with much passion—on the innocence of the accused, but if the prosecution's case was strong, he argued for the jury's consideration of mitigating circumstances. Although the defense was supposedly permitted to invoke only those extenuating conditions recognized

---

9. Cruppi, *La Cour d'assises*, 80–108; Baudat, *De la réforme*, 66–82, 112–13; Sheehan, *Criminal Procedure*, 26–30, 81–85; Saillard, *Le Rôle de l'avocat*, 141–92.

by law, the président rarely enforced this injunction. The three sides could speak in rebuttal, with the defense having the last word. The accused then had a final chance to address the jury. To conclude the trial, the 1808 criminal code directed the président to summarize the evidence himself for the jury, but his presumed objectivity was often distinct partiality toward the prosecution. By the law of June 19, 1881, the Third Republic eliminated the président's *résumé* and restricted his role after the closing arguments to instructing the jury—explaining the applicable law, specifying the questions of guilt or innocence to be answered, and charging the jurymen to act upon a *conviction intime*.[10]

The laws of September 16 and 29, 1791, introduced the jury de jugement to France, and during the succeeding century and a half, the procedures by which twelve men were chosen and then deliberated a verdict underwent substantial modification. The Revolution simply declared all "active citizens" eligible for jury duty. Bonaparte wanted only the loyal and severe as jurors and turned their selection over entirely to his prefects. The Restoration struck a lasting compromise (subject to slight variation): The law of May 2, 1827, required a list of *jurés titulaires* (regular jurors) and *jurés suppléants* (substitute jurors) to be established annually in each department by the présidents of the tribunaux de première instance, the juges de paix, the mayors, the *conseillers généraux* (departmental councillors), and the *conseillers municipaux* (town councillors). For the Department of the Seine (including Paris), there would be three thousand jurés titulaires and three hundred jurés suppléants; for the other departments, four hundred to six hundred jurés titulaires and fifty jurés suppléants. The Ministry of Justice advised selecting only men "who by their proven morality, independent and firm character, and sufficiently broad intelligence are capable of fulfilling the high mission of justice confided to them by society."[11]

Although eligibility appeared broad—a French citizen at least thirty years old in full possession of his political and civil rights—the range of potential jurors was narrow. The definition eliminated the unenfranchised (the bulk of the male population before the Second Republic and all women before 1944), criminals and many misdemeanants (because the penalty included loss of civil rights for a

10. Esmein, *Continental Criminal Procedure*, 534, 555–56.
11. André Cambréal, *Le Jury criminel: Comment se forme, délibère, et statue le jury de cour d'assises* (Paris, 1937), 11–23, the quotation from 20; Esmein, *Continental Criminal Procedure*, 532.

time), the recently bankrupt (because that status also carried the loss of civil rights), domestics (for lack of "independence"), and the illiterate. Further language exempted members of the national legislature, all members of the armed forces on active duty, and anyone associated with judicial proceedings, by virtue of their professions, and "excused" from consideration all manual laborers, on the ground that they could not afford to serve. Men from the working classes were admitted to jury duty only after the laws of March 19, 1907, and July 17, 1908, provided for their lodging during the trial and indemnified them for lost wages. Who was left? Jean Cruppi, a respected magistrate who became a mediocre politician, analyzed 1,500 jurors from the Seine in 1898 and found that 849 (56.6 percent) were merchants, manufacturers, and business employees; 281 (18.7 percent) proprietors and rentiers; 174 (11.6 percent) professors, engineers, and government bureaucrats; 64 (4.3 percent) retired; 57 (3.8 percent) architects; 53 (3.5 percent) veterinarians, physicians, and pharmacists; and 22 (1.5 percent) artists. Despite the obvious distortion of applying statistics from the capital to the whole country, Cruppi was undoubtedly correct in concluding that criminal justice had "a true class jury . . . the jury of the middle class." Nevertheless, a quantitative analysis of verdicts before and after 1908 reveals that working-class representation had little effect on the attitude of juries toward crime and criminals.[12]

At the chef-lieu of each department the names of the potential jurors were deposited in two urns, corresponding to the two lists, and during a public ceremony at least ten days before the cour d'assises convened, a panel of judges blindly drew thirty-six jurés titulaires and four jurés suppléants to make up the final jury list for the trial. Advanced age (seventy years or older), sickness, absence from the department, and service as a juror the previous year were acceptable reasons for removal from the list. Any other attempt to avoid jury duty was heavily fined: Fr 500 for the first offense, Fr 1,000 for the second, and Fr 1,500 for the third or more. The jury de jugement was impaneled from the remaining names, with the first juror seated becoming the foreman. During the trial the jurymen had the right to ask questions of the accused and the witnesses (through the prési-

12. Charropin, *De la participation du jury*, 11–25; Esmein, *Continental Criminal Procedure*, 559–60; Cruppi, *La Cour d'assises*, 1–79, 205–331, the analysis of the Seine jurors from 22, the quotation from 256. For the quantitative analysis see James M. Donovan, "Justice Unblind: The Juries and the Criminal Classes in France, 1825–1914," *Journal of Social History*, XV (1981), 92–94, 102–103.

dent) but did so extremely rarely, and until they left to deliberate the verdict, they were absolutely forbidden to discuss the proceedings or even to manifest their opinions at all.[13]

After withdrawing to a separate room, the jurors had to resolve three issues to determine their verdict: Were the facts of the case established? Was the accused guilty as a result of these facts? And did the facts fall under the specific provisions of the law? The last could involve a question of values as much as legalities: The jurors might decide that certain acts, particularly *crimes passionnels*, were simply outside the limits of the law and therefore not punishable. If the case or the law was unusually complex, the foreman could request that the président enter the jury room to answer questions. Because this consultation might prove prejudicial to the defense, legislation was ultimately enacted on December 10, 1908, requiring that the defense attorney, the prosecutor, and the greffier, who maintained an official record, accompany the président. During the jury's first forty-four years of existence, jurors voted their *conviction intime* orally before the foreman, the président, and the prosecutor, but the laws of September 9, 1835, and May 13, 1836, established a secret ballot. For conviction, the laws of 1791 required the votes of ten jurors; the 1808 criminal code seven; the law of March 4, 1831, eight; that of March 9, 1835, seven; the decree of March 6, 1848, nine; a further decree of October 18, 1848, eight; and the law of June 10, 1853, seven, the number at which the level remained until 1940. Originally the jury's competence extended only to the verdict, but confronted with an exceptionally severe penal code, many jurors were reluctant to convict when the punishment seemed too harsh for the crime. To lessen this hesitation, the law of April 28, 1832, permitted the jury to accompany a guilty verdict with a finding of extenuating conditions that bound the justices to reduce the possible penalty by one degree and authorized them to reduce it by two degrees. Except in the most flagrant and vicious crimes, juries routinely discovered grounds for mitigating circumstances. A century later, in 1932, the jury would gain the right to deliberate with the justices on the actual sentence.[14]

From 1791 onward, juries were consistently criticized as irra-

13. Cambréal, *Le Jury criminel*, 22–40.
14. *Ibid.*, 40–55; Halton, *Etude sur la procédure criminelle*, 171–76; Esmein, *Continental Criminal Procedure*, 531–33, 561; Sheehan, *Criminal Procedure*, 185–86; Cruppi, *La Cour d'assises*, 94–108; Charropin, *De la participation du jury*, 52–77.

tional, undependable, and lax. No case came before the cour d'assises until after an extensive investigation by the juge d'instruction and the concurrence of the chambre des mises en accusation. Yet the conviction rate barely exceeded 70 percent, and extenuating conditions were found for nearly 80 percent of the guilty. Jurors were frequently swept toward acquittal by the rhetoric of an eloquent defense attorney. More often, no matter how strong the prosecution's case, they embraced the innocence of an accused who dramatically confronted the witnesses against him. Juries alternated between extreme severity (toward all forms of armed robbery) and extreme sympathy (toward *crimes passionnels*, infanticides, and abortions). They refused almost absolutely to convict if the penalty appeared to be disproportionate to the crime: For infanticide, a simple guilty verdict meant the guillotine; a finding of mitigating circumstances, merely imprisonment for life at hard labor. Stern moralists and many judicial officials railed at this incoherence, but most Frenchmen recognized that juries placed the penalties of criminal justice in agreement with contemporary social morality and thereby made them acceptable to popular opinion, an essential element in a nation where government (in this case, the repression of crime) depended greatly upon the consent of the governed.[15]

When the jury returned, its verdict was read aloud to the court by the greffier. If the accused had been found guilty, the defense attorney asked for mercy in the sentencing. The avocat général could reply for the state, but the defense had the right to a final plea. The justices then withdrew to decide on a sentence, which was announced without dissenting opinion. Depending upon the crime and any finding of extenuating conditions, they imposed a penalty ranging from death to imprisonment for at least five years, added a substantial fine, stripped such dignities as membership in the Légion d'honneur, and awarded damages to the partie civile. The Ministry of Justice and most prosecutors urged severity in sentencing, because of the perception that juries were lenient and because "all the greatest interests of society are at stake."[16] Most of the justices displayed such ferocity toward convicted criminals that the encouragement was hardly necessary.

15. Emile Yvernès, *Le Crime et le criminel devant le jury* (Paris, 1894), 7–21; Esmein, *Continental Criminal Procedure*, 564; Charropin, *De la participation du jury*, 78–91; Cruppi, *La Cour d'assises*, 205–31.
16. Ernest Roullet, *Des devoirs des magistrats* (Lyon, 1886), 11.

The Courts

The definitive nature of the jury's verdict was a basic principle in French justice, and the outcome of a trial before the cour d'assises was subject to appeal only on the basis of procedural error. Although infrequent because expensive and unlikely of success, such a *pourvoi en cassation* (petition for reversal) could be filed by the prosecution and the partie civile as well as the defense. Intention to appeal had to be signaled within five days of the verdict, and the complete brief submitted within ten days, to the chambre criminelle of the Cour de Cassation, which heard oral arguments and considered a summation prepared by one of its fifteen conseillers. The chambre criminelle usually disregarded minor flaws in procedure, but for a grave irregularity it quashed the original judgment and ordered a retrial during the next session of the department's cour d'assises. The ruling on procedure by the chambre criminelle was not binding on the retrial, but if the issue led to a second appeal, the full bench of the Cour de Cassation deliberated the petition. A decision that upheld the chambre criminelle quashed the second judgment and bound the third trial.

Immediately after the 1808 criminal code became effective, prosecutors attempted to create an exemption to the definitive jury verdict through what could be called, anachronistically, *correctionnalisation* in reverse. Frustrated by an acquittal in the cour d'assises, the parquet would use the same evidence to bring the accused before a cour correctionnelle charged with a *délit*. By its decision of October 29, 1812, the Cour de Cassation quickly prohibited the tactic. Two less serious infringements on the jury's verdict remained. One was a curious survival of the ancien régime's royal lettres de réduction and lettres de grâce that gave the chief of state (under the Third Republic, the president) the right to commute a sentence of death as he saw fit. The other was a rare appeal, the *pourvoi en revision*, which the 1808 criminal code permitted in three specific circumstances—if an important witness committed perjury, if two irreconcilable verdicts existed on the same crime, and if an alleged homicide victim was in fact alive. The law of June 8, 1895, added a fourth, the discovery of new evidence previously unavailable. The Cour de Cassation was empowered to order a new trial, or exceptionally, to overturn the original verdict and terminate all proceedings when the person convicted was dead and a retrial obviously impossible or when no credible evidence would continue to exist that a crime had ever been committed. The 1895 law also required the state to publicize widely any finding from a pourvoi en revision that the conviction proceeded from judicial error and to make a monetary reparation for the injury and suffering as a result.[17]

The persistently erratic quality of jury verdicts can be illustrated impressionistically through an examination of cases taken from the late 1920s and the 1930s, almost a century and a half after the trial jury was instituted. When the case involved a relatively straightforward *crime passionnel*, juries were predictably sympathetic. Sidney Conquy, a couturier in the Faubourg St. Honoré, shot and killed his wife, Gisèle, when she demanded a divorce to marry his assistant manager. Léonie Gérard killed her lover of forty years, Victor Deprez, by whom she had had three children, after he abandoned her for a girl eighteen years old. Charles Jeziorski shot his wife dead and then futilely attempted suicide upon learning that she had betrayed him. All three were tried before the cour d'assises of the Seine and acquitted. Juries outside the capital were equally forgiving, occasionally at the price of remarkable credulity. Raymond Falcou became incensed when his mistress, a Mme Boutet, left him for a rival, and took revenge by burning her automobile—with her inside. A jury at Rouen accepted his claim of meaning only to destroy her property and acquitted him. Camille Tharault killed her lover, the champion cyclist Henri Pélissier, with a pistol shot but insisted that she was merely trying to wound him after he struck her. A jury at Versailles voted for acquittal. When a death, however great the passion behind it, had the marks of premeditation, all tolerance could disappear. Another jury at Versailles judged the case of Gaston Langevin and Gilberte Tessier, who together murdered her husband in a plot reminiscent of Balzac's *Thérèse Raquin,* and condemned both lovers to the guillotine.[18]

The response was harder to predict when a *crime passionnel* was more complicated. In 1931 a jury in Nice heard the trial of Charlotte

---

17. Esmein, *Continental Criminal Procedure,* 538–39, 565–69; Sheehan, *Criminal Procedure,* 90–94; Millié, *Le Guide du Palais,* 78–83; Saillard, *Le Rôle de l'avocat,* 193–209; F. Crouzillac, *De la cassation sans renvoi après revision des procès criminels et correctionnels* (Paris, 1910). When the Cour de Cassation declared Alfred Dreyfus innocent on July 12, 1906, and ended all judicial proceedings against him, it acted through a pourvoi en revision.

18. *La Gazette des Tribunaux, Journal de Jurisprudence et des Débats judiciaires,* July 5–6, 1927, on Conquy; April 2, 1927, on Gérard; July 2, 1929, on Jeziorski; March 9–12, 1933, on Falcou; May 27, 1936, on Tharault; March 10–11, 1937, on Langevin and Tessier.

Nash, who eight years earlier, at the age of seventeen, had held the title Miss St. Louis. She had married F. Nexon Nirdlinger three times. In January, 1924, the ceremony was invalidated because he already had a wife. In December, 1925, they married after his divorce, but they agreed to a divorce of their own six months later in May, 1926. They remarried in July, 1928. Over the next two and a half years, he threatened to beat her, forbade her the use of cosmetics, and, during a final argument in March, 1931, accused her of taking lovers. She shot him, and she was acquitted. A jury in Rouen came to a different verdict in a similar case. Gisèle Bourdet was twenty years old and the mother of an infant son. Her husband menaced her with his revolver for having visited her mother, whom he hated. After he fell asleep, she took the revolver and fired several bullets into his head. Although the jury agreed that extenuating conditions existed, it did not acquit, and she was condemned to prison for five years. Two cases from Paris provide a second comparison. Charles Harscoet, a restaurateur who had fought publicly with his wife many times, shot her dead in the midst of a violent quarrel. At his trial he appeared to be genuinely remorseful about her death and yet displayed a wit that won the sympathy of the jury. He wore evening dress for the interrogatoire, and to testimony that he had once hurled a Camembert at his wife, he replied that he had far too much respect for that cheese ever to throw it. The jury returned an acquittal. Georgette Hodot, a Paris beauty queen, was tried for killing her former lover, the wealthy jeweler Isaac Eichisky. When he rejected her to marry another woman, she demanded Fr 200,000 for having been his mistress, but he scornfully answered that Fr 20,000 was sufficient for the pleasure he had received. In a rage she pulled a pistol from her purse and shot him. The jury showed little compassion, and she was sentenced to twenty years in prison at hard labor.[19]

The ambiguity of a *crime passionnel* was conveyed most compellingly by the case of Jane Weiller, née Boyer, which came before the cour d'assises of the Seine in October, 1929. Thirty-eight years old, slender, elegant, well educated, she was on trial for the murder of her husband, Robert. Both were born to the haute bourgeoisie, and both had descended to a nether world. Jane Weiller's first husband died in an automobile accident; her second, eight years her junior, by whom she had two children, divorced her. At some point during

19. *Ibid.*, May 21, 1931, on Nash; May 28, 1930, on Bourdet; November 22, 1932, on Harscoet; March 27–28, 1931 on Hodot.

the second marriage, she adopted the habit of occasionally prostituting herself at a discreet *maison de rendez-vous,* less for the money than for the sensation. She met Robert Weiller there, and they lived together for four years until her pregnancy led them to marry. Weiller was an unstable idler, subject to crises of exaltation and depression, prone to make threats and to talk loosely of suicide. He had been married and divorced three times before. At the trial the second and third wives testified that he forced them into sexual relations with other men while he watched. Some witnesses recounted how the Weillers boasted of arranging orgies. On the night of his death Weiller became violent and tried to strangle his wife. She escaped his grasp and shot him in self-defense. After he fell wounded, she fired a bullet through the back of his skull. During the interrogatoire, she excused herself by explaining that Weiller had asked her to administer a coup de grâce if he ever attempted suicide and failed. Shocked by these sordid revelations, the jury could not hold Jane Weiller entirely to blame for the second shot, or entirely blameless either. She was found guilty with extenuating conditions and sentenced to five years in prison.[20]

Although French juries could be lenient toward many *crimes passionnels,* they turned ferocious when the accused more clearly had a criminal intent and especially when an *assassinat* or *meutre* accompanied larceny. In such a case the jury frequently returned a verdict that permitted the justices to impose a sentence of forced labor —and, until 1937, transportation to the penal colony in Guiana—for a period ranging up to life. Forced labor was the fate that juries in Paris determined for Charles Mestorino, who killed the jeweler Gaston Truphème while committing armed robbery; for Marcel Nourric, his wife Blanche, and her brother, who murdered a bank messenger for the currency he carried, and threw his body into the Seine River; for Georges Legay, a mentally disturbed adolescent who shot dead his mother and wounded two women servants. But the decision was not always taken without hesitation. A jury at Aix-en-Provence felt a certain sympathy for Dr. Pierre Bougrat, a member of the Légion d'honneur and an authentic hero with six wounds from World War I. Desperate for money after his wife divorced him because of his infatuation with a lower-class prostitute, he killed a patient to steal ten thousand francs and was sentenced to hard labor for the rest of his life. At Orléans, Michel Henriot, the son of the city's pro-

20. *Ibid.,* October 31–November 1, 1929.

cureur de la République, was charged with the murder of his wife, Georgette. The trial revealed that during a marriage lasting only seven months, he devised sadistic tortures and finally stabbed her to death with an iron poker. The jury's preference was almost certainly for execution, but it was swayed by evidence of Henriot's mental instability and condemned him to forced labor for twenty years. Louis Plateaux got forced labor for life after being found guilty in Laon of killing a mute girl, fourteen years old, who was under treatment at the hospital in Soissons where he was an orderly. She resisted his attempt at rape, and he strangled her accidentally.[21]

Certain crimes—multiple murders or the murder of parents, children, or police officers—impressed most juries as so particularly heinous that they deserved the ultimate sanction of the law, execution at the guillotine. Anne-Marie David, angry at her renter, a Mme Baud, forced a piece of sponge down the throat of the woman's ten-month-old child until it choked to death. Blanche Vabre stabbed her stepson, Jean, fifteen years old, ten times in the neck and reported that he had been attacked by robbers. Louise Ducrozet, called the Ogress of Jasseron, drowned her eight-year-old daughter. Pierre Delafet, clearly an ogre himself, used a knife, a hatchet, and a rifle as he massacred his wife, son, daughter, mother, grandmother, and uncle—and was ruled sane. Violette Nozière, a thin, short girl nineteen years old, drugged her parents with Veronal and left them shut in their house after opening the gas taps. Her father suffocated; her mother was barely revived. At the trial Nozière claimed that she had committed a *crime passionnel* in killing a father who had molested her and seeking to kill a mother who had permitted it. The prosecution countered that she schemed and murdered to gain an inheritance of Fr 180,000. She was supporting two lovers in the Latin Quarter and was also the mistress of several unnamed wealthy businessmen. Arthur Mahieu killed a patrolman who surprised him at burglary. Camille Maueurer and Calixte Joulia, known as the Bandits of Marseille, shot dead three police officers while robbing a train station. Dr. Pierre Laget poisoned two successive wives. Christine and Léa Papin slaughtered the family that employed them as servants and mutilated the bodies horrifically. Bruno Weidmann committed six unusually brutal murders. In all ten cases the juries

---

21. *Ibid.*, June 5–9, 1928, on Mestorino; March 10–16, 1928, on Nourric and his family; February 9–11, 1930, on Legay; March 23–30, 1927, on Bougrat; June 28–July 2, 1935, on Henriot; February 24, 1938, on Plateaux.

rendered verdicts entirely devoid of any recommendation for mercy. The president of the Republic spared all of the women and Delafet by commuting their sentences to forced labor for life. The remaining men went to the guillotine, with Weidmann's execution on June 16, 1939, the last under the Third Republic.[22]

22. *Ibid.*, November 8, 1928, on David; November 23, 1928, on Vabre; April 11, 1933, on Ducrozet; March 7, 1933, on Delafet; October 11–13, 1934, on Nozière (whose case was the subject of a feature film, *Violette Nozière*, released by Gaumont in 1978, directed by Claude Chabrol, with Violette played by Isabelle Huppert); March 24, 1936, on Mahieu; January 23–28, 1934, on Maueuer and Joulia; June 4–9, 1931, on Laget; September 29, 1933, on the Papin sisters; March 11–April 1, 1939, on Weidmann. Ducrozet was tried in Lyon, Delafet in Agen, Maueuer and Joulia in Marseilles, Laget in Montpellier, the Papin sisters in Le Mans, and the others in Paris.

6

The Magistrature

Writing in 1871, Odilon Barrot, the liberal "banquet campaigner," bluntly denounced France's judiciary: "No, the magistrature, such as it is constituted, does not offer sufficient guarantees to the protection of law and rights in our country; the best men within it are lost in the immensities of the judicial ranks and are paralyzed by a vicious organization and by a mode of procedure more vicious still."[1] The main target of this condemnation was the method by which magistrates were promoted, a method that effectively immersed the judicial bureaucracy, and occasionally justice itself, in favoritism and politics. Barrot wrote in hope—shared by the many other critics of the judicial system—that the new Third Republic might end the abuses practiced by the various imperial, royal, and republican regimes during the first seven decades of the nineteenth century. To the contrary, by attempting to purge the magistrature of judges and prosecutors whose republican loyalty was suspect, the new regime exacerbated the practices Barrot decried.

1. Barrot, *De l'organisation judiciaire en France*, 12. For other expressions of the reform that a republic might bring, see Prévost-Paradol, *La France nouvelle*; Jules Favre, *De la réforme judiciaire* (Paris, 1877); Picot, *La Réforme judiciaire en France*; Philouze, *Etude sur l'organisation*; Roullet, *Des devoirs des magistrats*. See also Martin, "The Courts, the Magistrature, and Promotions," 977–1009.

During the nineteenth century and through the Third Republic, entrance into the ranks of the magistrature was relatively easy. The candidate had to complete his *licence ès lois* (law degree), serve a *stage d'avocat* (twelve-month clerkship), pass an unchallenging *examen d'aptitude* (competency test), attain the age of twenty-two, and win recommendation from a chief judge or justice. Such a recommendation usually required at least limited political influence. Beginning in 1875, the Ministry of Justice experimented with a *concours* for recruitment, but discontinued this competitive examination in 1879 because its use restricted discretionary (and often purely political) appointments. A ministerial decree of August 18, 1906, imposed a second *examen d'aptitude* on candidates, but this test hardly restored a *concours*, because almost everyone passed it. Although a few scholarship students at the law schools pursued careers in the magistrature, the ministry preferred to entrust the maintenance of order to men who had much to lose from disorder, and most young judges and prosecutors came from bourgeois families that discouraged deviation from *idées reçues, bien pensant*, and *fils à papa*. Their fathers were frequently either magistrates themselves or *propriétaires* (the propertied, usually rentiers as well) who could afford to provide their sons with a professional education and private wealth. An outside income of at least Fr 2,000 was essential, because the salary for the lowest ranks was quite meager (from Fr 2,800 to Fr 3,000 as late as 1914), and magistrates were expected to maintain a proper image. When Jules Favre wrote in 1877 that only the rich could afford to be magistrates, he did not greatly exaggerate.[2]

The framework of courts and the ranks of the magistrature were overseen by the Ministry of Justice at the Place Vendôme. The ministry traced its lineage to the office of chancellor under the ancien régime, but it more properly dated from a series of decrees (January 9 and 19, April 27, and May 25) in 1791 that established its modern functions: to register the laws ("keep the seals"; thus the title *garde*

---

2. Favre, *De la réforme judiciaire*, 48. On the subject of magistrates, their recruitment, and their services, see Jean Pierre Royer et al., *Juges et notables au XIXe siècle* (Paris, 1982), 24–31, 139–47; Martial Bergeron, *La Réforme de la magistrature* (Paris, 1908); Jacques Du Boishamon, *Du recrutement de la magistrature* (Rennes, 1902); Maurice Dehesdin, *Etude sur le recrutement et l'avancement des magistrats* (Paris, 1908); G. Demartial, *La Nomination des magistrats* (Paris, 1907); Paul Lallemand, *Le Recrutement des juges* (Paris, 1936); F. L. Malepeyre, *La Magistrature en France et projets de réforme* (Paris, 1900); Georges Marchand, *Le Recrutement de la magistrature en France* (Paris, 1910); and Jean Mendiondou, *Etude des projets de réforme de la magistrature sous la Troisième République* (Paris, 1912).

des sceaux for the minister of justice), to publish and distribute these laws to the jurisdictions, and to maintain correspondence with, and direction of, the system of courts. The Revolutionary and Napoleonic periods brought numerous reorganizations, as both Jacobins and Bonapartists realized the importance of controlling the administration of justice. Napoleon even made the minister of justice *grand juge*, enabling him to preside over the Cour de Cassation or any appellate court as the needs of the state required. None of the changes fundamentally altered the structure set down in 1791. The ministry was instead confirmed in its functions and began developing a bureaucracy to discharge them. The most important aspect of this evolution was the creation, prefigured as early as 1794, of two great units within the ministry, the *direction des affaires civiles* (which had control of civil cases) and the *direction des affaires criminelles* (which had control of criminal cases), each entrusted to a *directeur* (director) ranking immediately beneath the minister. The decision to split the administration of justice so high in the bureaucratic structure meant that the justices and judges, who heard both civil and criminal cases, were subject to quite different pressures from the ministry, depending upon the jurisdiction of a given case. Additionally, the directeurs came to have significant power concentrated in their hands.

The remaining apparatus of the ministry was also elaborated by the beginning of the nineteenth century, though it underwent various modifications. Initially, a *secrétaire général* (secretary general) for the ministry acted as an intermediary between the minister of justice and the other high officials, eventually becoming influential enough to undermine the independence of the two directeurs. Ministerial decrees of December 30, 1884, and November 22, 1890, first restored the balance by creating the *cabinet du ministre*, an advisory council in which the secrétaire général sat with the directeurs and chefs de division, and then replaced the office of secrétaire général entirely with a weaker one, the *chef du cabinet* (chief assistant to the minister). On June 8, 1894, the Division of Personnel was elevated to the status of a *direction*, and on June 9, 1909, after some preliminary experimentation, the Division of Accounting was placed under its authority. Despite these increased responsibilities, the directeur for personnel remained a lesser figure than the directeurs for civil and criminal affairs. His tasks were viewed as a *marchepied* (training ground) for future succession to those more demanding and politically delicate *directions*. The final major change before the end of the Third Republic was the decision by the government to transfer supervision of the prisons from the Ministry of the Interior to the Ministry of Justice. The process began with a decree on July 13, 1913, but it was fully accomplished only on December 28, 1935.

Officials in the bureaucracy at the Place Vendôme worked short hours, from 11 A.M. to 5 P.M., and never numbered many more than one hundred until the mid-1920s. The total rose to nearly two hundred by the late 1930s because of the new administration for the prisons. In ascending order, the positions were those of *expéditionnaire* (copying clerk), *commis d'ordre* (clerk), *vérificateur* (verifier), *rédacteur* (head clerk), *sous-chef* (deputy department head), *chef de bureau* (department head), *chef de division* (division head), and *directeur*. Magistrates were usually placed in the principal offices. Prior to June 5, 1909, the other positions were not filled through a competitive examination but did have educational prerequisites: for the expéditionnaires, commis d'ordre, and vérificateurs, the baccalaureate and a twelve-month probationary period in a legal office; for rédacteurs, the *licence ès lois* and a *stage d'avocat*, as was mandated for magistrates. After 1909 a *concours* was established for all ranks through rédacteur, but to compete to become a rédacteur, a candidate had to serve two years with the ministry in a lower position or be a magistrate. The Ministry of Justice thereby defended its median and higher ranks from outside infiltration while bowing to demands for competitive placement.[3]

In France a great distinction existed between the bar and the magistrature. A law student usually decided before completing the *licence ès droit* which direction his career was to take; crossovers were infrequent. With all the positions of the bench (the *magistrature assise*) and the parquet (the *magistrature debout*) guaranteed to them, magistrates developed a strong esprit de corps. At the same time, because they were clearly part of the state bureaucracy, they were not commonly regarded, among themselves or by outsiders, as an independent judiciary. Rather than staking out precedents, judges relied on the text of the law codes. A panel of at least three judges heard a case and rendered its verdict without public dissenting opinions. Conseillers frequently felt compelled to defer to the wishes of the premier président, because he recommended promotions for the

---

3. On the Ministry of Justice see Pascal Durand-Barthez, *Histoire des structures du ministère de la justice, 1789–1945* (Paris, 1973), and Louis Rouvier, *La Chancellerie et les sceaux de France* (2nd ed.; Marseille, 1950).

bench. A prosecutor had even less space for independence. The written pleadings he presented for a case could be dictated by his superior, and though he was free to formulate his own oral arguments in open court, to contradict his original submission was highly imprudent. Within each *ressort,* prosecutors reported to the procureur général, who prepared the annual evaluations for the parquet, and in turn, the procureurs généraux were accountable directly to the minister of justice. The laws of April 28, 1810, and March 1, 1852, established the principle of *inamovibilité* (irremovability) for the magistrature assise, with exceptions for insanity or incapacitating illness, and set a mandatory retirement age of seventy (seventy-five for the Cour de Cassation). But this protection was not extended to the magistrature debout. A prosecutor who incurred the displeasure of his superiors could be ejected from the magistrature, but more often he was assigned to the bench at the lowest rank and could consider his career broken.

The desire for promotion and fear of dismissal dominated the mind of many a magistrate. Ordinarily, his first positions were on the parquet or bench of a provincial tribunal. The inadequate salary and backwater society contrasted acutely with the comfortable world in which he had been reared and educated. He could dream of a brilliant career, culminating in appointment to the Cour d'appel de Paris or even the Cour de Cassation, but that required rapid elevation. He learned that advancement came fastest to the magistrature debout and that it was not difficult to shift from the bench to the parquet and back again. The caveat was that service in the magistrature debout carried with its opportunities an uncertain degree of risk. In quest of promotion, a young magistrate had to maintain at least correct relations with the premier président and the procureur général of his *ressort,* because mediocre or indifferent recommendations from them were difficult to overcome. Naturally he began to develop that exaggerated respect for superiors and aversion to wrong ideas so characteristic of the ambitious in the French magistrature. Outward conformity to the trilogy of *famille honorable, aisance large,* and *bonne vie et moeurs* (family, wealth, and morality) was mandatory. Marriage was the proof of stability, divorce worse than a succession of love affairs. Hypocrisy was regarded as a virtue. With the many changes of regime before 1871 and the shifting factions of the Third Republic afterward, the safest political loyalty was to order and to the government in power. Georges Sorel described all the magistrates involved in the Dreyfus affair as "domestiques judiciaires," and in 1940, only one of approximately 2,500 magistrates refused the oath of allegiance to Philippe Pétain.[4]

Compliance and conformity were all the greater as a consequence of extraordinary dismissals that provided dramatic evidence of how political persuasion could make or unmake careers. The republicans, both Opportunist and Radical, who since January, 1879, had controlled the Chamber of Deputies, the Senate, and the presidency, resolved to punish magistrates who refused to carry out the new anticlerical laws, especially those of March 29, 1880, aimed at the religious congregations. Between April and December, 1880, a total of 259 parquet officers resigned rather than prosecute the Jesuits and other male communities. Approximately 300 more created delays or obstructions to the proceedings. Similarly, nearly 400 judges and justices blocked enforcement of the laws. Some of this recalcitrance arose from sincerely held religious conviction; some of it derived from antirepublican sentiment among magistrates who had been appointed during the imperial regime of Louis Napoleon and who hoped for a return of the Bonapartes or for a royalist restoration. The republicans responded with a thorough purge of the parquets. Beginning in February, 1879, with Philippe Le Royer as minister of justice, and continuing to December, 1882, through the ministries of Théodore Cazot and Gustave Humbert, 82 percent of the magistrature debout (1,763 of 2,149) was dismissed or replaced.[5]

There remained the magistrates of the bench. The law of August 30, 1883, that raised salaries for the lowest-ranking judges and prosecutors also eliminated 614 positions of the magistrature assise. Their irremovability was suspended for three months, and the Cour de Cassation was empowered to expel any magistrate who had served on the notorious *commissions mixtes* (summary courts composed of military and civilian judges formed to try the insurrectionists who opposed Louis Napoleon's coup d'état of December 2, 1851) and the most prominent judges and justices who had manifested hostility to the principles or form of republican government. Like the clergy, the bench was an easy target for Opportunist and Radical legislators, who associated it with the repression of the Second Empire. Jules Simon, one of the more moderate legislators, did note one dif-

4. Georges Sorel, *La Révolution dreyfusienne* (Paris, 1911), 51; Casamayor, *Les Juges*, 88; Royer et al., *Juges et notables*, 46–49, 103–18.
5. Georges Picot, *La Magistrature et la démocratie, une épuration radicale* (Paris, 1884), 6–52; Georges Légée, *La Loi du 30 août 1883 sur la magistrature* (Paris, 1904), 83–102; Royer et al., *Juges et notables*, 359–64, 376–86.

ference: Hatred of the clergy was collective, that of the judges individual.[6] Each deputy and each senator had his chosen victims. Denunciations from them, from prefects, and even from Radical newspapers, piled high at the Place Vendôme, and the minister of justice, Félix Martin-Feuillé, had difficulty choosing which 614 "irremovables" to revoke. One expedient was to dismiss the most visible. Thus 10 of 26 premiers présidents of the cours d'appel and 122 of 359 présidents of the tribunaux de première instance were removed. At Angers the conseillers rallied behind the premier président, with the result that 18 of the 28 justices on the court were replaced. By early 1884, between 900 and 1,000 additional members of the magistrature assise had resigned in sympathy. Monarchists in the legislature alleged that many judges were dismissed merely for being practicing Catholics and therefore suspect as "clericals." When questioned before the Senate in December, 1883, Martin-Feuillé did not deny the charge.[7]

For magistrates who put promotion above principle, the ideological battles of the Third Republic made it difficult to know where to place their allegiance. Opportunist Republican ministers were likely to reward Opportunist Republican magistrates, less likely to reward Radicals, and very unlikely to reward monarchists. Because the Third Republic saw numerous shifts of power among these contending political groups, the stakes of loyalty were high. They weighed most heavily on the parquet, which had to conduct the prosecution in sensitive cases, but the bench also faced crises of conscience. Most of the truly important politicians were members of the bar and continued to practice law while holding office. Judges depended ultimately upon the minister of justice for promotion; the minister of justice depended upon these powerful politicians for legislative support. There was always the implied threat that a decision rendered against the clients of an important politician-barrister could destroy a magistrate's career.

---

6. Henri Fourchy, *Observations sur la suspension de l'inamovibilité de la magistrature* (Paris, 1882), 7.

7. *JOS*, Débats parlementaires, December 26, 1883, question from Ernest Denormandie. See Albert Desjardins, *L'Inamovibilité de la magistrature dans l'ancienne France* (Paris, 1890), and *La Magistrature élue* (Beauvais, 1882); Victor Jeanvrot, *La Magistrature, l'inamovibilité* (Paris, 1882); Eugène Ninard, *De l'inamovibilité de la magistrature et de l'indépendance du magistrat* (Bordeaux, 1884); B. Schadet, *Nos magistrats, ce qu'ils soient, ce qu'ils doivent être* (Paris, 1882), and *Encore nos magistrats, ce qu'ils seront par le suffrage universel* (Paris, 1882); Royer et al., *Juges et notables*, 365–75.

During the nineteenth century, the promotion of magistrates was dominated by patronage and favoritism. However inequitable, the process was an advance over the venality of the ancien régime, when magisterial positions were considered proprietary and hereditary. But the step was hardly great, because before 1908 almost no rules governed consideration for advancement other than the ministerial circular of May 15, 1850, directing the premier président and the procureur général to prepare an annual report on each magistrate of the *ressort*. In it they were to provide detailed information about his background, training, competence, *caractère* (character), "conduite privée et publique" (behavior private and public), "position sociale et de fortune" (family, social position, and wealth), "appréciation politique" (appraisal of political beliefs and influence), and "observations et appréciations du chef de la cour" (the evaluator's personal assessment). The last two categories were the most significant.[8]

Political influence could be measured by the number and range of recommendations submitted on the magistrate's behalf and the stature of the references. The most effective letters were from ecclesiastics, until anticlerical republicans took charge in 1879, and from legislators, with Daniel Wilson, the son-in-law of President Jules Grévy and notable for his scheme to sell government decorations, principally the Légion d'honneur, composing an unusually large number.[9] Odilon Barrot declared in 1871, "I have known magistrates whose appointment to the Cour de Cassation can only be attributed to political influence." Thirty-one years later, in 1902, a young jurist, Jacques Du Boishamon, expressed a broadly held opinion within the judicial world when he wrote in his doctoral thesis, "We have seen numerous abuses committed by unscrupulous ministers of justice who sacrificed recognized merit in favor of incapacity recommended by the influential or fawning subservience to the current government." Political beliefs were even more critical. With each change of regime during the nineteenth century, there was a greater or lesser purge of the magistrature. Adolphe Crémieux, a republican of great rigor, presided over two of them, in April and May, 1848, and from September, 1870, to February, 1871. The purges were followed by a clear shift in the pattern of desirable political traits.[10]

---

8. Royer et al., *Juges et notables*, 7, 33–46.
9. Even a casual reading of the personnel files in the series BB 6 II at the AN reveals an extraordinary quantity of letters from Wilson.
10. Barrot, *De l'organisation judiciaire en France*, 105; Du Boishamon, *Du recrutement de la magistrature*, 146; Royer et al., *Juges et notables*, 50–80.

The Magistrature

Foremost among the complaints about judicial promotions was the charge that the minister of justice, with the advice of his directeurs and pressured by the importuning of deputies and senators for their favorites, advanced magistrates as he chose, without oversight and without accountability. Of the sixty-nine men who were gardes des sceaux from 1870 to 1940, fifty-one (74 percent) were politician-attorneys, and only eight (12 percent) were from the magistrature. The frequently made assumption that stability and continuity were greater among the principal assistants is not entirely true. During the same period, there were twenty-one directeurs des affaires civiles, thirty-five directeurs des affaires criminelles, and fifty-one directeurs du personnel. (See Tables 29–32.) Almost invariably these assistants were far more conversant with the personnel files than the minister was, but the dossiers reveal that the minister himself made the final decision on promotions to all important positions. Memoranda in the files also indicate that directeurs were as willing as the ministers of justice to place patronage over merit in the promotion of friends or political allies—though the ministers and directeurs did not always agree on specific individuals.

Proposals to reform the process of promotion called for the election of magistrates, as had been effected under the Constitution of 1791, or for a scheme of co-optation, with each court filling its own vacancies from the bench and parquet of lower courts. But even republicans were unwilling to trust the selection of judges to manhood suffrage, and co-optation was opposed for its tendency to create a caste of magistrates. Most important, either change threatened to remove the control of justice from the government itself, a gain of the 1789 Revolution that no political faction was willing to renounce. Yet there was widespread dissatisfaction with the ministry's unregulated favoritism and a general admission that irremovability was an insufficient guarantee of independence for the bench as long as promotion had to be chased.[11]

To deflect the continuing criticism, a ministerial decree of February 13, 1908, established a "system of presentations," by which every summer the premier président and procureur général of each *ressort* recommended up to one-half of the magistrates under their supervision for a specific promotion. Any magistrate not on the list could protest his exclusion directly to the ministry. Working from

11. For examples of reform proposals see Favre, *De la réforme judiciaire*, 25–121, and Picot, *La Réforme judiciaire en France*, 303–57.

TABLE 29
Ministers of Justice, 1870–1940

Minister of Justice	Dates of Service
Isaac Moïse (*dit* Adolphe) Crémieux	September 12, 1870–February 19, 1871
Jules Dufaure	February 19, 1871–May 25, 1873
Jean Ernoul	May 25, 1873–November 26, 1873
Octave Depeyre	November 26, 1873–May 22, 1874
Adrien Tailhand	May 22, 1874–March 10, 1875
Jules Dufaure	March 10, 1875–December 12, 1876
Louis Martel	December 12, 1876–May 17, 1877
Albert de Broglie	May 17, 1877–November 23, 1877
François Le Pelletier	November 23, 1877–December 13, 1877
Jules Dufaure	December 13, 1877–February 4, 1879
Philippe Le Royer	February 4, 1879–December 28, 1879
Théodore Cazot	December 28, 1879–January 30, 1882
Gustave Humbert	January 30, 1882–August 7, 1882
Paul Devès	August 7, 1882–February 21, 1883
Félix Martin-Feuillée	February 21, 1883–April 6, 1885
Henri Brisson	April 6, 1885–January 7, 1886
Charles Demôle	January 7, 1886–December 11, 1886
Jean Sarrien	December 11, 1886–May 30, 1887
Charles Mazeau	May 30, 1887–December 12, 1887
Armand Fallières	December 12, 1887–April 3, 1888
Jean-Baptiste Ferrouillat	April 3, 1888–February 5, 1889
Jean Guyot-Dessaigne	February 5, 1889–February 22, 1889
François Thévenet	February 22, 1889–March 17, 1890
Armand Fallières	March 17, 1890–February 27, 1892
Louis Ricard	February 27, 1892–December 6, 1892
Léon Bourgeois	December 6, 1892–April 4, 1893
Eugène Guérin	April 4, 1893–December 3, 1893
Antonin Dubost	December 3, 1893–May 30, 1894
Eugène Guérin	May 30, 1894–January 26, 1895
Jacques Trarieux	January 26, 1895–November 1, 1895
Louis Ricard	November 1, 1895–April 29, 1896
Jean-Baptiste Darlan	April 29, 1896–June 28, 1898
Jean Sarrien	June 28, 1898–November 1, 1898
Georges Lebret	November 1, 1898–June 22, 1899
Ernest Monis	June 22, 1899–June 7, 1902
Ernest Vallé	June 7, 1902–January 24, 1905
Jacques Chaumié	January 24, 1905–March 14, 1906
Jean Sarrien	March 14, 1906–October 25, 1906
Jean Guyot-Dessaigne	October 25, 1906–December 21, 1907
Aristide Briand	January 4, 1908–July 24, 1909
Louis Barthou	July 24, 1909–November 3, 1910
Théodore Girard	November 3, 1910–March 2, 1911
Antoine Perrier	March 2, 1911–June 27, 1911

TABLE 29
Continued

Minister of Justice	Dates of Service
Jean Cruppi	June 27, 1911–January 14, 1912
Aristide Briand	January 14, 1912–January 21, 1913
Louis Barthou	January 21, 1913–March 22, 1913
Antony Ratier	March 22, 1913–December 9, 1913
Jean-Baptiste Bienvenu-Martin	December 9, 1913–June 9, 1914
Alexandre Ribot	June 9, 1914–June 13, 1914
Jean-Baptiste Bienvenu-Martin	June 13, 1914–August 26, 1914
Aristide Briand	August 26, 1914–October 29, 1915
René Viviani	October 29, 1915–September 12, 1917
Raoul Péret	September 12, 1917–November 16, 1917
Louis Nail	November 16, 1917–January 20, 1920
Gustave Lhopiteau	January 20, 1920–January 16, 1921
Laurent Bonnevay	January 16, 1921–January 15, 1922
Louis Barthou	January 15, 1922–October 5, 1922
Maurice Colrat	October 5, 1922–March 29, 1924
Edmond Lefebvre du Prey	March 29, 1924–June 9, 1924
Antony Ratier	June 9, 1924–June 14, 1924
René Renoult	June 14, 1924–April 17, 1925
Théodore Steeg	April 17, 1925–October 11, 1925
Anatole de Monzie	October 11, 1925–October 29, 1925
Camille Chautemps	October 29, 1925–November 28, 1925
René Renoult	November 28, 1925–March 9, 1926
Pierre Laval	March 9, 1926–July 19, 1926
Maurice Colrat	July 19, 1926–July 23, 1926
Louis Barthou	July 23, 1926–November 3, 1929
Lucien Hubert	November 3, 1929–February 21, 1930
Théodore Steeg	February 21, 1930–March 2, 1930
Raoul Péret	March 2, 1930–November 17, 1930
Henry Chéron	November 17, 1930–January 27, 1931
Léon Bérard	January 27, 1931–February 20, 1932
Paul Reynaud	February 20, 1932–June 3, 1932
René Renoult	June 3, 1932–December 18, 1932
Abel Gardey	December 18, 1932–January 31, 1933
Eugène Penancier	January 31, 1933–October 26, 1933
Albert Dalimier	October 26, 1933–November 26, 1933
Eugène Raynaldy	November 26, 1933–January 30, 1934
Eugène Penancier	January 30, 1934–February 9, 1934
Henry Chéron	February 9, 1934–October 15, 1934
Henry Lémery	October 15, 1934–November 8, 1934
Georges Pernot	November 8, 1934–June 7, 1935
Léon Bérard	June 7, 1935–January 24, 1936

(continues)

TABLE 29
Continued

Minister of Justice	Dates of Service
Yvon Delbos	January 24, 1936–June 4, 1936
Marc Rucart	June 4, 1936–June 22, 1937
Vincent Auriol	June 22, 1937–January 18, 1938
César Campinchi	January 18, 1938–March 13, 1938
Marc Rucart	March 13, 1938–April 10, 1938
Paul Reynaud	April 10, 1938–November 1, 1938
Paul Marchandeau	November 1, 1938–September 13, 1939
Georges Bonnet	September 13, 1939–March 21, 1940
Albert Sérol	March 21, 1940–June 16, 1940
Charles Victor Jules Frémicourt	June 16, 1940–July 12, 1940

SOURCE: *Journal Officiel*, Lois et Décrets, 1870–1940.

TABLE 30
Directeurs des Affaires Civiles, Ministère de la Justice, 1870–1940

Directeur des Affaires Civiles	Dates of Service
Duvergier	1869–October 19, 1881
Eugène Jean Marie Gonse	October 19, 1881–February 22, 1888
Alphonse Bard	February 22, 1888–April 16, 1892
Charles Falcimaigne	April 16, 1892–November 29, 1894
Louis Octave Laborde	November 29, 1894–October 4, 1900
Honoré Marie Louis Henri Ditte	October 4, 1900–July 31, 1901
Georges Louis Mercier	July 31, 1901–April 22, 1904
Victor Fabre	April 22, 1904–July 16, 1904
François Edmond Paillot	July 16, 1904–May 31, 1906
Ferdinand Monier	May 31, 1906–June 19, 1907
Georges Eugène Lucien Lecherbonnier	June 19, 1907–May 24, 1910
Maurice Deligne	May 24, 1910–April 22, 1912
Paul Boulloche	April 22, 1912–November 2, 1915
Hippolyte Gaston Péan	November 2, 1915–July 24, 1918
Jean Baptiste Joseph Coudert	July 24, 1918–January 11, 1919
Fernand Constant Bricout	January 11, 1919–September 30, 1923
Germain Eucher Léon Fleys	September 30, 1923–May 20, 1926
Marie Louis Charles Donat-Guigue	May 20, 1926–February 4, 1928
Charles Victor Jules Frémicourt	February 4, 1928–May 6, 1932
Louis Loriot	May 6, 1932–November 20, 1935
Pierre Henri André Brack	November 20, 1935–August 29, 1940

SOURCE: *Journal Officiel*, Lois et Décrets, 1870–1940.

TABLE 31

Directeurs des Affaires Criminelles, Ministère de la Justice, 1870–1940

Directeur des Affaires Criminelles	Dates of Service
Jean Charles Babinet	1863–July 31, 1871
Jean Claude Petit	July 31, 1871–June 30, 1873
Marie Joseph Alexis Gast	June 30, 1873–August 4, 1874
Camille Godelle	August 4, 1874–June 1, 1875
Alexandre Ribot	June 1, 1875–January 21, 1876
Marie François Jules Lacointa	January 21, 1876–May 21, 1877
Joseph Amédée Benoist	May 21, 1877–December 18, 1877
Picot	December 18, 1877–February 11, 1879
Pierre Charles Sevestre	February 11, 1879–February 21, 1880
Célestin Louis Tanon	February 21, 1880–December 12, 1881
Pierre Achille Vételay	December 12, 1881–October 10, 1882
Ernest Jean Poux-Franklin	October 10, 1882–March 8, 1884
Etienne Edmond Jacquin	March 8, 1884–January 8, 1889
Marius Joseph Dumas	January 8, 1889–October 6, 1892
André Boulloche	October 6, 1892–October 17, 1896
Marie Jules Adrien Couturier	October 17, 1896–October 18, 1898
Hubert Petitier	October 18, 1898–July 31, 1901
François Malepeyre	July 31, 1901–October 12, 1903
Gabriel Geoffroy	October 12, 1903–March 21, 1905
François Joseph Saint-Aubin	March 21, 1905–October 16, 1906
Jules Emile Bourdon	October 16, 1906–January 13, 1908
Albert Anatole Tissier	January 13, 1908–July 29, 1909
Maurice Deligne	July 29, 1909–May 24, 1910
Théodore Lescouvé	May 24, 1910–January 18, 1911
Paul Boulloche	January 18, 1911–April 22, 1912
Paul André	April 22, 1912–February 28, 1914
Léon Joseph Courtin	February 28, 1914–February 20, 1917
Jean Baptiste Joseph Coudert	February 20, 1917–July 24, 1918
Eugène Leroux	July 24, 1918–November 28, 1922
Abel Prouharem	November 28, 1922–October 18, 1923
Maurice Gilbert	October 18, 1923–November 23, 1926
Paul Henri Mouton	November 23, 1926–May 1, 1930
Georges Ruteau	May 1, 1930–July 18, 1934
Edouard Ferdinand Raymond Bacquart	July 18, 1934–February 3, 1938
Nicolas Battestini	February 3, 1938–December 22, 1940

SOURCE: *Journal Officiel*, Lois et Décrets, 1870–1940.

TABLE 32
Directeurs du Personnel, Ministère de la Justice, 1870–1940

Directeur du Personnel	Dates of Service
Mausat-Laroche	1868–January 1, 1874
Valot	January 1, 1874–February 8, 1879
Durand-Desormeaux	February 8, 1879–June 28, 1881
Etienne Edmond Jacquin	June 28, 1881–March 8, 1884
Jules Auguste Clément Marie Roulier	March 8, 1884–August 7, 1885
Marie Emile Forichon	August 7, 1885–January 11, 1887
Charles Georges Persac	January 11, 1887–January 24, 1888
Jean Laroze	January 24, 1888–April 14, 1888
Marius Joseph Dumas	April 14, 1888–January 8, 1889
Pierre Ernest Boyer	January 8, 1889–April 3, 1890
Jean Laroze	April 3, 1890–March 7, 1892
Paul Louis Poupardin	March 7, 1892–January 12, 1893
Eugène Louis Marie Duval	January 12, 1893–April 24, 1893
Pierre Ernest Boyer	April 24, 1893–December 24, 1893
Louis Victor Mercier	December 24, 1893–June 9, 1894
Louis Octave Laborde	June 9, 1894–November 29, 1894
André Sauvajol	November 29, 1894–February 2, 1895
Jean Bruno Lacombe	February 2, 1895–November 11, 1895
Hubert Petitier	November 11, 1895–May 2, 1896
Marie Jules Adrien Couturier	May 2, 1896–October 17, 1896
Emile Flach	October 17, 1896–May 13, 1897
Gustave Lombard	May 13, 1897–July 5, 1898
Gabriel Geoffroy	July 5, 1898–November 5, 1898
Henry Milliard	November 5, 1898–March 21, 1900
Victor Fabre	March 21, 1900–August 6, 1900
Jules Emile Herbaux	August 6, 1900–October 4, 1900
François Malepeyre	October 4, 1900–July 31, 1901
Georges Eugène Lucien Lecherbonnier	July 31, 1901–July 25, 1902
Gabriel Geoffroy	July 25, 1902–October 12, 1903
Jean Baptiste Paul Dupré	October 12, 1903–February 20, 1906
Jean Baptiste Joseph Coudert	February 20, 1906–January 27, 1907
Jean Huguet	January 27, 1907–May 9, 1908
Maurice Deligne	May 9, 1908–July 29, 1909
Théodore Lescouvé	July 29, 1909–May 24, 1910
Paul Boulloche	May 24, 1910–January 18, 1911
Monmon	January 18, 1911–July 20, 1911
Fernand Constant Bricout	July 20, 1911–January 18, 1912

TABLE 32
Continued

Directeur du Personnel	Dates of Service
Albert Anatole Tissier	January 18, 1912–January 23, 1913
Léon Siben	January 23, 1913–March 28, 1914
Eugène Leroux	March 28, 1914–July 24, 1918
Charles Joseph Demangeat	July 24, 1918–November 25, 1919
Abel Prouharem	November 25, 1919–November 28, 1922
Germain Eucher Léon Fleys	November 28, 1922–September 30, 1923
Maurice Gilbert	September 30, 1923–October 18, 1923
Eugène Paul Henri Mancel	October 18, 1923–August 30, 1924
Raymond Robert Pierre Dreyfus	August 30, 1924–September 15, 1925
Marie Louis Charles Donat-Guigue	September 15, 1925–May 20, 1926
Paul Henri Mouton	May 20, 1926–November 23, 1926
Charles Victor Jules Frémicourt	November 23, 1926–February 4, 1928
Louis Loriot	February 4, 1928–May 6, 1932
Edouard Ferdinand Raymond Bacquart	May 6, 1932–July 18, 1934
Pierre Henri André Brack	July 18, 1934–November 20, 1935
Paul Octave Louis Brouchot	November 20, 1935–July 16, 1937
Georges Fillaire	July 16, 1937–August 20, 1940

SOURCE: *Journal Officiel*, Lois et Décrets, 1870–1940.

these recommendations and from the annual reports, the minister of justice, assisted by the directeurs of the ministry and by the premier président, the procureur général, and four conseillers from the Cour de Cassation, drew up the table of advancement for the year during the first two weeks of November.[12] The system was a cosmetic reform. Mere inscription on the table of advancement did not mean promotion, because there were many more names than positions to be filled. And the biggest plums—the entire Cour de Cassation, the premiers présidents and procureurs généraux of the cours d'appel, and the président and procureur de la République of the Tribunal de la Seine (a total of 110 positions)—remained entirely discretionary. The games of influence played out in secret at the Place Vendôme

12. The ministerial decree of February 13, 1908, was amended by decrees of December 10, 1908, March 9, 1910, and July 21, 1927, but the system remained essentially the same.

could continue. Proper patronage could still ensure a brilliant career in which each promotion leapfrogged the fortunate magistrate several ranks and brought him to the politically central courts of Paris. Without it, even the most talented judge or prosecutor was doomed to a slow climb, position by position, and a long residence in the provinces.

Although one republican ideal in 1871 was the creation of a magistrature in which merit and not patronage or favoritism would be the basis of advancement, the personnel dossiers present ample evidence that this goal was not sincerely pursued.[13] From the birth of the Third Republic, and particularly after they captured the vital organs of state in 1879, the republicans had to defend the regime from its monarchist and clerical enemies. The Seize Mai ministry of Duke Albert de Broglie, the plots of royalist extremists like Baron Athanase de Charette, and the charismatic electoral campaign of the potentially Caesarean General Georges Boulanger did not appear in the 1870s and 1880s to be so utterly lacking in political reality as they do in retrospect. Ideals had to give way to stern practicality. As Henri Albert Dauphin, who was appointed procureur général of the Cour d'appel de Paris in February, 1879, and who directed from there the first expulsion of antirepublicans, recalled, "I entered the magistrature because I was an *homme politique* [politician], and at that time, the government needed politicians at the head of the great parquets."[14]

During the next ten years, the Republic was defended and a "republican system of justice" created, as clericals, monarchists, and

---

13. The way in which the game of promotion was played can be judged in detail from the personnel dossiers of the magistrates, which are now kept in the AN, Series BB 6 II. The dossiers were begun in 1848 to record the progress of individual magistrates and to hold evaluations, letters of recommendation, and memoranda about their suitability for advancement. The series is divided into three parts: Cartons 1 to 434 contain the dossiers of magistrates who left the magistrature (through death, retirement, resignation, or dismissal) between 1842 and 1883; Cartons 435 to 611, the dossiers of magistrates who left the magistrature between 1883 and 1900; and Cartons 612 to 1294, the dossiers of magistrates who left the magistrature betwen 1900 and 1942. Under the law of January 3, 1979, that revised the rules for the use of archival material, only the first two parts and the dossier of any magistrat in the third part born at least 125 years before the request are freely available. Access to the remaining dossiers of the third part is subject to special application. Mme Ségolène de Dainville-Barbiche is the archivist for the BB 6 II series.
14. Dauphin to Eugène Guérin, minister of justice, April 22, 1893, in AN, BB 6 II, 480, dos. Henri Albert Dauphin.

The Magistrature

even those whose political opinions were too vague to be calculated exactly were systematically replaced.[15] Republicans who had themselves been dismissed from the magistrature during the Seize Mai crisis were rehabilitated.[16] Questions of merit were made entirely secondary to political reliability. The litmus test was the phrase "dévoué aux institutions républicaines" (dedicated to republican institutions), and it came to excuse even the sins of drunkenness, sexual misconduct, and bankruptcy—all of which would normally have occasioned harsh disciplinary action.[17] However necessary to the firm establishment of republican government these methods might have been before 1890, they were an infection in the magistrature that became deep-seated. One measure of the debilitation that resulted from continued favoritism, political patronage, nepotism, and condoning questionable morality can be taken by examining the careers of eleven magistrates born between 1846 and 1864, men who came of age with the solidification of the Third Republic.

Félix Pierre Joseph Leydet (1855–1919) began his career as a rédacteur at the Ministry of Justice in 1877. After eight years, in 1885, he requested assignment to the court system and was appointed juge d'instruction for the Tribunal de Nantes. This move began a series of advances that within thirteen years brought him back to Paris: procureur de la République at Dreux in 1887, then at Pontoise in 1893, and substitut on the parquet of the Tribunal de la Seine in 1898. Two years later he was made juge d'instruction in Paris, a position preferable to technically superior ones on appellate courts in the provinces. His rise had not been spectacular (he was forty-five years old), but he had made a successful career. The evaluations from his superiors spoke not of any outstanding ability—that was never cited—

---

15. For examples of the treatment of "clericals," see AN, BB 6 II, 447, dos. Xavier Marie Thomas de Cantorbury Béquet; *ibid.*, 452, dos. Marcel Victor Marie Bilard; and *ibid.*, 531, dos. Pierre François Gustave de la Gorce. For the treatment of monarchists, see *ibid.*, 550, dos. Jean Léopold de Masfrand; *ibid.*, 600, dos. Placide Léopold Thoreau La Salle; and *ibid.*, 447, dos. Jean Marie Louis Vincent Hubert Bécanne. On the treatment of magistrates with ambiguous political views, see *ibid.*, 467, dos. Pierre Chaize; *ibid.*, 559, dos. François Emile Moreau; and *ibid.*, 577, dos. Henri Auguste Xavier Prinet. See also Royer et al., *Juges et notables*, 275–304.

16. For examples of this rehabilitation, see AN, BB 6 II, 500, dos. Jean Marie Léon Fayot; *ibid.*, dos. Joseph Paulin Guisol; and *ibid.*, 549, dos. Georges Martin-Sarzeaud.

17. For examples of the treatment accorded those accused of drunkenness, sexual misconduct, and bankruptcy, see AN, BB 6 II, 484, dos. Charles Alfred Delacour; *ibid.*, 449, dos. Jean Charles Paul Béra; and *ibid.*, 549, dos. Jean Antoine Gustave Martin.

but rather of his politics ("good republican") and his connections (his father-in-law was a deputy from the Eure-et-Loir).[18]

As a juge d'instruction in the capital, Leydet demonstrated considerable dexterity in handling cases with political overtones. In 1907 important Radical Republican politicians, Gaston Thomson at the Naval Ministry and Jean Guyot-Dessaigne, the minister of justice, praised his capacity to prepare prosecutions while simultaneously burying scandals: "en évitant les indiscrétions pour les faits essentiels." Victor Fabre, procureur général of the Cour d'appel de Paris, proposed Leydet for promotion to one of the twelve vice-presidencies on the Tribunal de la Seine, a *marchepied* for the bench of the cour d'appel.[19] Leydet was passed over in 1907, and the following year he ruined his career by trying to protect his mistress, Marguerite Steinheil, who was accused in the double murder of her husband and her mother. Leydet arranged his assignment to the case and contrived to disregard evidence against Mme Steinheil in what was admittedly a baffling mystery. Unluckily for him, these intrigues came to the attention of the newspapers, and he was removed from the investigation. The press called for Leydet's dismissal, but his friends within the magistrature, Fabre foremost, convinced the current minister of justice, Aristide Briand, to order his reduction in rank to juge on the Tribunal de la Seine.[20]

Although Mme Steinheil was acquitted, the scandal made Leydet a pariah. His health deteriorated, and in 1911 he wrote a pathetic letter to Théodore Girard, the new minister of justice, begging for any promotion. Henri Ditte, président of the Tribunal de la Seine, seconded this appeal with a recommendation noting that Leydet had "cruelly paid for his mistake." But in the ministry's opinion, he was "a magistrate of mediocre value, of feeble authority." A year later the painful request was renewed, with Leydet writing to Briand, who was once again the minister of justice, "I want to tell you what hopes I place in your good will and also how much happiness I will owe to an elevation." Briand took pity and raised him to président de la section on the Tribunal de la Seine, the smallest advance possible.

18. AN, BB 6 II, 1025, dos. Félix Pierre Joseph Leydet, annual evaluations of 1887, 1892, 1896.

19. *Ibid.*, Thomson notation, December 18, 1907, Guyot-Dessaigne notation, February 10, 1907, and Fabre recommendation, August 12, 1907.

20. *Ibid.*, notations, October 15 and December 17, 1908, and Fabre's comment on the issue, March 24, 1909. For additional information see AN, BB 18, 2369, Affaire Steinheil. See also Martin, *The Hypocrisy of Justice*, 24–35.

The Magistrature

World War I opened many places in the ranks of the magistrates, often leading to rapid promotion, but not for Leydet.[21] He died in 1919, a testimony to how the system could reward the appropriately connected, but just as rapidly abandon the irremediably indiscreet.

The career of Leydet's champion, Victor Albin Fabre (1852–1916), also illustrates this process. Despite serious defects in character and judgment that became evident later, Fabre was appointed a substitut for the Tribunal de Digne in 1879, after Charles Bessat, the procureur général at Aix, pronounced him "one of the excellent examples of our republican youth." Promotions came rapidly: substitut général for the Cour d'appel d'Aix in 1880, procureur de la République at Draguignan midway through the same year, and avocat général at Aix in 1882. The Ministry of Justice, firmly in republican hands, took particular note that Fabre was from "a family absolutely dedicated to the government." This pedigree outweighed a report that he was "violent, passionate, without education, devoured by ambition, imprudent in his remarks, incapable of discretion, excessive in his acts."[22]

In 1892, Fabre's wife, née Marie Callamand, sued for divorce, charging that he had seduced her twenty-two-year-old sister, Jeanne. She publicized this allegation broadly, and by early 1893, Fabre's authority in Aix had been seriously eroded. The divorce was so embittered by a struggle for custody of their daughter that Mme Fabre threatened to shoot her estranged husband when his fellow magistrates sided with him. Additional embarrassment for the government lay in Jeanne Callamand's plans to marry a certain de Belval, whose monarchist connections were certain to exploit her tales of republican turpitude. Moving Fabre was imperative, but he protested his complete innocence of the "infamies against him" and refused to accept any change of position unless it had the semblance of a promotion. The ministry acquiesced in June, 1893, by naming him a juge on the Tribunal de la Seine.[23]

Fabre's political allies made certain that his advancement was not long delayed by the minor inconvenience of scandal. He was ele-

---

21. AN, BB 6 II, 1025, dos. Leydet, clipping from *L'Action française*, September 29, 1909; Leydet to Girard, January 31, 1911; Ditte to Girard, February 15, 1911; annual evaluation of 1912; Leydet to Briand, October 7, 1912; notations of 1918.

22. AN, BB 6 II, 850, dos. Victor Albin Fabre, Bessat notation, March 17, 1879; annual evaluation of 1892; and notation, August 17, 1886.

23. *Ibid.*, notations, letters, and reports of Fabre's marital problems, August, 1892–April, 1893. Fabre lost his custody suit in the lower court but won on appeal.

vated to a vice-presidency of the tribunal in 1898 and then to avocat général of the Cour d'appel de Paris in 1901. At that time Fabre wrote to the minister of justice, Ernest Monis: "Thanks to you, I am finally going to participate wholeheartedly in the defense of republican institutions. I have always thought that a magistrate could do that, without forgetting any of his duties to justice."[24] Such sentiments won him a place in the highest ranks of the ministry, as directeur des affaires civiles in 1904. Later that year he was given the powerful position of procureur de la République for the Tribunal de la Seine. In 1906 he reached the zenith of his prestige with appointment to be procureur général for the Cour d'appel de Paris.

Fabre's brilliant career was shipwrecked on the Rochette affair. In 1911, for complicated reasons that smacked of corruption, the premier, Ernest Monis, to whom Fabre owed his promotion, and the finance minister, Joseph Caillaux, requested that Fabre arrange for an extraordinary postponement in the appeal hearing of financier Henri Rochette. Fabre bent to their pressure but was dismayed at this particular defense of "republican institutions." He prepared a memorandum recounting the incident and in 1912 presented it to Briand, who was then minister of justice and who in turn passed it to Louis Barthou, his successor at the Place Vendôme and, like him, Caillaux's enemy. During a vicious press campaign against Caillaux in 1914, *Le Figaro* alluded to the existence of this memorandum several times. After Caillaux's wife, Henriette, shot and killed *Le Figaro*'s editor, ostensibly to prevent its revelation, Barthou read the document aloud before the Chamber of Deputies. In the uproar that followed, Fabre was demoted to premier président of the Cour d'appel d'Aix, and the minister of justice, Jean-Baptiste Bienvenu-Martin, angrily denounced him for having disgraced the magistrature—but whether the offense was bowing to political pressure or revealing that he had done so was unclear.[25] Fabre retained an attorney to plead his case for future promotion to the Cour de Cassation, but Bienvenu-Martin would not consider the request. Fabre had no opportunity to renew the appeal, because his health failed suddenly in 1915, and he died the following year.[26]

The Caillaux affair of 1914 also contributed to the destruction of

24. *Ibid.*, Fabre to Monis, March 16, 1901.
25. *Ibid.*, notations, March–April, 1914. See also Martin, *The Hypocrisy of Justice*, 161–76.
26. AN, BB 6 II, 850, dos. Fabre, notation of December 27, 1914. Fabre retained Paulin Silvau in his unsuccessful attempt to reach the Cour de Cassation.

another magistrate's career, that of Jean Marie Louis Albanel (1854–192?). Albanel began as a substitut on the Tribunal de Sens in 1880 and continued to serve on the parquet at Coulommiers (1882), Paris (1886), and Pau (1888). He moved to Paris permanently in 1896 as a juge on the Tribunal de la Seine. Later that year he was elevated to juge d'instruction, a position he held until 1910. He was frequently assigned to investigations involving minor violations of propriety that the Ministry of Justice preferred to have buried. He was, in effect, a political hack. His superiors were not unaware of his value, but warned against confiding more difficult cases to him. His work was described as "insufficient" and "superficial."[27] In 1907 he fell into legal difficulties of his own in connection with an acrimonious suit over the dowry of his son's wife. Documents in Albanel's file make it clear that he acted with few scruples in the matter, and he did everything possible to delay a hearing of the suit.[28]

Despite this record, Albanel was promoted to conseiller of the Cour d'appel de Paris in 1910, largely through the influence of two powerful political friends, Jean Cruppi and Joseph Caillaux. Immediately there was a suspicious change of tone in the evaluations of his work. For the first time in his career he was fulsomely praised, though his experience on the magistrature assise was almost nil. In 1914 the ministry named him président of the cour d'assises to try Henriette Caillaux for the murder of *Le Figaro*'s editor, Gaston Calmette. The decision was obviously partisan: Albanel owed his promotion to Caillaux, and Caillaux had served in the same cabinet with Bienvenu-Martin, who made the selection. During the trial Albanel was so protective of the defense that one of the assesseurs, Louis Dagoury, rebuked him in open court. When *Le Figaro* published the remark, Albanel demanded a formal retraction from Dagoury, who refused. A duel was barely avoided.[29]

Albanel never received another promotion. On his retirement in 1921, he asked the dignity of appointment as *conseiller honoraire* (honorary justice). The moment was not propitious. Caillaux had been convicted of improper conversations with German agents during World War I, and the conservative Bloc National controlled the government. The response at the ministry was dismissive: "The name of M. Albanel is linked in memory to the trial of Mme

27. AN, BB 6 II, 616, dos. Jean Marie Louis Albanel, notation of 1903.
28. *Ibid.*, documents dated 1899–1909.
29. *Ibid.*, annual evaluation of 1912, and documents dated July 25–31, 1914. See also Martin, *The Hypocrisy of Justice*, 179–206.

Caillaux, over which he presided in the Cour d'assises de la Seine in July, 1914. The incidents to which it gave place are well known. The best that one can say of M. Albanel is that on this occasion he was unequal to the duties of his office. He called attention to himself through a lamentable lack of authority. He was, in addition, a mediocre magistrate to whom the judicial world has accorded only feeble consideration."[30] This opinion notwithstanding, Albanel was made a conseiller honoraire in 1925, when Caillaux's friends returned to power in the Cartel des Gauches.

The practice of appointing to high position on the bench magistrates whose experience was primarily with the parquet carried an accompanying risk, that the habits learned and the pressures encountered in the magistrature debout did not encourage the calm reflection and objectivity necessary for the magistrature assise. Albanel was one example of the problem; Ferdinand Monier (1859–1919) was a more egregious case. After fifteen years on the parquets of provincial tribunals and appellate courts, Monier became chef du cabinet at the Ministry of Justice in 1898. He had in his favor a wealthy wife and the recommendation that "the political dedication of M. Monier is certain; he is sincerely attached to republican institutions." The notation that he required "more maturity of spirit" was ignored.[31]

From the ministry, Monier moved to a vice-presidency of the Tribunal de la Seine (1898) and to conseiller of the Cour d'appel de Paris (1903). In 1906, Jean Sarrien named him directeur des affaires civiles. The following year he was rewarded with the position of procureur de la République for the Tribunal de la Seine. When Monier was elevated to président of the tribunal in 1911 and then to premier président of the Cour d'appel de Paris in 1916, he reached the highest levels of power and influence among the magistrates. He had been made a *chevalier* of the Légion d'honneur in 1901 and was promoted to *officier* in 1907 and to *commandeur* in 1913. The announcement in November, 1917, of his dismissal by the full bench of the Cour de Cassation, acting as the Conseil supérieur à la magistrature, the disciplinary board for accusations of malfeasance and dereliction of duty, was consequently a shocking assault on the reputation of the judiciary. His offense was to have illegally amended a contract in January, 1916, between Charles Humbert and Paul Bolo-Pasha, both

---

30. AN, BB 6 II, 616, dos. Albanel, memorandum of April 12, 1921.
31. AN, BB 6 II, 1083, dos. Ferdinand Monier, notations of 1884, 1887, 1896.

of whom were exposed as German sympathizers; Bolo-Pasha was shot as a traitor.[32]

The Ministry of Justice and the magistrature as a whole acted with self-righteous hypocrisy toward Leydet, Fabre, Albanel, and Monier. As long as the flaws and indiscretions of a magistrate remained concealed from the great majority of the public, he might advance and prosper, particularly if he had the appropriate ideas and friends. In fact, a healthy propensity toward amorality, not to say immorality, could be useful to the government in sensitive matters. But if a magistrate disgraced "justice," he could expect little consideration from the ministry or his colleagues. The line between embarrassment and disgrace was not carefully drawn; the identical behavior of different magistrates was not judged the same way every time. The careers of François Gaston Bonnet (1849–1914) and Paul Adolphe Trouard-Riolle (1857–1922) offer illumination.

Bonnet, who came from a wealthy republican commercial family, held an unusually attractive first appointment as substitut général for the Cour d'appel de Nancy in 1880. Within six months he was promoted to avocat général at the Cour d'appel de Rennes. Such rapid advancement was rare, but Bonnet was a good friend of René Waldeck-Rousseau, the protégé of Léon Gambetta. Even so, he chafed at not reaching the heights with greater dispatch. After four years at Rennes he complained to the Ministry of Justice that his superiors were "blocking" his career. The procureur général of the cour d'appel could reply only that he had consistently commended Bonnet and had thought him a friend. The pressure was effective, because in 1885, Bonnet was made a président de chambre for the Cour d'appel de Riom. But Riom was not Paris, and two years later Bonnet again openly protested his treatment. His colleagues, in turn, accused him of "plots" and of lacking "the reserve essential in a small town." Bonnet's arrogance provoked a serious incident in April, 1892, when he pronounced judgment in a case before the court without having heard all of the arguments. The bar of Riom called for his censure, and an unpleasant amount of publicity appeared in the local newspapers.[33] In spite of these blemishes on his record, Bonnet never received a reprimand. Primarily through his political connections, he reached Paris in 1894 as a conseiller on the cour d'appel. In

---

32. *Ibid.*, documents from the Conseil supérieur à la magistrature, November 6–9, 1917.
33. AN, BB 6 II, 690, dos. François Gaston Bonnet, notation of April 15, 1892, reports of June, 1884, 1887, and April–December, 1892.

1903 he was advanced to président de chambre and in 1913 to conseiller of the Cour de Cassation.

Trouard-Riolle's career was also marked by questionable episodes and by patronage from the powerful. It began modestly with positions on the parquet of tribunaux at Rambouillet, Evreux, and Le Havre. In 1886 he was named a substitut for the Tribunal de la Seine. By then he had married Marie Lebey, whose father was director of the Agence Havas, and could count on income of forty thousand francs a year from her dowry. Daniel Wilson was among his political friends. These fine prospects were jeopardized in August, 1890, when the Paris press reported that he had fought a duel in Switzerland. He resigned his office, but a secret arrangement was made for his reappointment three months later.[34]

Trouard-Riolle served five more years with the parquet of the Tribunal de la Seine before he was promoted to substitut général for the Cour d'appel de Paris. He had gained the favor of Félix Faure, the president of the Republic—some whispered that Faure coveted Trouard-Riolle's wife. The duel was explained away as having occurred "pour des motifs étrangers." Another advancement came in 1901, to avocat général, and in this capacity he presented the case against Marguerite Steinheil in 1909. Compared with the consummate performance of Mme Steinheil from the defendant's rail, any prosecutor would have seemed pallid, but Trouard-Riolle's final arguments were particularly weak. Even Victor Fabre, ever solicitous to defend the members of his parquet, merely offered this disingenuous comment: "Whatever has been said of it, and in spite of several imperfections of detail, this summation, which lasted six hours, was eloquent. The case was among the most difficult, having been poorly prepared [a reference to Leydet's work]."[35] There was one last promotion for Trouard-Riolle, to avocat général of the Cour de Cassation in 1917. His wealthy wife having died five years earlier, he celebrated his new dignity by marrying for a second time. Despite this elevation to the highest court, his fellow magistrates never recognized him as a jurist of distinction.

The career of Manuel Achille Baudouin (1846–1917) is evidence that the least taxing and most rapid means of attaining the highest level of the judiciary was through nepotism. His father, Louis Bau-

---

34. AN, BB 6 II, 1256, dos. Paul Adolphe Trouard-Riolle, notations of 1884, 1885, documents of August–November 1890.

35. *Ibid.*, notations of November 14, 1895, and 1896; memorandum of December, 1909. See also Martin, *The Hypocrisy of Justice*, 45, 64–66.

douin, was a member of the Cour de Cassation from 1873 to 1886, ultimately as procureur général; his father-in-law, Tiengon de Tréferion, was a conseiller of the Cour d'appel de Rennes. Substantial wealth on both sides of the family was an additional recommendation. After Baudouin *fils* gained seasoning as a substitut for tribunaux at Châteaulin and Quimper, he quickstepped through an extraordinary series of promotions: substitut général for the Cour d'appel de Rennes in 1878, avocat général for the Cour d'appel de Lyon in 1880, procureur général for the Cour d'appel de Limoges in 1885, and avocat général for the Cour de Cassation in 1890—at the age of forty-four. Three years later he was made président of the Tribunal de la Seine. In 1901 he duplicated his father's achievement of becoming procureur général for the Cour de Cassation, and in 1911 he was elevated to premier président.[36] With such a career, he was the most successful magistrate during the first half of the Third Republic.

Baudouin's counterpart for the second half of the Republic was Théodore Paul Lescouvé (1864–1940), whose father, Adrien Alfred Lescouvé, retired in 1896 as a conseiller of the Cour de Cassation. Lescouvé was hailed as a "magistrate of the future" as early as 1894, after only four years of service on provincial parquets. He solidified his chances through an advantageous marriage to the wealthy Blanche Morand, clear allegiance to the republican cause, and friendship with Louis Barthou. The Ministry of Justice moved him to Paris permanently in 1896, with an appointment as the *chef adjoint du cabinet* (deputy chief assistant to the minister). Between 1897 and 1909 he held positions on the parquet of the Tribunal de la Seine and of the Cour d'appel de Paris before returning to the ministry, first as directeur du personnel and, in 1910, as directeur des affaires criminelles. From the Place Vendôme he was promoted to procureur de la République for the Tribunal de la Seine (1911), procureur général for the Cour d'appel de Paris (1917), and procureur général for the Cour de Cassation (1920). Eight years later he reached the summit as premier président.[37]

Bernard Théodore Médéric de Valles (1853–1929) represents a less successful variation of this nepotism. He had only a mediocre career until his marriage in 1884 to Yvonne de Marcère, whose father, Emile de Marcère, a close associate of Léon Gambetta and other

36. AN, BB 6 II, 650, dos. Manuel Achille Baudouin.
37. AN, BB 6 II, 1020, dos. Théodore Paul Lescouvé.

founders of the Republic, was designated a senator for life that year. Thereafter, de Valles moved swiftly through provincial parquets and was named to the Tribunal de la Seine as a substitut in 1894 and as a juge d'instruction in 1897. He obtained a separation from his wife in late 1894, and a divorce followed four years afterward, but de Valles's progress was not slowed for long. In 1903 he concluded a strategic marriage with the daughter of a chef de bureau at the Ministry of Justice. The following year de Valles was elevated to the Cour d'appel de Paris as a conseiller. In 1909 he presided over the trial of Mme Steinheil and was one of the few magistrates involved in the case to emerge with his prestige intact.[38] A final promotion in 1916 made him a président de chambre of the cour d'appel.

Political reliability and social or political connections were not the only means of advancement. Some magistrates, such as Louis Marie Joseph Blondel (1851–19?), climbed through the ranks solely on merit. Although his father was a mere *avoué* (solicitor) in Blois and his father-in-law a *propriétaire* of middling wealth, Blondel was endowed with a mellifluous voice that made his oral presentations memorable and with an insistence on exactitude that further impressed his superiors. Even so, he spent twenty-one years with provincial parquets before he was named a substitut général for the Cour d'appel de Paris in 1896. More visible in the capital, he was promoted to avocat général of the cour d'appel in 1901 and then of the Cour de Cassation in 1907. He was advanced to président de chambre of the court in 1922.[39]

Another career made through talent belonged to Louis Emile Henri Boucard (1862–19?), whose specialty was the investigation of criminal charges. This ability brought him an appointment as a juge d'instruction for the Tribunal de la Seine in 1894 at the age of thirty-one. During the next twenty-three years, he won nearly universal praise as the most perspicacious magistrate of the rank. In June, 1910, Ditte, the président of the Tribunal de la Seine, assured the ministry that Boucard could be entrusted with "the weightiest tasks in the certitude that he would complete them honorably while safeguarding particular interests placed in peril."[40] Boucard needed all

38. AN, BB 6 II, 1267, dos. Bernard Théodore Médéric de Valles, notations of 1884, 1887, 1896, 1903, 1912. See also Martin, *The Hypocrisy of Justice*, 44–68.
39. AN, BB 6 II, 679, dos. Louis Marie Joseph Blondel, notations of 1881, 1887, 1892.
40. AN, BB 6 II, 695, dos. Louis Emile Henri Boucard, notations of 1896, 1906, 1912. The memorandum from Ditte, June, 1910, referred specifically to Boucard's skillful handling of the controversy over the death of nationalist deputy Gabriel Syveton in 1904.

The Magistrature

of his dexterity in 1914, when he was juge d'instruction for the shooting of Gaston Calmette by Henriette Caillaux. By diligently conducting the inquiry against her while ignoring any evidence implicating her husband, he demonstrated remarkable political equipoise. Nevertheless he would have to wait until 1917 for promotion to the Cour d'appel de Paris as a conseiller. He became a président de chambre in 1925 and was elevated to the Cour de Cassation in 1929, a year before his retirement.[41]

The extent to which this anecdotal material from personnel dossiers represents the promotion pattern of the magistrature as a whole can be judged by analyzing the appointments to and from the Cour de Cassation and the Cour d'appel de Paris for the period 1871 to 1940.[42] Table 33 displays in tabular form this information about 957 individual magistrates and 1,643 changes in status. Many of the promotions appear to have been in-step advancements predicated on previous experience and attainment. The great majority of appointments to the Cour d'appel de Paris (78 percent, or 853 of 1099) were either elevations from the Tribunal de la Seine (47 percent, or 517 of 1099) or promotions from within the court (31 percent, or 336 of 1099). Substituts and vice-présidents from the Tribunal constituted, respectively, 80 percent (185 of 231) of the substituts généraux and 35 percent (204 of 581) of the conseillers. The avocats généraux were chosen from among the substituts généraux (96 of 113), and the présidents de chambre from among the conseillers (125 of 147), at the rate of 85 percent for each rank. Similarly, most of the appointments to the Cour de Cassation (79 percent, or 333 of 421) were promotions from within the court (21 percent, or 89 of 421) and elevations from the Cour d'appel de Paris (27 percent, or 115 of 421) or from the provincial cours d'appel (31 percent, or 129 of 421). Avocats généraux from the Cour d'appel de Paris (44 percent, or 28 of 64) and procureurs généraux from provincial cours d'appel (31 percent, or 20 of 64) made up 75 percent (48 of 64) of the avocats généraux for the Cour de Cassation. The previous position for 43 percent (125 of 290) of the conseillers was président de chambre of the Cour d'appel de Paris (19 percent, or 56 of 290) or premier président of a provincial cour d'appel (24 percent, or 69 of 290). Présidents de chambre were

---

41. Ibid., reports of April, 1914. See also *Le Figaro*, March–May, 1914, and Martin, *The Hypocrisy of Justice*, 175–78.
42. AN, BB 6 I, 524[4], Personnel de la magistrature, 1864–99, Cour de Cassation et cours d'appel; BB 6 I, 524[5], Personnel de la magistrature, 1899–1914, Cour de Cassation et cours d'appel; *JO*, 1871–1940.

TABLE 33
Patterns of Senior Judicial Promotion, 1871–1940

Previous Position \ Promotion	Premier Président, Cassation	Procureur Général, Cassation	Président de Chambre, Cassation	Conseiller, Cassation	Avocat Général, Cassation	Premier Président, Paris	Procureur Général, Paris	Président de Chambre, Paris	Conseiller, Paris	Avocat Général, Paris	Substitut Général, Paris	Président, Seine	Procureur de la République, Seine	Premier Président, Provincial	Procureur Général, Provincial	Directeur des Affaires Civiles	Directeur des Affaires Criminelles	Directeur du Personnel	TOTALS
Procureur Général, Cassation	6	—	0	0	0	0	0	0	0	0	0	0	0	0	0	0	0	0	6
Président de Chambre, Cassation	2	9	—	0	0	0	0	0	0	0	0	0	0	0	0	0	0	0	11
Conseiller, Cassation	1	2	23	—	0	3	6	0	0	0	0	1	0	0	0	0	0	0	36
Avocat Général, Cassation	0	0	8	38	—	0	2	0	0	0	0	1	0	0	0	0	0	0	49
Premier Président, Paris	1	0	1	2	0	—	0	0	0	0	0	0	0	0	0	0	0	0	4
Procureur Général, Paris	0	1	5	3	0	1	—	0	0	0	0	0	0	2	0	0	0	0	12
Président de Chambre, Paris	0	0	0	56	0	1	0	—	0	0	0	1	2	2	0	0	1	1	64
Conseiller, Paris	0	0	0	1	0	2	0	125	—	3	0	1	2	12	8	3	6	6	169
Avocat Général, Paris	0	0	0	17	28	0	2	13	8	—	0	0	6	2	3	3	2	3	87
Substitut Général, Paris	0	0	0	0	0	0	0	0	85	96	—	0	0	0	15	1	2	10	209
Président, Seine	0	2	1	1	0	1	0	0	0	0	0	—	0	0	0	0	0	0	5
Procureur de la République, Seine	0	0	0	9	2	0	6	0	0	0	0	0	—	0	0	0	0	0	17

Vice-Président, SEINE	0	0	0	0	0	0	0	0	204	2	0	0	0	0	0	0	0	0	206
Juge d'Instruction, SEINE	0	0	0	0	0	0	0	0	112	0	3	0	0	0	0	0	0	0	115
Juge, SEINE	0	0	0	0	0	0	0	0	3	0	0	0	0	0	0	0	0	0	3
Substitut, SEINE	0	0	0	0	0	0	0	0	1	0	185	0	0	0	0	0	0	0	186
Premier Président, PROVINCIAL	0	0	0	69	0	0	0	1	18	1	0	0	0	—	0	0	0	0	89
Procureur Général, PROVINCIAL	0	0	0	32	20	0	0	2	27	1	4	0	0	0	—	0	0	0	87
Président de Chambre, PROVINCIAL	0	0	0	6	0	0	0	1	35	1	0	0	0	0	0	0	0	0	43
Conseiller, PROVINCIAL	0	0	0	0	1	0	0	0	8	0	0	0	0	0	0	0	0	0	9
Avocat Général, PROVINCIAL	0	0	0	1	0	0	0	0	3	2	21	0	0	0	0	0	0	0	27
Substitut Général, PROVINCIAL	0	0	0	0	0	0	0	0	0	0	1	0	0	0	0	0	0	0	1
Président de Tribunal, PROVINCIAL	0	0	0	0	0	0	0	0	19	0	0	0	0	0	0	0	0	0	19
Procureur de la République, PROVINCIAL	0	0	0	0	0	0	0	1	14	0	9	0	0	0	0	0	0	0	24
Directeur des Affaires Civiles	0	0	0	10	1	0	1	0	0	0	0	2	1	0	0	—	0	0	15
Directeur des Affaires Criminelles	0	0	0	14	4	0	0	1	0	0	0	0	1	0	3	—	0	0	23
Directeur du Personnel	0	0	0	0	1	0	0	3	11	4	1	0	0	0	1	6	13	—	40
Professeur de Droit	0	1	0	11	0	0	0	0	3	0	0	0	0	0	0	0	0	0	15
Politician	1	0	0	3	1	0	1	0	0	0	0	0	0	0	0	0	0	0	6
Avocat	0	0	0	3	0	0	0	0	7	0	2	0	0	0	0	0	0	0	12
Miscellaneous	1	2	0	14	6	0	0	0	23	3	5	0	0	0	0	0	0	0	54
TOTALS	12	17	38	290	64	8	19	147	581	113	231	6	12	18	27	16	24	20	1,643

SOURCES: Archives Nationales, BB 6 524⁴–524⁵; *Journal Officiel*, *Lois et Décrets*, 1871–1940.
NOTE: This table covers 1,643 changes in status involving 957 individual magistrates.

selected from among the conseillers of the court at a rate of 61 percent (23 of 38). The significance of these examples lies in the maintenance of the magistrates either on the bench or with the parquet, where their seniority and achievement had been earned.

Conversely, this responsible pattern was short-circuited for certain men whose performance in especially sensitive positions entitled them to extraordinary consideration. Magistrates who served as high officials within the Ministry of Justice, for however short a period, frequently emerged from the Place Vendôme with exalted dignity after their exposure to the politically powerful. Between 1871 and 1940, about 22 percent (11 of 51) of the directeurs du personnel were immediately named conseiller of the Cour d'appel de Paris; 43 percent (24 of 56) of the directeurs des affaires civiles and affaires criminelles were elevated to conseiller of the Cour de Cassation. Almost all had entered the ministry at a much lower rank.[43] A record on the parquet of dealing skillfully with critical or delicate cases often brought a magistrate the reward of promotion to high position on the bench, where his objectivity was open to question. For the Cour d'appel de Paris, 41 percent (85 of 209) of the substituts généraux promoted were advanced to conseiller of the court. Of the avocats généraux promoted, 20 percent (17 of 87) were elevated to conseiller of the Cour de Cassation, 15 percent (13 of 87) and 9 percent (8 of 87) to président de chambre and conseiller, respectively, of the cour d'appel. And 10 of the 12 procureurs généraux who were promoted received even more handsome treatment: 1 (8 percent) advanced to premier président of the cour d'appel, 9 (75 percent) to the Cour de Cassation (1 to procureur général, 5 to président de chambre, 3 to conseiller). The ministry also promoted 112 juges d'instruction from the Tribunal de la Seine directly to conseiller of the Cour d'appel de Paris.

In Table 34 the years 1871 to 1940 are divided into nine periods to permit organization of the data from Table 33 according to the changing political coloration of the Third Republic. From 1871 through 1878 the forces of "Moral Order" were in power, and monarchist sentiment was strong (much less so, of course, after the failure of the Seize Mai ministry in 1877). The Opportunist Republicans,

---

43. Royer et al., *Juges et notables*, observes that in the late nineteenth century, "the magic staircase" to the Cour de Cassation was appointment to a high administrative post in the Ministry of Justice that involved a close association with the minister (184).

moderate but clearly republican liberals, dominated during the following decade and a half, 1879–1894. A relaxing of hostility toward suitably disposed Catholic monarchists and conservative republicans (the Ralliement) distinguished the years 1895 through 1898. Between 1899 and 1911, Radical Republicans held control. The return of moderate republicans, the Union Sacrée of World War I, and the conservative Bloc National combined to produce a constrasting period from 1912 through 1923. Radical Republicanism revived as the Cartel des Gauches in 1924 and 1925. The years from 1926 through 1935 were marked by ministries and policies without a clearly ideological basis. The Popular Front swept to a brief moment of power in 1936 and 1937. Drift and incoherence characterized 1938–1940, the last years before the collapse in World War II. Table 34 also displays the average number of promotions annually to and within the Cour de Cassation and the Cour d'appel de Paris for each period (a low of 16.2 [1899–1911], a high of 59.5 [1936–1937], and a mean of 21.7).

Table 35 assembles information from Table 34 by political period for those promotions that may be considered suspicious: a change from the parquet to the bench (Type 1), the promotion of a juge d'instruction to the bench (Type 2), and an out-of-step advancement for a directeur leaving the Ministry of Justice (Type 3). Because the periods are of such different lengths (from two to sixteen years), the statistics must be interpreted cautiously. Nevertheless, two conclusions are readily apparent. The average number of suspicious promotions per year varied greatly from period to period (from a low of 4.6 [1899–1911 and 1938–1940] to a high of 14.5 [1936–1937], with a mean of 6.2) and varied directly with the number of total promotions per year for each period. But the percentage of the total represented by the suspicious promotions varied within a relatively narrow range (from 24.4 percent [1936–1937] to 32.4 percent [1895–1898], with a mean of 28.6 percent) and was remarkably consistent throughout the Third Republic.

Before they came to power, the Opportunist Republicans traditionally charged that the judiciary was widely exploited by the ministries of "Moral Order." Yet the averages and percentages for the years 1871–1878 and 1879–1894 are nearly identical. Likewise, conservatives (republican and otherwise) denounced the "pork-barrel" promotions by the Radicals in the decade before World War I, but the averages and percentages for 1895–1898 and 1912–1923 are clearly higher than the ones for 1899–1911. An expansion of the

TABLE 34
Promotions Within the Magistrature by Political Period, 1871–1940

Promotion	Previous Position	1871–1878	1879–1894	1895–1898	1899–1911	1912–1923	1924–1925	1926–1935	1936–1937	1938–1940	Totals
Premier Président, CASSATION	Procureur Général, Cassation	0	1	0	1	1	0	1	2	0	6
	Président de Chambre, Cassation	1	0	0	1	0	0	0	0	0	2
	Conseiller, Cassation	1	0	0	0	0	0	0	0	0	1
	Premier Président, Paris	0	0	0	0	0	1	0	0	0	1
	Politician	0	1	0	0	0	0	0	0	0	1
	Miscellaneous	0	1	0	0	0	0	0	0	0	1
	Totals	2	3	0	2	1	1	1	2	0	12
Procureur Général, CASSATION	Président de Chambre, Cassation	1	4	0	1	1	0	2	0	0	9
	Conseiller, Cassation	0	0	0	0	1	0	0	1	0	2
	Procureur Général, Paris	0	0	0	0	1	0	0	0	0	1
	Président, Seine	0	0	0	1	0	0	0	1	0	2
	Professeur de Droit	0	1	0	0	0	0	0	0	0	1
	Miscellaneous	1	0	0	1	0	0	0	0	0	2
	Totals	2	5	0	3	3	0	2	2	0	17

Président de Chambre, CASSATION	Conseiller, Cassation	4	6	0	4	2	2	2	2	1	23
	Avocat Général, Cassation	2	1	0	1	2	0	1	1	0	8
	Premier Président, Paris	0	1	0	0	0	0	0	0	0	1
	Procureur Général, Paris	0	3	0	1	0	0	1	0	0	5
	Président, Seine	0	0	0	0	0	0	1	0	0	1
	Totals	6	11	0	6	4	2	5	3	1	38
Conseiller, CASSATION	Avocat Général, Cassation	5	8	2	4	10	0	7	1	1	38
	Premier Président, Paris	1	1	0	0	0	0	0	0	0	2
	Procureur Général, Paris	0	0	0	2	0	0	1	0	0	3
	Président de Chambre, Paris	6	7	3	5	7	3	13	6	6	56
	Conseiller, Paris	0	1	0	0	0	0	0	0	0	1
	Avocat Général, Paris	0	0	0	0	0	1	8	5	3	17
	Président, Seine	0	0	0	1	0	0	0	0	0	1

(continues)

TABLE 34
Continued

Promotion	Previous Position	1871–1878	1879–1894	1895–1898	1899–1911	1912–1923	1924–1925	1926–1935	1936–1937	1938–1940	Totals
	Procureur de la République, Seine	1	4	1	1	0	0	2	0	0	9
	Premier Président, Provincial	9	10	6	9	15	5	7	5	3	69
	Procureur Général, Provincial	3	7	1	4	3	2	7	1	4	32
	Président de Chambre, Provincial	5	1	0	0	0	0	0	0	0	6
	Avocat Général, Provincial	0	0	0	0	1	0	0	0	0	1
	Directeur des Affaires Civiles	0	3	0	3	3	0	1	0	0	10
	Directeur des Affaires Criminelles	2	5	1	4	2	0	0	0	0	14
	Professeur de Droit	1	2	0	0	2	0	4	0	2	11
	Politician	0	3	0	0	0	0	0	0	0	3
	Avocat	0	2	0	1	0	0	0	0	0	3
	Miscellaneous	4	6	0	0	1	0	0	3	0	14
	Totals	37	60	14	34	44	11	50	21	19	290

										Total
Avocat Général, CASSATION										
Avocat Général, Paris	0	7	2	4	6	0	7	1	1	28
Procureur de la République, Seine	0	0	1	1	0	0	0	0	0	2
Procureur Général, Provincial	4	4	1	3	5	0	1	0	2	20
Conseiller, Provincial	0	1	0	0	0	0	0	0	0	1
Directeur des Affaires Civiles	0	0	0	0	1	0	0	0	0	1
Directeur des Affaires Criminelles	3	0	0	0	0	0	1	0	0	4
Directeur du Personnel	0	1	0	0	0	0	0	0	0	1
Politician	0	1	0	0	0	0	0	0	0	1
Miscellaneous	3	0	0	0	1	0	1	1	0	6
Totals	10	14	4	8	13	0	10	2	3	64
Premier Président, PARIS										
Conseiller, Cassation	1	0	1	0	1	0	0	0	0	3
Procureur Général, Paris	0	1	0	0	0	0	0	0	0	1
Président de Chambre, Paris	0	0	0	0	0	0	0	1	0	1

(continues)

TABLE 34
Continued

Promotion	Previous Position	1871–1878	1879–1894	1895–1898	1899–1911	1912–1923	1924–1925	1926–1935	1936–1937	1938–1940	Totals
	Conseiller, Paris	1	0	0	1	0	0	0	0	0	2
	Président, Seine	0	0	0	0	1	0	0	0	0	1
	Totals	2	1	1	1	2	0	0	1	0	8
Procureur Général, PARIS	Conseiller, Cassation	0	2	0	1	1	0	1	1	0	6
	Avocat Général, Cassation	0	1	0	1	0	0	0	0	0	2
	Avocat Général, Paris	0	1	0	0	1	0	0	0	0	2
	Procureur de la République, Seine	0	2	0	2	1	0	0	1	0	6
	Procureur Général, Provincial	1	0	0	0	0	0	0	0	0	1
	Directeur des Affaires Civiles	0	0	0	0	0	0	1	0	0	1
	Politician	0	1	0	0	0	0	0	0	0	1
	Totals	1	7	0	4	3	0	2	2	0	19

Président de Chambre, PARIS	*Conseiller, Paris*	7	10	6	14	21	9	34	18	6	125
	Avocat Général, Paris	2	6	1	1	2	0	1	0	0	13
	Premier Président, Provincial	0	0	0	0	0	0	1	0	0	1
	Procureur Général, Provincial	0	0	0	0	0	1	1	0	0	2
	Président de Chambre, Provincial	0	1	0	0	0	0	0	0	0	1
	Procureur de la République, Provincial	0	0	0	1	0	0	0	0	0	1
	Directeur des Affaires Criminelles	0	0	0	1	0	0	0	0	0	1
	Directeur du Personnel	0	1	0	0	0	1	0	1	0	3
	Totals	9	18	7	17	23	11	37	19	6	147
Conseiller, PARIS	*Avocat Général, Paris*	2	2	1	3	0	0	0	0	0	8
	Substitut Général, Paris	11	14	6	13	20	3	13	4	1	85
	Vice-Président, Seine	20	32	10	29	30	17	44	15	7	204

(continues)

TABLE 34
Continued

Promotion	Previous Position	1871–1878	1879–1894	1895–1898	1899–1911	1912–1923	1924–1925	1926–1935	1936–1937	1938–1940	Totals
	Juge d'Instruction, Seine	7	13	3	11	21	9	34	10	4	112
	Juge, Seine	0	0	0	1	1	1	0	0	0	3
	Substitut, Seine	0	0	0	0	0	0	1	0	0	1
	Premier Président, Provincial	3	4	2	8	1	0	0	0	0	18
	Procureur Général, Provincial	3	10	2	4	2	1	5	0	0	27
	Président de Chambre, Provincial	4	10	2	8	3	0	5	2	1	35
	Conseiller, Provincial	0	8	0	0	0	0	0	0	0	8
	Avocat Général, Provincial	0	2	1	0	0	0	0	0	0	3
	Président de Tribunal, Provincial	0	0	0	0	1	3	12	2	1	19
	Procureur de la République, Provincial	0	0	1	1	6	0	1	4	1	14

											Total
	Directeur du Personnel	1	3	3	4	0	0	0	0	0	11
	Professeur de Droit	0	1	0	1	0	0	0	0	0	3
	Avocat	0	3	0	3	0	1	1	0	0	7
	Miscellaneous	4	4	1	3	2	0	4	4	1	23
	Totals	55	106	32	89	87	34	120	42	16	581
Avocat Général, PARIS	Conseiller, Paris	0	0	0	1	1	0	0	1	0	3
	Substitut Général, Paris	5	22	3	10	19	3	23	8	3	96
	Vice-Président, Seine	0	0	0	1	1	0	0	0	0	2
	Premier Président, Provincial	0	1	0	0	0	0	0	0	0	1
	Procureur Général, Provincial	0	1	0	0	0	0	0	0	0	1
	Président de Chambre, Provincial	0	1	0	0	0	0	0	0	0	1
	Avocat Général, Provincial	1	1	0	0	0	0	0	0	0	2
	Directeur du Personnel	0	0	1	1	1	1	0	0	0	4
	Miscellaneous	2	0	0	1	0	0	0	0	0	3
	Totals	8	26	4	14	22	4	23	9	3	113

(*continues*)

TABLE 34
Continued

Promotion	Previous Position	1871–1878	1879–1894	1895–1898	1899–1911	1912–1923	1924–1925	1926–1935	1936–1937	1938–1940	Totals
Substitut Général, Paris	Juge d'Instruction, Seine	0	2	0	1	0	0	0	0	0	3
	Substitut, Seine	14	33	8	22	35	8	44	15	6	185
	Procureur Général, Provincial	0	0	1	2	1	0	0	0	0	4
	Avocat Général, Provincial	0	7	1	2	6	0	4	1	0	21
	Substitut Général, Provincial	0	1	0	0	0	0	0	0	0	1
	Procureur de la République, Provincial	1	2	1	4	1	0	0	0	0	9
	Directeur du Personnel	0	1	0	0	0	0	0	0	0	1
	Avocat	0	2	0	0	0	0	0	0	0	2
	Miscellaneous	0	1	1	2	1	0	0	0	0	5
	Totals	15	49	12	33	44	8	48	16	6	231
Total Promotions		147	300	74	211	246	71	298	119	54	1,520
Average Per Year		18.4	18.8	18.5	16.2	20.5	35.5	29.8	59.5	18.0	21.7

Sources: See Table 33.

TABLE 35
Parquet-to-Bench and Out-of-Step Promotions, 1871–1940

Type of Change	1871–78		1879–94		1895–98		1899–1911		1912–23	
	No.	Per Year	No.	Per Year	No.	Per Year	No.	Per Year	No.	Per Year
Type 1	29	3.6	59	3.7	16	4.0	37	2.8	47	3.9
Type 2	7	0.9	13	0.8	3	0.8	11	0.9	21	1.8
Type 3	6	0.8	13	0.8	5	1.2	12	0.9	7	0.6
TOTALS	42	5.3	85	5.3	24	6.0	60	4.6	75	6.3
% of Total Promotions	28.6		28.3		32.4		28.4		30.5	

Type of Change	1924–25		1926–35		1936–37		1938–40		1871–1940	
	No.	Per Year	No.	Per Year	No.	Per Year	No.	Per Year	No.	Per Year
Type 1	8	4.0	50	5.0	18	9.0	10	3.3	274	3.9
Type 2	9	4.5	34	3.4	10	5.0	4	1.3	112	1.6
Type 3	2	1.0	3	0.3	1	0.5	0	0.0	49	0.7
TOTALS	19	9.5	87	8.7	29	14.5	14	4.6	435	6.2
% of Total Promotions	26.8		29.2		24.4		25.9		28.6	

SOURCES: See Table 33.
Type 1: Promotion from parquet to bench. Type 2: Promotion of a juge d'instruction to the bench. Type 3: Out-of-step advancement for a directeur leaving the Ministry of Justice.

courts, and a series of deaths and retirements, respectively, permitted the Cartel des Gauches and the Popular Front to make a large number of appointments during quite few months, but the percentage of suspicious promotions actually declined. Under the Popular Front it reached its lowest level, just under one-fourth. The very consistency of this record is the most damning evidence; the indictment contained in these numbers affects each of the nine periods. Over the seventy years of the Third Republic, there were 435 questionable advancements for the Cour de Cassation and the Cour d'appel de Paris alone, slightly more than 6 per year and 28.6 percent of all the promotions to France's two most powerful courts. An analysis of the other cours d'appel and the important tribunaux, particularly the Tribunal de la Seine, would surely reveal many more.

The promotion policies elucidated in these statistics and case histories demonstrate that the magistrature of the Third Republic was not, and could not claim to be, an unsullied guardian of right. The probity and impartiality of the judges and prosecutors to whom this ideal was entrusted could not be guaranteed as long as their careers were frequently the instruments of political rancor and reward. But to conclude that they therefore floated in a miasma of corruption would be erroneous. Despite dramatic lapses, the magistrature appears to have performed reasonably well in the majority of cases brought before it, especially when politics did not play a role.[44] The examples of Leydet, Fabre, Albanel, and Monier indicate that magistrates could believe so much in their own importance and immunity that they overstepped the bounds, thinking that they could do so with impunity. The examples also suggest that such behavior could lead to their disgrace at what should have been the pinnacle of their careers. In addition, almost all of France's leaders recognized that the 1883 purge had to serve more as a cautionary tale than as a standing threat. The system could not have survived many such shocks without the loss of all public esteem and confidence. But while the promise of irremovability implied independence, the chase for promotion assured governmental control. The ideal of a magistrature free from favoritism and politics could be honored in the breach. To introduce his three-volume analysis of the French ju-

44. AN, BB 18, 1796–2529, Correspondance de procureurs généraux avec la garde des sceaux (division criminelle), 1871–1913. If it is possible to generalize about such a mass of documents, there appears to have been an effort at objectivity in nonpolitical cases; there is clear evidence of favoritism and even corruption in the handling of politically sensitive cases.

The Magistrature

dicial system, Raoul de La Grasserie, the distinguished jurist from Rennes, wrote in 1914 what he could have written at any point from 1800 to 1940: "Le juge doit être indépendant . . . au cas contraire, il lui faudra de héroïsme pour être juste."[45] Heroism is always a limited quantity.

45. La Grasserie, *De la justice en France et à l'étranger*, I, 7.

7

The Bar

When Vincent de Moro-Giafferi, known—for his demeanor—as the Lion of the Palais de Justice, was taxed for using his formidable talents to secure the acquittal of notorious murderers and swindlers, he countered with this reply: "I would be overjoyed to defend only archbishops and the children of the Virgin Mary, but such individuals are rarely charged before the cour d'assises." Every *accusé* deserved a defense, and from barristers of Moro-Giafferi's caliber it was often a brilliant one. But the sentiment has seldom won lawyers esteem from a society victimized by crime or a state determined to repress it. In 1804, Napoleon wrote to his principal judicial adviser, Duke Jean-Jacques Régis de Cambacérès, "I would like to cut out the tongue of any barrister who uses it against the government." Even to their clients, lawyers were an expensive and usually unpleasant recourse. Henri Robert, former *bâtonnier* (president) of the Paris bar, called his colleagues "the professional witnesses of bad times, the necessary confidants to whom family secrets and shameful, if petty, depravities had to be revealed."[1]

In France, the *hommes de loi* (men of the law) were separated by

---

1. André Damien, *Les Avocats du temps passé* (Paris, 1973), 470; Henry Buteau, *L'Ordre des avocats: Ses rapports avec la magistrature, histoire, législation, jurisprudence* (Paris, 1895), 173; Henri Robert, *L'Avocat* (Paris, 1923), 8–9.

function into three discrete professions, *notaires* (notaries), *avoués* (solicitors), and *avocats* (barristers). This division dated from the spread of royal judicial power in the 1500s and 1600s and was based to some extent on distinctions arising from Roman law. The notaires and avoués were *officiers ministériels* (officials of the court) exercising a monopoly of their duties within a geographical area. The venality of their *études* (law offices) did not end with the ancien régime but continued through the Third Republic. Both organized themselves regionally into professional corporations to defend these privileges. Avocats had their own corporate bodies to register and discipline their membership. The right to *plaider*, to make oral arguments before a court, was restricted to these *ordres des avocats*, which were also called the *barreau* (the bar).[2]

Almost as a civil priest, a notaire ministered to the financial rites of passage—the divisions of property attendant upon birth, marriage, and death. The essence of his function was to guarantee the authenticity of legal documents, and in doing so, he was responsible for witnessing signatures, drawing up contracts and depositions, and acting as a depositary for official papers. Typically, a consultation with a notaire produced a notarial act, the fee for which was divided unequally into taxes (much the greater part) and the notaire's income. In the 1780s approximately forty thousand notaires were scattered throughout France, some holding a royal, others a seigniorial, office. Most, particularly notaires in small villages, had to supplement their professional dignity by working as artisans or by running small businesses. When the National Assembly abolished the venality and heritability of the études on September 29, 1791, it established *notaires publics* to be chosen for life through a *concours*. Because the confusion of the revolutionary years hindered a systematic enforcement of this legislation, the practice of many notaires from the ancien régime was unaffected until Bonaparte imposed a reorganization on 25 Ventôse XI (March 16, 1803). He eliminated the *concours* and reserved to himself the appointment of notaires, strictly limited their number (to slightly fewer than fourteen thousand), and ordered them in typically Napoleonic categories: About 4 percent, the *première classe*, had their études in the seat of a cour d'appel and the right to practice throughout its *ressort*; another 13 percent, the

---

2. Philip Dawson, "The *Bourgeoisie de Robe* in 1789," French Historical Studies, IV (1965), 1–21; Isser Woloch, "The Fall and Resurrection of the Civil Bar, 1789–1820s," French Historical Studies, XV (1987), 241–62.

deuxième classe, were located in towns with a tribunal de première instance and could act within the entire arrondissement; the vast majority, the *troisième classe,* were limited to a single canton. And Bonaparte did not object to the return, de facto, of an attenuated venality, in which a notaire could sell his étude and the official certification from the government to an acceptable successor. Under the Restoration the law of April 28, 1816, granted de jure recognition to this practice but also empowered the state to reduce the number of officiers ministériels if appropriate.

Although an homme de loi, a notaire rarely had a law degree or any formal legal training, and usually prepared for the profession by serving a *stage* (clerkship) in an étude. The official requirements were to have attained the age of twenty-five, to hold French citizenship, and to produce certificates of morality and aptitude, but the essential qualification was sufficient capital to purchase a notarial practice. By the end of the nineteenth century, the cheapest cantonal étude cost at least Fr 15,000, one in central Paris Fr 700,000, with the great majority between Fr 40,000 and Fr 100,000. But this substantial investment, increased by the mandatory posting of a security bond ranging from Fr 1,800 to Fr 50,000, did not always generate a successful income. Despite the existence of supervisory professional groups, many notaires went bankrupt, particularly after 1870, or fled with money embezzled from their clients. The government responded by abolishing the least profitable études when their owners were unable to find buyers, and by 1940 the number of notaires had fallen to approximately seven thousand, half the total under Napoleon.[3]

Avoués (called, confusingly, *procureurs* during the ancien régime) first appeared as officiers ministériels in the early 1600s, when royal courts required that every party to a lawsuit retain their representation. Procureurs alone were given the right to *postuler et conclure*— to prepare and file the multitudinous documents of civil litigation and to submit written briefs about the facts of the case—and purchased this monopoly from the crown. Although the procureur was essentially a technician of judicial procedure and commanded less social prestige than an avocat, who could speak before the court and argue legal principles, his étude was often lucrative because he could compel clients to assign him certain property rights as a condition of

3. Zeldin, *France, 1848–1945,* I, 43–52; Dawson, "The *Bourgeoisie de Robe* in 1789," 3–5.

representation. The National Assembly ended venality and heritability for procureurs on January 29, 1791, but the argument for guaranteeing procedural uniformity led to maintaining the requirement that civil litigants engage a solicitor (called from this date an *avoué*) and the state's prerogative to designate him. More thoroughgoing, the Convention eliminated what it presumed to be these survivals of the ancien régime by the law of 3 Brumaire II (October 24, 1793), which abolished the office of avoué. Because the National Assembly had granted the right to counsel in criminal proceedings on October 8–9, 1789, and had suppressed the ordres des avocats on September 2, 1790, every Frenchman could then be his own lawyer or retain anyone else he chose, and could present both oral and written arguments before the Revolution's new system of courts.

When Napoleon established the tribunaux de première instance by the law of 27 Ventôse VIII (March 18, 1800), the legislation also granted him the power to appoint a list of avoués for each tribunal (with the total approximately 2,700), thereby reviving the office. Six months later the law of 18 Fructidor VIII (September 5, 1800) restored the status of 1791: Avoués were required for all civil litigation and, because the avocats had lost their privileges, permitted to make oral and written pleadings. During the next decade, Napoleon decided reluctantly—so much did he mistrust the eloquence of barristers—to restore the ordres des avocats. As a preparation, by the law of July 19, 1810, he limited the avoués to the competence of the prerevolutionary procureurs. They were forbidden to *plaider* but exclusively were able to *postuler et conclure*. As with the notaires, Napoleon authorized the avoués to sell their études and so countenanced a form of venality. The law of April 28, 1816, extended to the avoués the same legal recognition of this practice that it did to the notaires. In addition to the capital to purchase an étude, the government required that the proposed successor be at least twenty-five years old, hold French citizenship, present certificates of morality, submit proof of having completed an abbreviated course of study with a law faculty and a *stage* with an avoué, and post a security bond.

Avoués did not regain completely the formidable power of procureurs to compel payment from clients, but their incomes were hardly affected. With litigiousness almost a national characteristic of the French, all but a few of the études were filled with bulging dossiers, and their avoués multiplied motions—and consequently fees—to draw out lawsuits for years and occasionally decades. The average price of an étude d'avoué at the end of the nineteenth century was

Fr 50,000 to Fr 70,000 (slightly less than that of an étude de notaire), and for a lawyer, it was a steady and secure investment. In 1808, Napoleon reduced the number of avoués by 112 (all in Paris), but the total thereafter remained nearly constant at slightly more than 2,600 through 1940. The professional organizations of avoués had little to do other than defend their members from the charge of encouraging litigation (for which fees were high) instead of settlement out of court (for which fees were much lower). The scope for profit was enlarged by a ruling of the Cour de Cassation on July 24, 1897, granting avoués the privilege of making oral arguments in any criminal proceeding, but only slightly, for the *accusés* preferred an avocat to sway the jury.[4]

On October 23, 1902, Georges Clemenceau proposed that the Senate adopt legislation to end the monopoly (and thus the venality) of notaires, avoués, and the sixty special avocats whose sole right to argue cases before the Cour de Cassation and the Conseil d'Etat dated from the laws of June 11, 1806, and September 10, 1817. Doing so, he argued, would open the professions to competition and lower the cost to clients. His bill claimed that the state would owe no compensation to the officiers ministériels, because the offices had not been *sold*—the initial holders having been *appointed* by Napoleon—and by the law of April 28, 1816, the state could reduce the number as it desired. Opponents had on their side tradition, inertia, a threat to enormous investments, and the reply that the existing system, though admittedly counter to the republican ideal of *égalité*, had the virtue of guaranteeing to the public that the men in whom they placed their affairs and trust had the certification of the state, the disgrace of a few notaires notwithstanding. Clemenceau's project died quickly, as all previous such efforts during the nineteenth century had, and the officiers ministériels survived until the end of the Third Republic.[5]

Among the hommes de loi of the ancien régime, the highest social

---

4. Georges Boutiron, *De la responsabilité des avoués* (Paris, 1912), 9–76; Edouard Avond, *De la vénalité des offices ministériels et de sa suppression* (Paris, 1905), 48; M. Chadefaux, *De la séparation des fonctions d'avocat et d'avoué* (Paris, 1912), 3–101; Michael P. Fitzsimmons, *The Parisian Order of Barristers and the French Revolution* (Cambridge, Mass., 1987), 76–82, 95–100, 132–34, 152–53; Woloch, "The Fall and Resurrection of the Civil Bar," 243–53; Dawson, "The *Bourgeoisie de Robe* in 1789," 5–6.

5. *JOS*, Documents parlementaires, 1902, No. 321. The Conseil d'Etat is an appellate court to hear cases brought from lower administrative courts involving citizens seeking damages against the state or state officials.

The Bar

position belonged to the avocats, who boasted that their corporate bodies, the ordres des avocats, which regulated membership and discipline, dated from the 1100s, considerably earlier than many claims of nobility. There were thirteen of the ordres, each constituting the barreau of a parlement, and within the *ressort,* the avocats were free to *plaider* before any court. This right to make oral arguments and invoke legal principles distinguished them from avoués. Avocats could also submit written briefs that raised issues beyond fact, but that risked tension with the procureur for the case. Even so, some avocats actually specialized in the preparation of memoranda detailing the precedents applicable in particular instances, and a very few others, usually the most learned of the ordre, were primarily consultants for abstruse legal problems. But it was the *plaidoirie* (oral pleading) that was the essence of the title avocat.

The *license ès lois,* the degree awarded after three years of study with a law faculty (Roman law the first year, canon law the second, French law the third) permitted an aspiring avocat to begin a *stage* lasting from two to four years. The rules of this probationary period varied from one ordre to another and were largely unwritten, but the *stagiaire* (law clerk) was expected to supplement what was often a mediocre legal education by attending a series of *conférences* (lectures), to learn the customs and usages of the profession by watching carefully at court sessions, and to demonstrate the qualities of discretion and diligence by attaching himself to a senior avocat as an unpaid assistant while becoming familiar with matters of routine. Successful completion of the *stage* led to full membership in the ordre and enrollment on the Tableau (list) des avocats. Because the typical *plaidoirie* was filled with quotations from Roman law, references to French legislation and precedent, and invocations from historical analogy, the avocat was regarded as the most cultured of the hommes de loi. Social position and culture did not necessarily, however, bring clients. Only the most established avocats, whose eloquence and experience were a reassurance, argued many cases. Some avocats did not practice the profession at all, having joined the ordre merely to increase their dignity. No objection was raised, because this membership, unlike that in the corporate bodies of avoués and notaires, had no proprietary basis.[6]

6. Lenard R. Berlanstein, *The Barristers of Toulouse in the Eighteenth Century (1740–1793)* (Baltimore, 1975), 1–31; Fitzsimmons, *The Parisian Order of Barristers,* 1–32; Pierre Avril, *La Personalité morale de l'ordre des avocats* (Grenoble, 1902).

But though not proprietary, the ordres des avocats were privileged, and so came under attack during the Revolution. As early as the famous evening session of August 4, 1789, the National Assembly made clear its general intention to reorder and regenerate France by replacing the inequity of corporate privilege with liberty and equality for the individual. On July 5, 1790, the Assembly granted every citizen the right to make his own pleas in court and on September 2 opened the profession of barrister to all, without restrictions of education or experience, by dissolving the ordres des avocats. The privileges of the avocats had never been considered property and were therefore abolished without compensation. Within two years, most of the prerevolutionary avocats withdrew entirely from legal affairs. Some of the others sought election, often successfully, to the bench or parquet of the new courts. Proudly, but almost pathetically, the small number who continued to plead cases tried to maintain the traditions of their ordres by refusing to associate with men who would not have qualified for the profession before 1790.

In the Bonapartist reorganization of the hommes de loi and the judicial system, the turn for the avocats came on 22 Ventôse XII (March 13, 1804), when the right to *plaider* was restricted to avoués and to men listed on a new Tableau des avocats. The profession was restored, but without the independence in which it had gloried under the ancien régime. The state, not ordres, imposed the qualifications (essentially a *licence ès lois*) for the Tableau des avocats and exercised all disciplinary powers. Any hope for greater autonomy depended on Napoleon's goodwill, and that was lost when several avocats were prominent in the defense of General Jean Victor Moreau at his trial for treason in May, 1804. Their role aroused Napoleon's suspicion of all avocats, not merely his anger at a few. It was only on December 14, 1810, that he permitted the ordres to reconstitute themselves, and even then most of the powers of membership and discipline remained with the state. The premier président and the procureur général for the cour d'appel of the *ressort* established the Tableau des avocats, with advice from six senior members of the ordre. The avocats could assemble as a body only upon the convocation of the departmental prefect to select candidates for their *conseil de l'ordre* (executive committee and council of discipline). From them, the procureur général chose the members of the conseil and ordre's bâtonnier (the name derived from a long baton carried on ceremonial occasions). The conseil heard avocats charged with misconduct, and its decisions could be challenged before the cour d'appel, not before the entire ordre as during the ancien régime. Napoleon further undermined the profession's corporate nature by demanding that the avocat's oath be taken individually instead of collectively: "neither to say nor to publish anything, as counsel for the defense, contrary to laws, morality, public tranquillity, or the security of the state, and never to show disrespect for the courts or legitimate authorities."[7]

More so than any other social group in France, the avocats welcomed the Restoration. The Bourbons, they believed, would return to the ordres privileges lost during the preceding quarter century, and this confidence was not misplaced. By the laws of November 20, 1822, and August 27, 1830 (the latter promulgated by Louis Philippe but prepared under Charles X), the ordres des avocats regained the power to determine the membership of the profession by establishing the Tableau des avocats, to choose their own conseils and bâtonniers, and to assemble as a corporation to take the oath of the avocat. The only remaining Napoleonic restraint was the right to protest disciplinary sanctions before the cour d'appel. With avoués limited to written pleadings since July, 1810, the avocats had essentially regained the position they had held among the hommes de loi prior to 1790. Yet they remembered with such keenness the humiliations imposed by first the Revolution and then Napoleon that for more than a century they would bristle fiercely at threats, however mild, and justify their prerogatives as the vital ramparts of an independent legal profession.[8]

The avocats were inevitably suspicious and quickly resentful at the coming of a new Bonaparte. In 1850, as president of the Second Republic, Louis Napoleon authorized a *patente* (license fee) for avocats, the first time they had been singled out for taxation, and approved the law of January 22, 1851, that provided for *assistance judiciaire*—counsel for *accusés* too poor to pay for a defense—by requiring the avocats to assume their cases without charge. For more than two centuries, the ordres had encouraged such service *pro bono publico*, but the responsibility was now expanded enormously. During the 1850s, these cases amounted to as many as one of three before the cours d'assises; by the 1890s, they amounted to one of two. After the coup d'état of December 2, 1851, Louis Napoleon was ex-

7. Berlanstein, *The Barristers of Toulouse*, 148–82; Fitzsimmons, *The Parisian Order of Barristers*, especially 51–63, 76–78, 88–90, 149–58, 177–92.

8. Damien, *Les Avocats du temps passé*, 500–20. See also Donald R. Kelley, *Historians and the Law in Postrevolutionary France* (Princeton, 1984).

ceptionally sensitive about criticism. He feared, like his uncle before him, the eloquence of the avocats and, on March 22, 1852, placed new restraints on them. To secure control of the ordres by senior, and presumably conservative, avocats, he limited candidates for the conseils to men who had been listed on the Tableau des avocats for at least five years—and, for the Paris ordre, ten years. The conseils punished breaches of conduct by imposing one of four penalties: *avertissement* (warning) or *blâme* (reprimand) in minor incidents, *suspension* (suspension) for up to a year in more serious violations, and *radiation* (disbarment) in the most serious. Louis Napoleon created an additional state sanction, *suspension* for up to ten years, which, though rarely invoked, remained a threat to avocats who were political opponents until it was withdrawn in April, 1870, as a reform of the Liberal Empire. The *patente, assistance judiciaire*, and the rules for the conseils remained in force until 1940.[9]

Such relatively minor annoyances aside, the avocats attained their greatest prestige and political power during the seventy years of the Third Republic. Industrial development and increasing urbanization generated an abundance of clients by providing additional issues for litigation and a new context for serious crime. The national taste for oratory admired the legislative address of three hours and the *plaidoirie* of four. Often the same man delivered both, for this was the time of the *avocats-rois*—the politician-barristers who dominated the ministries as well as the courts: Léon Gambetta, Jules Dufaure, René Waldeck-Rousseau, Alexandre Ribot, Emile Loubet, Armand Fallières, Raymond Poincaré, Louis Barthou, René Viviani, Aristide Briand, Alexandre Millerand. The number of avocats increased, from barely 1,700 throughout the country in 1789 to approximately 7,000 in 1914, and especially in Paris, from slightly more than 600 to nearly 2,500. This eminence, which they considered entirely appropriate and even delayed, made them all the more resentful of any intrusion upon their autonomy.[10]

In mid-November, 1897, Jeanne Chauvin, holder of a *doctorat ès lois*, petitioned to become a stagiaire of the Paris ordre des avocats but was rejected on the basis of her gender, even though all of the other higher professions in France (medicine, pharmacy, and the professoriat) had already admitted women. Viviani and Poincaré, them-

9. Damien, *Les Avocats du temps passé*, 403–404, 470–97; Buteau, *L'Ordre des avocats*, 173–81.
10. Damien, *Les Avocats du temps passé*, 359–62, 432–45; Buteau, *L'Ordre des avocats*, 297–327.

selves members of the Paris ordre, sponsored legislation to end what they called this "unrepublican" discrimination, and it became law on December 1, 1900, despite the opposition of many avocats. Chauvin petitioned a second time and was inscribed as a stagiaire on December 19, but not as the first woman. Out of resentment, the ordre granted that precedence to Mme Eugène Petit, whose husband was an avocat. In the annual address of the bâtonnier, the word *avocate*, created in 1900, would not be spoken until 1926, when the number of women in the Paris ordre had reached 150.[11]

There was a change of attitude during the 1920s and 1930s, when inflation and depression at home combined with weakness and passivity abroad to reduce possibilities and to destroy certainties and confidence. The ordres welcomed the intervention of the state in the form of laws to require that an avocat reside within the *ressort* of his barreau and actively practice his profession or be disbarred (June 20, 1920), that anyone falsely claiming to be an avocat would be imprisoned (March 26, 1924), and that immigrants to France were ineligible to become avocats until ten years after their naturalization (July 19, 1934). The two decades before 1940 led the ordres des avocats, like some other elements of French society, toward a failure of nerve.[12]

The career of every avocat began with a *stage*, when he received his initiation into the profession. By its very act of accepting his petition to become a stagiaire, the ordre admitted him to a strictly defined elite. He possessed a *licence ès lois*, the proof of legal studies. He could not be a member of the military or the clergy, because he might have to obey commands in conflict with the rules of the ordre; he agreed never to involve himself in any commercial venture, because the dignity of a businessman was considered beneath that of an avocat. His private life, and that of his wife if he were married, was without irregularity. He had no record of arrests, drunkenness, or large debts. Very likely he was from a bourgeois family and possessed a private income. The expense of education, the length of the *stage*, and the unlikely prospect of immediate financial success after opening an office deterred almost anyone not from a comfortable background. But because the practice of law was too demanding for dilettantes, few aristocrats were attracted. In 1883 a handbook for

11. Fernand Carcos, *Les Avocates* (Paris, 1934), 11–42.
12. Louis Crémieu, *Traité de la profession d'avocat* (Paris, 1939).

avocats claimed that the advantages of the profession were honorability, purity of income, and association with natural law and classical authors such as Horace. As late as the mid-1890s, Charles Damiron, a stagiaire at Lyon, believed that the bar was reserved for men of wealthy circumstances.[13]

Early in the nineteenth century the ordres began prescribing that the stagiaire spend his first twelve months in an étude d'avoué, where he could hone his knowledge of procedure and where he frequently solidified his fortune by marrying the avoué's daughter. For two to four more years, he prepared dossiers for a senior avocat and made himself available to the public, without charge, for consultation on minor legal matters at the *secrétariat de l'ordre* (the administrative offices of the bar). By the middle of the century, the tradition that stagiaires attend a series of *conférences* was reversed in Paris. They began to deliver the lectures themselves as a competition in the eloquence and sophistication of thought that would be necessary to attract and then win cases. The twelve best speakers were named *secrétaires de la conférence* (secretaries of the series), and this distinction came to be the mark of future eminence at the bar and sometimes in politics as well: Gambetta, Ribot, Poincaré, Barthou, Millerand, and Viviani were winners.

The *stage* was also an immersion in the strict etiquette of the profession. An avocat had to wear his robe—and until the beginning of the twentieth century, his toque—at all times when performing his functions: in court, in his office, and in the offices of magistrates. By custom it was worn negligently and until it was threadbare, as if the avocat could afford to adopt an air of indifference. His office had to be appropriately near the law courts, and the oversight committee of the ordre established a standard for the furnishings. It even recommended the contents of his personal library—twelve books on the philosophy of law, fifty-nine on history, and forty on modern legislation.[14]

The etiquette was most elaborate about the relationship of avocat to client. In civil litigation the client was completely free to choose his avocat, and the avocat completely free to accept or refuse the case. In criminal justice, the institution of *assistance judiciaire* in

---

13. Félix Liouville (ed.), *Abrégé des rèles de la profession d'avocat* (Paris, 1883), 70, 89; Charles Damiron, *Souvenirs d'un avocat de province* (Lyon, 1949), 18.

14. Damien, *Les Avocats du temps passé*, 271–97; Robert, *L'Avocxat*, 78–88. See also Fernand Payen and Gaston Duveau, *Les Règles de la profession d'avocat et les usages du barreau de Paris* (Paris, 1926).

1851, which assigned avocats to plead the cases of indigents, constrained this traditional independence, with one important reservation. If the client confessed his guilt to the avocat, the rules of the ordres required the avocat to retire from the defense and to ask that another member of the barreau take on the case. He could not withdraw for any other reason, even if his own examination of the evidence convinced him overwhelmingly of the client's culpability, and he could not divulge to anyone a client's avowal. For both French law and the ordres maintained the absolute inviolability of *secret professionnel* (confidentiality between avocat and client). The emphasis was so strong that avocats were reluctant to equip their offices with telephones or typewriters when they became generally available in the last two decades of the nineteenth century. With the telephone, there was always the possibility that unauthorized use might be made of an extension. As for the typewriter, because hardly a single avocat could operate it, the transcription of notes would mean entrusting confidential details to a secretary. As late as World War I, nearly all of an avocat's files were in longhand, and almost no legal business was transacted by telephone.[15]

The ordres perpetuated a myth from the ancien régime that an avocat's decision to plead a case represented less a business contract than a mission of honor and that the *honoraires* (professional fee) due the avocat should be viewed as a spontaneous gift from the grateful client. The corollary was clear: An avocat was unlike businessmen, professionals such as physicians, and even the other hommes de loi (avoués and notaires) in that he offered his services instead of selling them. The barreau could concentrate on the lofty themes of law and justice, not base, quotidian details like billing clients. To uphold this fiction, the ordres surrounded the settlement of accounts with artificial conventions. The preferred term was *honoraire* (honorarium) rather than *honoraires* (fee). An avocat did not present his client with a statement of charges; he had to receive the honoraires personally and in cash (an exception was made for a cashier's check), and he could not provide a receipt. The use of receipts, representatives, or personal checks would imply payment for services rendered instead of a gift made out of appreciation. For the same reason, avocats were forbidden to act for a contingency fee. These rules were often ignored, particularly after 1914. The avocat simply

---

15. Damien, *Les Avocats du temps passé*, 321, 423–25; Robert, *L'Avocat*, 69–77. See also Louis Pimienta, *Le Secret professionel de l'avocat* (Paris, 1937).

specified his honoraires confidentially, basing them on his reputation and the difficulty of the case. Of course, payment could not be asked or accepted for a defense undertaken through *assistance judiciaire*. In his memoirs—nearly the only specific evidence available about honoraires—Charles Damiron recalled that at the end of the nineteenth century in Lyon, an uncomplicated civil suit cost three hundred to five hundred francs and that the office of a successful avocat had gross receipts of forty thousand to fifty thousand francs a year. Honoraires in Paris for the most celebrated avocats were almost certainly much higher.[16]

Stagiaires learned that the barreau had only a limited respect for the magistrature. Any open disdain toward the bench or the prosecution always brought disciplinary action by the conseil de l'ordre, and the courts themselves punished incidents of outright contempt. But privately many avocats considered the majority of magistrates to be servilely sensitive to political pressure and more concerned with promotion than justice. Henri Robert alluded to this opinion circumspectly when he wrote in 1923 that a magistrate without a personal fortune was "in a critical and painful position." Avocats also complained that appointment to the bench was sometimes regarded as a sinecure. Damiron retailed anecdotes about justices of the Cour d'appel de Lyon habitually falling asleep during the presentation of oral arguments and waking up only at the end of the session. One conseiller, urged by the premier président to take coffee with his meals, declined, explaining that it kept him awake. Another, jostled out of his sleep by a colleague, murmured to an astonished court, "Non poulette, pas ce soir!" Damiron concluded: "A successful career as a magistrate requires influential references but not necessarily intelligence. A successful career as an avocat requires intelligence but not necessarily influential references."[17]

Once the *stage* was completed, the new avocat's opportunity to demonstrate this intelligence came with his first case, usually one assigned through *assistance judiciaire*. Almost invariably, it was minor and hopeless, tried before the bench of a cour correctionnelle in no mood to hear a long *plaidoirie*. Albert Naud, a celebrated avocat in Paris during the 1940s and 1950s, began his career in 1934 defending a bicycle thief. Although required if conviction could result

16. Damien, *Les Avocats du temps passé*, 372–74; Robert, *L'Avocat*, 111–15; Damiron, *Souvenirs*, 87–108; Albert Naud, *Les défendre tous* (Paris, 1973), 33.
17. Buteau, *L'Ordre des avocats*, 258–97; Robert, *L'Avocat*, 116–26, the quotation from 120; Damiron, *Souvenirs*, 179–251, the quotations from 182 and 250–51.

in a prison sentence, the presence of an avocat was actually of little benefit in the trial of a *délit* because the three-judge panel was rarely swayed by rhetoric. But the accused did have the pleasure of hearing himself defended before he was found guilty. A request from an established avocat to assist in a case to be tried by the cour d'assises presented a much grander chance. As the junior member of the defense, the new avocat assumed responsibility for many of the pretrial details, particularly attending the interrogation of the *inculpé* and witnesses by the juge d'instruction. His reward was the privilege of delivering a *plaidoirie* before a jury and before the newspaper reporters who always packed the cour d'assises to cover lurid crimes. In 1935, Vincent de Moro-Giafferi asked Naud to join him in defending a woman accused of robbery and murder. When the trial opened, the proceedings went so swiftly that by late afternoon on the first day, Naud was about to begin his *plaidoirie*. Aware that many of the reporters would already have left to file their stories, Moro-Giafferi contrived delays. Naud's *plaidoirie* was postponed until the following morning, when he spoke brilliantly. The press acclaimed him, and so a reputation was made.[18]

Throughout the nineteenth century and well into the twentieth, most avocats concluded a defense before the cour d'assises by declaiming an impassioned *plaidoirie*, quite literally a "pleading." The jurymen were asked to understand, or at least to pity, the *accusé*, who was standing, they were always reminded, where they might one day have to stand. The cultural Romanticism dominating the early part of the nineteenth century and lingering on until its end encouraged this style of address and stimulated an appreciation for florid oratory lasting into the 1940s. The stagiaire learned that the ideal *plaidoirie* consisted of five elements (introduction, narration of the case, argument for the defense, refutation of the prosecution, and conclusion), that it should be written out and then memorized so thoroughly that the delivery would seem spontaneous, and that, in Damiron's words, it "touched all the strings of the lyre: emotion, virtuous indignation, irony, sarcasm, insolence, tears, gestures." The *plaidoirie* became so widely admired that Ferdinand Brunetière, editor of the belletristic *Revue des Deux Mondes*, felt compelled to remark stuffily in 1888 that it could not be considered literature. Henri Robert caused a sensation among avocats in December, 1890,

---

18. Robert, *L'Avocat*, 58–68; Damiron, *Souvenirs*, 49–60; Naud, *Les défendre tous*, 66–72, 97–145; Saillard, *Le Rôle de l'avocat*, 71–123.

by giving a simple synopsis of the evidence as his *plaidoirie* in the trial of Gabrielle Bompard, who was charged with her lover, Michel Eyraud, in the murder of the bailiff Gouffé. This tempered approach was imitated by the brilliant politician-barrister René Waldeck-Rousseau but by few others. When Robert wrote his memoirs in 1923, he called "the fire of conviction" the essential ingredient of a *plaidoirie* and testified to the continuing ascendancy of the melodramatic appeal.[19]

During the first two-thirds of the nineteenth century, most avocats were "instinctive Talleyrands, displaying perhaps nostalgia for the [prerevolutionary] past but . . . accommodating themselves to constitutional transformations." Patiently and successfully, they sought to restore first the existence and then the prerogatives of their ordres. Victims of the 1789 Revolution, they opposed radical change and supported conservative policies. They adjusted easily to the revolution of 1830, they were generally appalled by the revolution of 1848, and after some hesitation, they reconciled themselves to the coup d'état of 1851 and the proclamation of empire a year later. Dominated by rural notables, political life under these royal and imperial regimes could offer them only a very limited scope, but the appointment of prominent avocats to important positions in the magistrature was widely regarded as proof of their assimilation. When Pierre Paul Henrion de Pansey, sixty-eight years old and a specialist in feudal law, agreed in 1810 to become premier président of the Cour de Cassation (he remained in that position until his death nineteen years later), the avocats of the ancien régime symbolically made their peace with Napoleon. The decision by André Dupin, bâtonnier of the Paris ordre in 1829, to accept the post of procureur général for the Cour de Cassation in 1830 was a bridge for the avocats to cross from the Bourbons to the Orléanists.[20] The imperial appointment of Gustave Charles Chaix d'Est-Ange, himself bâtonnier of the Paris ordre in 1842, as procureur général of the Cour d'appel de Paris in 1857 marked a broad conciliation between Louis Napoleon and the ordres.

But for a minority of avocats, accommodation, particularly to Bonapartist government, was out of the question, and they tried to turn

19. Damiron, *Souvenirs*, 64–81, the quotation from 64; Damien, *Les Avocats du temps passé*, 302, 432–57, the reference to Brunetière from 453; Robert, *L'Avocat*, 24–32, the quotation from 26; Fernand Payen, *Le Barreau et la langue française* (Paris, 1939), 232–80.
20. Kelley, *Historians and the Law*, 57–63.

important trials into occasions of embarrassment and propaganda. The outstanding examples, separated by half a century, were that imprudent alacrity to defend General Moreau in 1804 and Jules Favre's eloquent *plaidoirie* for Felice Orsini, whose bungled attempt to assassinate Louis Napoleon and Eugénie on January 14, 1858, left 8 bystanders dead and nearly 150 wounded. The number of "political" avocats increased during the Second Empire because the barreau's republicans—Favre, Jules Grévy, Léon Gambetta, and Jules Ferry foremost—recognized that the courts could be used, more safely and spectacularly than the tightly controlled elections, to rouse popular opinion against the regime. Their example linked politics and law more closely than ever before and contributed to the rise of the avocats-rois, who were so conspicuous throughout the Third Republic and especially before World War I. During the trial of Henriette Caillaux in July, 1914, the relationships of politicians and avocats reached such an involution that Joseph Caillaux, a former premier (1911), had a heated confrontation with Louis Barthou, an avocat as well as a second former premier (1913), and the president of the Republic, Raymond Poincaré, another avocat and a third former premier (1912), submitted a sworn deposition that was introduced into evidence.[21]

Henri Robert's list of the most distinguished avocats between 1870 and 1923 revealed strikingly the changes in status and attitude during this period.[22] Eight of the eighteen he named were avocats-rois: Gambetta, Dufaure, Waldeck-Rousseau, Poincaré, Barthou, Briand, Millerand, and Viviani. Each had been premier at least once, and two had been president of the Republic. Far from having to accommodate themselves to the regime, avocats were its leaders. Of the remaining ten, four—Henri Du Buit, Fernand Labori, Maurice Bernard, and Charles Chenu—had willingly associated their names with cases or clients that were notorious. Certainly, every *accusé* deserved a defense, but until the final quarter of the century a great many avocats accepted unsavory cases only reluctantly, if at all. The loss of this inhibition was closely related to the emergence of the cour d'assises as a form of theater. The most ambitious avocats vied for the role of defense counsel, even if a defense appeared hopeless or

21. Roger L. Williams, *Manners and Murders in the World of Louis-Napoleon* (Seattle, 1975), 81–89, 192; Martin, *The Hypocrisy of Justice*, 183, 193–94.
22. Robert, *L'Avocat*, 33–38. See also Roger Allou and Charles Chenu, *Barreau de Paris: Grands avocats du siècle* (Paris, 1894), and Edmond Rousse, *Avocats et magistrats* (Paris, 1903).

repugnant. The newspaper accounts could burnish a reputation, and juries were sufficiently unpredictable that a stunning acquittal was always possible.

Beginning in 1898, Henri Du Buit became the principal avocat in civil litigation for Frédéric and Thérèse Humbert and unwittingly protected their grand "Crawford" deception that defrauded investors of more than one hundred million francs. Although Waldeck-Rousseau, among others, had raised suspicions about the Humberts, Du Buit professed to have no doubts until May, 1902, when they fled France to escape criminal charges. But if Du Buit's sensibilities had finally been offended, both Charles Chenu and Fernand Labori were willing to plead for them, and to receive the unusually generous honoraires for which the Humberts were well known, after their apprehension seven months later in Spain. Chenu argued and won a case in which there was actually sympathy for them—the suit brought in February, 1903, by the banker Elie Cattauï, who had charged 63.14 percent interest on the money he loaned them. In August, Labori, who had been a notable Dreyfusard as much out of ambition, perhaps, as conviction, defended the Humberts at their trial for fraud by denouncing the cheated investors as usurers and describing the charges as the product of a mysterious political intrigue involving the current minister of justice, Ernest Vallé, who had once been Cattauï's avocat, and Waldeck-Rousseau, who had been premier from June, 1899, until May, 1902. The jury returned a verdict of guilty with mitigating circumstances that limited the sentence imposed on the Humberts to five years in prison.

Eleven years later, in 1914, Labori was even more successful with his tactic of assailing the victim when he won Henriette Caillaux's acquittal by blaming Gaston Calmette for provoking the six pistol shots that killed him. Maurice Bernard argued for Cattauï in the suit against the Humberts and, in 1910 and 1911, defended the notorious financier and swindler Henri Rochette. As Joseph Caillaux's avocat, he negotiated his envenomed divorce from Berthe Gueydan in 1911 and assisted Labori's preparations for Henriette Caillaux's trial. By contrast, Edgar Demange governed his career according to an entirely different ethical code. Although a devout Catholic and a conservative, he accepted the unpopular defense of Alfred Dreyfus, from the first court-martial in 1894 to the exoneration by the Cour de Cassation in 1906, and of Joseph Caillaux, in 1920, against charges of treason after satisfying his conscience that each was innocent. Labori, Du Buit, Chenu, and Bernard gained great wealth; Demange died all but penniless.[23]

The following is a list of thirty prominent avocats in Paris between 1870 and 1940 who regularly accepted criminal cases.[24]

Antony Aubin	Raymond Hubert
Henri Barboux	Jacques Isorni
Maurice Bernard	Fernand Labori
André Berthon	Jean-Charles Legrand
César Campinchi	Désidéré Lente
Charles Chenu	Vincent de Moro-Giafferi
Edouard Clunet	Henri Robert
Edgar Demange	Jeanne Rospard-Legrand
Maurice Flach	Raoul Rousset
René Floriot	Emile de Saint-Aubin
Maurice Garçon	Justin Seligman
Albert Gautrat	Odette Simon
Henri Geraud	Jean-Louis Thaon
Georges Guilhermet	Lucile Tinayre-Grenaudier
André Hesse	Henry Torrès

After World War I the nature of the profession seemed to change. The reign of the avocats-rois slowly came to an end as the increasing growth and complexity of government made simultaneous distinction in law and politics extremely difficult. Ethical considerations about a defense, particularly the assumption of a client's innocence, that had been paramount in the nineteenth century lost much of their force in the twentieth. Even the most eminent avocats were less scrupulous: The willingness before 1914 to plead in distasteful cases having political overtones was supplanted during the 1920s and 1930s by an avidity to defend *accusés* charged with heinous, repellent crimes. At least Henri Rochette, Thérèse Humbert, and Henriette Caillaux had not been *common* criminals. After the war, if a case was not intrinsically sensational, the avocat—or avocate—did so much to generate publicity that some of them became celebrities. Individualism replaced corporate loyalty. Many of the giants from

---

23. Martin, *The Hypocrisy of Justice*, 99–100, 117–19, 134–40, 161–64, 184–206, 218–19; Jean-Denis Bredin, *L'Affaire* (Paris, 1983), translated by Jeffrey Mehlman as *The Affair: The Case of Alfred Dreyfus* (New York, 1986), 397–99, 445–49, 497–98.

24. The list was culled from *La Gazette des Tribunaux*, 1870–1940.

the Belle Epoque were gone. Labori died prematurely of heart disease in 1917. Demange collapsed at his desk in 1925. Robert, who was bâtonnier of the Paris ordre throughout the war, suffered from a progressive blindness and by the mid-1920s rarely took cases. The simple eloquence of his restrained *plaidoiries* was recognized by his election in 1923 to the Académie Française, and after his death in 1936, the short street linking the Pont Neuf to the Place Dauphine, appropriately midway between the Palais de Justice and the Institut de France, was named for him. The new stars of the cour d'assises were César Campinchi, Henry Torrès, Raymond Hubert, Maurice Garçon, and, above all, Moro-Giafferi, who first gave proof of his great talent during the trial of the Bande à Bonnot in February, 1913.[25]

Raymond Hubert and Henry Torrès were known for quiet but fervent *plaidoiries*, entreating the jury to acquit, never insisting imperiously, as Demange and Labori often had. César Campinchi adopted something of Henri Robert's approach, a pithy, logical, occasionally literary style. All three made a specialty of defending the "undefendables," *accusés* whose guilt was overwhelming and for whom plausible extenuating circumstances had to be devised. That could mean portraying the act as a *crime passionnel*. Campinchi and Torrès won acquittals for men (Léopold Ordioni and Désiré Maguère, respectively) who shot wives they claimed were adulterous. Hubert defended the widow of an avocat (Yvonne Langue) who killed her brother-in-law for cheating her in business. The jury accompanied its guilty verdict with a finding of so many mitigating conditions that the judges imposed a sentence of merely three years in prison. More frequently, the goal was simply avoiding a condemnation to the guillotine. They saved the heads of *accusés* who killed in the commission of armed robbery (Pierre Nathan and Marie-Louise Gérin by Torrès, Marcel Nourric and Pascal Fuscol by Campinchi, and Charles Mestorino by Hubert) or who admitted multiple murders (Jacques Beauvilliers and Jeanne Bouquillon by Hubert).[26]

The most idiosyncratic member of the Paris ordre was Maurice

---

25. Georges Guilhermet, *Souvenirs et histoires vécues* (Paris, 1956), 163–72; André Toulemon, *Portraits d'avocats* (Paris, 1964), 35–56.

26. Maurice Hamburger, *La Défense: Nos grands avocats* (8th ed.; Paris, 1930), 25–30, 101–104, 145–49; Madeleine Jacob, *Quarante ans de journalisme* (Paris, 1970), 245–48, 250–53; *La Gazette des Tribunaux*, March 26, 1930, for Ordioni; February 22–23, 1938, for Maguère; February 12–13, 1930, for Langue; June 18–24, 1935, for Nathan and Gérin; March 10–16, 1928, for Nourric; January 23–28, 1934, for Fuscol; June 5–9, 1928, for Mestorino; May 4, 1929, for Beauvilliers; November 26–27, 1930, for Bouquillon.

Garçon. As an adolescent, he declared his devotion to poetry, but at the urging of his father, Emile Garçon, the distinguished professor of criminal law at the Sorbonne, he agreed to study for the *licence ès lois* and become an avocat. From the first, he displayed a remarkable mastery of language. His briefs and *plaidoiries* were elegant, meticulously constructed, and compellingly argued. Although he consciously adopted the offhand gestures of nonchalance, languidly sketched figures during court sessions, and had the air of an aging *lycéen*, the force of his brilliance impressed magistrates and juries. He became one of the most celebrated avocats in the twentieth century, but law was never his primary affection. He read deeply in the literature of diabolism and wrote authoritatively about it and about the history and the legal controversies of his own time. The suspicion of dilettantism hung around him, but every word he spoke or wrote had the mark of keen intelligence. His election to the Académie Française, which came in 1946, was nearly inevitable.[27]

Garçon was slender, aloof, controlled, intellectual, always prepared. Vincent de Moro-Giafferi, the only avocat of greater professional stature during the 1920s and 1930s, was very much his opposite: obese, expansive, Corsican, emotional, an improviser. By passionately maintaining the innocence of Eugène Dieudonné at the Bande à Bonnot trial and of Henri-Désiré Landru, the wartime bluebeard, in 1921, he assured his reputation. Although both were convicted, Moro-Giafferi was right about Dieudonné. He pleaded in other sensational cases (particularly those of Pierre de Ryssac, Jane Weiller, Marcel Sauret, Georgette Hodot, and José Browermann), but he did not have a client so notorious as Landru again until Bruno Weidmann in 1939, whom he defended unsuccessfully on grounds of insanity. His fame spread beyond France, and in 1927 he lent his name to the American committee seeking clemency for Sacco and Vanzetti. Called the Lion of the Palais de Justice, he dominated the cour d'assises with majestic bearing as he roared questions, adjurations, and commands in a full, deep voice. But he also took pleasure in useless diversionary tactics—always wasting a peremptory chal-

---

27. Hamburger, *La Défense*, 75–80; Jacob, *Quarante ans de journalisme*, 241–45. Among Maurice Garçon's many works, see especially *La Justice contemporaine* (Paris, 1933), *Sur les faits divers* (Paris, 1945), *Histoire de la justice sous la Troisième République* (Paris, 1957), *Histoires curieuses* (Paris, 1959), *L'Avocat et la morale* (Paris, 1963), and *Nouvelles histoires curieuses* (Paris, 1964). Many of his private papers and files have been deposited in the AN, 304 AP, Papiers Maurice Garçon. Access is dependent upon authorization from his son Pierre Maurice-Garçon, a magistrate.

lenge on the first potential juror—and permitted himself extraordinary impudence toward the bench: Asked once to specify the articles of the criminal code on which he based his argument, he replied, "Sur tous!"[28]

Moro-Giafferi was the outstanding example of the evolution taken by avocats after the late nineteenth century. The focus of the profession had shifted permanently from the corporate ordre to the avocat celebrity and from the ideal of a richly cultured, highly ethical defense to the acknowledgment that an acquittal was the goal, however guilty the *accusé*. The avocat had become a modern lawyer and had moved far from the dignity and decorum that his predecessors had sought to retain from the ancien régime.

28. Jacob, *Quarante ans de journalisme*, 236–41, the exclamation by Moro-Giafferi from 239; Toulemon, *Portraits d'avocats*, 11–34; Hamburger, *La Défense*, 57–66; *La Gazette des Tribunaux*, February 3–28, 1913, for Dieudonné; November 8–December 1, 1921, for Landru; October 26–28, 1928 for Ryssac; October 31–November 1, 1929, for Weiller; May 3, 1930, for Sauret; March 27–28, 1931, for Hodot; June 30, 1937, for Browermann; March 11–April 1, 1939, for Weidmann.

8

The Punishments

"To find the suitable punishment for a crime is to find the disadvantage whose idea is such that it robs for ever the idea of a crime of any attraction. It is an art of conflicting energies, an art of images linked by association, the forging of stable connections that defy time: it is a matter of establishing the representation of pairs of opposing values, of establishing quantitative differences between the opposing forces, of setting up a complex of obstacle-signs that may subject the movement of the forces to a power relation."[1] So Michel Foucault wrote as one of the least controversial declarations in his *Surveiller et punir: Naissance de la prison* and one of the few with which citizens of the Third Republic would have readily agreed. For they had devised a hierarchy of penalties that were designed to deter crime, and if these punishments had at the same time the effect of exacting a social vengeance, that was accounted an additional benefit.

A defendant found guilty of a serious *délit* by the three-judge panel of a cour correctionnelle faced *emprisonnement*, a term of confinement in a *maison de correction* (departmental prison) that could last, depending upon the offense and the circumstances under which it was committed, from several days to five years. Emprisonne-

---

1. Michel Foucault, *Surveiller et punir: Naissance de la prison* (Paris, 1975), translated by Alan Sheridan as *Discipline and Punish: The Birth of the Prison* (New York, 1977), 104.

ment was sometimes accompanied by an *amende*, literally a "fine" but better translated as a "reparation." Unlike the other penalties available to French criminal justice—death, forced labor, transportation, imprisonment, and, after 1891, the occasional suspended sentence for a first offender—an amende did not meet the test of *égalité*, because it bore less heavily on the rich than on the poor. Nevertheless a conviction for aggravated assault and wounding when the victim was incapacitated for more than twenty days but suffered no permanent injury meant a sentence of two to five years in a maison de correction and an amende of from sixteen to two thousand francs; for extortion without threat of violence, one to five years and from fifty to three thousand francs; for abuse of confidence, two months to two years and from twenty-five francs to one-fourth of the money or property placed in jeopardy; for theft from the mails by a postal employee, three months to five years and from sixteen to five hundred francs; for concealment of a birth when the infant was stillborn, six days to five years.

A guilty verdict on a felony charge by a jury in the cour d'assises opened a range of harsher penalties. The least severe was *réclusion*—confinement in a *maison centrale* (state prison) for a period extending upward from five years for such crimes as simple highway robbery, simple grand larceny, simple theft from a church, aggravated assault and wounding when the victim suffered permanent injury, girl molestation committed without violence, obtaining or assisting in an abortion if not a physician or a pharmacist, perjury in a criminal trial, fraud in a private document, and abuse of confidence by a public official.

The considerably harsher penalty of *travaux forcés*, hard labor of a painful and exhausting character for a period of at least five years, served by male offenders in the penal colonies of French Guiana and New Caledonia, was imposed when aggravated conditions accompanied the commission of the felony: girl molestation by a relative or guardian or with violence; the assistance of a physician or a pharmacist at an abortion; accepting money for perjury in a criminal trial; highway robbery, grand larceny, or theft from a church when carried out armed, at night, with violence, or as a member of a band. Travaux forcés was also the standard sentence for crimes regarded as intrinsically heinous but not capital: manslaughter with or without premeditation, arson of a nondwelling, rape, pillage, counterfeiting, fraud in a commercial or a public document, and embezzlement or

The Punishments

malfeasance by a government official. The punishment was all the more severe because a convict condemned to travaux forcés for five to eight years had to remain in the colony for an equal period after serving his sentence, a penalty appropriately called *doublage*. Any sentence to more than eight years of travaux forcés carried with it the prohibition of ever leaving the colony. The death rate was so high among hard-labor convicts that many did not survive even five years. Few ever returned to France.

The ultimate punishment, *la peine de mort*—death rendered by the guillotine—was reserved for arson of a dwelling and for murder in its various guises, premeditated, unpremeditated, parricide, infanticide, and poisoning.[2]

This hierarchy of penalties had been elaborated during the years since the National Assembly adopted a revised Code pénal on September 25, 1791, that swept away the traditional punishments of French criminal justice. Banishment, branding, flogging, and condemnation to the Mediterranean galley fleet were abolished forever, and so too the refinements for capital crimes—breaking on the wheel, mutilation, drawing, quartering, and burning at the stake—that brought infinite suffering before death. Punishment would be simplified and in its forms made equal for all. Decapitation, previously reserved for aristocrats, became the sole method of execution, but a machine, the guillotine, replaced the headsman with his ax. For all noncapital offenses the sentence would be imprisonment.

Initially, choosing prison to be the focus of punishment was for want of a better alternative. Although confinement as a penalty was not unknown in the eighteenth century, it was directed almost exclusively against vagabonds and beggars, particularly when privation dramatically increased their number and brought fears of brigandage. Otherwise, prisons were used for defendants held "temporarily" pending their trials, for debtors until they could (or would) pay their creditors, and for the unlucky who, blamelessly or not, incurred the wrath of the powerful and were subjected to royal lettres de cachet or to an even more arbitrary local equivalent. But a multifaceted rationale for imprisonment quickly developed. The essence of prison, the loss of freedom, was the obverse to the ideal of *liberté* that the 1789 Revolution purportedly granted France, and was therefore the

2. E. Garçon (ed.), *Code pénal annoté*.

proper penalty for transgression of a free society's laws. The length of the sentence could be varied to fit the severity of the crime. And like the guillotine, prison satisfied the ideal of *égalité*.

Eighteenth-century prisons indiscriminately mixed men, women, and children, leaving them to pass their days in idleness and vice. Infectious diseases were rampant in the almost complete absence of sanitary facilities and the permanent condition of filth. The warders were extortionists, willing to supply any luxury, including escape, for a price. Prisoners with money or friends outside the walls might survive their incarceration with relatively little hardship. The poor or friendless shivered in rags and died from a diet that was undisguised starvation. The National Assembly proposed to replace this promiscuous inconsistency with a uniform rigor. There was substantial sentiment for the utmost severity: The worst offenders would endure *le cachot*, being chained alone, hand and foot, in a dark cell, fed bread and water—but for no more than twenty-four years; when somewhat less harshness was appropriate, *la gêne* would be imposed—a lighted cell, a more nourishing diet, a single chain about the waist, and occasional contact with other inmates; "simple confinement" would suffice for the rest. Because the majority rejected le cachot as inhumane, the Code pénal of 1791 (and that of 1810 under Napoleon) distinguished only two forms of imprisonment. The most serious noncapital crimes would be punished by travaux forcés, made more grievous by the weight of ball and chain, to be performed in the penal dockyards called *bagnes* at Toulon, Rochefort, and Brest, where *galériens*, men sentenced to the galleys, had been held since the ships were decommissioned in 1748. For lesser *crimes* and *délits*, convicts would suffer réclusion or emprisonnement.[3]

The National Assembly had concerned itself with punishment, but unlike the brutal retributions it replaced, prison implied the possibility of reforming the criminal. The brief pain of branding could only engender fear or anger; years spent under the proper regimen in prison might effect a transformation of character. During the 1780s and 1790s, the medical profession in France adopted "disciplinary thought," symbolized above all by the decision of Philippe Pinel, superintendent at the asylum of Bicêtre in Paris, to remove

3. Gordon Wright, *Between the Guillotine and Liberty: Two Centuries of the Crime Problem in France* (New York, 1983), 24–33; Patricia O'Brien, *The Promise of Punishment: Prisons in Nineteenth-Century France* (Princeton, 1982), 13–20; Foucault, *Discipline and Punish,* 232; Pierre Deyon, *Le Temps des prisons: Essai sur l'histoire de la délinquance et les origines du système pénitentiaire* (Paris, 1975).

The Punishments

the chains from the insane. In the place of physical fetters, he imposed mental ones of "surveillance, hard labor, and submission to rules." The analogy to prisons was obvious and was made by Jeremy Bentham's *Panopticon* in 1791, the French translation appearing the same year. By the early 1800s, the debate about prisons was concentrated on the conditions that would characterize this discipline.[4]

The first and essential problem was where to incarcerate convicts. The solution was simplified by the Revolution's confiscation of church property and by the example of the abbey at Mont Saint-Michel, which the monarchy had used since the 1400s to confine enemies among the nobility. The conversion of monastic buildings spared the erection of prisons and was pursued with alacrity. Maisons centrales were created from the abbey of St. Bernard at Clairvaux, from the Benedictine abbey at Frontvrault, from the Cistercian abbey at Loos, from the convent of the Soeurs de St. Nicolas at Melun, from the convent of the Cordeliers at Riom, and from a citadel designed by Vauban at Nîmes. Their age—Frontvrault dated from 1099, Clairvaux from 1115, Nîmes, the most recent, from 1687—and general insalubrity were no bar, because prisons were to be punishment. The new departments of the nation similarly expropriated whatever large structures were available to establish the maisons de correction.

Few of these prisons were suitable for their new use, and conversion usually meant little more than the addition of bars and locks. At night convicts slept together in barracks. During the day, they worked in common at whatever tasks could be provided. The first penologists pointed out that such a regimen was unlikely to bring about any change in moral qualities. Immediately after the Restoration in 1814, Duke François Alexandre Frédéric de La Rochefoucauld-Liancourt extolled the results achieved at the Quaker Walnut Street penitentiary in Philadelphia, where each inmate was isolated night and day in a small cell except for visits from "prison missionaries." La Rochefoucauld-Liancourt had not actually crossed the Atlantic Ocean to view the prison personally, but he was convinced of its merit. A decade and a half later, Gustave de Beaumont and Alexis de Tocqueville spent a year in the United States studying various Ameri-

---

4. Michael Ignatieff, *A Just Measure of Pain: The Penitentiary in the Industrial Revolution, 1750–1850* (New York, 1978), 69; Jeremy Bentham, *Panoptique: Mémoire sur un nouveau principe pour construire des maisons d'inspection* (Paris, 1791), initially published as *Panopticon; or, The Inspection House* (3 vols.; London, 1791).

can experiments in penal administration. After their return in 1832, they reported the failure of the Walnut Street plan—only a few convicts responded to the exhortation of the missionaries—but praised two other prisons, Cherry Hill in Philadelphia and Auburn in New York. Although inmates at Cherry Hill were kept in solitary confinement as at Walnut Street, they were made to perform work in their cells, to bring them new self-respect through productive labor. At Auburn the inmates worked in groups during the day under an absolute rule of silence and returned to individual cells at night. For Tocqueville and Beaumont, the critical factor was the necessity of this isolation, to protect convicts from further corrupting one another.

During the next half century, legislators, penologists, bureaucrats, and other interested parties of many types wrangled over which regimen was best suited to France. Claiming Tocqueville and Beaumont themselves, supporters of the Philadelphia system commanded the largest faction, for the effectiveness of solitary confinement in promoting self-rehabilitation and thereby reducing recidivism was widely admitted. Unfortunately, building cellular prisons was extremely expensive, and arranging individual work for each inmate was often difficult. Some physicians also warned that continuous isolation bred madness. Charles Lucas, who eventually became France's best-known prison reformer and always attracted a significant following, used the problems of organizing work and mental breakdown to argue for the Auburn system. Others, budget-conscious functionaries and a few police officials, contended that the traditional common prison, a barracks and workhouse surrounded by walls, was sufficient and that any effort to impose silence on a Latin race such as the French was liable to stimulate an uprising among the inmates. While the debate continued, the state constructed some cellular prisons, most notably the Petite-Roquette and Mazas in Paris, while the departments, ever short of money, clung to the traditional form.

In the late 1840s the Philadelphia system almost won legislative endorsement as the prescribed form of imprisonment, and though the revolution of 1848 prevented its passage by interrupting the final proceedings, Jules Dufaure, the minister of the interior, issued a circular the following year calling for the rebuilding of existing departmental prisons on the cellular model. Under the Second Empire there was an abrupt shift. In 1853, Jean Gilbert Victor Fialin de Persigny, himself minister of the interior, ordered a return to the common prison, ostensibly as an economy measure. Victory for the Philadelphia system had to await the law of June 5, 1875, when the Third Republic's National Assembly declared that all new prisons would be cellular and that current prisons, state or departmental, would have to be converted. The departments found means to delay, and even in 1940, sixty-five years later, some of them were not in compliance. The national administration began paying the ordinary operating expenses of the departmental prisons in 1855, and on February 4, 1893, was "authorized" by the legislature to assume complete control of them, an authorization it chose not to exercise until 1946. Although the basic punishment in France after conviction of a *délit* or a *crime* was imprisonment, there was inconsistency in the form of its imposition.[5]

The second fundamental problem to resolve was how the discipline of regular work that was almost universally believed—though without much evidence—to have a moralizing influence on the inmates could be provided. During the nineteenth century, this work was organized most often through the system of *entreprise*, by which the state commissioned an *entrepreneur* to establish manufacturing jobs within the prison. He received a stipend based on the number of inmates, assumed all the costs of production, and divided any profit with the government. In many instances he also acted as the *fournisseur* for the prison, contracting to provide food, clothing, laundry, heat, and light. These arrangements led to frequent abuse. An *entrepreneur* had little interest in establishing manufactures that taught a trade and might prepare inmates for work after their release. His presence tended to undermine the closed prison society of convicts and warders. He could, and did, severely compromise the goods and services he supplied as *fournisseur*. The eagerness of businessmen in bidding to become *entrepreneurs* testified to its lucrative nature and for long successfully tempted the government not to insist upon changes, because *entreprise* was cheap. The alternative was for the state to organize and supervise the work directly, a system called *régie*. It had the advantage of much greater accountability, and prison directors did try to make the labor an apprenticeship. But this solicitude raised the cost, and few of the directors had real business abil-

5. Wright, *Between the Guillotine and Liberty*, 53–81, 99–103, 129–37; Armand Mossé, *Exposé pratique du régime pénitentiaire en France* (Paris, 1927), 39–40, and *Les Prisons et les institutions d'éducation corrective* (Paris, 1939), 188–91; Georges Bonneron, *Notre régime pénitentiaire: Les Prisons de Paris* (Paris, 1898), 9–18; Joseph Magnol, *De l'administration pénitentiaire dans ses rapports avec l'autorité judiciaire et de son rattachement au ministère de la justice* (Toulouse, 1900); Foucault, *Discipline and Punish*, 238–39.

ity. Despite recognizing that *entreprise* was seriously flawed, the Ministry of the Interior, which was responsible for the prisons before they were transferred to the Ministry of Justice in 1913, resisted a general adoption of *régie* for the maisons centrales until 1906. *Entreprise* continued at departmental prisons into the late 1920s.

Whichever the system, the issue was as controversial outside as inside the walls. Although inmates were required to work, penologists insisted that they be paid, to fix the association of reward for accomplishment. During most of the nineteenth century this payment was approximately Fr 0.75 a day in the maisons centrales, and it rose to slightly more than Fr 7 by 1940. The inmate was permitted the use of about half this pittance, either to send to his family or to spend at the prison commissary for additional food and such items as writing paper. The remainder was placed in a savings account, his *pécule*, which he received at the end of his sentence to assist in beginning a new life. Manufacturers who had to compete against the products of prison labor complained that the *entrepreneur* (or the state in *régie*) had unfair advantages in a captive labor force whom he could pay so little. Their workers bitterly agreed that the competition brought reduced wages or unemployment. The needle trades were particularly affected near the maisons centrales for female inmates at Montpellier and Rennes, with the ironic result that women who lost their jobs were often forced into prostitution and, when convicted for it, made to work at their former occupation. While acknowledging that both *entreprise* and *régie* could cause localized problems, the government concluded that prison work was too vital a part of the reformative process to curtail.[6]

But any improvement in character engendered by isolation in the cell and by the system of work was subverted by the conditions that existed in the prisons. The director of one maison centrale recalled that part of his was known as "'le quartier de misère,' and when I thought about the abominations that transpired there, I swear I was chilled to the bone." Until the last quarter of the nineteenth century, the government and many penologists insisted that the prisons were models of rehabilitative punishment under rigid yet humane discipline, but the accounts of inmates and resident physicians make clear that they were truly dreadful places. Prisons were surely pun-

---

6. O'Brien, *The Promise of Punishment*, 150–90; Bonneron, *Notre régime pénitentiaire*, 19–34; Albert Delmas, *De la rémunération du travail pénitentiaire et du pécule des détenus* (Toulouse, 1935), 11–82; Lucien Berthet, *Le Travail dans les prisons* (Grenoble, 1903), 11–129.

ishment but rarely rehabilitative; the discipline was neither rigid nor humane and was under the control of the inmates as well as the warders. Through the use of tattooing, graffiti, and an argot, the inmates evolved a subculture embedding first offenders in a texture of criminality that dominated their lives in prison. After release, convicts, all of whom were subject to the stigmatization of residence restrictions and special police surveillance lasting up to twenty years, often preferred to maintain this network of relationships in an underworld of crime rather than seek social reintegration. The warders were unable to monitor, and certainly unable to control, the inmate milieu, because they were perpetually undermanned and because they became part of it.[7]

The objective of prison life was an absolute subjugation to rules and schedules. Convicts wore the penal costume (broad stripes). If male, their heads and faces were shaved. They were forbidden to speak unless questioned by a warder. They could be searched at any time. Food was limited to the minimum necessary for the maintenance of strength. Tobacco was contraband. A bath was permitted once a month, a footbath every two weeks. Letters could be written on only one day each week and, except for correspondence with an avocat or avoué, were read and censored by the director. Work, under the system of *entreprise* or *régie*, was mandatory barring illness that required confinement in the infirmary. Illiterates less than forty years old were given classes in elementary education during what would otherwise have been their rest hours. Beginning in 1841, all prisoners were compelled to attend Catholic services; in 1882, Protestants, Jews, and nonbelievers were exempted, and in 1885, religious participation became entirely voluntary. Minor infringement of the regulations led to the loss of commissary or correspondence privileges. Flagrant disobedience brought transferral to a punishment cell for up to fifteen days or restriction to bread and water.

By choice in the nineteenth century and by law in the twentieth,

7. Francis Carco, *Les Hommes en cage* (Paris, 1936), the quotation from 66, and *Prisons des femmes* (Paris, 1931); Charles Perrier, *Emprisonnement et criminalité: La Maison centrale de Nîmes, ses organes, ses fonctions, sa vie* (Paris, 1896), and *Les Criminels*; J. Caillet, *Contribution à l'étude de la simulation des troubles mentaux chez les criminels* (Bordeaux, 1908); André Marty, *Dans les prisons de la République* (Paris, 1924); Bizzard, *Souvenirs d'un médecin*; Emmanuel Bourcier, *La Cage aux femmes: Choses vues* (Paris, 1928); Robert Boucard, *Les Dessous des prisons de femmes* (Paris, 1930); Robert Loewel, *Condamnés: Secrets de prisons* (Paris, 1930); Georges Salan, *Trente-trois ans de centrale, 1938–1970* (Paris, 1971); Bonneron, *Notre régime pénitentiaire*, 141–381; O'Brien, *The Promise of Punishment*, 75–108, 226–57.

the prison administration recruited its warders from the army's retiring noncommissioned officers, men who were presumably accustomed to an isolated and regimented life. Most were appointed at the lowest rank, *gardien*, and most served only a few years before resigning—the turnover rate was the highest of the civil service. Warders who remained and wanted to make a career could be sent for special training to the Ecole supérieure des gardiens at the Conciergerie prison in Paris, after which they could be considered for promotion to *gardien-chef* (chief warder) and eventually to *directeur* (prison director). Salaries were comparable, respectively, with those for an inspecteur, brigadier, and sous-chef of the Paris Sûreté (see Table 15), but working conditions were far more disagreeable. The directeur, the gardien-chef, and all unmarried gardiens were required to live within their prison. Almost without relief, their daily existence was defined by contact with convicted and frequently dangerous criminals. There were never enough gardiens at any prison for proper security. Consequently, men of high caliber were difficult to attract and hold. Some warders began as, and some warders became, little different from the convicts. They merged easily into the inmate milieu, selling contraband goods, ignoring (for a price, like the warders of the ancien régime) serious violations of prison rules such as homosexuality and rape and, most serious, tolerating the imposition of the criminal subculture on first offenders. Toward the end of the nineteenth century the prison administration attempted to eliminate the worst of the warders—by resignation rather than prosecution—and to improve the rest through additional training and oversight. There was limited success for a limited time until the lack of money and dedication to change left them much as they had been.[8]

By then the high rate of recidivism had called into question the basic premise of the prison, that either the threat or the experience of incarceration could deter a life of crime. An increasing number of penologists and medical scientists concluded that many inmates, whether for reasons of heredity or degeneracy, simply could not be reformed in prison or anywhere else and would have to remain excluded from the rest of society. This belief and fear led to the law of May 27, 1885, which created the status of *relégation*, permanent exile for the habitual criminal. Conviction, within a ten-year period, of two *crimes* and two *délits*, or as determined by a scale measuring

---

8. Mossé, *Exposé pratique du régime pénitentiaire*, 53–100; Bonneron, *Notre régime pénitentiaire*, 35–78; O'Brien, *The Promise of Punishment*, 204–25.

The Punishments

the outrage done society, of from four to seven *délits*, condemned the recidivist without reprieve to become a *rélégué* in French Guiana or, until 1897, New Caledonia. Because the prisons themselves were decried as a breeding ground for crime, where efforts at rehabilitation struggled vainly against corrupting influences, the cours correctionnelles were authorized by the law of March 26, 1891, to suspend the sentences for first offenders convicted of certain *délits*. By arguing passionately in favor of this right to "condamner avec sursis," René Bérenger, its sponsor, admitted the failure of his own half-century's campaign for prison reform.[9]

A similar retreat began from the practice of imprisoning children. The law of April 12, 1906, made eighteen the minimum age for confinement to a maison de correction or maison centrale and twenty-one for a sentence of travaux forcés. Although segregated from adult inmates or placed in special youth prisons such as the Petite-Roquette of Paris, juvenile offenders had not been spared the austerity of penal discipline and suffered an appalling mortality. Many of them had been guilty only of having angered a father who, invoking the privilege of *correction paternelle*, could have his child confined for a month (six months if at least age sixteen) merely by declaring him wayward. Some judges, and they became more numerous late in the nineteenth century, saved convicted children from prison by sending them to the *colonies pénitentiaires* (agricultural reform schools) run either by the state or by private benefactors (such as the famous Mettray in the Indre-et-Loire). Further legislation of July 22, 1912, created a separate system of juvenile courts and granted them wide discretionary power. A child less than thirteen years old would be released without formal charges if the arrest was his first; a child under the age of eighteen convicted of a *délit* could be placed on probation and turned over to the custody of his parents, or to a state agency if more appropriate, after a judicial finding that he acted *sans discernement* (without capacity to understand the consequences).[10]

---

9. Nye, *Crime, Madness, and Politics in Modern France*, 72–96; Wright, *Between the Guillotine and Liberty*, 109–28, 143–52; O'Brien, *The Promise of Punishment*, 259–67. On these issues see also Michelle Perrot (ed.), *L'Impossible prison: Recherches sur le système pénitentiaire au XIXe siècle* (Paris, 1980), and "Délinquance et système pénitentiaire."

10. Mialane, *La Criminalité juvénile*, 179–235; Mossé, *Exposé pratique du régime pénitentiaire*, 158–200; Loewel, *Condamnés*, 25–64; O'Brien, *The Promise of Punishment*, 109–49. For a popular account see Michelle Perrot, "Les Enfants de la Petite-Roquette," *L'Histoire* C (May, 1987), 30–38.

For convicts sentenced to travaux forcés in French Guiana or New Caledonia, there was little sympathy and no attenuation of punishment until the 1930s. Public opinion believed that their crimes had marked them as the most dangerous of criminals, men who deserved their fate and of whom France was well rid. The precedent for their penal transportation was established by two brief experiments, seventy years apart, during the eighteenth century—shipping criminals to Louisiana from 1718 to 1722, and exiling first nonjuring priests and then the most vicious of the Jacobins to Guiana during the Revolution. In the aftermath of the June Days in 1848 and the coup d'état of December, 1851, the Second Republic revived the practice by sending a total of more than twenty thousand insurgents to Algeria for confinement. Under the Second Empire, the law of May 30, 1854, closed the three bagnes (Brest, Rochefort, and Toulon) for travaux forcés and ordered that present and future bagnards serve their sentences in the colonies. The rationale then and later was simple: to inspire fear through a noncapital punishment that would impose great suffering, to contribute the labor of these criminals to the development of the French colonial empire, and, most important, to eliminate them from France entirely. Implementation was more difficult, because the prison administration was forced to choose between productive work and exemplary suffering. At first Guiana was the destination for most of the bagnards, but the death rate was so high that from 1867 to 1887 only convicts from the African and Asian colonies were sent there. Although the climate of New Caledonia was better suited to Europeans, penal officials decided by the 1890s that the island was too pleasant, that its prospect was insufficiently intimidating to bagnards and, since 1885, to relégués. And so from 1897 on, all transported convicts were taken to Guiana.

Whether on New Caledonia or in Guiana, transportation was a failure. The free colonists objected to the presence of so many dangerous criminals. The overseas bagnes came to be an enormous expense, one that was hardly balanced by the building of a few roads through convict labor. The bagnards had no incentive to work hard, because most understood that they would either die quickly of disease or never be permitted to leave the colony. No one could believe that the bagnes served any rehabilitative function: All the rigors and barbarities of the prisons in France were multiplied manyfold. International opinion turned decisively against transportation by the beginning of the twentieth century. Other than France, only Portugal continued to ship prisoners beyond its borders. French sentiment was excited against the bagnes by sensational disclosures in the late 1920s and early 1930s. Nevertheless, with penal officials divided, reform was delayed until the law of June 17, 1938, which ordered that all future sentences of travaux forcés be served in France, with at least three years spent in solitary confinement. No mention was made of relégués, but the prison administration did not transport anyone after 1937. The Fourth Republic would complete the liquidation of the penal colonies in 1946 by returning to France the last of the bagnards.[11]

When the *peine de mort* was pronounced against an *accusé*, his avocat filed a pourvoi en cassation and, if that failed, petitioned the president of the Republic to commute the sentence to life at travaux forcés—a clemency always granted to women. While awaiting the result of these appeals, which could take up to two months but was usually much faster, the condemned was placed in a special cell under constant surveillance to prevent any attempt of suicide. Some of the prison rules were relaxed for him: He could smoke, purchase as much as his money allowed from the commissary, and receive frequent visits from the chaplain. If there was no reprieve, the prison director and the executioner were alerted and made their preparations during the night. On the following morning, the condemned was awakened just before dawn and told: "Your appeal has been rejected. Be brave!" He was permitted, if he wished, a final cigarette, a final glass of rum, a final letter, and a final confession to the chaplain. He was then dressed in the clothes he had worn when the court imposed sentence and handed over to the executioner and his assistants. They tied his hands behind his back, hobbled his ankles with a short cord, trimmed any hair that extended down his neck, and cut away the collar of his shirt. Carefully, almost solicitously, he was led out to the guillotine and strapped upon it. Seconds later, the broad triangular steel blade, weighted by a sixty-six-pound wood block, was released from the uprights by the executioner and fell from the height of fourteen feet nine inches to sever the head of the condemned from his body. Until the decree of June 24, 1939, ended public executions, a large crowd, sometimes in the thousands, in-

11. Henri Russier, *Transportation et colonisation pénale: Essai sur l'évolution des préoccupations économiques dans notre système pénitentiaire colonial* (Paris, 1904), i–xvii, 97–103; Maurice Thamar, *Les Peines coloniales et l'expérience guyanaise* (Rodez, 1935), 191–97; Mossé, *Exposé pratique du régime pénitentiaire*, 200–12, and *Les Prisons et les institutions d'éducation corrective*, 369–79; O'Brien, *The Promise of Punishment*, 258–96; Wright, *Between the Guillotine and Liberty*, 91–95, 138–52, 183–89.

variably gathered to watch. Often women rushed forward to dip their handkerchiefs in the blood.

The guillotine performed France's executions from 1792 until 1981, when capital punishment was abolished during the first months of François Mitterrand's presidency. Even then a substantial majority of the French people seem to have favored its retention; certainly they did so throughout the Third Republic. Between 1870 and 1940 the legislature seriously considered ending the *peine de mort* only once, in 1908, but then public opinion quickly convinced the deputies to vote decisively against doing so. Opponents of capital punishment claimed that killing a criminal in the name of the state was uncivilized, that judicial error could lead to the execution of an innocent man, and that the death penalty had little value as a deterrent because it was carried out infrequently—if the atypical years 1871, 1914–1918, and 1939–40 are set aside, the guillotine's blade fell 519 times during the Third Republic, an annual average of slightly more than 8. Defenders replied that society had a right to self-defense by eliminating the worst of its kind, that an execution was performed only after scrupulous examination of a criminal and his crime by the jury of the cour d'assises, the Cour de Cassation, and the president of the Republic, and that without the threat of the guillotine, burglars and robbers would murder witnesses. The *peine de mort* represented, they insisted, the essential apex for the hierarchy of penalties: It was the ultimate symbol of society's determination to exact vengeance for crime, the final sanction of justice.[12]

12. Alister Kershaw, *A History of the Guillotine* (London, 1958), 74–79, 121–42; Montarron, *Tout ce joli monde*, 81–82; Alexandre Lacassagne, *Peine de mort et criminalité: L'Accroissement de la criminalité et l'application de la peine capitale* (Paris, 1908), 11, 140–41, 165–66; Wright, *Between the Guillotine and Liberty*, 166–74; Nye, *Crime, Madness, and Politics in Modern France*, 214–26, 265–309.

Conclusion

In tradition, justice is personified by a blindfolded goddess holding the scales on which truth will be weighed against falsehood. But the ideal so symbolized must be accomplished through the acts of humans, not immortals, and must rest on the decisions of fallible minds, not divine balances. Justice is the entire process by which a crime is investigated and tried, and because it should mean that guilt and innocence will be duly apportioned, the manner and degree to which it departs from this maintenance of right in a society is the measure of its hypocrisy. For Third Republic France, the Dreyfus affair of the fin de siècle seemed to provide that standard and description. Despite his convictions by courts-martial for a treason he did not commit, the eventual exoneration and vindication of Alfred Dreyfus by civilian courts, after intense political and social dislocation, implied that for the French, the rendering of justice to a single, and unpopular, individual was paramount, even at the cost of disgracing the army and important segments of the government that had conspired to perpetuate this wrong.

But the outcome of the Dreyfus affair did not prove that justice reigned in France or that it was about to reign. Instead, the plot of the affair—the innocent falsely convicted, the guilty improperly acquitted—was not uncommon before and after in French courts. The injustice Dreyfus suffered arose from a combination of factors. The investigation by the army of the alleged treason was inadequate. Because an arrest and conviction were essential to the political career of General Auguste Mercier, the minister of war, evidence was fabricated, perjury suborned, and trial procedures violated. Constrained by the solidarity of the officer corps and by the hierarchy of rank, all the court-martial boards convened during the affair conformed their verdicts to the openly avowed position of the high command. Doubts and misgivings were largely overcome by the argument that admitting these grievous faults would seriously damage the public image of the army. Prejudice against Jews, above all, but also against civilians, intellectuals, and politicians of the Left injected a blinding venom. The conduct of criminal justice was routinely haunted by similar failings. The police were appallingly incompetent, responsible for such alarming laxity that the army's investigation appears almost professional in comparison. The judges and prosecutors were civil servants struggling for promotion and under as much pressure from superiors as the court-martial boards. Exigent political influence could descend from a position as exalted as that occupied by Mercier. The prejudices exacerbating the Dreyfus affair differed only in particulars (if that) from the prepossessions affecting jury deliberations.[1]

Crime rates in France increased rapidly after 1945, as they did throughout the Western world, making the years of the Third Republic and even the preceding regimes of the nineteenth century seem orderly and safe. To a victim, however, the most important crime is the one he has suffered, and during the time of the Third Republic there were victims aplenty, most shockingly among young girls. Molestation, grand larceny, and the various forms of murder have no justification (as opposed to the mitigating conditions often found by juries). No civilized nation can permit the perpetration with impunity of these and other felonies. Failure to seek the apprehension, prosecution, and punishment of the guilty leads inexorably to the Hobbesian state of nature, of a war each against all. Here is the rationale for the apparatus of criminal justice. As the social defense against crime, the system ought to be fair and effective, to reassure the innocent and make the blameworthy tremble. Criminal justice in France did neither sufficiently.

Although chronically undermanned and using equipment that

1. See my "The Dreyfus Affair and the Corruption of the French Legal System," in Norman L. Kleeblatt (ed.), *The Dreyfus Affair: Art, Truth, and Justice* (Berkeley, 1987), 37–49, and *The Hypocrisy of Justice*, 1–14, 228–35. For the Dreyfus affair in general, see Bredin, *The Affair*, and Douglas Johnson, *France and the Dreyfus Affair* (London, 1966).

Conclusion

was often ludicrously outmoded, the Paris Sûreté and the Sûreté Générale were still able to make some spectacular arrests because they had a few intuitive detectives like François Goron, Jean Belin, and Charles Chenevrier, who cut the pattern for Georges Simenon's Inspector Maigret. Usually with less notice, as many other cases were bungled by the precursors of Peter Sellers' Inspector Clouseau. Reforms, some carried out but most of them simply promised, never attacked the fundamental flaw of the Police judiciaire, the enduring legacy of Vidocq. The great majority of detectives were simply brutal and corrupt, depending solely upon informers, prostitutes, and beatings to "solve" their cases. They were not above creating evidence against those they wished to be rid of or destroying evidence against those who, for one reason or another, had to be freed. Anatole France's character Crainquebille had, and was widely regarded as having, much basis in fact: a poor carter arrested, tried, convicted, and imprisoned on charges trumped up by a sergent de ville irritated that his path was briefly blocked by the sidewalk traffic in vegetables.[2]

Most prosecutors and many judges knew of these abuses firsthand, but they rarely acted or even spoke against them. Like the police, magistrates knew that arrests and convictions, no matter how obtained, quieted the public outcry that always followed a crime wave or a well-publicized murder. There were also compelling personal reasons for acquiescence. The material collected by the Paris Sûreté for the "dossiers blancs" and the Sûreté Générale for "les roses" deterred nearly everyone powerful enough to threaten these empires. And as Louis Casamayor, himself a magistrate, warns in one of his books on French justice: "If you write about the police, you do not know what you are risking. You must suspect the taxi you take—it might have an accident. You cannot enter a public urinal—you might find there individuals who will declare that you made them indecent advances. You dare not speak to a woman—she might place you in an equivocal position and destroy your home. You must lose all hope of making a career, for you will be mysteriously switched onto a siding, yet happy enough not to find in your dossier some subtle snare that will cause you to be reprimanded, demoted, and broken."[3] Inspectors Lucien Mariani and Pierre Bonny, Director of the Sûreté André Benoist, Prefect of Police and former Director of the Sûreté Générale Jean Chiappe were criminals whose record makes Casamayor's caution chilling.

2. Jacques Anatole Thibault [Anatole France], *Crainquebille, Putois, Riquet* (Paris, 1904).
3. Louis Casamayor, *Le Bras séculier: Justice et police* (Paris, 1960), 38–39.

Passing from the justice of the police to the justice of the magistrates offered no more guarantees. The process of preparing a prosecution, though amended by the Revolution, was a survival of the ancien régime. This "inquisitorial" method is not inherently inferior to the Anglo-Saxon "accusatory" procedure; the problem lay in its execution. The instruction of a felony was supposed to be a dispassionate analysis of the evidence by a judge. Unfortunately, most juges d'instruction were young magistrates, relatively inexperienced and junior in rank. "Dispassionate" characterized too few of them. They feuded with the Police judiciaire during investigations. Like the lieutenants criminels before 1789, they tended to assume that anyone arrested was guilty and tried to prove it while leaving him in custody for months. They recommended indictments except when the suspects were clearly innocent, because careers were made by sending them to trial, not by releasing them. They were too often amenable when parquet officials, with promotion recommendations in their gift, urged the ignoring or overemphasizing of ambiguities to establish the conditions for a conviction or a dismissal of charges. In all the most notorious and controversial criminal cases of the Belle Epoque in Paris (the death of Emile Zola, the swindles by the Thérèse Humbert family, the suicide of Gabriel Syveton, the murders of the Marguerite Steinheil affair, and the assassination of *Le Figaro*'s editor by Henriette Caillaux), the responsible juge d'instruction distorted his findings in a manner that was politically motivated. It is impossible to believe that similar manipulations did not occur in provincial cases that had a merely local prominence.

The primary reforms of the Revolution in criminal justice were the public trial of charges and the use of a jury in felony cases, but custom and procedure placed the defense at a disadvantage. The very arrangement of the courtroom, the color of the judicial gowns, and their common status as magistrates implied that the judges and the prosecution were in alliance. The *interrogatoire* compelled the *accusé* either to answer, risking self-incrimination, or to remain silent, almost ensuring conviction. In compensation he had wide latitude to comment on the testimony of witnesses and experts and, at least before the cour d'assises, to influence the jury through an emotional performance. All trials are theater, each participant assuming the role of an abstract quality: the prosecutor as avenging rectitude, the *accusé* as aggrieved virtue or repentant sin, the judges and jury as society's moral standard, a complex amalgam of attitudes and prejudices toward the law and toward specific laws, penalties, and indi-

Conclusion

viduals. All trials are contests as well, the prosecution against the defense. Neither aspect is necessarily associated with justice. The verdict alone provides that measure in a trial. Inevitably the *accusé* bore an assumption of guilt based on the pretrial inquiry of the procureur de la République or the juge d'instruction. His presence in the cour correctionnelle meant that he would nearly always be found guilty; in the cour d'assises the result was less predictable but would likely be guilty with extenuating circumstances. Rather than a search for truth, the public trial was usually only the final stamp on a destiny already determined by arrest and indictment.

From the Place Vendôme, the minister of justice oversaw a bureaucracy of the parquet and the bench that ranged from the lowliest substitut for a provincial tribunal de première instance to the premier président of the Cour de Cassation. Despite theoretical safeguards, these magistrates were frequently elevated because the deputies who intervened for them were necessary to the cabinet's legislative majority. In consequence, magistrates blatantly curried favor with every deputy in their circles. Because many of the deputies were also avocats-rois, practicing before the same judges who sought patronage, the risk of favoritism in the rendering of justice was grave. Eugen Weber has insisted that in France, "justice" was not expected always to be just, that in certain great criminal trials justice became "the occult meshing of political power, the judicature, and the administration of law." Agreed: such a diabolical mixture is as easy to condemn as to cite its examples. But the notion that even in routine cases criminal justice might be reduced to nothing more than "judicial proceedings," banal in their lack of ideals and unfair almost by definition, is more troubling and more difficult to situate on the moral plane. Although written about literary criticism, H. L. Mencken's aphorism is appropriate: "Injustice is relatively easy to bear; what stings is justice."[4]

The cynical reply is true: "Miscarriages of justice occur under any system."[5] But there is substantial evidence that the meaning and process of criminal justice were debased in nineteenth- and twentieth-century France. This argument is not meant to rehabilitate or defend the miscreants who were responsible for abominable crimes. Rather it requires the cynical to distinguish why the Drey-

---

4. Eugen Weber, Review of Benjamin F. Martin's *The Hypocrisy of Justice in the Belle Epoque*, in *Louisiana History*, XXV (1984), 436–37; Henry Lewis Mencken, *Prejudices: Third Series* (New York, 1922), 101.

5. David Robin Watson, Review of Benjamin F. Martin's *The Hypocrisy of Justice in the Belle Epoque*, in *English Historical Review*, CII (1987), 750.

fus case should not also be dismissed by the phrase "Miscarriages of justice occur" and to recognize how close they stand to Fernand Labori, who before the Chamber of Deputies in 1908 brushed aside the implications of injustice even when it might lead an innocent man to the guillotine: "Error is everywhere in life . . . and in judicial matters, alas, too frequent. I know it and you know it." Labori had made his reputation as a passionate avocat for Dreyfus. Now he declared with remarkable detachment that if Dreyfus had been shot instead of having been sent to Devil's Island, "there would have remained for us the right of defending his memory, and that, I imagine, would not have been an indifferent satisfaction to his family."[6] Although Dreyfus experienced to the full the injustice of military justice, it is worth considering carefully whether he would have fared any better under civilian criminal justice.

How did matters reach such a pass? The most important reasons were institutional and administrative. The system of criminal justice had its roots deep in the ancien régime. The modifications made after 1789 tempered but did not change this essence—an inquisition designed to convict every person unlucky enough to fall within its grasp. The tradition of political interference in the processes of justice was also inherited from the ancien régime, then nurtured by the Revolution and Napoleon before becoming cemented through the creation of a bureaucratic magistrature. The oppression of the system, terrible to those in its coils, was tolerable for the society at large because it did not engulf many, particularly in a nation widely held to be an early model of "the policed state." Even with its serious flaws, the system appears to have satisfied the overwhelming majority of French men and women, because there was never a general call for its radical transformation.

The motto of the 1789 Revolution, "Liberté, Égalité, Fraternité," was all but ubiquitous under the Third Republic: stamped onto coins, woven through flags, carved into the stone of buildings. But these ideals were conspicuously absent from the system of criminal justice. Western societies often condemn the rest of the world for judicial charades, for rendering a travesty of justice, and claim themselves to be the guarantors of fairness and impartiality, the guardians of the blindfolded goddess with the scales. The example of France during this period makes mock of that boast.

6. *JOC*, Débats parlementaires, November 4, 1908.

Afterword

Gangsters and Anarchists in the Belle Epoque: The Bande à Bonnot

On May 14, 1912, Xavier Guichard, the dark and angular director of the Paris Sûreté, led fifty of his men into the eastern suburb Nogent-sur-Marne. Earlier in the day a report had been passed to him that Octave Garnier and René Valet, the only members of the murderous Bonnot gang still at large, were suspected of hiding there. An informant had noticed Garnier's mistress, Marie Vuillemin, at the market and had followed her to a house near the river. Under the cover of dusk the commissaires and inspecteurs surrounded the building. Guichard was completing the preparations when Vuillemin appeared carrying five *baguettes*. Her screams as she was taken captive alerted Garnier and Valet in the house. Within seconds, the two thrust Valet's mistress, Celeste Dondon, outside to join Vuillemin in the custody of the police. After a pause, they fired six rifle shots and shouted that they would not be taken alive.

Throughout the next hours, Garnier and Valet picked off their attackers with sniperlike accuracy while moving from room to room in the house to frustrate the returning fire. Guichard ordered up a company of infantry from the nearby Vincennes barracks and then several *mitrailleuses*. The news that the famous bandits were under siege spread through Paris. By midnight the soldiers and police were joined by sensation-seeking men and women in evening dress who caustically dissected each tactic. Reporters and photographers vied for vantage points. Near 2:30 A.M., a Sûreté inspecteur crept close to the house and planted dynamite against the wall. When the bomb was detonated, there was a great explosion. Guichard gave the order for a mass charge. Garnier and Valet were found dead in the rubble. After the bodies were carried away, the curious in fancy clothes, the soldiers, and the Sûreté detectives picked apart the ruined house for souvenirs.[1]

The deaths of Garnier and Valet were hardly the last chapter in the history of the Bande à Bonnot, because there would be an acrimonious and widely publicized trial in February, 1913, for the surviving members of the gang. During the following two months, three of the leaders would die beneath the guillotine and almost all of the others depart for varying terms of imprisonment or for hard labor in Guiana. This wretched denouement obscures a certain high-minded sentiment in their lives. Styling themselves anarchists against an unjust society, they lived out a radical creed of *illégalisme,* proudly flouting the law. The justification for theft, called by them *reprise individuelle* (expropriation), was a collectivism of the elite: sharing the booty among members of their closed group. But ultimately any quest for an association of equal and loyal friends was superseded by an individualism so extreme that each was free to determine for himself which trammels of the unjust world to break. Murder became merely a form of *égoisme à outrance.*[2]

The anarchist circles of the Belle Epoque were remarkably amorphous. Almost anyone was welcome because the right of asylum was considered sacred. It was easy to find among them true intellec-

---

1. APP, E A/141, Bande à Bonnot, report of May 15, 1912; *Le Figaro,* May 15–16, 1912.
2. Much of the story of the Bande à Bonnot was a war between the anarchists and the police, and it is important to examine the conflict from both sides. For the police, there are the appropriate dossiers at the AN, F 7, 12094–12097, 13053–13068, Anarchistes, and at the APP, E A/141, Bande à Bonnot. For the anarchists, there are many sources. The most important memoirs are David Bellonie, "Souvenirs et révélations," *Le Journal,* May 2, 1913; Raymond Callemin, "Notes," *Le Journal,* April 6, 24, 26, 27, 1913; Eugène Dieudonné, *La Vie des forçats* (Paris, 1930); Octave Garnier, "Lettre à M. Xavier Guichard," *Le Matin,* March 21, 1912; Claire ("Rirette") Maîtrejean, "Souvenirs d'anarchie," *Le Matin,* August 18–26, 1913, and "Commissaire Guillaume, ne réveillez pas les morts," *Confidences,* March 11, 18, 1937; and Victor Kibaltchiche [Victor Serge], *Mémoires d'un révolutionnaire, 1901–1941* (Paris, 1941). Contributions from contemporaries extend the perspective: André Roulot [Lorulot], *Chez les loups* (Paris, 1922); and Emile Michon, *Un peu de l'âme des bandits* (Paris, 1914). The activities of the gang were the crime sensation of 1911 and 1912, and the newspapers of the period provided detailed reporting. See especially *La Croix, L'Ex-*

tuals, students, poets, workers down on their luck and seeking shelter, workers who had heard the gospel of anarchism and believed—as well as informers and provocateurs from the police. Some were violent, some were not; there was the propaganda of the word, and there was the propaganda of the deed. Just as the divide between speech and action could be a narrow one, so was that between the serious and the ridiculous. Exaltation of the individual and hatred of a hypocritical and constricted society made many an anarchist argue for free love and defend prostitution. But a few went so far as to advocate contracting venereal diseases in order to spread them to the bourgeoisie. Here was the serious internal contradiction of anarchism: For every disciple who glimpsed in the movement a utopia of completely free individuals, there were far more tagalongs for whom anarchy was the revenge of the resentful. The newspapers described the Bande à Bonnot as "anarchist criminals"—more criminal than anarchist, to judge from the record. More tellingly, they were also termed "les bandits tragiques," tragic because the anarchist formulas to which they turned, and practiced literally, after having been slighted or condemned by society, led them into crimes that they almost certainly would not otherwise have committed.[3]

Ironically, the titular head of the gang, Jules Bonnot, was an anomaly among the rest, and was the least influenced by anarchy. Born to a poor family on October 14, 1876, at Pont-de-Roide, he was a rebellious young man who by age seventeen had a long record of arrests for fighting. Army service appeared to change him. He had regular meals for the first time, and the uniform attracted women. Proud of being the best shot in his regiment, Bonnot accepted military discipline as the price for his improved life. He developed a compulsion for neatness, and even while driving to commit robberies, he would

---

celsior, Le Figaro, Le Gaulois, L'Illustration de l'époque, L'Intransigeant, Le Journal, and Le Matin. For the trial in February, 1913, see La Gazette des Tribunaux. There have been a number of popular histories. The best are Georges Adam, "La Bande à Bonnot," in Gilbert Guilleminault (ed.), Le Roman vrai de la Troisième République: Avant 14, Fin de la Belle Epoque (Paris, 1957), 138–95; Emile Becker, La Bande à Bonnot (Paris, 1968); Arthur Bernède, Bonnot, Garnier, et Cie. (Paris, 1930); F. Dumas-Vorzet, La Bande à Bonnot (Paris, 1930); Henri Coudon [Victor Méric], Les Bandits tragiques (Paris, 1926); and Bernard Thomas, La Bande à Bonnot (Paris, 1968). See also my "The Bande à Bonnot: Les Bandits tragiques," Laurels (American Society of the Legion of Honor Magazine), LIII (Fall, 1982), 73–98, for excellent illustrations.

3. For an introduction to these circles of anarchism, see Jean Maitron, Histoire du mouvement anarchiste en France, 1880–1914 (2nd ed.; Paris, 1955), and Raymond Manévy and Philippe Diolé, Sous les plis du drapeau noir (Paris, 1949).

carry with him a small toilet kit to remain well brushed. After he was mustered out, he settled down in marriage with Sophie Burdet to work as a mechanic, but the old habits of defiance returned to him, and by 1902 he was blacklisted. A child born to the couple that year died after only four days. Bonnot turned to a local union of mechanics for assistance and managed to hold temporary jobs during the next two years. Sophie then eloped with the union head, a certain Besson, in 1904, taking with her a son whose paternity was clearly open to question.

Bonnot could think of nothing but revenge against a society that, in his view, had stripped everything from him. Working with an Italian anarchist, Joseph Platano, he devised a clever ruse. Automobiles were becoming increasingly common, and they would steal one, dress in fine clothes, and ride to the house of a notary on the pretext of consulting him about a business they intended to establish. Once inside, they discovered how they could return to burglarize at night. For several years, the plan worked so successfully that they never attracted suspicion. Meanwhile Bonnot found solace for his disappointed love in Judith Thollon of Vienne. He hid the money from his burglaries in her house and planned to elope with her when his capital was large enough, a figure he constantly revised upward. In November, 1911, when the police finally picked up their trail, Bonnot and Platano fled, leaving Thollon behind because she knew nothing of the crimes. A stolen Buick carried them almost to Châlons-sur-Saône before breaking down on a deserted road. While Bonnot repaired the engine, Platano negligently toyed with a revolver. After warning him to be careful, Bonnot tried to wrestle the pistol away, but it discharged and wounded his partner severely. Rather than risk taking him to a hospital, Bonnot impulsively fired a fatal shot. Even from the perspective of a criminal on the run, he committed a serious blunder. The police hunt for murderers with great persistence.

Bonnot's flight brought him to Paris. Like many another fugitive in this period, he knew that anarchists extended shelter to all who asked. He frequented their cafés and soon met a large, round-faced man with a huge moustache, Eugène Dieudonné, twenty-seven years old, a carpenter, and a member of the group who published the newspaper *L'Anarchie*. Although recognizing that Bonnot was only a common criminal, Dieudonné took him to a safe room at 24 Rue Nollet. From Paris, Bonnot wrote Judith Thollon, but in doing so, he led the police to her. They had connected Bonnot to Platano's murder and were watching for his letters. When they searched Thollon's house, they found twenty-five thousand francs under a mattress and arrested her for complicity. With his world as shattered as it had been in 1904, Bonnot turned for companionship and assistance to the anarchists he met through Dieudonné.[4]

L'Anarchie appeared for the first time on April 13, 1905, founded by Joseph Albert, who called himself Libertad. He had come to Paris in 1897 at the age of twenty-two and lived in Montmartre, where his sandals and long hair blended with the appearance of the artists and performers. His anarchism was based not on throwing bombs but on questioning, in a penetrating Socratic manner, the bases of bourgeois society. The circle he formed about himself and L'Anarchie reflected these pacific but corrosive views. After Libertad's premature death in 1908, direction of L'Anarchie passed to a lieutenant, André Roulot, known as Lorulot. He continued the interrogative tradition of the newspaper, but to justify a rejection of the established social order, he adopted more advanced opinions about anarchist individualism. From them, it was not far to *illégalisme:* Could an unjust society demand adherence to its laws? After 1910, the members of the circle debated *illégalisme* heatedly among themselves and in the columns of L'Anarchie. The issue was splitting the group, but Lorulot lacked the brilliance to impose a solution. He was increasingly undermined by Claire ("Rirette") Maîtrejean and Victor Kibaltchiche, who persuasively argued an ambiguous position that appealed to both adherents and detractors of *illégalisme.* Lorulot's direction of the newspaper grew more lethargic, and in 1911 he left to form a rival group that would publish L'Idée libre.[5]

Rirette Maîtrejean, born in 1889, married an anarchist intellectual at age seventeen and, between 1906 and 1908, bore him two daughters. She was petite and almost pretty in her black ringlet curls, but she was also an incisive thinker who frequently contributed to L'Anarchie. In 1909, when her husband was in prison convicted of counterfeiting, she met Kibaltchiche, a brooding, dour young man with ice-gray Slavic eyes, and took him for her lover. He had come to Paris from Brussels, where his father, a Russian émigré, lectured at the university. Kibaltchiche had been nurtured on the writings of Herzen, Belinsky, and Chernychevsky, and this revolutionary tradi-

4. Coudon, Les Bandits tragiques, 217–19.
5. Ibid., 90–107; Maitron, Histoire du mouvement anarchiste, 348–413; Kibaltchiche, Mémoires d'un révolutionnaire, 26–39.

tion was augmented by the penury in which his father's imprudent dealings with usurers left the family. From his mother, a descendant of minor Polish nobles, he acquired unsatisfiable sensibilities and a taste for refinement. His was a perfect background for an advanced sense of bitterness at the "injustice" of society. To express these feelings, he might have turned to one of the various brands of French socialist thought prevalent in Brussels, but he found Jules Guesde's Marxism too dryly utilitarian and Jean Jaurès' reformism too meek. There would have to be a revolution in the conduct of mankind, but a moral one. For this, he turned to the appealing vision of anarchism: "To take what you want while leaving behind in its place what you are able." The writings of Libertad became his guide.

In 1909, at the age of nineteen, Kibaltchiche left for Paris. He had with him ten francs, a change of shirt, and the photographs of a few friends. Along the way, he begged lodging with a working-class couple in Armentières. Lying in the next room, he was shocked by the violence of their copulation, hearing the husband beat his wife, who cried out in pain but also in desire. The experience was a searing reinforcement of his conviction that drastic changes were necessary to make a better world. In Paris he joined the *L'Anarchie* circle, became Maîtrejean's lover, and joined her in writing columns for the newspaper. He haunted Left Bank bookshops, complementing the education he had received from his father by reading remaindered volumes placed on tables outside. He was deeply affected by the trial and execution of Constant Liabeuf, a twenty-year-old who had been sent to prison on a trumped-up charge of pandering. In revenge he shot at four policemen after his release. Although none of them died from their wounds, Liabeuf was guillotined as an example.[6]

When Maîtrejean and Kibaltchiche took over direction of *L'Anarchie*, they moved the office and presses of the newspaper from Montmartre to a large house at 16 Rue de Bagnolet in the northeast suburb of Romainville. Kibaltchiche invited two of his friends from Brussels, Raymond Callemin and Edouard Carouy, to join them, and they brought along Octave Garnier. All five, and occasionally other friends such as Dieudonné and his often errant wife, Louise, lived in the upper floors of the house as an anarchist commune. By November, 1911, cold weather, the inconvenience of being two miles out in the suburbs, and a mixture of boredom and quarrels made the arrangement unpleasant. Callemin, Carouy, and Garnier had grown up

6. Kibaltchiche, *Mémoires d'un révolutionnaire*, 7–25.

in a poverty similar to that known by Kibaltchiche, but in working-class families. The resentments they felt were more vicious, and they had fewer scruples about violence. The issue of *illégalisme* arose again, but it was no longer merely a question of intellectual debate, because Carouy had begun a series of burglaries. He had even hidden some of his loot in the house at Romainville, and he was defended by Callemin and Garnier. Frightened by the possibility of arrest, Kibaltchiche and Maîtrejean decided to disavow *illégalisme* clearly. They broke up the commune and moved *L'Anarchie* back to Paris, this time to 34 Rue Fessart, deep in the poor northeastern section of the city. Callemin, Carouy, and Garnier also returned to Paris, and one evening Dieudonné introduced them to an authentic *illégaliste*, Bonnot, who invited them to become his partners in crime.[7]

Raymond Callemin was slight and clean-shaven, and his skin had a pinkish hue that earned him the nickname Bébé rose. He was born on March 26, 1890, the son of a shoemaker in Brussels. As an adolescent he began reading the nineteenth-century propagandists for science, moved to the prophets of revolution, and discovered his spiritual guide in Félix Le Dantec. Now forgotten, Le Dantec was a popularizer of the Barrèsian *culte du moi:* One of his titles, *L'Egoisme, seule base de toute société*, sums up the basic argument. Callemin, who always wore a carefully knotted cravat and pomaded his hair, looked like nothing so much as a *collégien* (schoolboy) and had the intellectual pretensions for the role. None of his development necessarily set him on a fatal path until he had a passionate, but Platonic, love affair with a Russian student in Brussels. With desperate innocence, he believed that she would make over her life for him, and when she returned to Russia instead, he added a thick layer of cynicism over his romantic nature. He became "Raymond la science," determined to use the new technology of the bomb to change the world that had disappointed him. Cold, aloof, insolent, Callemin was trapped by his own sense of grievance.

Edouard Carouy, born on January 28, 1885, in Sens-sur-Dendre in Belgium, was a swarthy, heavily muscled metal worker with a nose like a trumpet. He devoted most of his youth to minor crime, drink, and prostitutes, but as he happened to walk through a public park one afternoon during the speech of an anarchist, he heard the admo-

---

7. *Ibid.*, 35–44; Maîtrejean, "Souvenirs d'anarchie"; Coudon, *Les Bandits tragiques*, 108–39.

nition to read Ernest Haeckel's *Enigma of the Universe*. Carouy puzzled through the book to find for himself a message of coming revolution. He immediately joined the group of anarchists that included Kibaltchiche and Callemin. Under their influence he cultivated a latent sensitivity. He began to spend his free hours wandering in the woods and even adopted vegetarianism. But he was hardly intelligent and filtered every doctrine through his particular experience. Anarchism provided a solidarity with comrades that he had not previously known; *illégalisme* would be the justification for continuing his crimes.

The most curious of the three was the handsome, dark-haired Octave Garnier. Born on Christmas Day, 1889, he was reared by his mother in Fontainebleau. His hard, strong body was proof that poverty compelled him to begin work early in life, but the crudeness that characterized Carouy was altogether lacking. In its place there was about him a certain gentleness. At Romainville he cared for Maîtrejean's daughters. He enjoyed attending the theater in Paris. Although his formal education was limited, he discussed ideas and ideology at length with Kibaltchiche. Like Callemin and Crouy, Garnier had experienced a marker event that made him reject society and commit himself to anarchism. At the age of nineteen he was beaten by the police as he participated in a nonviolent strike. He developed an intense antipathy toward all authority, and the following year he went to Belgium rather than report for required military service. More so even than Bonnot, Garnier would reveal an implacable violence during the crimes of 1911 and 1912. "Pas de témoins" (no witnesses) was his rule.[8]

When Bonnot approached Callemin, Carouy, and Garnier, they were already inclined to join him. Since January, 1911, Carouy had carried out a series of successful burglaries in the Paris region and ranging as far as Nancy in the east and Méru (Oise) in the north. He occasionally worked alone, but more often he enlisted men who hung about the fringes of the anarchist movement. One of these was a restaurant cook, Marius Metge, who wanted presents for his mistress, a twenty-year-old Breton girl, Barbe Le Clerch. Together, Metge and Carouy broke into the post office at Romainville during the night of October 17–18 and into a house in the suburb on November 11. It was these burglaries, so close to the office of *L'Anarchie*, that alarmed Kibaltchiche and Maîtrejean. They feared that the po-

8. Callemin, "Notes."

Afterword

lice would search the commune and discover what Carouy had stored there from other robberies. In fact, Carouy had a network of confederates to hold or to fence stolen goods and used the commune as a hiding place only for brief periods. Callemin and Garnier were members of this network, and so were Dieudonné and Jean Dettweiller, a metal worker and locksmith who was preparing to open a repair garage at the southern edge of Paris.[9]

On the night of December 13–14, 1911, Callemin, Garnier, and Bonnot stole the magnificent Delaunay-Belleville automobile belonging to a certain M. Normand in the western suburb of Boulogne-sur-Seine. Several days earlier Bonnot had seen it on the Paris streets and had insisted that it be taken for use in his plan to rob a bank courier. Bonnot had never driven such a fine automobile, and he could not resist touring through the suburbs with Callemin and Garnier before heading to the unfinished garage at 5 Avenue de l'Harmonie, where Dettweiller and Carouy waited to hide it. A week later, in the early morning of December 21, the three picked up the automobile, and just before 9 A.M., Bonnot parked near the branch of the Société Générale at 146 Rue Ordener in Montmartre. Further down the sidewalk, Ernest Gaby, a courier, was approaching the bank. Garnier stepped from the Delaunay, waited until Gaby was within a few feet, and then raised a pistol in his left hand. He fired twice, wounding him in the chest and neck. Shouts came from the bank office, where an assistant, Peemans, and the doorman, Tavac, saw the attack. After tearing two security pouches from Gaby's grasp, Garnier returned to the Delaunay, and as he swung onto the running board, Bonnot accelerated down the Rue Ordener. Callemin fired his own pistol at the witnesses who had been attracted by the first two shots. The Bande à Bonnot had created a new variety of crime, the motorized bank robbery.

Bonnot drove northwest approximately one hundred miles until he reached Dieppe. Along the way, Callemin and Garnier searched through the security pouches. One contained Fr 318,722 in securities, but the serial numbers would make them difficult to negotiate. The other had Fr 5,526 in small bills, an amount far below their expectations. From newspaper accounts of the robbery, they would learn that Gaby had been carrying a third pouch inside his coat, this one holding Fr 20,000 in large bills and rolls of gold. Bonnot's origi-

---

9. *La Gazette des Tribunaux,* February 3–4, 16, 1913; *Le Figaro,* January 31, February 7, 1913.

nal plan had been for them to escape by crossing the Belgian border, but they agreed on returning to Paris for at least one more bank robbery. Because the Delaunay was too conspicuous, they would have to travel by train, and Bonnot regretfully left it on a mud lot at the end of the Avenue Alexandre Dumas in Dieppe.[10]

Back in Paris, the gang decided that they needed to have a large stock of arms. On the following night, December 23–24, Carouy, their burglary expert, led three of his henchmen, Dettweiller, Marcel Poyer, and Jacques Bernard, into the Foury gun shop at 70 Avenue Lafayette, and they came away with twenty pistols. Most of them were distributed to gang members, but three were given to Kibaltchiche and Maîtrejean in token of old friendship. Garnier was dissatisfied because he wanted rifles as well, and he organized a raid into the Smith and Wesson shop at 54 Boulevard Haussman during the night of January 8–9, 1912. This time, in addition to more pistols, there were three Winchester carbines and Fr 1,600 in cash.[11]

By the time of the second burglary, Carouy was in deep hiding, and Dettweiller was in custody. On December 30, after an informant reported having seen the now-famous Delaunay at the garage, Sûreté detectives arrested Dettweiller, his wife, and their boarder, Jeanne Giorgis, who readily admitted that she was Carouy's mistress. Octave Hamard, the director of the Sûreté, believed with good reason that the Rue Ordener robbery had been solved, because Carouy was a suspect in five burglaries and, at Alfortville several months before, had escaped capture only by firing a pistol at the pursuing policeman. Hamard was scheduled to be promoted within the Paris police hierarchy on January 1, 1912, and he was able to end his nine years as head of the Sûreté by grandly announcing to the newspapers that he had provided his successor, Xavier Guichard, with the name of the man who shot Gaby.[12]

Carouy was incensed at this false allegation but far more so at the arrest of his mistress. He vowed to wreak terrible vengeance against the bourgeois society that would have such police for its servant. He recruited Metge, and on the morning of January 2 they began walking toward the southern suburbs of Paris. Along the way, Carouy told of hearing about an elderly man, a M. Moreau, who lived in Thiais and often kept large amounts of money in his house. By mid-

10. Coudon, *Les Bandits tragiques*, 17–24; *La Gazette des Tribunaux*, February 3–4, 9–12, 1913; *Le Figaro*, December 22–23, 1911, January 31, February 1, 1913.
11. *La Gazette des Tribunaux*, February 3–4, 8, 1913.
12. *Le Figaro*, January 1, 1912.

Afterword

afternoon they reached Choisy-le-Roi and stopped a middle-aged woman to ask the way and then, carelessly, whether she knew Moreau's house. The woman, a certain Mme Dragon, mistrusted them and replied vaguely. As they started off, she distinctly heard Carouy say how unfortunate that it was daylight and too dangerous to find out what money she was carrying. Although frightened by these words, she did not alert the police, not even when she glimpsed the men a second time, near 8 P.M., on the road toward Thiais.

Locating Moreau's house was not difficult, and soon after midnight Carouy and Metge climbed the wall around the garden and forced open the back door. In one bedroom they found Moreau, who was ninety-one years old, and stabbed him so many times that they were covered with his blood. The noise of their butchery woke Moreau's serving woman, Mme Marie Arfeux, herself seventy-two years old, but Carouy strangled her. For an hour they searched the house, leaving bloody fingerprints everywhere and taking away more than sixty thousand francs in cash and bonds that Moreau had cached in his library.

The lack of activity at the house on the following morning caused a worried neighbor to call the police, and the horrific crime was discovered. The news spread rapidly through the area, and Mme Dragon came forward with descriptions of the two men she had seen at Choisy-le-Roi. Because Carouy seemed to be involved, the Sûreté sent out a special alarm to all police units. By unusual luck, Metge was apprehended immediately. Carouy had taken more precautions, and realizing that Paris was too dangerous for him, he sought refuge with friends in Nancy. When he returned to the southern suburbs in March, he was recognized, and on April 4 he was arrested at the Lozère train station.[13]

Before Carouy left for Nancy, he gave the bonds from Moreau's library to Henri Crozat de Fleury, a handsome, vain young man of good family, who had fenced stolen goods for him before. Crozat de Fleury was an example of another fringe element in the anarchist movement: members of the middle class who rejected bourgeois values and played at a romantic revolt against society. For him, that meant learning a trade (locksmithing), spending time in filthy clothes drinking in anarchist cafés, and writing a diatribe, *Comment on nous ruine*, against the wealth that permitted him to do as he pleased. For three months Crozat de Fleury uneasily planned various schemes

13. *La Gazette des Tribunaux*, February 3–4, 15, 1913; *Le Figaro*, January 4, 1912, February 2, 1913; Coudon, *Les Bandits tragiques*, 25–29.

to cash the bonds, but on April 3 he finally turned to Jean Tardieu, his own father's broker. With no reason to be suspicious, Tardieu was about to liquidate them when he found their serial numbers on the list circulated by the police. He quietly informed the Sûreté, which arrested the miserable romantic revolutionary.[14]

Bonnot, Garnier, and Callemin also had bonds to liquidate, from the Rue Ordener robbery. Knowing that French banks were watching for the Société Générale securities, Callemin tried to arrange a transaction in the Netherlands. With Jean Deboé, a typesetter and anarchist friend from Brussels, he traveled to Amsterdam on January 12. There, they met with an underworld figure, a certain Vandenbergh, who told them that even Dutch banks had the serial numbers. He did agree to hold the bonds while looking into a means of cashing them, but despite Callemin's promise of a very large commission, he hesitated to involve himself in such a notorious case. At the beginning of March, Callemin sent two other confederates, David Bellonie and Léon Rodriguez, to pick up the bonds from Vandenbergh. By then, the Sûreté had learned enough about the gang to have Bellonie under watch. When he and Rodriguez returned to France on March 11, they were arrested and the bonds recovered.[15]

With Metge in jail and Carouy hiding in Nancy, three other members of the gang were forced into greater prominence, and the most important of them was André Soudy. Twenty-three years old, pale and tubercular, Soudy had a poor and unhappy childhood in Loiret that was complicated by a suppressed lust for his pretty first cousin. When he was twenty, he entered the Saint-Louis sanatorium for treatment. A friend sublet his one-room apartment and used it to store stolen objects. When the friend was arrested, the police and the court assumed that Soudy was an accomplice. The injustice of eight months in prison embittered him and led him to anarchism. Callemin and Maîtrejean were his closest friends.

The two other gang members to gain importance were René Valet and Antoine Monier, known as Simentof, who were both twenty-two years old in early 1912. Fair, strapping, quiet, but prone to violence, Valet came from the poorest section of Verdun. Like Garnier, he went to Belgium to avoid military service, and the two became fast friends. They would die together in the shoot-out of May 14 in Nogent-sur-Marne. The dark, tall Monier was from the Mediter-

14. *La Gazette des Tribunaux*, February 3–4, 7, 1913; *Le Figaro*, February 2, 1913.
15. *La Gazette des Tribunaux*, February 3–4, 8, 1913; *Le Figaro*, February 1, 1913; Bellonie, "Souvenirs et révélations."

ranean coast of France and spoke with a heavy southern accent. He was a careful observer and acted as the intelligence officer for the gang.[16]

As the anarchists plotted further crimes, the Sûreté's new director, Guichard, and his men came under increasing criticism from the public and the Paris press for their failure to apprehend any of the participants in the Rue Ordener robbery. During the first two weeks of January, 1912, the Sûreté actually had few leads to follow, but after the Société Générale offered a reward, letters from informants piled up in the offices along the Quai des Orfèvres. In one week alone, the assistant director, Louis Jouin, opened 2,427. Most were worthless, but one led to the arrest of Marie Schoofs, née Vuillemin, the pretty, plump, full-lipped girl who had left her husband to live with Garnier. She was incapable of discretion, and from her the Sûreté learned the names of Bonnot and Garnier and obtained photographs of them.[17]

On January 24, Guichard, Jouin, and Maurice Gilbert, the juge d'instruction assigned to the case, led a group of newspaper reporters to Gaby's hospital bed. He examined the photographs and positively identified Garnier as the man who shot him. The other witnesses, Peemans and Tavac, also picked out the picture of Garnier. In their January 25 editions, the Paris press published the photographs of Bonnot and Garnier on the front page, but the criticism of the Sûreté continued because no arrests followed. Frustrated themselves by the lack of progress, the Sûreté chiefs and Gilbert ordered a descent on the office of *L'Anarchie*. Bursting in at 6 A.M. on January 31, the sixty detectives found Kibaltchiche, Maîtrejean, and several anarchist comrades quietly sipping their morning chocolate. A search that lasted until noon turned up the three pistols from the Foury gun shop burglary but nothing else incriminating. Although the entire *L'Anarchie* circle was arrested, only Kibaltchiche and Maîtrejean were held after questioning. For its efforts, the Sûreté had a case of receiving stolen property against the two anarchist editors, but otherwise not even the name of Callemin.[18]

What Guichard and Jouin could not know was that the fortunes of the Bande à Bonnot were about to turn. Even as the Sûreté was tear-

---

16. *La Gazette des Tribunaux*, February 6, 1913; *Le Figaro*, February 6, 1913; Coudon, *Les Bandits tragiques*, 117–29.
17. *Le Figaro*, February 2, 1913.
18. *La Gazette des Tribunaux*, February 3–4, 1913; *Le Figaro*, January 25, 1912; Kibaltchiche, *Mémoires d'un révolutionnaire*, 43–44; Coudon, *Les Bandits tragiques*, 30–39.

ing through the *L'Anarchie* office, Bonnot, Callemin, Garnier, and Deboé were in Ghent. Their plan was to steal an automobile, drive to Brussels, and mount another motorized bank robbery. From the first, everything went wrong. As they were taking the automobile, its chauffeur unexpectedly appeared. Garnier shot him dead, but all four were unnerved. Approaching Brussels, Bonnot recklessly skidded through a curve and ran into a tree. The worst injuries were bruises, but the gang was now on foot. It was late at night, and they could not find another automobile to steal. The only means of returning to their hideouts in Paris was by train, but station guards had pictures of Bonnot and Garnier and were watching for them. They took the risk, ready to shoot their way free if necessary. Bonnot and Garnier kept their heads low, hats pulled down over their faces, and the five-hour ride to Paris was merely anxious.

There the gang learned that Kibaltchiche and Maîtrejean were in custody and that the Sûreté was beginning to penetrate the anarchist milieu. Still, they continued to cling to their dream of sharing the loot from a great robbery and to believe that Bonnot's basic plan could succeed. On February 15, Callemin and Deboé, who had not yet been identified, traveled to Béziers and stole the Peugeot of a M. Malbec. They hid it carefully in Paris until the night of February 22, when Bonnot, Garnier, and Dieudonné joined them. They proposed to drive in the dark to Nîmes and rob the large Société Générale bank in the center of the town, but they had as little luck as they had had three weeks earlier in Belgium. The Peugeot broke down at Arnay-le-Duc, and though Callemin and Dieudonné located a garage, the problem was too complicated for rapid repair. Once again the gang had to abandon a stolen automobile and risk the train ride back to Paris. This time, there was a witness who could pick out Callemin and Dieudonné, and on the back seat of the Peugeot, Deboé left a collar bearing his laundry mark.[19]

The second successive failure severely shook the confidence of the gang. Garnier, Callemin, and Bonnot considered fleeing to the Midi and sent Monier to reconnoiter his native districts. In the last week of February he telegraphed that the Bande à Bonnot was almost unknown in the region. Bonnot had already located an automobile he thought suitable for the trip, another Peugeot, this one belonging to a M. Buisson in the Saint-Mandé suburb near the Bois de Vincennes. The three stole it on the night of February 26–27 and headed south

19. *La Gazette des Tribunaux*, February 3–4, 1913; *Le Figaro*, February 2, 1913.

Afterword

toward Allais. They were hardly on the road when Bonnot, always the driver, ran into a ditch and damaged the right front axle. He fixed it temporarily, but at Pont-sur-Yonne they had to stop overnight for repairs. By the following day, February 28, they changed their minds about meeting Monier in the Midi and returned to Paris. They were riding down the Rue d'Amsterdam toward the Place du Havre, near the Saint Lazare station, when Bonnot grew careless again and lightly bumped an autobus. As a crowd gathered, he desperately backed up the Peugeot and tried to drive it out of the square toward the Rue Tronchet. The policeman directing traffic at the Place du Havre stepped onto the running board to demand that he stop. Callemin and Garnier shot him at point-blank range. As he fell dead, Bonnot accelerated rapidly. The last pursuers lost sight of them as they passed through the Place de la Concorde.

Bonnot drove Callemin and Garnier aimlessly through the Paris suburbs until it was dark. All of the money from the Rue Ordener robbery had long before been spent, and three botched attempts since, at the price of two murders, had yielded not a single franc. The killing of a policeman would bring even greater pressure to apprehend them. They needed action to release their tensions, and Bonnot suggested that they burglarize the house of Henri Tintant, a notary he knew of in Pontoise. At 3 A.M. he stopped the Peugeot near the corner house, and Garnier began to work at the door with a skeleton key. Tintant awoke at the noise, looked from his second-floor bedroom window, and then fired his hunting rifle at the three bandits. Callemin shot back with his pistol, one bullet grazing Tintant's ear. When a neighbor shouted for the police, the gang retreated to the Peugeot and drove off. They abandoned it later, half-burned on a deserted street in Saint-Ouen.[20]

The latest outrages by the Bande à Bonnot, and their escape, stimulated even louder criticism of the Sûreté. Along with photographs of Bonnot, Garnier, and now Callemin, the Paris newspapers published pictures of the automobiles the gang had stolen, noting bitterly that the police could find them more easily than they could bandits. Jouin, who had direct command of the investigation, needed some quick success to allay public opinion, and he had it within two weeks. On March 11, Bellonie and Rodriguez were arrested carrying the bonds from the Société Générale. Three days later an informant

20. *La Gazette des Tribunaux*, February 3–4, 12, 1913; *Le Figaro*, February 2, 1913; Coudon, *Les Bandits tragiques*, 40–45.

led detectives to Dieudonné and his wife, Louise. After gathering reporters around Gaby's hospital bed for a second time, Jouin brought in Dieudonné and two Sûreté inspecteurs, all dressed alike. He thought Gaby might identify him as one of the Rue Ordener robbers who remained in the Delaunay. To everyone's astonishment, Gaby declared that it was Dieudonné who had shot him. As the reporters raced to write up this development, Dieudonné protested his entire innocence of the crime. But Jouin preferred to believe in the revised identification, because he could claim credit for a more important arrest.[21]

There was so much euphoria at the Quai des Orfèvres that when Gilbert decided to release both Louise Dieudonné and Marie Vuillemin, against whom there were no formal charges, Jouin neglected to have them shadowed. Louise went to Callemin's hideout and began a liaison with him that had its origin in a casual affair during the days at Romainville. Although frequently unfaithful to her husband, Louise never allowed her affections to wander far from him. For Callemin the relationship meant a great deal more, his first love for a woman since the departure of the Russian student in Brussels. He and Louise ignored the most basic rules of concealment, even attending the theater. It was romance, but also self-destruction.

Marie Vuillemin returned to her lover Garnier and was able to tell him and the other members of the gang about the questioning she had undergone. From that, they could gauge the progress of the Sûreté's investigation. The newspapers had published Dieudonné's photograph on their front pages and had exchanged criticism of Guichard and Jouin for praise. Garnier responded with a signed letter to *Le Matin*, which had one of the largest circulations in Paris, declaring that he alone shot Gaby and that Dieudonné did not even participate in the robbery. To prove the letter genuine, Garnier suggested that Alphonse Bertillon, the renowned specialist in scientific criminal detection, examine it for fingerprints. When Bertillon verified Garnier's claim, Jouin came under withering ridicule. He submitted his resignation to Guichard, who accepted it, but Louis Lépine, the prefect of the Paris police, tore the resignation into bits and told Jouin to work even harder.[22]

After more than three weeks of inaction, the Bande à Bonnot struck again on March 25. Near dawn Bonnot, Callemin, Garnier, Soudy, Monier, and Valet hid along the road leading from Paris to the

21. *Le Figaro*, March 15, 1912.
22. Garnier, "Lettre à M. Xavier Guichard."

Afterword

southern suburb of Montgéron. At approximately 8 A.M., a Dion automobile appeared in the distance, and three of the gang stood in the road, motioning for it to stop. When the chauffeur stepped down to demand an explanation, he was shot dead by the other gang members, who attacked from the flank. The passenger and owner of the Dion, a M. Cérisoles, jumped from the back seat and ran away as two bullets wounded him slightly.

With Bonnot driving, the gang rode in a great semicircle through the eastern suburbs and then north to Chantilly. At several minutes after 10 A.M., Bonnot parked on the Place de l'Hospice de Condé, across from their target, the Société Générale bank, and remained with the Dion. Soudy, carrying one of the Winchester carbines, waited outside, while the other four, pistols drawn and ready, went in. After ordering the three cashiers to raise their hands, they began filling two bags with cash and rolls of coins. When the manager opened the door from his inner office, Callemin and Garnier feared an ambush. They started shooting, killing two of the cashiers, wounding the third and the manager. Soudy fired at any movement in the square.

In less than five minutes all of the gang were back in the Dion, and Bonnot took the road south toward Paris at great speed. In the rear seat, Soudy fainted from the tension. Valet revived him by applying alcohol to his forehead, but he rubbed so hard that he left red welts. Callemin and Garnier counted the money in the front seat: Fr 10,000 in gold, 4,000 in silver, 33,555 in bills—a total of Fr 47,555. Bonnot's plan had finally worked. At Asnières, just to the north of Montmartre, they divided the money in a hotel room and then took different routes back to their hideouts.[23]

Public reaction to the Montgéron-Chantilly crimes was close to hysteria. Bonnot, Callemin, and Garnier were "seen" everywhere. In the Chamber of Deputies, Henry Franklin-Bouillon, the representative from Montgéron, demanded that the government take action to ensure the safety of French citizens. Théodore Steeg, the minister of the interior, announced a new appropriation of Fr 800,000 for the Paris police and the Sûreté Générale. Soldiers were posted to stand guard at train stations and ports. The Société Générale increased its reward to Fr 100,000 for the capture of the bandits.[24]

Combined with the Sûreté's penetration of anarchist groups, these new measures had an immediate effect. An informant revealed that

23. *La Gazette des Tribunaux*, February 3–4, 13, 1913; *Le Figaro*, March 26, 1912, February 3, 1913; Coudon, *Les Bandits tragiques*, 46–53.
24. *Le Figaro*, March 26, 1912; *JOC*, Débats parlementaires, March 26, 1912.

Soudy was hiding at Berck-sur-Mer, and he was surprised in a rented room there on March 30. In his pockets, he had Fr 939, and around the room lay seven pistols, all loaded. On April 4, one of the soldiers at the Lozère train station recognized Carouy and sounded the alarm. When Carouy saw that he could not escape, he swallowed potassium cyanide, but the dose was too small to kill him. These two arrests, which received wide publicity, indicated that the Sûreté was finally close to crushing the gang. To secure her own welfare, Louise Dieudonné betrayed Callemin. Guichard himself led the fifteen detectives who surrounded Callemin on April 7 along the Rue La Tour d'Auvergne. He was so taken unawares that he never had a chance to draw the two loaded revolvers he kept in his coat pockets. Staring bitterly at Louise, he told the commissaire holding him: "My head is worth one hundred thousand francs. Yours is worth seven centimes [the price of a bullet]." Callemin was carrying Fr 5,300 in cash.[25]

After the arrests of Soudy, Carouy, and Callemin, Monier became ever more convinced that remaining in the Paris region was dangerous and that he could find safety only in the Mediterranean area, perhaps by going to Italy. Since late March he had been hiding with an anarchist sympathizer, Antoine Gauzy, who sold notions out of his ramshackle frame house at 63 Rue de Paris in the southeast suburb of Ivry. Thirty-eight years old, short, thick, and square-headed, Gauzy bore a remarkable resemblance to the future premier and collaborator Pierre Laval. Although not prosperous, his business was successful, and he had a good reputation among his neighbors. When Monier offered him Fr 1,300 to stay in his house, he agreed without asking any questions, but he should have suspected that he was selling asylum to a member of the Bande à Bonnot. On April 18, Monier said that he was leaving but that a friend, a "Russian revolutionary," might want to take his place. Then he registered under an alias at the Hôtel de la Lozère on the Boulevard Ménilmontant and began his arrangements to head south.

One of his meetings was with Bonnot, who was worried that the Sûreté had picked up his trail. Monier suggested Gauzy's house as a new hideout, and Bonnot went to Ivry on April 23 posing as the Russian revolutionary. After deciding that the house seemed safe and that Gauzy could be trusted, he moved into the single small room of the second floor. On the same day, a hotel employee, eager to share in the reward money and believing that he recognized Monier, went

25. *La Gazette des Tribunaux*, February 3–4, 1913; *Le Figaro*, March 31, April 5, 8, 1912, February 3, 1913.

Afterword

to the Sûreté with his information. Early the next morning Jouin, accompanied by seven inspecteurs, burst in upon Monier and made the arrest. Jouin wanted to know where he had been hiding before April 18, and in only a few minutes a café owner was found who recalled hearing him mention Gauzy. Three of the inspecteurs returned to the Quai des Orfèvres with Monier. Jouin and the rest drove to Ivry.

At the trial for the surviving members of the Bande à Bonnot, Gauzy would claim that he did not recognize the "Russian revolutionary" as Bonnot. He may have been telling the truth, because sixteen years earlier the army had discharged him for poor eyesight and the condition had grown worse. At approximately 9 A.M. on April 24, Gauzy saw Bonnot descend the staircase and head for the center of Ivry. He returned almost immediately, but it is impossible to be certain whether Gauzy, involved in the front of the house with his business, noticed him. Near 10:30 A.M., Jouin and the four inspecteurs arrived. They showed Gauzy a photograph of Monier, and when he did not at once recognize him, Jouin threatened severe treatment. Gauzy moved toward a window to have more light and declared that he had "employed" the man and had let him stay in the house for more than three weeks.

Jouin insisted on seeing the room where Monier slept. He left two inspecteurs, Hingand and Sevestre, to search the three ground-floor rooms, while he and the other two, Robert and Colmar, went upstairs. Gauzy led the way hesitantly, tried the door, and, finding it locked, turned the key twice. He stood aside as Jouin and Colmar entered the heavily shuttered room. For several seconds there was silence, until Jouin cried out, "C'est Bonnot!" What happened during the next minutes was confused. The sound of pistol shots came from the room, and Gauzy ran away. For reasons never satisfactorily explained, Sevestre and Hingand downstairs heard nothing. Robert looked through the doorway, saw three bodies, and then rushed to find the other inspecteurs. In his haste he neglected to determine whether Bonnot was actually wounded. While he was gone, Bonnot disappeared. Jouin was dead, and Colmar lay seriously wounded.

The report of Jouin's murder was telephoned to the Quai des Orfèvres, and Guichard brought a force of twenty-four commissaires and inspecteurs to Ivry. By the time they arrived, Jouin's body had been removed, Colmar taken to the nearest hospital, and the second-floor room searched thoroughly. Bonnot had left behind his wallet and a copy of *Crainquebille*, Anatole France's bathetic tale of the injustice meted out by the police and courts to a poor vegetable carter.

For the murderous Bonnot, it was an ironic choice. Almost a hundred men and women gathered around the house in curiosity. Their presence was a humiliation for Guichard and his men, who had lost their assistant director but had no trace of his murderer. When there was a murmur that Gauzy had returned, they had their scapegoat. Three detectives held him, and Guichard, losing all sense of dignity and proportion, struck his face twice. He was so overwrought that even as Gauzy was dragged roughly toward the local precinct building, he raged beside him, encouraging the crowd to pummel and spit upon the man he denounced vociferously as the accomplice to Jouin's murder. At the precinct Guichard hit Gauzy a third time and swore that the police would cause his house to be sold at auction, his children to beg in the streets, and his wife to prostitute herself.[26]

Bonnot could not be found, because he had run to the Ivry Métro station and taken a subway train to the Porte d'Italie. A mechanic named Dubois, one of Carouy's burglars, rented a garage nearby in Choisy-le-Roi that was set back from the road in a field. Bonnot walked there after dark and hid in an upstairs room. He cannot have doubted that the police would find him eventually. None of the anarchist groups was now free of informants, and Dubois's name was on a list at the Sûreté. For almost four days he waited like a cornered rat.

At dawn on April 28, twenty detectives walked toward the garage to search it, as they had other possible hideouts since Jouin's murder. Dubois was already outside working on a wrecked automobile and shouted a warning to Bonnot. When both opened fire with pistols, the detectives retreated out of range but kept the garage surrounded. By 9:30 A.M., Guichard came to take personal command, and he requested two companies of infantry and a *mitrailleuse*. When these forces were drawn up two hours later, he had a small army at his disposal. He was acutely aware that his superiors, Lépine and Hamard, were watching from the rear. The more than ten thousand raucous men and women who congregated at a distance generated a bizarre and macabre circus atmosphere. Everyone wanted to see a man die, whether police or criminal. Guichard hesitated, but by noon he was ready.

With three soldiers pushing an old wagon in front of him for cover, an explosives expert was able to reach the garage and place a dynamite charge against one wall. Then they worked their way back to the circumference of the field, pulling the wagon behind them as a shield.

---

26. *La Gazette des Tribunaux*, February 3–4, 7, 14–15, 1913; *Le Figaro*, April 24, 1912, February 3, 1913; Coudon, *Les Bandits tragiques*, 59–69.

Afterword

When the detonator was activated, nothing happened. A second try produced an explosion, but the garage remained standing. One more time the soldiers made their perilous approach, set the charge, and the garage burst into flames. Guichard bravely led the charge of police and infantry. Dubois was dead beside the wrecked automobile. They found Bonnot in the upstairs room. He had wrapped a mattress around himself for protection, but he was badly injured. In revenge for Jouin, Guichard shot him point-blank in the chest, and he died before he could be transported to a hospital. In his fist, he clutched a scrap of paper, which was dubbed the "Testament de Bonnot." It read simply: "Gauzy est innocent. Dieudonné aussi."[27]

The Sûreté cleaned up its files by arresting peripheral accomplices such as Metge's mistress, Barbe Le Clerch, while hunting for the only principal members of the gang left, Garnier and Valet. Both dyed their hair, and Garnier grew a moustache, but their faces were too well known, and the reward too great, for them to hide for long. After trying to lose themselves in the slums of Saint-Ouen, they moved to Nogent-sur-Marne. They were tracked down on May 14, and Paris applauded the second siege and dynamite-blasting of anarchist criminals in less than three weeks.[28]

During the next four months, Maurice Gilbert prepared the instruction against the twenty survivors. It was a disparate group that included genuinely dangerous criminals—Callemin, Soudy, Carouy, Metge, and Monier; intellectuals implicated by association—Kibaltchiche and Maîtrejean; less important elements involved in burglary and fencing—Dettweiller, Crozat de Fleury, Deboé, Bellonie, and Rodriguez; two whose guilt was problematic—Gauzy and Dieudonné; and truly minor figures such as mistresses and individuals who sheltered the criminals at one point or another. None of the twenty volunteered significant information during interrogation, but Gilbert had a large body of evidence from the Sûreté and many witnesses to the crimes. Because the court calendar for the fall and winter of 1912 was full, the date for the trial of the Bande à Bonnot was set for February 3, 1913.[29]

During the nine months between the siege at Nogent-sur-Marne and the opening of the trial, the way the public perceived the Bande à Bonnot underwent a curious transformation. When the gang mem-

---

27. *Le Figaro,* April 29, 1912; Coudon, *Les Bandits tragiques,* 70–81.
28. *La Gazette des Tribunaux,* February 3–4, 1913; Coudon, *Les Bandits tragiques,* 82–89.
29. *La Gazette des Tribunaux,* September 12, 1912.

bers were known only for their crimes, they were feared and despised. Once that fear was gone and details about them as individuals became clear, they were seen as more sympathetic figures, "les bandits tragiques." They were pitied as victims of social and economic injustice, men and women in revolt against a cruel society, and they were patronized as confused adolescents led to disaster by their misunderstanding of a dangerous ideology. The new perception was a form of subconscious guilt among the middle class, who were increasingly questioning the society they had made.[30]

This new sympathy heightened interest in the trial even though the verdict was all but foreordained. During the preceding decade, two other extraordinarily sensational cases had come before the cour d'assises of Paris. In 1902, Thérèse Humbert was convicted of fabricating a one-hundred-million-franc swindle over twenty years and of perverting the judicial system to lend it legitimation. In 1909, Marguerite Steinheil was dramatically acquitted of having plotted the mysterious deaths of her husband and mother. For both cases there was a packed courtroom to see a single notorious "heroine" defend herself.[31] The trial of the Bande à Bonnot could not offer that. Rirette Maîtrejean was hardly a central figure, and so many defendants blurred the focus. The special quality of this trial was that it could be understood not merely as a judgment on their alleged crimes but as a judgment on the alleged crimes of society. Some of the outstanding avocats of Paris eagerly donated their services in this *cause célèbre*. For the same reason, the procureur général of the Cour d'appel de Paris decided to present the state's case personally.

On the morning of February 3 the Palais de Justice was surrounded by military guards, and only those who had applied for and received a small white card were permitted to enter the cour d'assises. Even then, they had to wait until 11:45 A.M., only fifteen minutes before the session began, to take their seats. A startling display of evidence was in plain view: sixteen revolvers, ten Browning automatic pistols, three Winchester carbines, burglary tools, and skeleton keys.

At noon the twenty defendants were brought into the courtroom, each between two police guards. They seemed enchanted to be on display and had been thoroughly scrubbed and neatly dressed for the occasion. Rirette Maîtrejean made the most striking impression. Dressed in the black blouse and blue tie of a schoolgirl, she looked

30. See, for example, *Le Figaro*, February 1–4, 1913.
31. Martin, *The Hypocrisy of Justice*, 44–45, 123–24.

Afterword

sixteen years old, not twenty-three, as she sat down and folded her overcoat carefully on her lap. "C'est Claudine à l'école!" someone in the audience cried aloud. Among the men, only a few attracted much notice this first day. Callemin, like Maîtrejean, appeared young enough to belong in a classroom. Soudy, pale and tubercular, stood listlessly in a new suit. Beside him, shorter, darker, almost malevolent in his hatred of all outside the defendants' box, Kibaltchiche stared at the audience. In contrast, the gray-haired Gauzy was a broken man hardly capable of raising his eyes. How could these men and women be the bandits who had terrorized Paris for six months? They would have been easier to accept as criminals if they had all resembled Carouy.

There were sixteen black-robed avocats for the defense. Two of them, Vincent de Moro-Giafferi and César Campinchi, were among the most brilliant younger members of the Paris *ordre*. Five red-robed magistrates represented the state. The président of the three-judge panel was the stern Henry Couinaud. Victor Fabre, the procureur général, was a blunt-spoken, stocky native of the Midi. He was assisted by a substitut général, Raoul Bloque-Laroque. The twelve jurymen and two alternates were the final element of the court.

Fabre made the uncompromising nature of the prosecution's case evident immediately. He called the defendants a new breed of criminals who had declared war on society. After committing their crimes, they did not attempt to escape undetected or to avoid bloodshed. Instead, they made a conscious effort to kill, and to kill indiscriminately. The doctrines of anarchism were a facade for these crimes: *Reprise individuelle* was actually common theft. The bandits created for their war on society an underworld organization previously unequaled in its complexity. At the headquarters of this network, the office of *L'Anarchie*, they could take refuge, change clothes, adopt disguises; they could manufacture burglary tools and hide what they stole; they could meet and plan in secret. Society, Fabre argued, had a right and a duty to defend itself by waging war in return, as it had at Choisy-le-Roi and Nogent-sur-Marne and as it would do at this trial. Five days of the proceedings and part of a sixth, February 3–8, were taken up by the *interrogatoire*. Very early, the defendants split into groups rather than maintain solidarity. One motive lay in the natural division between those accused of capital crimes and those not. Another was the varying schemes of legal defense.

Kibaltchiche and Maîtrejean were the first to separate themselves.

The charges against them, receiving stolen property (the three revolvers) and associating with criminals, were only weakly substantiated by the evidence. The more damning accusation of preaching a dangerous doctrine, anarchism, even in one of its milder versions, was left unstated. If they could not both escape punishment entirely, Kibaltchiche was determined to take all of the blame himself and spare Maîtrejean further time in prison. During the interrogation, he subdued his anger. Offering the back issues of *L'Anarchie* as proof, he made clear that the anarchism he expressed in his articles and editorials could not be construed as an inspiration to crime. Both he and Maîtrejean claimed, perhaps truthfully, not to have known that the revolvers they accepted from "friends" had been stolen. Both insisted, falsely, that Maîtrejean had never exercised editorial control over the newspaper and had merely lent her name to the masthead. She strengthened this lie by seeming to be more "Rirette" than "Maîtrejean" during the questioning. The jury warmed to her as she told of learning Latin from the nuns who cared for the prisoners in Saint Lazare during her eleven months of pretrial confinement. Finally, Kibaltchiche drew a line between those anarchists such as himself and Maîtrejean, who emphasized "morality and affection," and others—he named Callemin, Carouy, and Garnier—who denied them.[32]

Dieudonné also stood apart. The prosecution had convincing evidence that he participated in several burglaries and received stolen property, but Fabre wanted to place him as the fourth man at the Rue Ordener robbery. The testimony of the eyewitnesses was in conflict, and Garnier's extraordinary letter to *Le Matin* asserted Dieudonné's innocence, but there were extraneous factors militating against him. He claimed to have been in Nancy during the period of the bank robbery, but he lacked corroboration. Moreover, on December 19, 1911, Callemin sent a telegram to him in Nancy—"T'attendons immédiatement, viens de suite"—which could be interpreted as calling him back to Paris for the robbery on December 21. Dieudonné declared that the telegram was a reference to his wife, who was waiting for him after ending another of her affairs, but this tolerance for adultery did not have a positive effect on the jury. He also could not deny his friendship with Callemin or arranging Bonnot's first hideout in Paris. He was in a difficult position. He had to dissociate himself from the gang, but he did not want to testify against them. In turn they could not prove his innocence without convicting themselves.

32. *La Gazette des Tribunaux*, February 3–4, 1913; *Le Figaro*, February 4, 1913; Becker, *La Bande à Bonnot*, 89–143.

Afterword

Callemin, Monier, Soudy, Carouy, and Metge, who faced capital charges, made up a third division. The evidence against all of them was overwhelming, and none of the five presented an effective refutation. Callemin was particularly disappointing. When he stood at his place for the *interrogatoire*, he resembled a student about to defend a thesis: notebook in his left hand, pencil in his right, spectacles slipping down his nose. Even to the most banal question, he responded laconically and only after consulting his notebook. He denied participating in the Rue Ordener robbery, the Chantilly robbery, or the shooting of the policeman at the Place du Havre. When Couinaud listed the many witnesses who had identified him, he replied contemptuously that next he would be accused of "having strangled Charlemagne and poisoned Louis XIV." His avocat, Georges Boucheron, interjected that the testimony of the witnesses had varied somewhat in regard to Callemin. Couinaud retorted, "Every day certain witnesses are unable to recognize an accused while others are able to do so," and, turning to Callemin, asked him to explain where he was during these crimes if indeed he had not committed them. Callemin sneered, "I have reflected about it, and I am unable to recall." He did make a special point of denying the report by a Sûreté detective that at his arrest he exclaimed: "It's a pity that you have surprised me. Otherwise, my pistols would have spoken."

In contrast to Callemin, Monier answered his questions at length. In a meridional accent that rendered his French nearly unintelligible, he spoke vaguely and endlessly, describing his life as a hawker of pamphlets and then denying all the charges against him. Asked why he cried "Je suis fait!" when arrested if he were innocent, he replied that he had evaded his required military service and thought that the police had finally caught up to him. Was fear of that arrest the reason he carried an arsenal of weapons? "Parfaitement" came the response. As an alibi for the Chantilly robbery, he claimed to have been working at Ivry for Gauzy, and in an afterthought he added that he had never known Bonnot.[33]

When Soudy's turn came, he delivered a short but vehement denial of the court's authority: "Gentlemen of the magistrature, gentlemen of the jury, I do not recognize your right to judge me. You are not gods or supernatural beings! You do not have the right to compel an innocent man like me to stand before this bar of grief." He continued with the story of his wretched childhood and complained that society had never granted him a position in which his intelli-

---

33. *La Gazette des Tribunaux*, February 5, 1913; *Le Figaro*, February 5, 1913.

gence could be appreciated. Poverty had forced him to steal: "If I had had money with which to live, I would not have used such means." This speech seemed to tire him, and with Couinaud's permission, his avocat, Jacques Doublet, brought him a cordial. After a moment's recovery, he repeatedly denied participating in the Chantilly robbery. He made only a halfhearted attempt at an alibi, saying that he was visiting a friend, but he claimed that he could never have shot at anyone because he had such an immense respect for human life. If that was true, why had he carried loaded pistols? Soudy answered bitterly that he had lost his liberty before—the eight-month prison term—and given the opportunity, would have committed suicide rather than surrender to the police: "If the detectives had allowed me time, I avow that there would have been a body at Berck— I would have left *my* body at Berck."

Carouy impressed the court as more brutal and common than his fellows, but he defended himself with some intelligence and wit. He talked of discovering through anarchism a joy in life and a concern for beauty. Did he frequent anarchist circles? "Oh, in the workshops, we discuss things like that a bit. You know how it is." Why had he occasionally adopted the alias "Maury"? "That is simple. Belgians do not work as hard as the French, and they are often not welcome in France. So, I took a French name. I have always had a great love for the French." Couinaud riposted, "You are accused of not being tender in this love!" When the questioning turned to the murders at Thiais, his avocat, Alexander Zévaès, who was as famous for his Radical politics as for his *plaidoiries,* protested the use of fingerprint evidence: "I trust that the procureur général is in accord with me on the scientific merit of M. Bertillon! He has disqualified himself by his actions in the Dreyfus affair!" This denunciation was a reference to Bertillon's disastrous dabbling with graphology in 1894, when he incorrectly identified Alfred Dreyfus as the author of the famous *bordereau* that offered the sale of French secrets to the Germans. Fingerprint analysis was entirely different, and Fabre replied, "I have the most profound respect for the science of M. Bertillon." The last question put to Carouy was why he had twice tried to commit suicide, first as he was captured and later in his cell. His voice firm, he answered that he sought death not because he considered himself guilty but because his faith in life had been shattered when anarchists began denouncing their comrades to the police in return for money.[34]

34. *La Gazette des Tribunaux,* February 6, 1913; *Le Figaro,* February 6, 1913.

Afterword

Metge, like Kibaltchiche, had a woman to protect. His mistress, Barbe Le Clerch, was accused with him of taking jewelry from a family named Schmidt in the Pavillon-sous-Bois. Metge insisted that he alone committed the crime and that Le Clerch had not known the earrings he had given her were stolen. As for the murders at Thiais and the fact that his fingerprints were found there, he denied everything. He had no alibi for that night, but he asked who could, in fact, recall where he was at every moment. His fervent avowal seemed to impress the jury: "The crime at Thiais was a horrible one, committed with an unheard-of violence. It was an act of vengeance. You cannot find the antecedents of such an act in my background. I am innocent."

The mistress Metge hoped to protect and the woman who left her husband for Garnier made up the fourth group of defendants. Le Clerch was charged with burglary and receiving stolen property, Vuillemin only with the latter. In court both were pathetic, more victims than criminals. Le Clerch had to fan herself with a handkerchief to keep from fainting as she answered through sobs. She was terrified because a guard had told her that in prison "we will have to eat rats." Pitilessly Couinaud bore down on the evidence. How could she not have been suspicious of earrings monogrammed with someone else's initials? The reply ended any question of her guilt: "I cannot read. I did not know what the marks were." Vuillemin, dressed completely in black, told the court, "I had no part whatsoever in *L'Anarchie*. I just cleaned the vegetables and was everyone's servant." Why had she remained with Garnier after the newspapers identified him as a murderer? "The more I believed him guilty, the more I made myself not think about it."

The testimony of the women was an interlude, and the atmosphere of the courtroom changed completely when Gauzy stood for his *interrogatoire*. In a blatantly partisan act, Couinaud began with a eulogy of Louis Jouin and all of the other police officers who had died in the line of duty. When Gauzy spoke, it was in a grave tremulous voice, his words underlined by sweeping gestures. He portrayed himself as a martyr, an innocent man trapped by circumstances beyond his control and blamed for their outcome. With ever-increasing emotion, he cried out his reputation as a merchant, as a husband and father, even as a chicken farmer. He had had a notions shop, Halles Populaires, in Ivry since 1910 and had won the respect of "all upright people, the mayor included." No one, he insisted, deplored the murder of Jouin more than he, and he should not be prosecuted for it. He knew nothing of either Monier or Bonnot when they "rented" his upstairs room. "If I were a juge d'instruction, I would have demanded their papers," but "you cannot inquire into everyone's background."

Couinaud read aloud from the police reports about the search through Gauzy's house and the shooting of Jouin. At every critical juncture he required Gauzy to explain his actions. Why had he failed to identify the picture of Monier when it was first presented to him? "I was released from the army for bad eyesight, my house is dark, and the obscurity of the photograph confused me for a moment." Why had he "paled"—according to the inspecteurs with Jouin—at the move to examine the second-floor room? Had not his face revealed the knowledge that Bonnot was waiting in ambush? Was not his flight afterward the final proof of his complicity? Heatedly, Gauzy attacked these conclusions. He "paled" because a police search brings disgrace, and he was an honest businessman never before accused of anything illegal. If the court and the jury could tour his house, they would recognize easily that he had no idea whether Bonnot had returned after leaving earlier in the morning. As for his panic at the shots, that was understandable in anyone not used to violence. If he had feared justice, he would not have come back voluntarily. Because the light and the arrangement of the rooms were critical to Gauzy's defense, his avocat, André Berthon, formally petitioned for a *transport sur lieux* to allow the jury a personal inspection. Fabre opposed the request, saying that a scale model would suffice and that anything else would be burdensome. Couinaud announced that he would rule on the motion after further consideration.[35]

The other nine defendants represented a virtual museum tour around the fringes of anarchism. Crozat de Fleury was charged with attempting to liquidate the bonds from the Thiais robbery and with receiving stolen property. He claimed to have been given the bonds by a friend in Rouen, of whom the police could not locate a trace. As a further defense, he offered his family's good name, his own comfortable situation—"I have cashed dividends while in prison awaiting trial"—and his reputation as a literary man. Poyer, Dettweiller, and Bernard, all accused of burglary, had no defense but denial and Dettweiller's declaration: "When the witnesses have spoken, all will be clear." Deboé and Bellonie were no more successful in justifying their attempt to liquidate the Rue Ordener securities. Deboé rambled confusingly and at length. Bellonie asked the jury to believe that he never looked at the "papers" he was carrying. Their accomplice, Rodriguez, provided one of the few humorous moments during the

35. *La Gazette des Tribunaux*, February 7, 1913; *Le Figaro*, February 7, 1913.

Afterword

trial. Asked about a record of ten previous convictions for minor crimes, he admitted, "My past life is lamentable, and I regret it." He said that he went to Amsterdam with Bellonie for the "sole purpose of earning enough money to open an institute at Lille for the teaching of modern languages, using the English method." Often he disarmingly interjected, "I don't know whether I am explaining myself properly, as I feel timid here." No matter what the verdict of this jury, he was certain to be convicted of counterfeiting in a later trial at Lille.

The last two defendants, Charles Reinert and Jacques Jourdan, were charged with providing illegal assistance to members of the gang. Reinert, from Nancy, was alleged to have sheltered Carouy, Callemin, and Garnier at various times during 1911 and 1912. The primary evidence against him was a deposition from his wife and another woman living in the neighborhood who recognized the men he sneaked into his house. Reinert could only counter, "A woman doesn't have a very solid head and is likely to say many stupid things." Jourdan, of Paris, was accused of selling a pistol to Callemin on March 25, 1912. His defense was that in spite of the wide publicity and the photographs, he had not known Callemin was wanted by the police. Fabre asked the jury to note that Jourdan lived openly with a woman of scandalous past who preached Malthusian doctrines.[36]

On February 8 the court began to hear the 249 witnesses, the most ever subpoenaed for a criminal trial in France. The first three dozen testified about the Rue Ordener robbery, from the theft of the Delaunay to the identification of the motorized bandits as they drove away. Dettweiller's wife admitted that her husband and his friends, particularly Carouy, made preparations to hide the Delaunay several days before it was actually stolen. Other witnesses described the robbery and placed Callemin in the automobile parked near the Société Générale bank. Gaby, whose dignity in spite of debilitating wounds commanded the jury's respect, pointed out Dieudonné as the man who attacked him and recalled seeing the pistol in his left hand. Dieudonné and his avocat, Moro-Giafferi, protested that Gaby was mistaken, that of the gang, only Garnier could shoot left-handed. Couinaud reminded Gaby that the identification might send Dieudonné to his death, but without hesitation he reaffirmed it. The other major witnesses at the bank, Peemans and Tavac, were less categorical but agreed.

Dieudonné's only hope for acquittal lay in establishing a credible

36. *La Gazette des Tribunaux*, February 8–9, 1913; *Le Figaro*, February 8–9, 1913.

alibi, but he was as unlucky with that as with Gaby's memory. His mother, who described her son as "good, honorable, and courageous," and four of his friends from Nancy swore that he was with them there on December 21, 1911, the day of the robbery. But a month before the trial, another of his friends, a certain Blanchet, killed a man, Joseph Bill. Two women, a Mme Sausse and Mlle Joséphine Belcot, told the court that Bill was murdered to prevent him from revealing that Dieudonné's alibi was a hoax. Neither woman had a good reputation, but their effect was to leave Dieudonné without convincing corroboration of his claim not to have been at the Rue Ordener.[37]

During the next four days of the trial, February 10–13, more than one hundred witnesses testified about the crimes at the Place du Havre, Montgéron, and Chantilly, and repeatedly identified Callemin, Monier, Dieudonné, and Soudy. In what was almost a litany, Couinaud asked the witness to designate the defendant he meant, and the witness pointed at one of the four. Once, when Carouy was mistakenly indicated, his avocat, Zévaès, reminded the jury: "See how the human memory can be fallible. It has already been established that Carouy was not at Montgéron." Before this absolutely damning evidence, Callemin reacted with resignation. Monier denounced it as "galimatias" (nonsense). Dieudonné pounded the rail of the defendants' box in frustration. After being identified eight times as the "homme de carabine" at Chantilly, Soudy finally exploded: "It's all the same to me! You may condemn me to death! I wanted to kill myself, but I shall not admit to what is untrue. I was not at Chantilly! I am innocent!" Only two witnesses during these four days broke the pattern. Louise Dieudonné, who was granted immunity from prosecution for betraying Callemin, insisted that the telegram of December 19, 1911, to her husband had nothing to do with the Rue Ordener robbery. As she spoke, she refused to meet Callemin's eyes. Lorulot gave Soudy an unlikely alibi for the Chantilly robbery, and his presence stimulated a furious outburst from Kibaltchiche, who had been silent since his *interrogatoire.* He demanded to know why, if he was on trial for his opinions, Lorulot was not beside him in the defendants' box. They had both edited *L'Anarchie,* and only months apart. "Justice is neither just nor logical. You wish to confound me with men on whom weighs the heavy accusation of murder!"[38]

37. *La Gazette des Tribunaux,* February 9, 1913; *Le Figaro,* February 9, 1913.
38. *La Gazette des Tribunaux,* February 10–14, 1913; *Le Figaro,* February 11–14, 1913.

Afterword

On February 13–14 the four inspecteurs who were with Jouin at Ivry told the court about Gauzy's involvement. Colmar, a stocky man who had recovered from his serious wound, recounted how Gauzy hesitated before admitting that he recognized Monier's photograph and was reluctant to go up the stairs. Asked whether he believed that Gauzy knew Bonnot waited in ambush, Colmar replied bluntly, "Oui, certainement." He did concede that Gauzy could not have warned Bonnot after Jouin arrived: "Cela était impossible." Robert, the other inspecteur to go upstairs, also maintained that Gauzy knew of Bonnot's presence: "He could not have been unaware of it. My impression is that he took my chief to his death. I believe that we were led to the slaughter." Sevestre, who was searching the rooms downstairs with Hingand, recalled seeing Gauzy turn pale at the demand to see the second-floor room: "I thought that we were going to find something compromising for him." Would he swear that Gauzy knew Bonnot was above? "I am absolutely convinced of it." Did Gauzy say anything as he ran away? "He told us nothing." Addressing the court, Berthon admitted, "I do not plead the virtue of my client, but for you to condemn him, he must have committed an illegal act." Once more, Gauzy defended his conduct: "I regret more than anyone what happened. I am desolate that M. Jouin's death was due to my imprudence, but I am not guilty of murder. I obeyed the detectives in everything." When Couinaud asked why, then, he ran away after the shooting, Gauzy answered that he simply became frightened. Berthon shrugged, "Some things are inexplicable."

To repair the damage done Gauzy's cause, Berthon raised the issue of mistreatment at the time of arrest. Guichard declared that the circumstances of Jouin's murder had made him so overwrought that he wanted to strike Gauzy, but he had not, in fact, done so. Sensing an opportunity to pose as a martyr, Gauzy told the jury: "M. Guichard not only struck me but left me to be beaten by the crowd. He hit me again at the precinct station and said to me, 'Your shop, it will be sold! Your wife will be forced into prostitution! Your children will beg in the streets!'" Guichard listened to this enumeration of grievances but disdainfully refused any further comment. That arrogance and the series of character witnesses attesting to his high standing in Ivry made Gauzy a considerably more sympathetic defendant, but Berthon understood that the testimony of the inspecteurs would be impossible to overcome unless the jury was taken to see the dark rooms and the isolated staircase at Gauzy's house. Any chance for an acquittal was almost certainly ended when Couinaud ruled against a *transport sur lieux* on the ground that re-creating exactly the conditions of light present at 10:30 A.M. on April 24, 1912, would be impossible.

Late in the afternoon of the same day, February 14, the prosecution presented testimony about the robbery and murders at Thiais. Except for Mme Dragon, who had seen them at Choisy-le-Roi, not in Thiais, the fingerprints taken for the Sûreté by Alphonse Bertillon were the only evidence conclusively linking Carouy and Metge to the crime. Bertillon explained to the jury the process of fingerprint identification and how the police of every country in Western Europe had adopted it. At Thiais the prints had been so clear that there could be no doubt of their belonging to the defendants. Carouy's avocat, Zévaès, taunted Bertillon about his error in the Dreyfus affair but elicited only the scornful reply, "That is the tarte à la crème of a defense counsel who has no serious arguments to advance."[39]

There were two more days of witnesses, more than one hundred of them, and the proceedings turned tedious. A witness would identify one or another of the defendants, who in turn would accuse the witness of lying. Only a single incident provoked vivid interest. Pierre Camboulin, who had been convicted of burglary in 1911, was brought from prison to make damaging allegations against Kibaltchiche. He testified that Carouy's burglars and fences were always around the office of *L'Anarchie* and helped pay the newspaper's bills. When Kibaltchiche and Maîtrejean vigorously disputed him, he admitted that he had never seen either of them actually accept money from the gang, but he added that the office was "a veritable entrepôt" because so many stolen objects passed through it. Some of them were disguised as ream bundles, but if *L'Anarchie* had used that much paper, "it would have printed as many copies as *Le Matin*."

This was testimony from a convicted burglar, but it might well affect the jury. The only mitigation that Kibaltchiche could offer was appearances by two fellow radical journalists in Paris, Pierre Martin and Séverine (Caroline Guebhard). Conspiratorially, Martin confided that for information, anarchist newspapers depended on individuals who often had something to hide, who came and went without bothering to identify themselves. To inspire the trust of these men, Kibaltchiche would surely have ignored what they wore, what they carried, and from where they might have come. Séverine declared that the secrets of a journalist were as sacred as those of a

---

39. *La Gazette des Tribunaux*, February 14–15, 1913; *Le Figaro*, February 14–15, 1913.

Afterword

priest or a physician. Unfortunately for Kibaltchiche, the secrets he had known or chosen to ignore could send him to prison.[40]

By February 18 all of the witnesses had been heard, and Fabre began his réquisitoire, the summation for the prosecution. He argued that anarchism was merely a philosophical facade behind which men did what they wished to a society they despised: "With them, anarchy was a form of refined and perfected banditry, serving as a pavilion for all atrocities. We should have no illusions about this: We are in the presence of vulgar criminals, but ones who constructed an underworld organization without equal. They are the successors to the brigands of legend, even to the Vandals." After this preface he reviewed the major crimes. Callemin and Dieudonné certainly participated in the robbery at the Rue Ordener; witness after witness pointed them out. Dieudonné was an extremely clever criminal who fired his pistol with his left hand because he needed the right to wrest the security pouches from Gaby. His alibis could not be substantiated, and a murder was probably committed to prevent the conspiracy on Dieudonné's behalf from being revealed. As for the monstrous crimes at Thiais, Carouy and Metge were undoubtedly guilty. Despite his unfortunate lapse during the Dreyfus affair, Bertillon's methods were completely reliable. According to the Académie des Sciences, there was only one chance in sixty-four million of duplicate fingerprints.

The next barbaric act was the murder of the policeman at the Place du Havre, Sergent de ville Garnier, "a young man recently married, whose respect for discipline extended to devotion, and the devotion to sacrifice. Such men are the glory of the Paris police and have a right to the gratitude and esteem of all." Later that night the gang attacked the house of a notary whom they believed to be rich but who was also courageous. Callemin's guilt in both of these episodes was certain, because he was in the automobile throughout its journey. As for who was actually the murderer at the Place du Havre, that was an interesting but not critical question. Witnesses testified that the three men carried loaded pistols. In a letter found after his death, Octave Garnier claimed to have killed Sergent de ville Garnier. "But there are responsibilities, solidarities, which are imposed by the fact that all of the bandits associated themselves in this criminal expedition. If Callemin did not fire the fatal shots, it was because

---

40. *La Gazette des Tribunaux*, February 16–19, 1913; *Le Figaro*, February 16, 18–19, 1913.

his companion was quicker than he. Callemin cannot be held less guilty." There could also be no question about the responsibilities in the Montgéron-Chantilly crimes. Soudy, Callemin, and Monier were recognized by many witnesses. At the time of their arrests they carried money from the robbery. Soudy's forehead bore the marks of the too-vigorous alcohol rub. Callemin and Monier had pistols that tests proved were fired in the bank at Chantilly.

The murder of Jouin presented a greater puzzle. The assistant director of the Sûreté had lived for danger. He had carried only a cane to defend himself, and he had "fallen on the field of honor. His death was fine and glorious, and it is with admiration that I salute his memory." Bonnot's end was Jouin's revenge, but there had to be more. Underneath the pose assumed by Gauzy was "an abominable criminal." He gave Bonnot time to prepare himself by delaying the identification of Monier's photograph. He tricked Jouin into relaxing his vigilance by accompanying him up the stairs. "His perfidy thus rendered the ambush possible. Gauzy was not the accomplice of Bonnot but in truth the coauthor of the murder. From a moral point of view, his guilt is the same."

This Bande à Bonnot was a society of criminals drawn from throughout France and Belgium for an association of evil. To a degree all of their crimes were identical: carried out openly against anonymous victims for the enrichment of bandits willing to kill anyone blocking their path. Their appearance was a new chimera facing society, men using the latest products of industry for the purpose of crime. "I have never confronted a more menacing threat," Fabre declared.

He concluded by tracing brief portraits of the seven major defendants. He called Dieudonné a leader, one of the most intelligent of the gang, so important that the Rue Ordener robbery was undertaken only after he could be summoned from Nancy by telegram to participate. Soudy, though young and seriously ill, was so resentful of society that he was willing to strike even the poor—chauffeurs and bank clerks. The Belgian Callemin's intellectual culture was only a costume over a bandit. He had often been heard to speak of murder—he not only spoke but murdered. Carouy, the other Belgian, committed acts at Thiais that were hardly human. He was so bold that he could even ask directions to the house where he would rob and kill. Metge and Monier were men who cared only for theft. Gauzy was a particularly nefarious figure because he lived an apparently regular existence. His house was open to any anarchist need-

Afterword

ing a hiding place. He sheltered Bonnot and led Jouin to his death. This act was "a masterwork that will merit him the admiration of all criminals, but now he must be held accountable to society." Of their own free will, these men embraced a life of crime. "I have vainly scrutinized their souls and their consciences to find anything but the idea of evil." The jury should show no pity, though in Gauzy's case it might consider mitigating conditions in light of his past and his family. Fabre's final words to the jury were the burden of his entire presentation: "This is not the moment to adopt a mistaken optimism. France, the model of civilization and progress, the home of art and industry, must not suffer such bandits. The contagion has to be halted. Thanks to your verdict, many may be spared a tragic death."

Bloque-Laroque, the substitut général, completed the réquisitoire by analyzing the roles played by the other thirteen defendants. He emphasized the guilt of Kibaltchiche and Maîtrejean. They had joined themselves to criminals, and as their part in the underworld, they provided cover to the others through *L'Anarchie*. Poyer, Bernard, and Dettweiller were the gang's burglars; Deboé, Bellonie, Rodriguez, and Crozat de Fleury the fences; Le Clerch and Vuillemin the receivers of stolen goods; Reinert and Jourdan the furnishers of asylum. Facing the defendants' box, he proclaimed: "You have too long escaped a valid repression while terrorizing your fellow citizens. Your hour has come to render an account before justice."[41]

During the next five sessions, the sixteen avocats delivered *plaidoiries*. No one contested the eloquence, but there were few serious arguments. Despite the harsh words of Fabre and Bloque-Laroque, gallantry was likely to lead the twelve jurymen to acquit Maîtrejean, Le Clerch, and Vuillemin. None of the three women had been closely linked to the crimes, and their avocats stressed that each was more involved with cooking and cleaning—in Maîtrejean's case, a flagrant falsehood. The evidence against all of the other defendants except Gauzy, Kibaltchiche, and Dieudonné was conclusive. In consequence the *plaidoiries* for them were entreaties to pardon the "follies" of youth, bombast holding an "unjust" society responsible, and disingenuous efforts to blame the crimes on those gang members already dead, Bonnot, Garnier, and Valet. The jury appeared unmoved. Pleas by Berthon for Gauzy and Charles Le Breton for Kibaltchiche were more substantial. Berthon attacked the illogic of Fabre's calling

---

41. *La Gazette des Tribunaux*, February 19–21, 1913; *Le Figaro*, February 19–21, 1913.

Gauzy the coauthor of Jouin's murder yet telling the jury to consider mitigating conditions for him. There was no concrete evidence that Gauzy knew of Bonnot's presence in the upstairs room, and his return to face probable arrest was a proof of his good character. He was, in fact, guilty only of offering asylum to an individual wanted by the police, but that was indeed how Victor Hugo was saved in 1851! Le Breton asked the jury to take note of how Kibaltchiche worked to make his newspaper a success. It published seven thousand copies of each edition, had two thousand subscribers, and made a profit of at least Fr 980 a month. Kibaltchiche might be a libertine and a theorist of anarchism, but he was not a criminal. "Look at him and recall his words," Le Breton demanded of the jury. "He has a quality that all of the others lack."

The most striking *plaidoirie* came from Moro-Giafferi, who was at the beginning of his great career. He was considered to have more talent than any other avocat of his generation, and he spoke brilliantly. Conceding that five witnesses along the Rue Ordener identified Dieudonné, he reminded the jury that eight others could not. Neither Peemans nor Tavac had been close enough to be certain. Gaby was a legitimate hero, but he had varied in his description of the man who attacked him. First, he believed it to be Garnier; now he claimed it was Dieudonné. Had the other witnesses pointed out Dieudonné to share in the Société Générale reward? Pausing dramatically, he faced the jury and exclaimed, "If I were at the witness bar, I would rather cut off my hand than condemn an innocent man!" Why, he continued, had the prosecution ignored Garnier's confession, especially when he was the only left-handed member of the gang? To condemn Dieudonné would be to commit a judicial error, one in a long line dating back to the hill at Golgotha! At that, the audience broke into sustained applause.[42]

When order was restored, Couinaud asked whether any of the defendants wished to make an additional statement. Callemin began: "The procureur général has said that beneath the skin of a philosopher he sees the sinews of a bandit. It is his kind that created the bandit. . . ." He foundered, threw his hands up, and sat down weeping. His avocat, Boucheron, immediately apologized for him: "He lacks aplomb, but he is the most loyal young man I have ever met." Soudy insisted once more: "You do not have the right to judge me. I

42. *La Gazette des Tribunaux*, February 21–26, 1913; *Le Figaro*, February 21–26, 1913.

am and will remain an anarchist, but I am not a bandit. You may condemn me if you desire, but I am innocent!" As he finished, he lapsed into coughing. Carouy said simply: "I was an honorable man until I became twenty-seven. Since that time, I have made several errors. The jurors will do with me what they will." Metge asked the acquittal of his mistress. Le Clerch cried out that her lover was innocent. Crozat de Fleury demanded back his good name. Vuillemin, sobbing, wanted only to return to her mother. Maîtrejean appealed, "I have two children!" Kibaltchiche, his voice icy to the end, argued again that anarchism was not banditry and told the jury that he expected "not your pity but your justice." No one else spoke. The proceedings had lasted twenty-one sessions, from February 3 to 26, at that time the longest criminal trial in French history.

The jury heard final instructions from Couinaud and at 3:30 P.M. retired to deliberate. The courtroom was cleared, but a crowd of reporters and the merely curious were permitted to remain in the corridors of the Palais de Justice. During the succeeding hours, some of them ordered hard-boiled eggs and champagne. Others spread blankets and slept. The defendants were held in an adjoining room under heavy guard. Soudy shyly passed Platonic love poems to Maîtrejean and blushed as she read them. Callemin announced that he forgave Louise Dieudonné for betraying him and said, "I would give up all of my theories for a woman worth the trouble." Turning suddenly mystical, Metge spent hours on his knees praying. In a corner by himself, Gauzy, whose gray hair had turned nearly white during the weeks of the trial, sat with a handkerchief clutched to his face.[43]

The jury returned at 4:30 A.M. the following morning, February 27. There were verdicts of innocent for the humorous Rodriguez, who still faced charges in Lille, and for the three women, Maîtrejean, Le Clerch, and Vuillemin, who were released. All of the other defendants were found guilty. Couinaud and the two assesseurs prepared the sentences and at 7:30 A.M. reconvened the court. Callemin, Dieudonné, Soudy, and Monier were brought in together to learn that they were condemned to die beneath the guillotine. When the sentence had been pronounced, Callemin asked permission to make a statement. "In regard to those matters that concern me, I have nothing to say, but I have a declaration about Dieudonné," he began. "I affirm to you that he did not attack Gaby. Gaby was mis-

---

43. *La Gazette des Tribunaux*, February 27, 1913; *Le Figaro*, February 27, 1913; Thomas, *La Bande à Bonnot*, 220–22.

taken in his identification. It was Garnier and I who accompanied Bonnot. I shall confirm this in writing. No, Dieudonné was not at the Rue Ordener, and I shall prove it. Gaby never noticed me, never recognized me, even though I was in plain sight. That is how much his testimony is worth!" The remaining defendants were then led in. Unaccountably, the jury distrusted the science of fingerprints and spared Carouy and Metge from the guillotine by finding mitigating conditions in their behalf. They were sentenced to forced labor in French Guiana for life. Deboé was to accompany them for ten years. All of the rest received sentences to prison: six years for Bernard; five years for Poyer, Dettweiller, Crozat de Fleury, and Kibaltchiche; four years for Bellonie; eighteen months for Gauzy and Jourdan; and twelve months for Reinert. By 8:30 A.M., the courtroom was empty again.[44]

Thirty minutes later Carouy was discovered dead in his cell. He had acquired a glove containing crystals of potassium cyanide—the means were never explained. Preferring death to the living hell of Guiana, this time he made certain of swallowing a lethal dose. A letter addressed to his mistress was beside him: "We shall no longer go out into the woods. Our enemy was ourselves. I have had weaknesses, and the knowledge of them makes me sad. My best to those who knew me. Tell them that Carouy was not a coward. To be strong and to die is difficult no matter what."[45]

Kibaltchiche stared wildly at the court as he heard the sentence of five years in prison for having held the wrong opinions and for choosing the wrong associates. Once back in his cell, he wrote a brief note to Maîtrejean: "My dear friend, I rejoice that you are free and that I alone remain to suffer. Everything will be all right. I shall come back. Enjoy the sun, the flowers, fine books, all that we loved together. But I ask of you, beg of you, never, never return to the milieu in which we lived." When he was released from prison in March, 1918, he took the name Victor Serge and became a professional revolutionary. Four months later he participated in the anarchist rebellion at Barcelona. He was next seen in Russia with the Bolsheviks in January, 1919. As a member of Trotsky's entourage, he was purged in 1926 by Stalin. After seven years in the background, he was exiled to Siberia in 1933, but he escaped, going first to France and finally to Mexico in 1941. He died there on November 17, 1947.[46]

44. *La Gazette des Tribunaux*, February 28, 1913; *Le Figaro*, February 28, 1913; Coudon, *Les Bandits tragiques*, 171–89.
45. *Le Figaro*, February 28, 1913; Thomas, *La Bande à Bonnot*, 232–33.
46. Thomas, *La Bande à Bonnot*, 229–31.

Afterword

Rirette Maîtrejean obeyed her lover's injunction and made an honorable life for herself as a small shopkeeper in the southern suburbs of Paris. She died in a rest home on June 15, 1968. Barbe Le Clerch returned to her native Brittany, where the publicity surrounding the Bande à Bonnot trial made her an object of derision. She began to suffer from acute depression and entered the hospital at Laennec in June, 1913. Like the fictional nineteenth-century heroines she could never know in her illiteracy, she soon died of chagrin. Le Clerch's lover, Metge, and Deboé were sent to the forced-labor camps of Guiana, but both fared better than usual. Metge was made one of the cooks at the Cayenne residency, and in 1931 he took advantage of the light supervision to escape. He was found dead two years later in the jungle. Deboé was sent back to France in 1920 and released early for good conduct. He returned to Brussels, married, and assumed his former trade of printing.

The cheerful reprobate Rodriguez was found guilty at Lille of counterfeiting, his eleventh conviction. After serving his sentence of eight years in prison, he surprised his associates and the police by renouncing crime. He became a successful wine merchant and lived until 1973. Gauzy's experience was an ironic counterpoint. He completed his term of eighteen months on July 8, 1914, was welcomed back by his neighbors in Ivry, and opened a new store. About three months later he encountered a certain Mazoyer, a former Sûreté detective turned petty thief. The two men exchanged insults, and Mazoyer shot Gauzy dead with three bullets to the abdomen. Crozat de Fleury, Poyer, Bernard, Dettweiller, Bellonie, Reinert, and Jourdan all served their time in prison. When they passed from under the administration of the penal officials, they disappeared from the records. Likewise, there is no information about Marie Vuillemin after she left the Palais de Justice with her mother.[47]

For the four men condemned to die, the dossier is full. A pioneering criminologist and member of the Société des Prisons, Emile Michon, spent many hours with them during the two months following the trial and wrote about his experience in *Un peu de l'âme des bandits*. When Michon began the study, his goal was to discover the psychological and sociological foundations of crime. Within two weeks he realized that he was drawing a psychological portrait of four criminals, not of crime, and that he would complete the process

---

47. Maîtrejean, "Souvenirs d'anarchie," and "Commissaire Guillaume, ne réveillez pas les morts"; Becker, *La Bande à Bonnot*, 161–89; Thomas, *La Bande à Bonnot*, 224–25.

of rendering them sympathetic. To Michon's stupefaction, Callemin, the best read of the bandits, passed much of his time in daydreams about learning to pilot an airplane or exploring volcanoes. Soudy played card games with his guards and coughed increasingly. Monier performed calisthenics and made a friend of the chaplain. Only Dieudonné appeared depressed. He worried about the future of his son, Jeannot, and prepared a treatise on maternal love for Louise. All four displayed a remarkable tolerance for cold air and, unlike other prisoners, maintained a scrupulous cleanliness. When Michon asked about their beliefs, none of them, not even Callemin, could define clearly what kind of world they had hoped anarchism would bring about. Their answers always returned to the nature of personal relations. For them, friendship was the most important value because it was based on a free choice. Man and woman paired in the same way: They were companions who traversed certain stages of their lives together. It followed naturally that the greatest fear was the loss of friendship or betrayal. Carouy had explained it well at the trial when he spoke of his first suicide attempt. The gist of their anarchism was a utopian society in which everyone was free to act as he pleased. Their understanding was no more profound.[48]

The avocats for the four men condemned to die filed pourvois en cassation, but there was no reason for hope except in Dieudonné's case. On April 9, Callemin testified formally in his cell that Dieudonné was not a participant in the Rue Ordener robbery. There was also Garnier's confession to the attack on Gaby. But because the evidence came from two murderers, one dead and the other under a sentence of death, the Cour de Cassation refused to grant it credence and on April 16 denied all four appeals. The avocats then petitioned the president of the Republic, Raymond Poincaré, to commute the death sentences. Soudy, Monier, and Dieudonné signed the required plea, but Callemin refused, calling the gesture and the wording too humiliating.[49]

After considering the files on April 19, Poincaré reduced Dieudonné's penalty to forced labor for life. He was sent to Saint-Martin de Ré two days later and boarded on a prison ship for Guiana. A tearful Louise watched from the pier. Dieudonné remained in Guiana for fourteen years, trying three times to escape until he finally succeeded in 1927. He made the extraordinarily dangerous trek across

48. Michon, *Un peu de l'âme des bandits*, 33–41, 48–90, 233–67, 277–78; Thomas, *La Bande à Bonnot*, 217–19, 223–25.
49. *La Gazette des Tribunaux*, April 5–19, 1913; *Le Figaro*, April 5–22, 1913.

Afterword

the Brazilian forests and wrote to Louise from Rio de Janeiro. The journalist Albert Londres took up his cause and waged a brilliant press campaign in his favor until the president of the Republic, Gaston Doumergue, granted a pardon. When Dieudonné's ship docked at Le Havre, Louise was waiting for him. Together they opened a furniture shop on the Rue du Faubourg Saint-Antoine.[50]

With a reprieve no longer possible, the condemned men were asked to draw up their wills. Callemin refused. Monier had only a revolver to pass on. Soudy saw an opportunity for jest. He left his skeleton key to the minister of war for opening the door to militarism, his brain to the faculty of medicine, his skull to the museum of anthropology, and his autograph to *L'Anarchie*. At dawn on April 21 they were awakened and warned to prepare themselves to die. Monier refused the traditional glass of rum and then embraced the chaplain with the words, "This is not for the priest but for the friend." He thanked the guards for their care and told them that they would see how a man from the Midi dies—with a smile. Callemin's face was extremely pallid, his mouth deformed by a rictus that had in it bitterness and grief, but his voice was strong and sincere. "At last, I am going to be free." Soudy said to the guards: "Reassure yourselves. I shall be courageous." He trembled but claimed that he was cold and asked for a warm drink. As he took it, he murmured, "What butchery there's going to be!" At the guillotine Soudy was strapped down first. He complained, "I am cold!" as the blade fell. Callemin was taken second, and he called out, "It's a fine thing, the death pangs of a man?" The blade fell again, and Monier's turn came. He saluted everyone, "Farewell to you all, and to society also."[51]

In his memoirs Kibaltchiche wrote of the trial, "This justice was odious to me; it was, in the widest sense, more guilty than the worst crimes."[52] From his perspective this judgment was undoubtedly valid. He considered French society of the Belle Epoque vile and spent almost the whole of his life attempting to undermine and overthrow the bourgeois world of which it was a part. To place trammels on his activity as a professional revolutionary was, to him, "criminal." The ghoulish hordes who gathered to watch the police

---

50. Thomas, *La Bande à Bonnot*, 237–38.
51. *Le Figaro*, April 22, 1913; Michon, *Un peu de l'âme des bandits*, 51–52, 229–32; Thomas, *La Bande à Bonnot*, 234–36; Coudon, *Les Bandits tragiques*, 203–19.
52. Kibaltchiche, *Mémoires d'un révolutionnaire*, 49.

shoot-outs at Choisy-le-Roi and Nogent-sur-Marne or to hear sentences of death pronounced in the cour d'assises were Kibaltchiche's final proof of a decay so pervasive that all had to be swept away and a new beginning made. But societies resist destruction and may be expected to deal severely with dangerous enemies. The language of the prosecution at the trial was harsh. The conduct of Couinaud, the président, was partisan. The retribution taken by the police against Bonnot, Garnier, and Valet was without quarter, and the court was hardly more merciful toward the convicted defendants. The jurors would not absolve Kibaltchiche, Gauzy, and Dieudonné of complicity despite conflicting evidence. One is known by the company one keeps: Those who run with the foxes must anticipate identification as predators.

It is interesting to consider the proposition that the Bande à Bonnot was a forebear of the Baader-Meinhof terrorists. Both committed murder and robbery in the name of ideology, common crimes wrapped in the black flag of anarchism. The members of each were characterized by an intense adolescent rebellion and resentment against society. They deluded themselves into believing that a propaganda by the deed—whatever the deed—was worthy and that by virtue of their status as cognoscenti of the ideal world to come, they should be held blameless for acts committed in the present despicable one. The approximately sixty years separating the two gangs made for differences. The Baader-Meinhof terrorists came almost exclusively from the middle class and were in revolt against an affluent West German society that gave them the leisure to do so, the rebellion of the sated in the name of cultural despair. With the exception of Crozat de Fleury, every one of the Bande à Bonnot was desperately poor. Their resentments had a material base in economic deprivation. But a psychological dimension links the two groups. Penetration to the core of their minds is impossible, but for Callemin, Soudy, Garnier, Kibaltchiche, and perhaps even Bonnot himself, disillusionments in love and life, combined with an utter lack of the realism and maturity that acknowledges the unfairness of things, drove them finally to their crimes. They call forth a certain sympathy because they were young, and tragedies are all the more tragic at twenty.

The Bande à Bonnot's history is a simple and sad tale of wasted lives and infecting doctrines leading to mistakes that could never be put right. Emile Michon quotes a letter that Deboé wrote from prison: "Nothing was more confused than the anarchist circles.

Afterword

Everyone was there, the dreamer and the cynic, the poet and the thief, the philosopher and the police spy, the charlatan and the idler. All were combined into a nonsense sometimes sublime, sometimes pretentious, often stupid. 'Anarchy' lent itself to humanitarian enthusiasms and to clever equivocations. For some, it was a banner courageously brandished against the old world. For others, it was the veil that dissimulated ferocious appetites." Anarchism was only a pretext, but a pretext that provided a rational foundation. Dieudonné understood how, when in April, 1913, under a sentence of death, he wrote to Louise, "I am no longer an anarchist, not because I am afraid, but because I now know that man will not find there the route to progress and a better future."[53]

53. Michon, *Un peu de l'âme des bandits*, 285, 281.

Glossary

Accusé. Defendant before a superior criminal court.

Amende. Fine; reparation.

Anthropométrie. Bertillon's system of physical measurements.

Assesseur. Associate justice at a criminal trial.

Avocat. Barrister.

Avocat général. Solicitor general.

Avoué. Solicitor.

Bagnard. Hard-labor prisoner.

Bagne. Penal dockyard; penal colony.

Barreau. The bar; the order of barristers.

Bâtonnier. President of the order of barristers.

Brigadier. Police sergeant.

Chambre des mises en accusation. Indictment court.

Chef de la Sûreté. Director of the Paris criminal investigation bureau.

Glossary

CLAMEUR PUBLIQUE. Common report of a crime.

COLONIE PÉNITENTIAIRE. Agricultural reform school.

COMMISSAIRE. Police captain.

COMMISSARIAT. Precinct station.

CONDAMNER AVEC SURSIS. Suspended sentence.

CONSEIL DE L'ORDRE. Executive committee and council of discipline for the order of barristers.

CONSEILLER. Associate justice for a court of appeal.

CONTRAVENTION. Minor misdemeanor.

CORRECTIONNALISATION. Trying a felony as a misdemeanor.

COUR CORRECTIONNELLE. Correctional court; lower magistracy court.

COUR D'APPEL. Court of appeal.

COUR D'ASSISES. Superior criminal court.

COUR DE CASSATION. Court of Cassation; court of final appeal.

CRIME. Felony.

CRIME PASSIONNEL. Crime of passion.

CUISINER. To interrogate a suspect roughly.

DÉLÉGATIONS JUDICIAIRES. Detectives assigned to examining magistrates.

DÉLIT. Misdemeanor.

DIRECTEUR DE PRISON. Prison director.

DOUBLAGE. Required residence in a penal colony equal to sentence at hard labor.

EMPRISONNEMENT. Confinement in a departmental prison.

EN FLAGRANT DÉLIT. In the act.

ENTREPRENEUR. Organizer of *entreprise* in a prison.

ENTREPRISE. Organization of prison work under private control.

ÉTUDE. Law office.

Glossary

FILLE PUBLIQUE INSOUMISE. Unregistered prostitute.

FILLE PUBLIQUE SOUMISE. Registered prostitute.

FLIC. "Cop."

FOURNISSEUR. Supplier of food, etc., to a prison.

GARDIEN. Warder.

GARDIEN-CHEF. Chief warder.

HONORAIRES. Barrister's fee.

HUISSIER. Bailiff.

INCULPÉ. Suspect in a felony case.

INDICATEUR. Informant; police spy.

INFORMATION. Judicial investigation.

INSPECTEUR. Police inspector.

INSPECTEUR PRINCIPAL. Principal police inspector.

INSTRUCTION. Judicial investigation of a felony.

INTERROGATOIRE. Direct examination of the defendant.

JUGE. Judge of a lower tribunal.

JUGE DE PAIX. Justice of the peace.

JUGE D'INSTRUCTION. Examining magistrate.

JURY DE JUGEMENT. Trial jury.

LICENCE ÈS DROIT. Law degree.

LIEUTENANT CRIMINEL. Examining magistrate of the ancien régime.

MAGISTRATURE ASSISE. The bench; judges.

MAGISTRATURE DEBOUT. The prosecution; prosecutors.

MAISON CENTRALE. State prison.

MAISON CLOSE. Brothel.

MAISON DE CORRECTION. Departmental prison.

MAISON DE RENDEZ-VOUS. Apartment or rooms for prostitution.

MAISON DE TOLÉRANCE. Brothel.

Glossary

Mandat d'amener. Arrest warrant.

Mandat d'arrêt. Fugitive arrest warrant.

Mandat de comparution. Summons.

Mandat de dépôt. Confinement warrant.

Maréchaussée. Mounted constabulary of the ancien régime.

Mouchard. Police spy; informant.

Mouche. Police spy; informant.

Notaire. Notary.

Observateur. Informant; police spy.

Officier de la paix. Police lieutenant.

Ordonnance de non-lieu. Decree dismissing charges.

Ordonnance de renvoi. Decree binding the defendant for criminal trial.

Ordre des avocats. Order of barristers.

Palais de Justice. Building containing courtrooms and the offices of magistrates and the police.

Parquet. Direction of prosecutions.

Partie civile. Civil litigant in a criminal trial.

Passage à tabac. Police brutalities toward a suspect.

Pécule. Required savings account of a prisoner.

Peine de mort. Death penalty.

Place Beauvau. Location of the Ministry of the Interior.

Place Vendôme. Location of the Ministry of Justice.

Plaider. To make oral arguments.

Plaidoirie. Summation for the defense.

Police des moeurs. Vice squad.

Police d'état. National police.

Police judiciaire. "Judicial police"; criminal investigation bureau.

Glossary

POLICE MOBILE.   Mobile brigades of the national criminal investigation bureau.

POLICE MUNICIPALE.   Units charged with order and administration.

POLICE SPÉCIALE.   Special duty members of the national criminal investigation bureau.

POSTULER ET CONCLURE.   To prepare and file written briefs.

POURVOI EN CASSATION.   Petition for reversal on the basis of procedure.

POURVOI EN REVISION.   Petition for reversal on the basis of new evidence.

PREMIER PRÉSIDENT.   Chief justice for a court of appeal.

PRÉSIDENT.   Chief judge for a lower tribunal.

PRÉSIDENT DE CHAMBRE.   Presiding justice for a chamber of a court of appeal.

PRÉSIDENT DE LA COUR D'ASSISES.   Presiding justice at a criminal trial.

PRÉVENU.   Suspect indicted by the chambre des mises en accusation.

PROCUREUR.   Solicitor of the ancien régime.

PROCUREUR DE LA RÉPUBLIQUE.   District attorney; public prosecutor.

PROCUREUR GÉNÉRAL.   Attorney general of a judicial district.

QUAI DES ORFÈVRES.   Headquarters of the Paris criminal investigation bureau.

QUESTION PRÉPARATOIRE.   Torture to elicit a confession.

RÉCLUSION.   Confinement in a state prison.

RÉCOLEMENT.   Verification of depositions.

RÉGIE.   Organization of prison work under state control.

RÉLÉGATION.   Transportation of habitual criminals.

RÉQUISITOIRE.   Summation for the prosecution.

RESSORT.   Judicial district.

Glossary

Rue des Saussaies. Headquarters of the national criminal investigation bureau.

Sans discernement. Without capacity to understand the consequences.

Sellette. Hard wooden bench on which the defendant knelt during a criminal trial of the ancien régime.

Sergent de ville. Police patrolman.

Serment. Oath taken by the defendant under the ancien régime.

Sous-brigadier. Police corporal.

Sous-chef de la Sûreté. Assistant director of the Paris criminal investigation bureau.

Stage. Clerkship.

Stagiaire. Law clerk.

Substitut. Assistant district attorney.

Substitut général. Assistant attorney general.

Sûreté. Paris criminal investigation bureau.

Sûreté Générale; Sûreté Nationale. National criminal investigation bureau.

Tableau d'avocats. Accredited barristers.

Travaux forcés. Confinement at hard labor.

Tribunal de police correctionnelle. Police court.

Tribunal de première instance. Lower tribunal; district court.

Vice-président. Presiding judge for a chamber of the Tribunal de la Seine.

Bibliography

I. Unpublished Government Documents

Archives Nationales, Paris

Series BB 6 I, Dossiers de mouvement des magistrats, Premiers Cours et Tribunaux, An VIII–1925.

524^4 Personnel de la magistrature, 1864–1899, Cour de Cassation et cours d'appel.

524^5 Personnel de la magistrature, 1899–1914, Cour de Cassation et cours d'appel.

Series BB 6 II, Dossiers personnels de magistrats, 1842–1942.

1–611 Abadie–Zoller.
616 Alacchi–Albrecht.
620 Ancelin–André.
621 André–Angeli.
650 Baudel–Bauer.
679 Bletry–Blondel.
690 Bonnefond–Bonnin.
695 Bottin–Boucly.
850 Fabre–Facdouel.
1020 Lescot–Lescure.
1025 Leydet–Liegeois.
1083 Mondot–Monier.
1092 Mouron–Muller.

1256 Trinquet–Trouche.
1267 Valès–Vallet.
Series BB 18, Correspondance de procureurs généraux avec la garde des sceaux (division criminelle).
1796–2529 (1871–1913).
Series F 7, Police générale.
12094–12097 Anarchistes.
13053–13068 Anarchistes.
Archives de la Préfecture de Police, Paris
Series B A.
81–85 Crimes.
497 Faits divers.
1165 Macé.
1612 Crimes.
Series E A.
66 Kuehn.
85 Affaire Stavisky.
88 Claude, Cochefert.
89 Goron, Guichard, Hamard, Jacob, Macé, Meyer.
90 Taylor.
141 Bande à Bonnot.
181 Meyer.
Unclassified.
26169 Jacob.
31900 Macé.
42472 Goron.
47940 Cochefert.
56248 Hamard.
65450 Ducrocq.
69513 Lacambre.
74408 Benoist.
75067 Guichard.
82932 Meyer.
Budget, Ville de Paris, Préfecture de Police, 1870–1940.
Archives du Ministère des Finances, Paris
Budget, Ministère de l'Intérieur, Sûreté Générale, 1860–1934.
Budget, Ministère de l'Intérieur, Sûreté Nationale, 1935–1940.
Ministère de la Justice, Paris.
Compte général de l'administration de la justice criminelle, 1825–1940.

Bibliography

II. Government Publications

Almanach National, 1800–1919.
Journal Officiel, Lois et Décrets, 1870–1940.
Journal Officiel, Chambre des Députés, Débats parlementaires, 1876–1940.
Journal Officiel, Chambre des Députés, Documents parlementaires, 1876–1940.
Journal Officiel, Sénat, Débats parlementaires, 1876–1940.
Journal Officiel, Sénat, Documents parlementaires, 1876–1940.

III. Newspapers

La Croix, 1911–1913.
L'Excelsior, 1911–1913.
Le Figaro, 1850–1940.
Le Gaulois, 1911–1913.
La Gazette des Tribunaux, Journal de Jurisprudence et des Débats judiciaires, 1850–1940.
L'Illustration de l'époque, 1911–1913.
L'Intransigeant, 1911–1913.
Le Journal, 1911–1913.
Le Libertaire, 1912–1913.
Le Matin, 1911–1913.

IV. Books, Articles, and Dissertations

Abadie, G. *L'Avocat devant le juge d'instruction*. Gaillac, 1898.
Abbiateci, André, et al. *Crimes et criminalité en France sous l'Ancien Régime, 17e et 18e siècles*. Cahiers des Annales, XXXIII. Paris, 1971.
Abbo, Albert. *Les Crimes des foules*. Menton, 1910.
Acollas, Emile. *Philosophie de la science politique*. Paris, 1877.
Adam, Georges. "La Bande à Bonnot." In *Le Roman vrai de la Troisième République: Avant 14, Fin de la Belle Epoque*, edited by Gilbert Guilleminault. Paris, 1957.
Alauzet, Isidore. *Essai sur les peines et le système pénitentiaire*. 2nd ed. Paris, 1863.
Albanel, Louis. *Le Crime dans la famille*. Paris, 1900.
Alcindor, Emile. *Questions diverses d'administration pénitentiaire*. Montpellier, 1909.
Allard, Paul. *L'Anarchie de la police*. Paris, 1934.

Allou, Roger, and Charles Chenu. *Barreau de Paris: Grands avocats du siècle*. Paris, 1894.
Améline, Léon. *Ce qu'il faut connaître de la police et de ses mystères*. Paris, 1926.
Ammar, Catherine. *La Tête qui roule*. Paris, 1951.
Ancel, Marc. *La Défense sociale nouvelle*. 2nd ed. Paris, 1971.
Anchel, Robert. *Crimes et châtiments au XVIIIe siècle*. Paris, 1933.
André, Louis. *La Récidive; théorie d'ensemble et commentaire détaillé*. Paris, 1892.
Andrier, G. *Intervention du défenseur dans l'instruction préparatoire*. Paris, 1903.
Andrieux, Louis. *Souvenirs d'un préfet de police*. 2 vols. Paris, 1885.
Anglade, Eugène. *Etude sur la police*. Paris, 1852.
Appel, Alfred, ed. *The Annotated Lolita*. New York, 1970.
Appert, Benjamin. *Bagnes, prisons et criminels*. 4 vols. Paris, 1836.
Appleton, Jean. *Traité de la profession d'avocat*. Paris, 1928.
Aubert, Georges. *Organisation et méthodes de la police française*. Tours, 1938.
Aujol, Jean-Louis. *Les Mains de Pilate: Adresse à la justice politique*. Paris, 1976.
Autrand, F. *Naissance d'un grand corps de l'Etat: Les Gens du Parlement de Paris, 1345–1454*. Paris, 1981.
Avond, Edouard. *De la vénalité des offices ministériels et de sa suppression*. Paris, 1905.
Avril, Pierre. *La Personalité morale de l'ordre des avocats*. Grenoble, 1902.
Aydalot, Maurice. *Magistrat*. Paris, 1976.
Aymard, Camille. *La Profession du crime*. Paris, 1906.
Ballanche, Pierre-Simon. *La Ville des expiations*. Paris, 1926.
Barrot, Odilon. *De l'organisation judiciaire en France*. Paris, 1871.
Batigne, Jacques. *Un juge récidive*. Paris, 1974.
Baudat, Fernand. *De la réforme de la procédure pénale à l'audience*. Paris, 1910.
Beauchet, Ludovic. *Transportation et colonisation pénale à la Nouvelle Calédonie*. Paris, 1898.
Beaumont, Gustave de, and Alexis de Toqueville. *Du système pénitentiaire aux Etats-Unis, et de son application en France*. Paris, 1833. Translated by Francis Lieber as *On the Penitentiary System in the United States and Its Application in France*. New York, 1970.

Becker, Emile. *La Bande à Bonnot.* Paris, 1968.
Belin, Jean. *Trente ans de Sûreté Nationale.* Paris, 1950.
Bellanger, A. *Les Théories modernes de la criminalité.* La Chapelle-Montligeon, 1905.
Bellonie, David. "Souvenirs et révélations." *Le Journal,* May 2, 1913.
Benjamin, René. *Le Palais et ses gens de justice.* Paris, 1919.
Benoist, André. *Au nom de la loi, ouvrez!* Paris, 1961.
―――. *Les Mystères de la police: Révélations par son ancien directeur.* Paris, 1935.
Bentham, Jeremy. *Panoptique: Mémoire sur un nouveau principe pour construire des maisons d'inspection.* Paris, 1791. Originally published as *Panopticon; or, The Inspection House.* 3 vols. London, 1791.
―――. *Sur le nouvel ordre judiciaire en France.* Paris, 1790.
Bérard des Glajeux, Marie-Anatole. *Souvenirs d'un président d'assises.* 2 vols. Paris, 1892.
Berenger, Alphonse. *De la justice criminelle en France.* Paris, 1818.
―――. *De la répression pénale, de ses formes et de ses effets.* 2 vols. Paris, 1855.
Bergeron, Martial. *La Réforme de la magistrature.* Paris, 1908.
Berjot, Eugène. "Cecilia." Translated by Bethany S. Oberst. *French-American Review,* VI (1982), 103–15.
Berlanstein, Lenard R. *The Barristers of Toulouse in the Eighteenth Century (1740–1793).* Baltimore, 1975.
―――. "Vagrants, Beggars, and Thieves: Delinquent Boys in Mid-Nineteenth-Century Paris." *Journal of Social History,* XII (1979), 531–52.
Bernard, Georges. *Vade-mecum du magistrat en matière criminelle et de l'officier de police judiciaire.* Paris, 1909.
Bernède, Arthur. *Bonnot, Garnier, et Cie.* Paris, 1930.
Beroud, Georges. *Laboratoire de criminologie de Marseille.* Marseille, 1949.
Berry, Georges. *Les Mendiants.* Paris, 1891.
Berthélemy, H. *Les Réformes administratives et judiciaires de 1926.* Paris, 1927.
Berthet, Lucien. *Le Travail dans les prisons.* Grenoble, 1903.
Besson, Antonin. *Le Mythe de la justice.* Paris, 1923.
Bishoff, Marc A. *La Police scientifique.* Paris, 1938.
Bizzard, Léon. *Souvenirs d'un médecin de la Préfecture de Police et des prisons de Paris, 1914–1918.* Paris, 1925.

Bibliography

Bluche, Frédéric. *Les Magistrats du Parlement de Paris au XVIIIe siècle, 1715–1771.* Besançon, 1960.
Bodin, Paul. *La Police moderne.* Paris, 1946.
Bondoux, René. *Les Incohérences de la justice.* Paris, 1946.
Bonger, W. A. *Criminalité et conditions économiques.* Amsterdam, 1905.
Bonneron, Georges. *Notre régime pénitentiaire: Les Prisons de Paris.* Paris, 1898.
Bonnerville de Marsangy, Arnould. *De l'amélioration de la loi criminelle.* 2 vols. Paris, 1855–1864.
Bonzon, Jacques. *Le Crime et l'école.* Paris, 1896.
———. *Des horreurs de la rélégation, des règles et des beautés de la profession de forçat.* Paris, 1896.
Boucard, Robert. *Les Dessous des prisons de femmes.* Paris, 1930.
Bouchardon, Pierre. *Le Magistrat.* Paris, 1926.
———. *Souvenirs.* Paris, 1953.
Boucher, Philippe. *Le Ghetto judiciaire.* Paris, 1978.
Bourcier, Emmanuel. *La Cage aux femmes: Choses vues.* Paris, 1928.
Bourdet-Pleville, Michel. *Des galériens, des forçats, des bagnards.* Paris, 1957.
Boutiron, Georges. *De la responsabilité des avoués.* Paris, 1912.
Bouzat, Pierre, and Jean Pinatel. *Traité de droit pénal et de criminologie.* 3 vols. Paris, 1970.
Brayer, F. *Dictionnaire général de police administrative et judiciaire.* Paris, 1910.
Bredin, Jean-Denis. *L'Affaire.* Paris, 1983. Translated by Jeffrey Mehlman as *The Affair: The Case of Alfred Dreyfus.* New York, 1986.
Bresler, Fenton. *The Mystery of Georges Simenon: A Biography.* London, 1983.
Brissaud, Jacques. *Guide-formulaire de la cour d'assises.* Paris, 1935.
Brissaud, Jacques, and Jean Béchade-Labarthe. *Visages et attitudes en justice.* Paris, 1942.
Brouilhet, Francis. *De la transportation, son organisation actuelle et ses résultats.* Paris, 1899.
Buisson, Henry. *Crimes célèbres, crimes oubliés.* 3 vols. Paris, 1953–1954.
———. *La Police, son histoire.* Vichy, 1949.
Buteau, Henry. *L'Ordre des avocats: Ses rapports avec la magistrature, histoire, législation, jurisprudence.* Paris, 1895.
Buteau, Max. *L'Avocat-roi.* Paris, n.d.

Bibliography

Caillet, J. *Contribution à l'étude de la simulation des troubles mentaux chez les criminels.* Bordeaux, 1908.
Callemin, Raymond. "Notes." *Le Journal,* April 6, 24, 26, 27, 1913.
Cambréal, André. *Guide formulaire de la pratique du droit et de la procédure criminelle.* Paris, 1932.
———. *Le Jury criminel: Comment se forme, délibère, et statue le jury de cour d'assises.* Paris, 1937.
Cameron, Iain A. *Crime and Repression in the Auvergne and the Guyenne, 1720–1790.* New York, 1981.
Canler, Louis. *Les Mémoires de Canler, ancien chef du service de Sûreté.* Paris, 1862.
Cannat, Pierre. *Nos frères, les récidivistes.* Paris, 1942.
———. *La Réforme pénitentiaire.* Paris, 1948.
Carco, Francis. *Les Hommes en cage.* Paris, 1936.
———. *Prisons des femmes.* Paris, 1931.
Carcos, Fernand. *Les Avocates.* Paris, 1934.
Carey, John A. *Judicial Reform in France Before the Revolution of 1789.* Cambridge, Mass., 1981.
Carol, Jean. *Le Bagne.* Paris, 1903.
Casamayor, Louis. *Le Bras séculier: Justice et police.* Paris, 1960.
———. *Les Juges.* Paris, 1956.
———. *La Justice, l'homme, et la liberté.* Grenoble, 1964.
———. *La Police.* Paris, 1973.
———. *Si j'étais juge.* Paris, 1970.
Castan, Nicole. *Justice et répression en Languedoc à l'époque des Lumières.* Paris, 1980.
Castan, Yves. *Honnêteté et relations sociales en Languedoc, 1715–1780.* Paris, 1974.
Cattelain, Philippe. *Mémoires inédits du chef de la Sûreté sous la Commune.* Paris, 1900.
Caullet, Louis. *Des fonctions du procureur de la République et de ses auxiliaires au point de vue de la police judiciaire.* Paris, 1909.
Caullet, Paul. *Cours de police administrative et judiciaire.* Paris, 1928.
Cere, Paul. *Les Populations dangereuses et les misères sociales.* Paris, 1971.
Chadefaux, M. *De la séparation des fonctions d'avocat et d'avoué.* Paris, 1912.
Chaprat, Jean. *La Composition écrite: Aide-mémoire sous forme de plans détaillés, droit pénal et procédure pénale.* 2nd ed. Paris, 1941.

Bibliography

Chardon, Henri. *L'Administration de la France: Les Fonctionnaires du gouvernement, le ministère de la justice*. Paris, 1908.
Charles, Raymond. *La Justice en France*. 4th ed. Paris, 1970.
Charrière, Henri. *Papillon*. Paris, 1969.
Charroppin, Henry. *De la participation du jury à l'application de la peine*. Poitiers, 1909.
Charvin, Robert. *Justice et politique: Évolution de leurs rapports*. Paris, 1968.
Chatelard, Claude. *Crime et criminalité dans l'arrondissement de St.-Etienne au XIXème siècle*. Saint-Etienne, 1981.
Chaulot, Paul, and Jean Susini. *Le Crime en France*. Paris, 1959.
Chauveau, Adolphe, and Faustin Hélie. *Théorie du Code pénal*. 8 vols. Paris, 1872.
Chauveron, Pierre de. *Du pouvoir de contrôle de la cour de cassation sur la qualification criminelle*. Paris, 1908.
Chêne, Christian. *L'Enseignement du droit français en pays de droit écrit (1679–1793)*. Geneva, 1982.
Chenevrier, Charles. *De la Combe aux Fées à Lurs: Souvenirs et révélations*. Paris, 1962.
Chesnais, Jean-Claude. *Les Morts violentes en France depuis 1826*. Paris, 1976.
Chevalier, Louis. *Classes laborieuses et classes dangereuses à Paris pendant la première moitié du XIXe siècle*. Paris, 1958.
Chiappe, Jean. *Paroles d'ordre*. Paris, 1930.
Chresteil, Georges A., ed. *Le Bâtonnier Georges Chresteil, 1878–1969: Notices et éloges*. Paris, 1974.
Clarétie, Georges. *Drames et comédies judiciaires: Chroniques du Palais, 1910–1911*. Paris, 1911–1912.
Cohen, David, and Eric A. Johnson. "French Criminality: Urban-Rural Differences in the Nineteenth Century." *Journal of Interdisciplinary History*, XII (1982), 477–502.
Colombain, René. *La Concurrence pénitentiaire en France*. Paris, 1904.
Commenge, O. *La Prostitution clandestine à Paris*. Paris, 1890.
Comte, Bernard. *Cours de criminologie*. Paris, 1953.
Coquet, James de. *La Justice poursuivant le crime*. Paris, 1977.
Corbin, Alain. *Les Filles de noce: Misère sexuelle et prostitution (19e et 20e siècles)*. Paris, 1978.
Cornateano, Visoiu. *Essai d'une théorie juridique et médico-légale de la préméditation criminelle*. Paris, 1910.

Corre, Armand. *Les Criminels, caractères physiques et psychologiques.* Paris, 1889.
Costa, Jean-Louis. *Liberté, ordre publique, et justice en France.* 3 vols. Paris, 1967.
Coudon, Henri [Victor Méric]. *Les Bandits tragiques.* Paris, 1926.
Courtois, Hélie. *Etude médico-légale des crimes passionnels.* Toulouse, 1910.
Crémieu, Louis. *Traité de la profession d'avocat.* Paris, 1939.
Crouzillac, F. *De la cassation sans renvoi après revision des procès criminels et correctionnels.* Paris, 1910.
Cruppi, Jean. *La Cour d'assises.* Paris, 1898.
Cuche, Paul. *De la possibilité pour l'école classique d'organiser la répression pénale en dehors du libre arbitre.* Grenoble, 1897.
———. *Traité de science et de législation pénitentiaire.* Paris, 1905.
Cudet, François. *Histoire des corps de troupe qui ont été spécialement chargés du service de la ville de Paris.* Paris, 1887.
Dallemagne, J. *Les Théories de la criminalité.* Paris, 1896.
Dally, Eugène. *Remarques sur les alienés et les criminels au point de vue de la responsabilité morale et légale.* Paris, 1864.
Damien, André. *Les Avocats du temps passé.* Versailles, 1973.
Damiron, Charles. *Souvenirs d'un avocat de province.* Lyon, 1949.
Daudet, Léon. *Le Palais de police.* Paris, 1931.
———. *La Police politique: Ses moyens et ses crimes.* Paris, 1934.
David, René, and Henry P. de Vries. *The French Legal System: An Introduction to Civil Law Systems.* New York, 1958.
Davidovitch, André. "Criminalité et répression en France depuis un siècle (1851–1952)." *Revue française de sociologie,* II (January, 1961), 30–49.
Dawson, Philip. "The *Bourgeoisie de Robe* in 1789." *French Historical Studies,* IV (1965), 1–21.
———. *Provincial Magistrates and Revolutionary Politics in France, 1789–1795.* Cambridge, Mass., 1972.
Debierre, A. *Le Crâne des criminelles.* Lyon, 1895.
Debois, E. *Des fonctions du président de la cour d'assises.* Poitiers, 1912.
Defert, Louis. *Code de police.* Paris, 1905.
Dehesdin, Maurice. *Etude sur le recrutement et l'avancement des magistrats.* Paris, 1908.
Deis, Maurice. *De la délégation des actes de l'instruction criminelle et des commissions rogatoires en droit pénal.* Lyon, 1895.

Delassus, Dr. *Les Théories modernes de la criminalité*. Paris, 1899.
Delmas, Albert. *De la rémunération du travail pénitentiaire et du pécule des détenus*. Toulouse, 1935.
Delorme, Roger. *Les Grands crimes sexuels*. Paris, 1969.
———. *Les Grandes énigmes criminelles*. Paris, 1976.
Delsat, Walter. *Le Procès: Comment le présenter au juge*. Thuillies, 1938.
Delvincourt, Augustin. *La Lutte contre la criminalité dans le temps modernes*. Paris, 1897.
Demartial, G. *La Nomination des magistrats*. Paris, 1907.
Demay, Lucien. *De l'attribution des pièces ou objets saisis au cours de procédure criminelle*. Paris, 1909.
Desgroupes, Pierre, and Pierre Dumayet. *En votre âme et conscience*. Paris, 1963.
Desjardins, Albert. *Les Cahiers des Etats Généraux en 1789 et la législation criminelle*. Paris, 1883.
———. *L'Inamovibilité de la magistrature dans l'ancienne France*. Paris, 1890.
———. *Le Juge d'instruction et le ministère publique dans le nouveau code d'instruction criminelle*. Paris, 1883.
———. *La Magistrature élue*. Beauvais, 1882.
Desmaze, Charles. *Le Châtelet de Paris, son organisation*. Paris, 1870.
———. *Le Crime et la débauchée à Paris, le divorce*. Paris, 1881.
———. *Les Criminels et leurs grâces: 1er série*. Paris, 1888.
———. *La Magistrature française: Les Premiers présidents de la Cour de Paris, 1802–1889*. Paris, 1889.
Despine, Prosper. *De la contagion morale*. Marseille, 1870.
———. *Psychologie naturelle: Étude sur les facultés intellectuelles et morales*. 3 vols. Paris, 1868.
Desportes, Fernand. *La Récidive, examen du projet de loi*. Paris, 1883.
———. *La Réforme des prisons*. Paris, 1862.
Desprez, Edouard. *De l'abolition de l'emprisonnement*. Paris, 1868.
Destrem, Jean. *Les Déportations du Consulat et de l'Empire*. Paris, 1885.
Detourbet, Edmond. *La Procédure criminelle au XVIIIe siècle: Histoire de l'ordonnance du 28 août 1670; son influence sur les législations qui l'ont suivie et notamment sur celle qui nous régit actuellement*. Paris, 1881.
Dévèse, Michel. *Cayenne, déportés et bagnards*. Paris, 1965.

Bibliography

Dewald, Jonathan. *The Formation of a Provincial Nobility: The Magistrates of the Parlement of Rouen, 1499–1610.* Princeton, 1980.

Deyon, Pierre. *Le Temps des prisons: Essai sur l'histoire de la délinquance et les origines du système pénitentiaire.* Paris, 1975.

Dhur, Jacques. *Visions de bagne.* Paris, 1925.

Diamant-Berger, Marcel. *Histoire de police.* Toulouse, 1977.

Dieudonné, Eugène. *La Vie des forçats.* Paris, 1930.

Dirand, Georges, and Pierre Joly. *Maître, vous avez la parole.* Paris, 1975.

Donnedieu de Vabres, Henri. *La Justice pénale d'aujourd'hui.* Paris, 1929.

Donovan, James M. "Justice and Sexuality in Victorian Marseille, 1825–1885." *Journal of Social History,* XXI (1987), 229–62.

———. "Justice Unblind: The Juries and the Criminal Classes in France, 1825–1914." *Journal of Social History,* XV (1981), 89–108.

———. "The Uprooting Theory of Crime and the Corsicans of Marseille, 1825–1880." *French Historical Studies,* XIII (1984), 500–28.

Douxchamps, Charles. *De la profession d'avocat et d'avoué.* Brussels, 1904.

Drapkine, Isaac Jacob. *La Stérilisation des criminels, défense sociale.* Paris, 1935.

Dreyfus, Ferdinand. *Un philanthrope d'autrefois: La Rochefoucauld-Liancourt.* Paris, 1903.

Dubief, Fernand. *La Question du vagabondage.* Paris, 1911.

Du Boishamon, Jacques. *Du recrutement de la magistrature.* Rennes, 1902.

Duché, Natacha, and Ariane Gransac. *Prisons de femmes.* Paris, 1982.

Duins, Michel. *Dans les coulisses de la Sûreté Nationale.* Verviers, 1959.

Dumas-Vorzet, F. *La Bande à Bonnot.* Paris, 1930.

Dupaty, Charles. *Mémoire justificatif pour trois hommes condamnés à la roue.* Paris, 1786.

Dupont, Edouard. *La Magistrature élective.* Paris, 1882.

Dupont, Etienne. *La Bastille des mers.* 5th ed. Paris, 1933.

Dupoy, Henri. *La Police des moeurs et la liberté individuelle.* Paris, 1913.

Durand, Claude. *Les Rapports entre les juridictions administratives et judiciaires.* Paris, 1956.

Durand-Barthez, Pascal. *Histoire des structures du ministère de la justice, 1789–1945.* Paris, 1973.
Duval, Maurice. *Religion, superstition, et criminalité.* Paris, 1935.
Duveau, Gaston. *De la protection du titre d'avocat.* Paris, 1913.
Ensor, R. C. K. *Courts and Judges in France, Germany, and England.* Oxford, 1933.
Errera, Roger. *Les Libertés à l'abandon.* Paris, 1973.
Esmein, Adhémar. *Histoire de la procédure criminelle en France, et spécialement de la procédure inquisitoire depuis le XIIIe siècle jusqu'à nos jours.* Paris, 1882. Translated by John Simpson as *A History of Continental Criminal Procedure with Special Reference to France.* Boston, 1913.
Euvrard, F. *Historique de l'institution des commissaires de police, son origine, leurs prérogatives.* Montpellier, 1911.
Fabre, Jules. *Le Barreau de Paris, 1810–1870.* Paris, 1895.
Faralicq, René. *Sur les pas sanglants: Souvenirs vécus.* Paris, 1933.
Farge, Arlette. *Délinquance et criminalité: Le Vol d'aliments à Paris au XVIIIe siècle.* Paris, 1974.
Faucher, Léon. *De la réforme des prisons.* Paris, 1838.
Fauconnet, Paul. *La Responsabilité: Étude de sociologie.* Paris, 1920.
Favard, Jean. *Le Labyrinthe pénitentiaire.* Paris, 1981.
Favre, Jules. *De la réforme judiciaire.* Paris, 1877.
Félix, Maurice. *Le Régime administratif et financier de Paris et du département de la Seine.* 3 vols. Paris, 1957–1958.
Féré, Charles. *Dégénérescence et criminalité: Essai physiologique.* Paris, 1888.
Ferré, Georges. *Bagnards, colons et canaques.* Paris, 1932.
Ferrus, Guillaume. *De l'expatriation pénitentiaire.* Paris, 1853.
———. *De la réforme pénitentiaire en Angleterre et en France.* Paris, 1853.
———. *Des prisonniers, de l'emprisonnement et des prisons.* Paris, 1850.
Field, Andrew. *Nabokov: His Life in Art.* Boston, 1967.
Firmin, Joseph, and François Pascal. *Ce que doit savoir l'agent de l'autorité et toute personne habitant la France.* Paris, 1938.
Fitzsimmons, Michael P. *The Parisian Order of Barristers and the French Revolution.* Cambridge, Mass., 1987.
Fleury, Maurice de. *L'Ame du criminel.* Paris, 1898.
Floriot, René. *Au banc de la défense.* Paris, 1959.

Fosdick, Raymond B. *European Police Systems*. London, 1915.
Foucault, Michel, ed. *Moi, Pierre Rivière, ayant égorgé ma mère, ma soeur, et mon frère . . .* Paris, 1973.
———. *Surveiller et punir: Naissance de la prison*. Paris, 1975. Translated by Alan Sheridan as *Discipline and Punish: The Birth of the Prison*. New York, 1977.
Fouillée, Alfred. *La France au point de vue morale*. Paris, 1900.
Fourchy, Henri. *Observations sur la suspension de l'inamovibilité de la magistrature*. Paris, 1882.
Franck, Adolphe. *Philosophie du droit pénal*. Paris, 1864.
Frémicourt, Charles. *Les Résultats de la loi sur la réforme de l'instruction criminelle (8 décembre 1897)*. Lille, 1904.
Friedman, Lawrence M., and Robert V. Percival. *The Roots of Justice: Crime and Punishment in Alameda County, California, 1870–1910*. Chapel Hill, 1981.
Gaillac, Henri. *Les Maisons de correction, 1830–1945*. Paris, 1971.
Galtier-Boissière, J. *Les Mystères de la police secrete*. Paris, 1936.
Gandon, Jacques. *Le Rôle de la police dans la recherche des preuves des infractions*. Bergerac, 1944.
Garçon, Emile, ed. *Code pénal annoté*. 2 vols. Paris, 1901–1911.
Garçon, Maurice. *L'Avocat et la morale*. Paris, 1963.
———. *Histoire de la justice sous la Troisième République*. 3 vols. Paris, 1957.
———. *Histoires curieuses*. Paris, 1959.
———. *La Justice contemporaine*. Paris, 1933.
———. *Nouvelles histoires curieuses*. Paris, 1964.
———. *Sur les faits divers*. Paris, 1945.
Garnier, Octave. "Lettre à M. Xavier Guichard." *Le Matin*, March 21, 1912.
Garraud, René. *Précis de droit criminel*. Paris, 1881.
———. *Le Problème moderne de la pénalité*. Paris, 1889.
Gaudry, Joachim Antoine Joseph. *Histoire du barreau de Paris depuis son origine jusqu'à 1830*. 2 vols. Paris, 1864.
Gide, André. *Souvenirs de la cour d'assises*. Bourges, 1914.
Girardin, Emile de. *Du droit de punir*. Paris, 1871.
Giuliani, Albert. *L'Adolescence criminelle*. Villefranche, 1908.
Gleizes, Vénuste. *Mémoire sur l'état actuel des bagnes en France*. Paris, 1840.
Gleys, Paul. *De l'organisation du travail dans les prisons et du pécule des détenus*. Toulouse, 1904.

Godfrey, James L. *Revolutionary Justice: A Study of the Organization, Personnel, and Procedures of the Paris Tribunal, 1793–1795.* Chapel Hill, 1951.
Goron, Marie François. *Les Mémoires de M. Goron.* 4 vols. Paris, 1897.
Gorsse, Pierre de. *La Justice égarée par les femmes.* Paris, 1946.
Granier, Camille. *La Femme criminelle.* Paris, 1906.
Grasset, J. *La Responsabilité des criminels.* Paris, 1908.
Grébaut, Roger. *De l'alcoolisme dans ses rapports avec la criminalité.* Paris, 1900.
Greenberg, David F. *Mathematical Criminology.* New Brunswick, N.J., 1979.
Gresset, Maurice. *Gens de justice à Besançon, 1674–1789.* 2 vols. Paris, 1978.
Grierson, Francis D. *La Police judiciaire française.* Paris, 1935.
Grosmolard, J. *La Lutte contre la criminalité juvenile au XIXe siècle.* Lyon, 1907.
Guénée, Bernard. *Tribunaux et gens de justice dans le bailliage de Senlis à la fin du moyen âge (vers 1380–vers 1550).* Paris, 1963.
Guilhermet, Georges. *Comment se font les erreurs judiciaires.* Paris, 1911.
———. *Souvenirs d'un avocat de la Belle Epoque.* Paris, 1952.
———. *Souvenirs et histoires vécues.* Paris, 1956.
Guillaume, Marcel Ludovic. *Trente-sept ans avec la pègre.* Paris, 1938.
Guillot, Adolphe. *Paris qui souffre: Les prisons de Paris et les prisonniers.* Paris, 1889.
Gutton, Jean-Pierre. *La Société et les pauvres: L'Exemple de la généralité de Lyon, 1584–1789.* Paris, 1971.
Guyau, Jean-Marie. *Esquisse d'une morale sans obligation ni sanction.* Paris, 1885.
Guyon, Etienne Félix. *L'Organisation de la police en France.* Paris, 1923.
Halton, Herbert W. *Etude sur la procédure criminelle en Angleterre et en France.* Paris, 1898.
Hamburger, Maurice. *La Défense: Nos grands avocats.* 8th ed. Paris, 1930.
Hamon, Louis. *Police et criminalité: Impressions d'un vieux policier.* Paris, 1900.
Harsin, Jill. *Policing Prostitution in Nineteenth-Century Paris.* Princeton, 1985.

Hélie, Faustin. *Pratique criminelle des cours et tribunaux.* 2nd ed. Paris, 1909.
Herman, Judith Lewis, with Lisa Hirshman. *Father-Daughter Incest.* Cambridge, Mass., 1981.
Hermite de Montmartre [pseud.]. *La Police de Sa Majesté Lépine Ier.* Meulun-Hardicourt, 1908.
Hervé, Léon. *De la nature juridique des offices ministériels.* Paris, 1903.
Hesse, Raymond. *Les Criminels peints par eux-mêmes.* Paris, 1912.
Hibbert, Christopher. *The Roots of Evil: A Social History of Crime and Punishment.* London, 1963.
Holtz, Louis. *Les Crimes passionnels.* Châteauroux, 1904.
Homberg, Théodore. *Etudes sur le vagabondage.* Nouvelle édition. Paris, 1880.
Huchon, Henri. *Quand j'étais au bagne.* Bordeaux, 1933.
Hullin, Frédéric. *Guide du juré: Jury criminel.* Troyes, 1897.
Husson, Jean. *Du rôle de la cour comparé à celui du jury en matière criminelle: Étude juridique et critique.* Paris, 1908.
Ignatieff, Michael. *A Just Measure of Pain: The Penitentiary in the Industrial Revolution, 1750–1850.* New York, 1978.
Imbert, Jean. *La Peine de mort.* Paris, 1972.
———, ed. *Quelques procès criminels des XVIIe et XVIIIe siècles.* Paris, 1964.
Imbert, Jean, and Georges Levasseur. *Le Pouvoir, les juges, et les bourreaux.* Paris, 1972.
Isorni, Jacques. *Les Cas de conscience de l'avocat.* Paris, 1970.
———. *Je suis avocat.* Paris, 1951.
Jacob, Madeleine. *Quarante ans de journalisme.* Paris, 1970.
Jacot, Charles. *L'Anarchie policière, 1891–1894: Mémoire d'un séquestre.* Paris, 1901.
Jeanvrot, Victor. *La Magistrature, l'inamovibilité.* Paris, 1882.
Johnson, Douglas. *France and the Dreyfus Affair.* London, 1966.
Joly, Henri. *Le Combat contre le crime.* Paris, 1892.
———. *Le Crime: Étude sociale.* Paris, 1888.
———. *La France criminelle.* Paris, 1889.
———. *Problèmes de science criminelle.* Paris, 1910.
Jousse, Daniel. *Traité de justice criminelle en France.* 4 vols. Paris, 1771.
Junosza-Zdrojewski, Georges O. *Le Crime et la presse.* Paris, 1943.
Kah, Philippe. *Aux enfers du crime.* Lille, 1930.
Kappenburg, Gerda. *Les Prisons des femmes.* Paris, 1926.

Karr, Alphonse. *Messieurs les assassins*. Paris, 1885.
Kelley, Donald R. *Historians and the Law in Postrevolutionary France*. Princeton, 1984.
Kershaw, Alister. *A History of the Guillotine*. London, 1958.
Kibaltchiche, Victor [Victor Serge]. *Les Coulisses d'une sûreté générale*. Paris, 1925.
———. *Mémoires d'un révolutionnaire, 1901–1941*. Paris, 1941.
Kinberg, Olof. *Les Problèmes fondamentaux de la criminalité*. Paris, 1959.
Kock, Gerald L., ed. *The French Code of Criminal Procedure*. South Hackensack, N.J., 1964.
Koral, Henri. *Essai de théorie générale de la correctionnalisation des crimes*. 2nd ed. Paris, 1919.
Kun, Jean. *Les Principales imperfections du code pénal en matière de crime et délits contre personnes*. Paris, 1933.
Labouret, H. *Des honoraires des avocats*. Lille, 1906.
Labrouche, Jean. *Instruction et criminalité*. Aire-sur-Adour, 1898.
Lacassagne, Alexandre. *Peine de mort et criminalité: L'Accroissement de la criminalité et l'application de la peine capitale*. Paris, 1908.
Laferrière, J. *Le Droit de propriété et le pouvoir de police*. Paris, 1908.
Laffey, John F. "The Problematic Bourgeoisie." *Historical Reflections/Réflexions Historiques*, XI (1984), 153–72.
La Grasserie, Raoul de. *De la justice en France et à l'étranger au XXe siècle*. 3 vols. Paris, 1914.
———. *Des principes sociologiques de la criminologie*. Paris, 1901.
Lallemand, Paul. *Le Recrutement des juges*. Paris, 1936.
Lalou, Jules. *Aperçu sur les motifs de la progression des cas de récidive en matière de criminalité*. Paris, 1870.
———. *De l'emprisonnement pour dettes*. Paris, 1857.
Lanessan, J. L. *La Lutte contre le crime*. Paris, 1910.
Langbein, John H. *Prosecuting Crime in the Renaissance: England, Germany, France*. Cambridge, Mass., 1974.
———. *Torture and the Law of Proof*. Chicago, 1977.
Langlois, Denis. *Le Cachot*. Paris, 1967.
———. *Les Dossiers noirs de la justice française*. Paris, 1977.
Lantier, Jacques [pseud.]. *Le Temps des policiers: Trente ans d'abus*. Paris, 1970.
Larnaude, Ferdinand. "La Séparation des pouvoirs et la justice en France et aux Etats-Unis." *La Revue des Idées*, May 15, 1905, pp. 1–15.

Bibliography

La Rochefoucauld, J.-D. de. *Le Duc de La Rochefoucauld-Liancourt, 1747–1827.* Paris, 1980.
La Rochefoucauld-Liancourt, Duc F.-A.-F. de. *Des prisons de Philadelphia, par un européen.* 4th ed. Paris, 1819.
Larrieu, Louis. *Service spécial de la gendarmerie, ses origines, son évolution, ses principes essentiels.* Paris, 1922.
Laurent, Emile. *L'Anthropologie criminelle et les nouvelles théories du crime.* 2nd ed. Paris, 1893.
Laurent, Jean Charles. *Principes de droit judiciaire français.* Paris, 1962.
Lauriot, André. *La Police à Paris et en province.* Paris, 1924.
Leauté, Jacques. *Criminologie et science pénitentiaire.* Paris, 1972.
———. *Droit pénal et procédure pénale.* Paris, 1965.
———. *Notre violence.* Paris, 1977.
Le Boucher, I. *Ce qu'il faut connaître du bagne.* Paris, 1930.
Le Clère, Marcel. *Histoire de la police.* Paris, 1964.
———. *La Vie quotidienne dans les bagnes, 1748–1953.* Paris, 1973.
Ledos, Eugène C. F. *Les Criminels et la criminalité.* Paris, 1908.
Le Favre, Georges. *Bagnards et chercheurs d'or.* Paris, 1925.
Légée, Georges. *La Loi du 30 août 1883 sur la magistrature.* Paris, 1904.
Lemaître, Prosper. *Criminalité, répression, du sens moral des criminels, prison cellulaire, exposition publique.* Limoges, 1900.
Lemoine, Léon. *De la révision des procès criminels et correctionnels.* Paris, 1896.
Lépine, Louis. *Mes souvenirs.* Paris, 1929.
———, ed. *Répertoire de police administrative et judiciaire.* 2 vols. Paris, 1896–1899.
Lepointe, Gabriel. *Histoire des institutions de droit public français au 19e siècle, 1789–1914.* Paris, 1953.
Le Poittevin, Gustave. *Dictionnaire-formulaire des parquets et de la police judiciaire.* 4th ed. Paris, 1912.
Leques, L. *Histoire de la gendarmerie.* Paris, 1874.
Leroy, Gaston. *Le Juge unique et la réforme de notre organisation judiciaire.* Paris, 1907.
Letellier, Albert, and R. Dubled. *Les Prisons des femmes.* Paris, 1923.
Letourneau, Charles. *L'Evolution de la morale.* Paris, 1887.
Leveillé, Jules. *La Guyane et la question pénitentiaire coloniale.* Paris, 1886.
Levilain, Marcel. "Histoire de l'organisation des services actifs de la police parisienne." 2 vols. Thèse droit, Université de Paris, 1970.

Lévy, Raoul. *Examen médico-légal d'un jeune criminel de vingt ans poursuivi pour viol et homicide volontaire.* Auxerre, 1907.

Lévy, Thierry. *Le Désir de punir: Essai sur le privilège pénal.* Paris, 1979.

Liard-Courtois, ex-forçat. *Souvenirs du bagne.* Paris, 1903.

Liègeois, Gaston. *Le Régime cellulaire en France et à l'étranger.* Nancy, 1900.

Linedecker, Clifford L. *Children in Chains.* New York, 1981.

Liouville, Félix, ed. *Abrégé des règles de la profession d'avocat.* Paris, 1883.

Locard, Edmond. *La Criminalistique à l'usage des gens du monde et des auteurs de romans policiers.* Lyon, 1937.

———. *La Défense contre le crime.* Paris, 1951.

———. *L'Enquête criminelle et les méthodes scientifiques.* Paris, 1920.

———. *Laboratoire de police et instruction criminelle.* Lyon, 1913.

———. *Traité de criminalistique.* 4 vols. Lyon, 1931–1933.

Loewel, Robert. *Condamnés: Secrets de prisons.* Paris, 1930.

Lombroso, Cesare. *L'Anthropologie criminelle.* 3rd ed. Paris, 1896.

London, Géo. *Aux portes du bagne.* Paris, 1930.

———. *Les Grands procès, 1927–1939.* 13 vols. Paris, 1928–1940.

Lucas, Charles. *De l'état anormal de la répression en matière de crimes capitaux.* Paris, 1885.

———. *De la réforme des prisons ou de la théorie de l'emprisonnement.* 3 vols. Paris, 1836–1838.

———. *Du système pénal et du système répressif en général, de la peine de mort en particulier.* Paris, 1827.

———. *Du système pénitentiaire en Europe et aux Etats-Unis.* 3 vols. Paris, 1828–1830.

Macé, Gustave. *La Police parisienne, aventuriers de génie.* Paris, 1884.

———. *La Police parisienne: Crimes impunis.* Paris, 1897.

———. *La Police parisienne: Femmes criminelles.* Paris, 1904.

Machelon, Jean-Pierre. *La République contre les libertés? Les Restrictions aux libertés publiques de 1879 à 1914.* Cahiers de la fondation nationale des sciences politiques, CCV. Paris, 1976.

McLaren, Angus. *Sexuality and Social Order: The Debate over the Fertility of Women and Workers in France, 1770–1920.* New York, 1983.

Maestro, Marcello T. *Voltaire and Beccaria as Reformers of Criminal Law.* New York, 1942.

Bibliography

Magnol, Joseph. *De l'administration pénitentiaire dans ses rapports avec l'autorité judiciaire et de son rattachement au ministère de la justice.* Toulouse, 1900.

Maîtrejean, Claire ("Rirette"). "Commissaire Guillaume, ne réveillez pas les morts." *Confidences*, March 11, 18, 1937.

———. "Souvenirs d'anarchie." *Le Matin*, August 18–26, 1913.

Maitron, Jean. *Histoire du mouvement anarchiste en France, 1880–1914.* 2nd ed. Paris, 1955.

Malepeyre, F. L. *La Magistrature en France et projets de réforme.* Paris, 1900.

Manévy, Raymond, and Philippe Diolé. *Sous les plis du drapeau noir.* Paris, 1949.

Mannheim, Hermann, ed. *Pioneers of Criminology.* Chicago, 1960.

Marchand, Georges. *Le Recrutement de la magistrature en France.* Paris, 1910.

Marcus, Steven. *The Other Victorians: A Study of Sexuality and Pornography in Mid-Nineteenth-Century England.* London, 1964.

Marcy, Charles. *Les Débuts de l'instruction criminelle.* Paris, 1899.

Marie, Armand, and Raymond Meunier. *Les Vagabonds.* Paris, 1908.

Marie, J. *Eléments de droit pénal et d'instruction criminelle.* Trévoux, 1913.

Marion, Marcel. *Le Brigandage pendant la Révolution.* Paris, 1934.

Maroger, Mireille. *Bagne.* Paris, 1937.

Marquet de Vasselot, Louis. *Ethnographie des prisons.* Paris, 1854.

Marquiset, Jean. *Le Crime.* Paris, 1948.

———. *Le Journal d'un juge.* Paris, 1958.

Martin, Benjamin F. "The Bande à Bonnot: Les Bandits Tragiques." *Laurels* (American Society of the Legion of Honor Magazine), LIII (Fall, 1982), 73–98.

———. *Count Albert de Mun: Paladin of the Third Republic.* Chapel Hill, 1978.

———. "The Courts, the Magistrature, and Promotions in Third Republic France, 1871–1914." *American Historical Review*, LXXXVII (1982), 977–1009.

———. "The Dreyfus Affair and the Corruption of the French Legal System." In *The Dreyfus Affair: Art, Truth, and Justice*, edited by Norman L. Kleeblatt. Berkeley, 1987.

———. *The Hypocrisy of Justice in the Belle Epoque.* Baton Rouge, 1984.

———. "Law and Order in France, 1980 and 1912." *Contemporary French Civilization*, VI (Winter, 1981), 205–12.

———. "The Record of Murders: Blood-Stained Dossiers at the Archives de la Préfecture de Police." *Third Republic/Troisième République*, X (Fall, 1980), 1–17.

———. "Sex, Property, and Crime in the Third Republic: A Statistical Introduction." *Historical Reflections/Réflexions Historiques*, XI (1984), 323–49.

Marty, André. *Dans les prisons de la République.* Paris, 1924.

Masson, Jeffrey Moussaieff. *The Assault on Truth: Freud's Suppression of the Seduction Theory.* New York, 1984.

———. "Freud and the Seduction Theory." *Atlantic*, CCLIII (February, 1984), 33–60.

Massu, Georges Victor. *Souvenirs du commissaire Massu: Aveux, Quai des Orfèvres.* Paris, 1949.

Maxwell, J. *Le Concept social du crime, son évolution.* Paris, 1914.

———. *Le Crime et la société.* Paris, 1909.

———. *Manuel du juré: Éléments de science criminelle et pénale à l'usage de la cour d'assises.* Paris, 1913.

Mazorie, Franck Duvoisin. *La Liberté individuelle dans le procès pénal.* Montpellier, 1903.

Mellor, Alec. *Les Grands problèmes contemporains de l'instruction criminelle.* Paris, 1952.

———. *La Pratique du procès pénal, plaintes et constitutions de partie civile.* Paris, 1959.

Mencken, Henry Lewis. *Prejudices: Third Series.* New York, 1922.

Mendiondou, Jean. *Etude des projets de réforme de la magistrature sous la Troisième République.* Paris, 1912.

Menut, René. *De la responsabilité civile des avoués.* Clermont-Ferrand, 1938.

Mering, Friedrich Everhard von. *Zur Geschichte der Stadt Köln am Rhein, von ihrer Gründung bis zur Gegenwart.* 4 vols. Cologne, 1838–1840.

Meritens, Léon de. *Causeries d'avocat.* Paris, n.d.

Merle, Roger, ed. *Les Mondes du crime: Introduction à la compréhension du fait criminel.* Toulouse, 1968.

Merle, Roger, and André Vitu. *Traité de droit criminel.* Paris, 1967.

Merlet, J. F. Louis. *Au bout du monde: Drames et misères du bagne.* Paris, 1928.

Mesclon, Antoine. *Comment j'ai subi quinze ans de bagne.* Paris, 1924.

Meunier, Georges. *Le Crime: Réquisitoire social.* Paris, 1890.

Mialane, Lucien. *La Criminalité juvenile, ses causes, ses remèdes.* Paris, 1926.
Michaux, Hubert-Ernest. *Etude sur la question des peines.* Paris, 1872.
Michon, Emile. *Un peu de l'âme des bandits.* Paris, 1914.
Millié, Henry. *Le Guide du Palais de Justice.* Paris, 1906.
Miltgen, Edouard. *Le Cerveau des criminels.* Clermont-Ferrand, 1938.
Molènes, Alexandre de. *De l'humanité dans les lois criminelles et de la jurisprudence.* Paris, 1830.
Moncelon, Léon. *Le Bagne et la colonisation pénale en Nouvelle-Calédonie.* Paris, 1886.
Monsieur Jean [pseud.]. *Les Bas-fonds du crime et de la prostitution.* Paris, 1901.
Montarron, Marcel. *Histoire des crimes sexuels.* Paris, 1970.
———. *L'Histoire vraie des brigades mobiles.* Paris, 1976.
———. *Tout ce joli monde: Souvenirs.* Paris, 1965.
Moreau-Christophe, Louis. *De l'état actuel des prisons en France.* Paris, 1837.
———. *De la réforme des prisons en France.* Paris, 1835.
———. *Du problème de la misère et de sa solution chez les peuples anciens et modernes.* 3 vols. Paris, 1851.
Morel, Benedict. *Traité des dégénérescences physiques, intellectuelles et morales de l'espèce humaine.* Paris, 1857.
Morel, Jules. *Etude sur la réforme de la magistrature et de l'organisation judiciaire.* Beauvais, 1882.
Morel, Pierre. *La Police à Paris.* Paris, 1907.
Morillot, André. *La Cour de Cassation: Conseil supérieur de la magistrature.* Toulouse, 1910.
Morizot-Thibault, Charles. *De l'instruction préparatoire.* Paris, 1906.
Mossé, Armand. *Exposé pratique du régime pénitentiaire en France.* Paris, 1927.
———. *Les Prisons et les institutions d'éducation corrective.* Paris, 1939.
———. *Variétés pénitentiaires.* Paris, 1931.
Mouneyrat, Edmond. "La Préfecture de Police." Thèse droit, Université de Paris, 1906.
Mousnier, Roland. *Les Institutions de la France sous la monarchie absolue.* 2 vols. Paris, 1974–1980.

Mousset, Paul. *Albert Londres; ou, L'Aventure du grand reportage.* Paris, 1972.
Nabokov, Vladimir Vladimirovich. *Lolita.* Paris, 1955.
Nadau, Henri. *Des enquêtes officieuses dans l'instruction criminelle.* Trévoux, 1913.
Nadaud, Marcel, and André Fage. *Les Drames passionnels: De Casque d'Or à Mata Hari.* Paris, 1926.
Naud, Albert. *Les défendre tous.* Paris, 1973.
Ninard, Eugène. *De l'inamovibilité de la magistrature et de l'indépendance du magistrat.* Bordeaux, 1884.
Normandeau, A. "Politique de réforme pénitentiaire: Le Cas de la France, 1789–1875." *Revue de science criminelle,* XXI (1970), 605–21.
Nye, Robert A. *Crime, Madness, and Politics in Modern France: The Medical Concept of National Decline.* Princeton, 1984.
———. "Crime in Modern Societies: Some Research Strategies for Historians." *Journal of Social History,* XI (1978), 491–507.
———. "Heredity or Milieu: The Foundations of Modern European Criminological Theory." *Isis,* LXVII (September, 1976), 335–55.
O'Brien, Patricia. "Crime and Punishment as a Historical Problem." *Journal of Social History,* XI (1978), 508–20.
———. "The Kleptomania Diagnosis: Bourgeois Women and Theft in Late Nineteenth-Century France." *Journal of Social History,* XVII (1983), 65–78.
———. *The Promise of Punishment: Prisons in Nineteenth-Century France.* Princeton, 1982.
Odin, Emile. *La Grande prostituée (dossier de la magistrature).* Paris, 1891.
Ollier, Jean. *Convient-il d'abolir la transportation à la Guyane?* Paris, 1932.
Olmi, Achille. *Tables des concordances de la statistique criminelle.* Paris, 1924.
Oudin, Bernard. *Le Crime et l'argent.* Paris, 1975.
Pagnier, Armand. *Du vagabondage et des vagabonds.* Lyon, 1906.
———. *Le Vagabond.* Paris, 1910.
Parias, L.-H. *Justice n'est pas faite.* Paris, 1953.
Pasquin, R. *Organisation de la défense dans l'instruction préparatoire.* Nancy, 1899.
Paulian, Louis. *Paris qui mendie: Mal et remède.* Paris, 1893.
Pauly, Alexandre. *De l'organisation du jury de cour d'assises.* Toulouse, 1901.

Payen, Fernand. *L'Anthologie des avocats français contemporains.* Paris, 1913.

——. *Le Barreau et la langue française.* Paris, 1939.

Payen, Fernand, and Gaston Duveau. *Les Règles de la profession d'avocat et les usages du barreau de Paris.* Paris, 1926.

Payne, Howard C. *The Police State of Louis Napoleon Bonaparte, 1851–1860.* Seattle, 1966.

Payraud, René. *Théorie et pratique: La Procédure criminelle dans les commissariats.* Paris, 1900.

Péan, Charles. *La Salut des parias.* Paris, 1935.

——. *Terre de bagne.* Paris, 1934.

Pearsall, Ronald. *The Worm in the Bud: The World of Victorian Sexuality.* London, 1969.

Pechard, Charles. *Figures et choses de mon temps: Souvenirs d'un commissaire de police.* Paris, 1928.

Pelatant, Léopold. *De l'organisation de la police: Étude historique, théorique, et pratique.* Dijon, 1899.

Perrier, Charles. *L'Affaire Deluze.* Lyon, 1907.

——. *Les Criminels, étude concernant 859 condamnés.* 2 vols. Paris, 1900–1905.

——. *Emprisonnement et criminalité: La Maison centrale de Nîmes, ses organes, ses fonctions, sa vie.* Paris, 1896.

Perrier, G. *La Police municipale, spéciale, et mobile: Historique et organisation.* 2nd ed. Paris, 1920.

Perrot, Michelle. "Délinquance et système pénitentiaire en France au XIXe siècle." *Annales: Economies, Sociétés, Civilisations,* XXX (January–February, 1975), 67–91.

——. "Les Enfants de la Petite-Roquette." *L'Histoire,* C (May, 1987), 30–38.

——, ed. *L'Impossible prison: Recherches sur le système pénitentiaire au XIXe siècle.* Paris, 1980.

Pherdac, Charles. *Les Jeux de l'amour et de la police: Souvenirs d'un commissaire.* Paris, 1908.

Philouze, Paul. *Etude sur l'organisation de nos institutions judiciaires.* Paris, 1882.

Picard, Edmond. *Scènes de la vie judiciaire.* Brussels, 1893.

Picon, Georges. *Pour une politique du crime.* Paris, 1966.

Picot, Georges. *La Magistrature et la démocratie, une épuration radicale.* Paris, 1884.

——. *La Réforme judiciaire en France.* Paris, 1881.

Pimienta, Louis. *Le Secret professionnel de l'avocat.* Paris, 1937.

Bibliography

Pinard, M. O. *Le Barreau au XIXe siècle.* 2 vols. Paris, 1864.
Pinchon, Paul. *Histoire et organisation des services de police en France.* Sens, 1949.
Pisier, Georges. *Les Déportés de la Commune à l'Ile des Pins, 1872–1880.* Paris, 1971.
Pitts, Jesse Richard. "The Bourgeois Family and French Economic Retardation." Ph.D. dissertation, Harvard University, 1958.
Pouyanne, Lydie. *Une prison de femmes.* Montpellier, 1928.
Prévost-Paradol, Lucien-Anatole. *La France nouvelle.* Paris, 1868.
Prins, Adolphe. *La Défense sociale et les transformations du droit pénal.* Brussels, 1910.
Proal, Louis. *Le Crime et la peine.* 3rd ed. Paris, 1899.
———. *La Criminalité féminine.* Paris, 1890.
———. *La Criminalité politique.* Paris, 1895.
Pugh, George W. "Administration of Criminal Justice in France: An Introductory Analysis." *Louisiana Law Review,* XXIII (December, 1962), 1–28.
———. "An Introductory Analysis of Characteristic Aspects of American Criminal Justice with Comparative Comments as to the French System." *Revue de la recherche juridique droit prospectif,* V (1985), 625–49.
Quéant, Olivier. *Le Monde inconnu des prisons.* Paris, 1970.
Raynal, Jean. *Histoire des institutions judiciaires.* Paris, 1964.
Raynaud, Ernest. *La Police des moeurs.* Paris, 1934.
———. *Souvenirs de police, au temps de Félix Faure.* Paris, 1925.
———. *Souvenirs de police, au temps de Ravachol.* Paris, 1923.
———. *Souvenirs de police: La Vie intime des commissariats.* Paris, 1926.
Reinach, Joseph. *Les Récidivistes.* Paris, 1882.
Reiss, R. A. *Contribution à la réorganisation de la police.* Paris, 1914.
Rémy, Henri. *Des principes généraux du Code pénal de 1791.* Paris, 1910.
Rhodes, Henry F. T. *Alphonse Bertillon: Father of Scientific Detection.* London, 1956.
Ribot, Théodule. *Les Maladies de la volonté.* Paris, 1884.
Richard, André. *Le Crime.* Paris, 1961.
Rivière, Louis. *Mendiants et vagabonds.* Paris, 1902.
Robert, Henri. *L'Avocat.* Paris, 1923.
Robert, Philippe, and René Lévy. "Histoire et question pénale." *Revue d'histoire moderne et contemporaine,* XXXII (1985), 481–526.
Robin, Elie. *La Question pénitentiaire.* Paris, 1873.
Rougé, Marcel. *La Sûreté Nationale.* Dijon, 1935.

Rougerie, Jacques. *Procès des Communards.* Paris, 1978.
Rouilleault, Armand. *La Suppression de la transportation.* Lyon, 1938.
Roullet, Ernest. *Des devoirs des magistrats.* Lyon, 1886.
Roulot, André [Lorulot]. *Chez les loups.* Paris, 1922.
Rousse, Edmond. *Avocats et magistrats.* Paris, 1903.
Rousseau, Louis. *Un médecin au bagne.* Paris, 1930.
Rousselet, Marcel. *Les Cas de conscience du magistrat.* Paris, 1967.
———. *Histoire de la justice.* Paris, 1948.
———. *Histoire de la magistrature française, des origines à nos jours.* 2 vols. Paris, 1957.
———. *La Magistrature sous la monarchie de juillet.* Paris, 1937.
Roussenq, Paul. *Vingt-cinq ans au bagne.* Paris, 1934.
Rouvier, Louis. *La Chancellerie et les sceaux de France.* 2nd ed. Marseille, 1950.
Roux, J. A. *Cours de droit pénal et de procédure pénale.* Paris, 1920.
———. *La Défense contre le crime.* Paris, 1922.
Roux, Roger. *Le Travail dans les prisons et en particulier dans les maisons centrales.* Paris, 1902.
Royer, Jean Pierre. *La Société judiciaire depuis le XVIIIe siècle.* Paris, 1979.
Royer, Jean Pierre, et al. *Juges et notables au XIXe siècle.* Paris, 1982.
Rozengart, Gecel. "Le Crime comme produit social et économique." Thèse droit, Université de Paris, 1929.
Ruff, Julius R. *Crime, Justice, and Public Order in Old Regime France: The Sénéchaussées of Libourne and Bazas, 1696–1789.* London, 1984.
Rush, Florence. *The Best Kept Secret: Sexual Abuse of Children.* Englewood Cliffs, N.J., 1980.
Russier, Henry. *Transportation et colonisation pénale: Essai sur l'évolution des préoccupations économiques dans notre système pénitentiaire colonial.* Paris, 1904.
Ryckère, Raymond de. *La Femme en prison et devant la mort.* Lyon, 1898.
———. *La Servante criminelle.* Paris, 1908.
Saillard, Paul. *Le Rôle de l'avocat en matière criminelle.* Paris, 1904.
Saint-Auban, Emile de. *L'Histoire sociale au Palais de Justice.* Paris, 1895.
Salan, Georges. *Trente-trois ans de centrale, 1938–1970.* Paris, 1971.
Saldona, Quintiliano. *La Criminologie nouvelle.* Paris, 1929.
Saleilles, Raymond. *L'Individualisation de la peine: Étude de criminalité sociale.* Paris, 1898.

Sanson, Louis Michel. *Considérations sur la réforme du système pénitentiaire au point de vue criminologique.* Bordeaux, 1924.

Sauvy, Alfred. *Histoire économique de la France entre les deux guerres.* 2 vols. Paris, 1965–1967.

Schadet, B. *Encore nos magistrats, ce qu'ils seront par le suffrage universel.* Paris, 1882.

———. *Nos magistrats, ce qu'ils soient, ce qu'ils doivent être.* Paris, 1882.

Schick, Thomas John. "The Parisian Court of Appeals and its Magistrates, 1848–1914." Ph.D. dissertation, Columbia University, 1977.

Seligman, Edmond. *La Justice en France pendant la Révolution.* 2 vols. Paris, 1901–1913.

Servais, J. J., and J. P. Laurend. *Histoire et dossier de la prostitution.* Paris, n.d.

Sevestre, André. *De la révision des procès criminels et correctionnels et des indemnités à accorder aux victimes d'erreurs judiciaires.* Paris, 1899.

Sheehan, A. V. *Criminal Procedure in Scotland and France: A Comparative Study.* Edinburgh, 1975.

Sice, Eugène. *Dictionnaire d'assises.* Paris, 1938.

Sicot, Marcel. *Servitude et grandeur policières: Quarante ans à la Sûreté.* Paris, 1959.

Sifnès, P. M. *L'Organisation de l'instruction et les garanties du prévenu.* Paris, 1900.

Signorel, Jean. *Le Crime et la défense sociale.* Paris, 1912.

Smedt, Marc de. *Essai de bibliographie médico-légale et criminologique.* Liège, 1953.

Sommer, André Daniel. *Les Rapports de l'acte et de la personne au point de vue médico-légale.* Clermont-Ferrand, 1941.

Sorel, Georges. *La Révolution dreyfusienne.* Paris, 1911.

Spierenburg, Pieter. *The Spectacle of Suffering: Executions and the Evolution of Repression from a Pre-Industrial Metropolis to the European Experience.* Cambridge, England, 1984.

Stead, Philip John. *The Police of France.* New York, 1983.

———. *The Police of Paris.* London, 1957.

———. *Vidocq: A Biography.* London, 1953.

Stefani, Gaston, et al. *Criminologie et science pénitentiaire.* 3rd ed. Paris, 1972.

Szabo, Denis. *Crimes et villes: Étude statistique de la criminalité urbaine et rurale en France et en Belgique.* Paris, 1960.

Bibliography

Tarde, Gabriel de. *La Criminalité comparée.* Paris, 1886.
———. *Etudes pénales et sociales.* Lyon, 1892.
———. *La Philosophie pénale.* Lyon, 1890.
Tasson, L. *Le Guet de Paris.* Paris, 1878.
Terral, Jean. *De la complicité des crimes et délits non-intentionnels.* Toulouse, 1905.
Thamar, Maurice. *Les Peines coloniales et l'expérience guyanaise.* Rodez, 1935.
Thévenin, Raymond. *Criminels, fous, et truands: Grands procès d'assises.* Paris, 1970.
Thibault, Jacques Anatole [Anatole France]. *Crainquebille, Putois, Riquet.* Paris, 1904.
Thomas, Bernard. *La Bande à Bonnot.* Paris, 1968.
Thulié, Henri. *La Lutte contre la dégénérescence et la criminalité.* Paris, 1912.
Tilly, Charles, et al. *The Rebellious Century, 1830–1930.* Cambridge, Mass., 1975.
Tobias, J. J. *Crime and Industrial Society in the Nineteenth Century.* New York, 1967.
Toulemon, André. *Portraits d'avocats.* Paris, 1964.
———. *La Question du jury.* Paris, 1930.
Ulmann, André. *Le Quatrième pouvoir: Police.* Paris, 1935.
Valbel, Horace. *La Police de Sûreté en 1889.* Paris, 1889.
Vallet, G. *Commentaire pratique de la loi des 8–10 décembre 1897.* Paris, 1898.
Vallet, G., and Emmanuel Montagnon. *Supplément au manuel des magistrats du parquet et des officiers de police judiciaire.* Paris, 1899.
Vidal, George Pierre Marie. *Considérations sur l'état actuel de la criminalité en France.* Paris, 1904.
———. *Cours de droit criminel et de science pénitentiaire.* 8th ed. Paris, 1935.
Vidocq, François-Eugène. *Mémoires.* Paris, 1828.
Viguié, P. *Essai sur la nature juridique des crimes punis de peines correctionnelles et des délits punis de peines de simple police en vertu d'excuses légales ou de circonstances atténuantes.* Toulouse, 1914.
Villiod, Eugène. *Comment on nous vole, comment on nous tue.* Paris, 1905. Translated by Russell T. Barnhart as *Crooks, Con Men, and Cheats.* Las Vegas, 1980.
Virmaître, Charles. *Paris police.* Paris, 1889.

Viterbo, Max. *Justice et police.* Paris, 1919.
Vohl, Pierre. *La Police française.* 5th ed. Paris, 1936.
Voulet, Jacques. *Les Prisons.* Paris, 1951.
Watson, David Robin. *Georges Clemenceau: A Political Biography.* London, 1974.
———. Review of Benjamin F. Martin's *The Hypocrisy of Justice in the Belle Epoque. English Historical Review,* CII (1987), 750.
Weber, Eugen. *France, Fin de Siècle.* Cambridge, Mass., 1986.
———. *Peasants into Frenchmen: The Modernization of Rural France, 1870–1914.* Stanford, 1976.
———. Review of Benjamin F. Martin's *The Hypocrisy of Justice in the Belle Epoque. Louisiana History,* XXV (1984), 436–37.
Weinreb, Lloyd. *Denial of Justice: Criminal Process in the United States.* New York, 1977.
Weisberg, D. Kelly. *Children of the Night: A Study of Adolescent Prostitution.* Lexington, Mass., 1985.
Werth, Léon. *Cour d'assises.* Paris, 1932.
Williams, Alan. *The Police of Paris, 1718–1789.* Baton Rouge, 1979.
Williams, Roger L. *Manners and Murders in the World of Louis-Napoleon.* Seattle, 1975.
Wills, Antoinette. *Crime and Punishment in Revolutionary Paris.* Westport, Conn., 1981.
Wolff, Larry. *Postcards from the End of the World: Child Abuse in Freud's Vienna.* New York, 1988.
Woloch, Isser. "The Fall and Resurrection of the Civil Bar, 1789–1820s." *French Historical Studies,* XV (1987), 241–62.
Wright, Gordon. *Between the Guillotine and Liberty: Two Centuries of the Crime Problem in France.* New York, 1983.
Wrigley, E. A., ed. *Nineteenth-Century Society: Essays in the Use of Quantitative Methods for the Study of Social Data.* Cambridge, England, 1972.
Yvernès, Emile. *Le Crime et le criminel devant le jury.* Paris, 1894.
Zehr, Howard. *Crime and the Development of Modern Society: Patterns of Criminality in Nineteenth-Century Germany and France.* Totowa, N.J., 1977.
———. "The Modernization of Crime in Germany and France, 1830–1913." *Journal of Social History,* VIII (1975), 117–41.
Zeldin, Theodore. *France, 1848–1945.* 2 vols. Oxford, 1973–1977.
———. *The French.* New York, 1982.
Zimmer, Lucien. *Un septennat policier.* Paris, 1967.

Index

Académie Française, 252, 253
Accusateur public, 138, 140, 163
Accusé: defined, 2; role in trial, 144–45, 156, 174–86; and attorney, 234, 241, 247, 249, 251–54, 267
Acte d'accusation, 137, 143–44, 178
Aguesseau, Henri François de, 161
Albanel, Jean Marie Louis, 157, 211–13, 232
Albert, Joseph [Libertad], 279–80
Allard, Paul, 122
Amende, 256
Anarchie, L': anarchist newspaper, 279–82; connection to Bande à Bonnot, 288, 298, 301, 304, 306, 309, 315
Andrieux, Louis, 44–45, 63, 76, 80
Anthropométrie. See Bertillon, Alphonse
Arrêt de renvoi, 143–44, 155–56, 178
Assesseurs, 138, 140, 143, 160, 168, 177–78, 211
Assistance judiciaire, 241, 244–46
Assizes court. *See* Cour d'assises

Attorney. *See* Avocat; Avoué; Procureur
Attorney general. See Procureur général
Auburn penitentiary, 260
Avertissement, 242
Avocat: role in trial, 146, 179–81, 184–85; evolution, 234–43; careers, 199, 243–54; and prisons, 263, 267
Avocat général: role in trial, 169, 177, 180, 184; individual magistrates, 152, 209, 214, 216, 217
Avocat-rois, 197, 242, 249–51
Avoué, 234–41, 244, 263. *See also* Procureur

Baader-Meinhof gang, 316
Badouin, Louis, 214–15
Badouin, Manuel Achille, 214–15
Bagnard, 43, 266–67
Bagne, 258, 266–67
Bailliage, 158–60, 162, 164, 167
Balthazard, Victor, 79
Bande á Bonnot, 90, 106, 113, 179, 252, 275–317

353

Index

Bar. *See* Barreau
Barreau, 234, 239, 243, 246, 248
Barrister. *See* Avocat
Barrot, Odilon, 151, 191, 198
Barthou, Louis, 174, 242, 244, 249
Bâtonnier, 240, 243
Bayle, Gaston Edmond, 92
Beaumont, Gustave de, 259–60
Beccaria, Cesare Bonesana di, 135
Belin, Jean: background, 89–90; investigations, 91, 94, 97, 100–101; as example, 106, 271
Bell, Alexander Graham, 49
Bellonie, David, 286, 289, 295, 302, 309, 312–13
Benjamin, René, 125
Benoist, André, 112, 115–17, 119, 121, 271
Bentham, Jeremy, 259
Bérenger, René, 265
Bernard, Jacques, 284, 302, 209, 312–13
Bernard, Maurice, 249–51
Berryer, Nicholas René, 41, 43
Berthoin, Jean, 102
Berthon, André, 302, 305, 309–10
Bertillon, Alphonse: classification system of, 57, 79–81, 92, 110; role in Bande á Bonnot trial, 290, 300, 306–307
Bessat, Charles, 209
Bienvenu-Martin, Jean-Baptiste, 210–11
Blâme, 242
Bloc National, 112, 114, 221
Blondel, Louis Marie Joseph, 216
Bloque-Laroque, Raoul, 297, 309
Boishamon, Jacques Du, 198
Bolo-Pasha, Paul, 91, 212
Bompard, Gabrielle, 70–71, 248
Bonaparte, Louis Napoleon, 47, 48, 55, 196, 242, 248
Bonaparte, Napoleon: Paris Prefecture of Police, 40, 42; criminal procedure and courts, 140–43, 145, 181, 258; magistrates, 165–66; attorneys, 234–41, 248
Bonnefoy-Sibour, Adrien, 99, 121
Bonnet, François Gaston, 213–14

Bonnot, Jules: as criminal, 277–95; referred to by gang members, 299–317
Bonny, Pierre: corrupt actions, 97–98, 101; as example, 117–18, 121–22, 271
Boucard, Emile Henri, 216–17
Boucheron, Georges, 299, 310
Boulanger, Georges, 57, 206
Bourg, Antoine du, 129
Bourgeois, Léon, 63
Briand, Aristide, 208, 210, 242, 249
Brigade de la voie publique, 50, 109
Brigade des moeurs, 41, 76–78, 109
Brigadier, 44–45, 50, 264
Broglie, Albert de, 206
Browermann, José, 253
Brunetière, Ferdinand, 247
Burdet, 278

Cabinet du ministre, 193
Cachot, le, 258
Cadiot, Raoul, 104
Cagoule, 106
Cahiers de doléances, 135–36, 138
Caillaux, Henriette, 157, 177, 210–12, 217, 249–51, 272
Caillaux, Joseph, 106, 157, 210–12, 249–51
Callemin, Raymond: crimes, 280–84, 286–92; trial, 295–99, 303–304, 307–308, 310–12; execution, 313–15
Calmette, Gaston, 157, 210, 217, 250
Cambacérès, Jean Jacques Regis de, 234
Camescasse, Jean, 63
Campinchi, César, 251–52, 297
Canon law, 239
Capital punishment. *See Peine de mort*
Captain. *See* Commissaire
Carouy, Edouard: crimes, 280–85, 292; trial, 295–300, 303–304, 307–308, 311–12; suicide, 312, 314
Cartel des Gauches, 118, 212, 221, 232

Index

Casamayor, Louis, 39–40, 150, 271
Cas prévôtal, 159
Cas royal, 158
Cassagnac, Paul-Julien de, 116
Cassation, 158
Cattauï, Elie, 250
Cavard, René, 83
Cazelles, Emile Honoré, 83
Cazot, Théodore, 196
Chaix d'Est-Ange, Gustave Charles, 248
Chamber of Deputies: police issues, 57, 102–103; criminal procedure, 151–55; magistrates, 196–97; penal code, 264–68; Bande à Bonnot, 291
Chambre des mises en accusation, 143, 151–53, 155–56, 167–68, 178, 184
Chambre du conseil, 143, 155
Charette, Athanase de, 206
Charles X, 241
Chauffeurs, 140
Chautemps, Camille, 99–102, 118–19
Chautemps, Pierre, 99
Chauvin, Jeanne, 242–43
Chef de bureau, 194
Chef de division, 193–94
Chef du cabinet, 193, 212
Chenevrier, Charles, 44, 98–101, 271
Chenu, Charles, 249–51
Cherry Hill penitentiary, 260
Chevalier, Louis, 21, 68
Chiappe, Jean: on informants, 44; as director of the Sûreté Générale and prefect of the Paris Police, 63, 97–102, 116–21; as example, 271
Clameur publique, 126, 133, 141
Claude, Antoine François, 48, 54–56, 112
Clemenceau, Georges, 82, 88–89, 99, 118, 238
Clerk. See Greffier
Cochefert, Armand Constant Théophile, 53–54, 60–61
Cochery, Alphonse, 61
Colbert, Jean Baptiste, 129, 132

Colmar (inspecteur), 293, 305
Colonie pénitentiaire, 265
Commis d'ordre, 194
Commissaire, 41, 44–48, 53–54
Commissaire du pouvoir exécutif, 140–42
Commissaire du roi, 138, 163
Commissariat, 45, 104
Commissions mixtes, 196
Commissions rogatoires, 149
Committee of General Security, 42
Committee of Public Safety, 164–65
Complete proof, 131
Conciergerie prison, 264
Condamner avec sursis, 265
Conseil d'Etat, 238
Conseil de l'ordre, 240–41, 246
Conseiller: ancien régime, 128–31, 137–38, 160; 1789 Revolution, 163–64; structure, 169–71, 194–95, 197, 220–21; Cour de Cassation, 167–69, 185; role in criminal trial, 143, 177–78, 184; individuals, 211, 213–16, 246
Conseil supérieur à la magistrature, 212
Constans, Ernest, 63, 71
Constitution of September, 1791, pp. 139, 164, 199
Constitution of 5 Fructidor III (August 22, 1795), 164–65
Constitution of 16 Thermidor X (August 4, 1802), 165
Contravention, 146–47, 163–66
Corporal. See Sous-brigadier
Correctionnalisation, 4, 33, 175, 185
Correction paternelle, 265
Couinaud, Henry, 297, 299–303, 305–306, 310–11, 316
Counsel. See Defense
Cour correctionnelle, 140, 146–47, 155, 165–67, 174–76
Cour d'appel, 165, 167–69
Cour d'assises: procedures, 143–45, 152, 155–56, 166–69, 177–86; drama and attorneys, 157, 211–12, 234, 246–47, 250–54
Cour de Cassation: origin, 144, 165; hears appeals, 169, 180, 250, 314;

Index

structure, 193, 195–96, 205, 212, 238, 273; procedure, 185–86, 268; pinnacle of promotion, 196, 198, 210, 214–15, 217
Court of the Châtelet, 134
Courts: ecclesiastical, 157–58; municipal, 157; seigniorial, 157; summary, 141–42, 159–60
Crémieux, Adolphe, 175, 198
Crime: statistical patterns analyzed, 1–38; cases from police files, 64–74; judicial treatment of, 129–45; jury verdicts for, 186–90, 252–54
Criminal Code of 1808: effective April, 1810, p. 166; specific provisions, 142–44, 149, 152, 155, 181, 183, 185
Criminality: and sex, 9–12; and age, 12–15; and marital status, 15–21; and residence, 21–23; and education, 23–27; and occupation, 27–33
Criminal procedure: ancien régime, 126–36; 1789 Revolution, 136–40; Napoleonic, 140–45; inquisitorial and adversarial systems compared, 145; procedures of district attorney, 145–48; procedures of juge d'instruction, 148–56
Crozat de Fleury, Henri, 285–86, 295, 302, 309, 311–13, 316
Cruppi, Jean, 182, 211

Dagoury, Louis, 157, 211
Daladier, Edouard, 99–100, 119
Dalimier, Albert, 117
Damiron, Charles, 244, 246
Darlan, Jean Baptiste, 152
Daudet, Léon, 45, 97
Dauphin, Henri Albert, 206
Deboé, Jean, 286, 288, 297, 302, 309, 312–13, 316–17
Defense: right to, 129, 132, 135–38, 140–43, 148, 151–55, 163; role in trial, 127, 129, 135, 144, 169, 175–84
Délit: judicial treatment of, 2, 138–50, 154–56, 162–67, 174–75, 185; and lawyers, 246–47; punishments, 255–56, 261, 264–65
Demange, Edgar, 250–51
Dénonciateur civique, 137–39
Dettweiller, Jean, 283–84, 297, 302–303, 309, 312–13
Dieudonné, Eugène: double of Jean Belin, 90; defense of makes career for Moro-Giafferi, 253; role in Bande à Bonnot, 278–81, 288, 290, 295, 298, 303–304, 307–17
Dieudonné, Louise, 280, 290–92, 304, 311, 314–15, 317
Directeur des affaires civiles, 193, 199, 210, 212, 220–21
Directeur des affaires criminelles, 193, 199, 215, 220–21
Directeur du personnel, 193, 199, 215, 220–21
District attorney. *See* Procureur de la République
Ditte, Henri, 208
Dossiers blancs, 44, 271
Doublage, 257
Doublet, Jacques, 300
Doumergue, Gaston, 100, 102–103, 315
Dragon, Mme (witness), 285, 306
Dreyfus, Alfred, and Dreyfus affair, 60, 118, 186n, 195, 269–70, 273–74, 300, 306–307
Du Buit, Henri, 249–51
Ducrocq, Charles, 112–14
Dufaure, Jules, 151–52, 175, 242, 249, 260
Dupin, André, 248

Ecole supérieure des gardiens, 264
Emprisonnement, 255–56. *See also* Prison
En flagrant délit, 126, 133–34, 141–42, 146, 175
Enquête flagrante, 146–47
Enquête officieuse, 147
Enquête préliminaire, 147
Entrepreneur, 261–62
Entreprise, 261–62

356

Index

Epices, 159, 161, 164
Etude d'avoué, 235, 237–38, 244
Etude de notaire, 235–36, 238
Expéditionnaire, 194
Eyraud, Michel, 70–71, 248

Fabre, Victor: career, 208–10, 213, 214, 232; role in Bande à Bonnot trial, 297–98, 300, 302, 307–309
Faivre, Jacques, 90
Fallières, Armand, 242
Faulds, Henry, 81
Faure, Félix, 153, 214
Favre, Jules, 192, 249
Felony. *See* Crime
Ferry, Jules, 151, 249
Figaro, Le, 157, 210–11, 272
Fille publique, 71–74, 76–78
Flandin, Pierre-Etienne, 104
Foucault, Michel, 255
Fournisseur, 261
France, Anatole. *See* Thibault, Jacques Anatole
Franco-Prussian War, 55, 59
François I, 127, 159–60
Franklin-Bouillon, Henry, 291
French Guiana, 256–57, 265–67, 312–14
Freud, Sigmund, 35
Fuscol, Pascal, 252

Gabrielli, Paul, 99
Gaby, Ernest, 283, 287, 290, 303–304, 307, 311–12, 314
Gages, 159
Galérien, 258
Galton, Francis, 81
Gambetta, Léon, 213, 215, 242, 244, 249
Garçon, Emile, 253
Garçon, Maurice, 251–53
Garde à vue, 146–48
Garde des sceaux. *See* Ministry of Justice
Garde Impériale, 42
Garde Nationale, 42
Garde Républicaine, 42
Gardes Françaises, 42
Gardes Suisses, 42

Gardien, 263–64
Gardien-chef, 264
Garnier, Octave, 90, 275–76, 280–83, 286–91, 295, 298, 303, 307, 309–10, 312, 314, 316
Garnier (sergent de ville), 289, 307
Gatrell, V. A. C., 4–5
Gauzy, Antoine, 292–95, 297, 301–302, 305–306, 308–13, 316
Gayet, Georges, 104
Geay, Antoine François, 100–102
Gendarmerie, 42, 46
Gêne, la, 258
Gérin, Marie Louise, 252
Gilbert, Maurice, 287, 290, 295
Giorgis, Jeanne, 284
Girard, Théodore, 208
Goron, Marie François, 53–54, 58–61, 69–71, 74–75, 81
Gouffé (bailiff), 70–71, 79, 248
Gragnon, Arthur, 63–64, 83
Grand juge, 193
Greffier: role in ancien régime, 128, 130, 132, 160; role with juge d'instruction, 142, 150, 153; role in trial, 178, 183–84
Grévy, Jules, 58, 63, 83, 198, 249
Guebhard, Caroline (Séverine), 306
Guesde, Jules, 280
Guichard, Xavier: career, 106–107, 110–13, 115–17, 119, 121; role in investigation and trial of the Bande à Bonnot, 275–76, 284, 287, 290, 292–95, 305
Guillaume, Marcel, 124
Guillotine, 257–58, 267–68, 315
Guyot-Dessaigne, Jean, 208

Hadden, T. B., 4–5
Haeckel, Ernest, 282
Half-proofs, 131–32
Hamard, Octave Henri Adéodat, 53–54, 60–61, 106–107, 284, 294
Haute cour de la nation, 164
Helly, Ernest, 104
Hennion, Célestin, 89, 96, 107–14, 121
Henri II, 159
Herschel, William, 81

Index

Hingand (inspecteur), 293, 305
Hodot, Georgette, 187, 253
Holmes, Sherlock, 44, 76
Hommes de loi, 234–41, 245
Hubert, Raymond, 251–52
Hudelo, Louis, 121
Hugo, Victor, 310
Humbert, Frédéric and Thérèse, 250–51, 272, 296
Humbert, Gustave, 196
Huissiers, 160, 178

Identité judiciaire, 57, 79–81, 110
Illégalisme, 276, 279, 281–82
Inamovibilité, 159, 166, 195
Inculpé, 149–54, 156, 247
Indicateurs, 44. *See also* Informers; Mouchards
Indictment, 145, 147, 150, 155
Information, 126–27, 130, 133, 136–37
Informers, 41
Inspecteur, 44, 50–51, 54, 264
Inspecteur principal, 44, 50–51, 54
Institut Médico-légal, 71, 79
Instruction, 130–56, 160
Interrogation, 127–32, 136, 153–54
Interrogatoire, 176, 179, 272

Jacob, Etienne Eugéne Lèopold, 53–56, 112
Jaurès, Jean, 280
Jouin, Louis, 287–95, 301–302, 305, 308–10
Jourdan, Jacques, 303, 309, 312–13
Judge: under ancien régime, 126–36, 145, 158–62; requirements for, 163, 192; total of, 164–65, 169–71, 174; irremovability, 165–66; trial procedures, 175–79; direction by ministry, 193–97, 199, 205–206
Judicial duel, 126
Juge: structure, 143, 166–67, 174; individuals, 208–209, 211
Juge d'instruction: investigating crimes, 75–76, 78; preparing indictments, 35, 142–51, 177, 179, 184, 247, 272; legislation affecting, 130, 139, 141–42, 151–56,

164; position in court structure, 165–67; promotion of, 220–21; individuals, 207, 211, 216–17
Juge de paix, 137–41, 162–67, 181
Juge rapporteur, 130, 132, 137
Juge unique, 174
Jurés suppléants, 181–82
Jurés titulaires, 181–82
Juror. *See* Jurés suppléants; Jurés titulaires
Jury, grand. *See* Jury d'accusation
Jury, trial. *See* Jury de jugement
Jury d'accusation, 137–41, 143, 163–64
Jury de jugement: renders verdict in cour d'assises, 4, 145, 152, 156–57, 163, 166, 169, 175, 177–78; legislation affecting, 138–45; procedures, 181–86; examples, 186–90
Justice retenue, 158
Juvenile courts, 265

Kératry, Emile de, 55
Kibaltchiche, Victor: as anarchist, 279–82, 287, 295; tried with Bande à Bonnot, 297–98, 301, 304, 309–12, 315–16
Kuehn, Pierre Marie, 88
Kuhn, Théophile Jean, 53–54, 57–58

Laboratoire de toxicologie, 79
Labori, Fernand, 249–52, 274
Labussière, André, 91–93, 96
Lacambre, Louis, 114–15
Lancelotti, Vincenzo and Michele, 91
Landru, Henri-Désiré, 91, 97, 253
Langéron, Roger, 63–64, 117, 122, 124
Lanterne, La, 58
Lantier, Jacques [pseud.], 39
La Rochefoucauld-Liancourt, François Alexandre Frédéric, 259
Laurent, Emile, 111, 121
Law of November 27, 1790, p. 164
Law of May 10, 1791, p. 164
Law of September 16, 1791, p. 181
Law of September 29, 1791, p. 181

Index

Law of 3 Brumaire II (October 24, 1793), 237
Law of 22 Prairial II (June 10, 1794), 139
Law of 3 Brumaire IV (October 25, 1795), 164
Law of 27 Ventôse VIII (March 18, 1800), 140, 143, 165, 237
Law of 18 Fructidor VIII (September 5, 1800), 237
Law of 7 Pluviôse IX (January 27, 1801), 141
Law of 18 Pluviôse IX (February 7, 1801), 141
Law of 25 Ventôse XI (March 16, 1803), 235
Law of 22 Ventôse XII (March 13, 1804), 240
Law of April 28, 1810, p. 195
Law of November 20, 1822, p. 241
Law of May 2, 1827, p. 181
Law of August 27, 1830, p. 241
Law of March 4, 1831, p. 183
Law of April 28, 1832, p. 183
Law of March 9, 1835, p. 183
Law of September 9, 1835, p. 183
Law of May 13, 1836, p. 183
Law of January 30, 1851, p. 176
Law of March 1, 1852, p. 195
Law of June 10, 1853, p. 183
Law of June 13, 1856, p. 155
Law of July 14, 1865, p. 149, 151
Law of June 19, 1881, p. 181
Law of August 30, 1883, pp. 169, 171, 196–97, 232
Law of June 8, 1895, p. 185
Law of December 8, 1897, pp. 153–56
Law of March 19, 1907, p. 182
Law of July 17, 1908, p. 182
Law of June 20, 1920, p. 243
Law of March 26, 1924, p. 243
Law of July 19, 1934, p. 243
Law of Suspects, 139
Le Breton, Charles, 309–10
Le Clerch, Barbe, 282, 295, 301, 309, 311, 313
Le Dantec, Félix, 281
Légion d'honneur, 123, 184, 188, 198, 212
Lépine, Louis Jean Baptiste: as prefect of police, 63–64, 77, 81, 106–107, 115, 121, 290, 294; comments about police, 40, 45, 90
Le Royer, Philippe, 196
Lescouvé, Adrien Alfred, 215
Lescouvé, Théodore Paul, 215
Lettres d'abolition, 158
Lettres de cachet, 257
Lettres de grâce, 158, 185
Lettres de réduction, 158, 185
Leullier, Robert, 121
Leydet, Félix Pierre Joseph, 207–209, 213, 214, 232
Liabeuf, Constant, 280
Libertad. See Albert, Joseph
Licence ès lois, 192, 239–40, 243, 253
Lieutenant. See Officier de paix
Lieutenant criminel, 127–30, 132–33, 136, 150, 160, 272
Lieutenant general of police, 40–42
Lieutenant particulier, 160
Lit de justice, 135, 137
Locard, Edmond, 44, 92, 96, 99, 100
Londres, Albert, 315
Lorulot. See Roulot, André
Loubet, Emile, 242
Loublié (police detective), 117, 122
Louis XI, 159
Louis XII, 127, 159
Louis XIV, 40, 129, 299
Louis XV, 159, 161–62
Louis XVI, 135, 140, 161–62
Louis Philippe, 241
Lozé, Henry, 63
Lucas, Charles, 260

Macé, Gustave Placide, 49–50, 53–60, 63, 79
Magistrature: relations with police, 124, 271; ancien régime, 127–36, 157–62; post-1789, pp. 136–45, 162–74, 272–74; role in preparing prosecutions, 145–56; role in trials, 174–86; recruitment, 191–92; structure, 192–95; promotion, 195–206; individuals, 206–17
Maguère, Désiré, 252

Index

Maigret, Jules, 49, 121, 271
Maison centrale, 256, 259, 262, 265
Maison close, 77
Maison de correction, 255, 265
Maison de rendez-vouz, 77, 188
Maison de Santé du Gardien de la Paix, 118
Maison de tolérance, 77
Maîtrejean, Claire ("Rirette"): as anarchist, 279–84, 286–87; tried with Bande à Bonnot, 295–98, 306, 309–13
Malvy, Louis, 118
Mandat d'amener, 149, 154
Mandat d'arrêt, 149, 154
Mandat de comparution, 149
Mandat de dépôt, 141, 146, 149, 154
Maréchaussée, 42, 47, 133, 160
Mariani, Lucien, 97, 271
Marin, Louis, 94
Martin, Félix, 152
Martin, Pierre, 306
Martin-Feuillé, Félix, 197
Massu, George Victor, 121
Matin, Le, 290, 298, 306
Maupeou, René Nicolas de, 161
Mazas prison, 74, 260
Mazoyer (former Sûreté detective), 313
Mencken, H. L., 273
Mercier, Auguste, 270
Mering, Friedrich Everhard von, 1, 9
Metge, Marius: crimes, 282–86; trial, 295, 299, 301, 306–308, 311–13
Mettray, 265
Meyer, Charles, 117
Michon, 313, 316–17
Millerand, Alexandre, 242, 244, 249
Ministry of Justice: statistics, 2, 27, 82; judicial power, 46–47; appointment of magistrates, 146, 168–69, 177; reforms, 151, 174; admonitions, 179, 181, 184; bureaucracy, 169, 191–97; promotions, 197–99, 205–11, 213–15, 217, 220, 273; prisons, 194, 261–62
Ministry of the Interior: police powers, 39, 46–47, 63; Sûreté Générale, 82, 85–86; Paris Prefecture, 106, 110, 122; prisons, 194, 261–62; individuals, 56–57, 115, 117, 119
Mise au secret, 149, 151–52
Mise hors de cour, 131, 145
Mitterrand, François, 268
Mona Lisa, 81, 91
Monier, Antoine ("Simentof"): crimes, 286–88, 290–93; trial, 295, 299, 301–302, 304–305, 308–309, 311, 314–15
Monier, Ferdinand, 212, 232
Monis, Ernest, 210
Monitoire, 133
Montesquieu, Charles Louis de Secondat, baron de, 135
Mont Saint-Michel, 259
Morain, Alfred, 121
Moral proof, 144–45
Moreau, Jean Victor, 240, 249
Moreau (murder victim), 284–85
Moro-Giafferi, Vincent de: "lion of the Palais de Justice," 234, 247, 252–53; defends Dieudonné, 297, 303, 310
Mouchards, 44. See also Indicateurs, Informers
Mougeot, Henri, 152
Mouton, Paul Henri, 110, 112–14

Nabokov, Vladimir, 37
Nathan, Pierre, 252
National Assembly: criminal procedure, 139; courts, 162–64, 166; hommes de loi, 235, 237, 240; prisons, 257–58
Naud, Albert, 246–47
Naudin, Armand, 121
New Caledonia, 256, 265–66
Notaire, 133, 235–38, 240, 245, 278, 289
Notary. *See* Notaire
Nourric, Marcel, 252
Nozière, Violette, 123, 189

Oedipus complex, 35
Officier de paix, 45, 53

Officier ministériel, 235–36, 238
Opportunist Republicans, 196–97, 220–21
Ordinance of Blois (1570), 158
Ordinance of Villers-Cotterêts (1539), 127–30, 135, 140, 159–60
Ordinance of 1498, p. 127
Ordinance of 1670, pp. 129–36, 140, 142, 152
Ordioni, Léopold, 252
Ordonnance de non-lieu, 155
Ordonnance de renvoi, 143, 155, 178
Ordres des avocats, 235, 237, 239–46, 248, 252, 254

Palais de Justice, 74, 234, 252, 296, 311, 313
Pansey, Pierre Paul Henrion de, 248
Paris Commune, 49, 55
Paris-Soir, 101
Parlement, 135, 151, 158, 160–65, 167
Parquet: Paris, 75, 98, 206–207, 210, 214–17; prosecutions, 145, 178; structure, 167, 169, 195; procedures, 175–76, 185; promotions, 196–97, 199, 273; individuals, 199, 205–207, 211–12, 214–16
Partie civile: civil suit in criminal trial, 126, 130, 133–34, 147, 184; role in trial, 128, 131, 149, 155, 175–76, 178–81, 185; and juge d'instruction, 149
Patrolman. *See* Sergent de ville
Paul, Charles, 79
Payne, Howard, 46
Pécule, 262
Peemans (witness), 283, 287, 303, 310
Peine de mort, 135, 189–90, 257, 267–68
Penal code, 166, 183, 255–59
Persigny, Jean Gilbert Victor Fialin de, 260
Peruggia, Vincenzo, 81, 91
Pétain, Philippe, 119, 196
Petit, Mme Eugène, 243
Petite-Roquette prison, 260, 265

Pherdac, Charles, 123
Philadelphia system, 259–61
Philosophes, 135–36
Piétri, Joachim, 48
Pinel, Philippe, 258
Place Vendôme. *See* Ministry of Justice
Plaidoirie, 108, 239, 242, 246–49, 253, 309–10
Platano, Joseph, 278
Plus ample information, 131–32, 145
Poe, Edgar Allan, 44
Poincaré, Raymond, 90, 92, 242, 244, 249, 314
Police (Paris): ancien régime, 40–42, 134; methods, 42–45, 64–78, 275–76, 284–88, 290–95; structure, 43–46, 48–53, 106–11; leadership, 53–64, 111–24; and science, 79–81, 300, 306–307. *See also* Police Judiciaire; Police Municipale; Prefecture of Police
Police d'état, 47, 91
Police inspector. *See* Inspecteur
Police Judiciaire: organization, 40–43, 45–46, 49–53, 63–64, 106–10, 121–24; leadership, 42–43, 53–61, 111–17; methods, 43–45, 64–78, 271–72, 275–76, 284–88, 290–95, 299, 306–308; relations with juge d'instruction, 74–76, 145–49, 152–54, 156
Police mobile, 82, 89–91, 105, 107
Police Municipale: organization and structure, 42, 45–46, 61, 63, 110–11, 117, 121; equipment and recruits, 52, 81, 94
Police Nationale, 39
Police spéciale, 86, 88, 91, 93, 95
Police spéciale de la frontière, 88
Police spéciale de l'intérieure, 88
Pollet gang, 82
Popular Front, 221, 232
Pourvoi en cassation, 185, 267
Pourvoi en revision, 185–86
Poyer, Marcel, 284, 302, 309, 312–313
Poyet, Guillaume, 127, 129, 159

Index

Prefecture of Police: organization, 40, 42–49, 82, 87, 104, 106–12; leadership, 53, 61–64, 117–21; methods, 51–61, 71, 73–81, 89–90, 96, 98–100, 121–24
Premier président: cour d'appel, 168, 177, 194, 197–98, 205, 217, 240, 246; Cour de Cassation, 169; présidial, 160; individual, 212
Président: tribunal criminel, 138, 141, 163; tribunal civil, 163; cour d'assises, 143–44, 157, 168, 177–81, 184; présidial, 160; tribunal de premiére instance, 166, 197, 205; cour correctionnelle, 176
Président de chambre: cour d'appel, 168, 177, 217; Cour de Cassation, 169; individuals, 213, 216
Présidial, 159–61, 164
Pressard, Antoine, 99–100, 102
Presumptions, proximate and remote, 131–32
Prévention, 158
Prévenu, 156
Prévôté, 158, 164
Prévôté des maréchaux, 159, 164
Prince, Albert, 100–102, 123
Principal inspector. *See* Inspecteur principal
Prison: as punishment, 255–57; debate over form, 257–61; conditions, 261–65
Procés-verbal, 147, 149–50, 154
Procureur, 236–39
Procureur de la République: preparation of prosecutions, 4, 145–49, 156, 174–75, 185, 273; and juge d'instruction, 35, 147–49, 155–56, 175; and police, 42, 46, 64; and trials, 184, 195; heads parquet for tribunal de premiére instance, 167, 205; individuals, 188–89, 207, 209–10, 212
Procureur du roi, 127–32, 135–36, 141, 160
Procureur général: heads parquet for cour d'appel, 195, 198, 205, 217, 220, 240; prepares prosecution before cour d'assises, 143, 146, 155, 169, 178; heads parquet for Cour de Cassation, 169; individuals, 206, 208–10, 215, 296–97
Procureur impérial, 142–43, 145
Procureur royal, 145
Prosecutor, public. *See* Procureur de la République

Quai des Orfévres, 49–50, 74, 78, 90
Quaker Walnut Street Penitentiary, 259
Question préparatoire, 130, 132, 134–35

Radiation, 242
Radical Republicans, 53, 57–58, 61, 106, 113, 116, 118–19, 196–97, 220–21
Rapport, 147
Raux, Fernand, 121
Raynaud, Ernest, 50–51, 63
Recidivism, 264
Réclusion, 256
Récolement, 127
Rédacteur, 194, 207
Régie, 261–63
Régnier, Marcel, 104, 122
Reinert, Charles, 303, 309, 312–13
Rélégation, 264, 267
Rénault, Léon, 83
Reprise individuelle, 276, 297
Réquisitoire, 180–81, 307–309
Réquisitoire aux fins d'inculpation, 148
Réquisitoire introductif, 147–48
Ressort, 143, 146, 166–68, 195, 198–99, 239–40
Résumé, 181
Revolutionary tribunals, 139, 164–65
Revolution of 1789: jury, 4, 181, 272; criminal procedure, 136–40, 142, 149, 272; courts, 157, 162–65, 174, 199, 237; hommes de loi, 235, 237, 240, 248; prisons, 257–59, 266; ideals, 274
Revolution of 1830, p. 248
Revolution of 1848, pp. 248, 260
Ribot, Alexandre, 154, 242, 244
Robert, Henri, 234, 246–49, 252
Robert (inspecteur), 293, 305

Rochette, Henri, 210, 251
Rodriguez, Léon, 286, 289, 295, 309, 311, 313
Roman law, 126, 235, 239
"Roses, les," 96–97, 271
Roulot, André (Lorulot), 279, 304
Ryssac, Pierre de, 253

Sacco, Nicola, 118, 253
Sadi-Carnot, François, 71
Saint Lazare prison, 77
Sarraut, Albert, 102–104, 122, 124
Sarrien, Jean, 212
Sauret, Marcel, 253
Scheffer, Henri Léon, 81
Sébille, Joseph, 89, 91
Second Empire: police, 47–48, 55, 83, 87, 106; courts, 167, 175, 196; avocats, 241–42, 249; prisons, 260, 266
Second Republic, 55, 181, 241, 266
Secrétaires de la conférence, 244
Secret professionnel, 179–80, 245
Seduction theory, 35
Seguenot, Françoise, 91
Seize mai ministry, 206
Sellers, Peter: and Inspector Clouseau, 271
Sellette, 129, 135, 137
Senate, 165, 196–97, 238
Sénéchaussée, 158–62, 164, 167
Sergeant. *See* Brigadier
Sergent de ville, 42, 45, 47
Serment, 128, 135, 149
Service des garnis, 41, 50, 74, 109
Sevestre (inspecteur), 293, 305
Sévigné, Marie de Rabutin-Chantal de, 134
Sicot, Marcel, 95–96, 106
Simenon, Georges, 44, 49, 121, 271
Simon, Jules, 196
Sorel, Georges, 195
Soudy, André: crimes, 286, 290–92; trial, 295, 297, 299–300, 304, 308, 310–11; execution, 314–16
Sous-brigadier, 45
Stage, 192, 236, 239, 242–44, 246–47
Stavisky, Serge Alexandre ("Sacha"), 98–102, 118–24

Steeg, Théodore, 291
Steinheil, Marguerite, 157, 179, 208, 214, 216, 272, 296
Substitut: role in parquet, 146, 166–67, 174–75, 273; individuals, 209, 211, 214, 216–17
Substitut général: role in parquet, 169; individuals, 209, 213–17
Sûreté. *See* Police Judiciaire
Sûreté Générale: organization, 47–48, 82–83, 86–93, 102–103, 114, 121–22; methods, 90–102, 122–24, 271, 291; under Jean Chiappe, 96–97, 117–19
Sûreté Nationale, 103–106, 122
Suspension, 242
Syveton, Gabriel, 272

Tableau des avocats, 239–40, 242
Tavac (witness), 283, 287, 303, 310
Taylor, Hippolyte Ernest Auguste, 54, 58–59
Theory of proof, 131–32, 160
Thermidoreans, 139, 164–65, 174
Thibault, Jacques Anatole [Anatole France], 271, 293
Thiers, Adolphe, 54–55
Thollon, Judith, 278–79
Thomé, Georges, 99, 102
Thompson, Basil, 101
Thomson, Gaston, 208
Tintant, Henri, 289
Toqueville, Alexis de, 259–60
Torrès, Henry, 252
Torture, 127–29, 133–35, 137, 140, 160
Transportation, 256–57, 264–67
Transport sur lieux, 180, 302, 305
Travaux forcés, 256–58, 265–67
Tribunal civil, 137, 140, 162–63, 165, 167
Tribunal criminel, 138, 140–41, 143, 163, 165–66
Tribunal d'exception, 164
Tribunal de Cassation, 164
Tribunal de Commerce, 167
Tribunal départemental, 174
Tribunal de police correctionnelle, 138, 140, 146, 163, 165–66
Tribunal de première instance:

structure, 140, 145, 148, 165–67, 174, 181, 236; personnel, 143, 168, 171, 177, 197, 273
Trouard-Riolle, Paul Adolphe, 213–14

Ulmann, André, 122–24
Union Sacrée, 221

Valet, René, 90, 275–76, 290–91, 295, 309, 316
Vallé, Ernest, 250
Valles, Bernard Théodore Médéric de, 215–16
Vandenbergh (underworld figure), 286
Vanzetti, Bartolomeo, 118, 253
Vérificateur, 194
Vice-président, 166, 168, 208, 217
Vidocq, François, Eugéne, 43–44, 271

Viviani, René, 152–53, 242, 244, 249
Voltaire, 135
Vuillemin, Marie (Schoofs), 275, 287, 290, 301, 309, 311, 313

Waldeck-Rousseau, René, 114, 213, 242, 249–50
Warder. *See* Gardien
Weber, Eugen, 273
Weidmann, Bruno, 106, 189, 253
Weiller, Jane, 187–88, 253
Wilson, Daniel, 58, 198, 214
Witness, 132–33, 136
World War I, 91, 111, 171, 188, 209, 211, 221, 245, 249, 251
World War II, 101, 221

Zehr, Howard, 3
Zévaès, Alexandre, 300, 304, 306
Zimmer, Lucien, 119
Zola, Emile, 272

LIBRARY OF DAVIDSON COLLEGE